Hindu Nationalism
A Reader

Hindu Nationalism
A READER

Edited by
Christophe Jaffrelot

PRINCETON UNIVERSITY PRESS
PRINCETON AND OXFORD

Published by
Princeton University Press, 41 William Street, Princeton,
New Jersey 08540

In the United Kingdom: Princeton University Press, 3 Market Place,
Woodstock, Oxfordshire OX20 1SY

In South Asia, published by
Permanent Black
D-28 Oxford Apartments, 11, I.P. Extension,
Delhi 110092
and
'Himalayana', Mall Road, Ranikhet Cantt,
Ranikhet 263645

Library of Congress Control Number 2006940297
ISBN-13: 978-0-691-13097-2 (cloth)
ISBN-10: 0-691-13097-3 (cloth)
ISBN-13: 978-0-691-13098-9 (pbk.)
ISBN-10: 0-691-13098-1 (pbk.)

British Library Cataloging-in-Publication Data is available

This book has been composed in Agaramond
Printed on acid-free paper. ∞
press.princeton.edu
Printed in the United States of America
1 3 5 7 9 10 8 6 4 2

For
Bruce D. Graham

Contents

Acknowledgements

The idea of this book was suggested to me by Rukun Advani more than four years ago, when he published my book *India's Silent Revolution*. The intention was to present, first, a selection of writings by historical figures of the Hindu nationalist movement, and second, a series of issues around which the movement had mobilized, intellectually as well as in the street.

This project made a lot of sense to me, not only because it gave me an opportunity to share with other readers old and fairly rare books that were lying on my shelves, but also because, in my previous work, I often felt frustrated at being able to quote only short passages from the ideologues of Hindu nationalism. In order to retrace the construction of this discourse over decades, even over centuries, it seemed necessary to reproduce pages, indeed whole chapters of the foundational texts.

When I started work on the Hindutva movement in the 1980s, I was struck by the lack of interest this stream of Indian politics had sparked thus far. There were very few books on the subject and the past history of the movement remained largely unknown. In my first book, *The Hindu Nationalist Movement and Indian Politics*, I built a narrative aiming to historicize the movement in order both to identify the contexts in which it was born—and relaunched in the course of time— and to analyse its rather consistent intellectual trajectory. Indeed, while some ideas have undergone transformations, the central corpus of Hindu nationalism has remained the same, as evident from the notion of a Vedic Golden Age, which is nascent in the first section of this reader dealing with Swami Dayananda—a nineteenth-century pioneer—and which still plays a pivotal role in the last section regarding a twenty-first-century controversy over the writing of history textbooks.

This ideological firmness is well in tune with the psychological rigidity of most leaders of this cadre-based movement.

I am grateful to the publishers, Rukun Advani of Permanent Black and Fred Appel of Princeton University Press, who have allowed me to substantiate my interpretation of the Hindu nationalist movement by quoting its architects at length.

This book is dedicated to Bruce Graham, who initiated me so generously into the study of Indian politics and complexities of the social sciences. His career stands as a model for all those who wish to cultivate intellectual and personal honesty.

Last but not least, I say 'thank you' to Cynthia Schoch for editing the Introduction to this reader in an effort to make it flow more naturally to the English-speaking ear!

Copyright Statement

PART 1

Introduction: The Invention of an Ethnic Nationalism

Introduction

The Invention
of an Ethnic Nationalism

The Hindu nationalist movement started to monopolize the front pages of Indian newspapers in the 1990s when the political party that represented it in the political arena, the Bharatiya Janata Party (BJP—which translates roughly as Indian People's Party), rose to power. From 2 seats in the Lok Sabha, the lower house of the Indian parliament, the BJP increased its tally to 88 in 1989, 120 in 1991, 161 in 1996—at which time it became the largest party in that assembly—and to 178 in 1998. At that point it was in a position to form a coalition government, an achievement it repeated after the 1999 mid-term elections. For the first time in Indian history, Hindu nationalism had managed to take over power. The BJP and its allies remained in office for five full years, until 2004.

The general public discovered Hindu nationalism in operation over these years. But it had of course already been active in Indian politics and society for decades; in fact, this *ism* is one of the oldest ideological streams in India. It took concrete shape in the 1920s and even harks back to more nascent shapes in the nineteenth century. As a movement, too, Hindu nationalism is heir to a long tradition. Its main incarnation today, the Rashtriya Swayamsevak Sangh (RSS—or the National Volunteer Corps), was founded in 1925, soon after the first Indian communist party, and before the first Indian socialist party. In fact, Hindu nationalism runs parallel to the dominant Indian political tradition of the Congress Party, which Gandhi transformed into a mass organization in the 1920s. Indeed, Hindu nationalism crystallized as an ideology and as a movement exactly at the time when the Congress became imbued with Gandhi's principles and grew into a mass movement. It then developed an alternative political culture to the dominant idiom in Indian politics, not only because it rejected non-violence as a legitimate and effective *modus operandi* against the British in the wake of the discourse of Bal Gangadhar Tilak (1856–1920) and his apologia in favour of a Hindu tradition of violent action,[1] but also because it rejected the Gandhian conception of the Indian nation.

Mahatma Gandhi looked at the Indian nation as, ideally, a harmonious collection of religious communities all placed on an equal footing. He promoted a syncretic and spiritual brand of the Hindu religion in which all creeds were bound to merge, or converge. Even though the leaders of India's minorities—especially Muslims—resisted this universalist appeal—in part because Gandhi articulated his views in a thoroughly Hindu style—the Mahatma insisted till the end that he spoke on behalf of all communities and that the Congress represented them all. In the early 1920s he even presided over the destiny of the Khilafat Committee, which had been founded to defend the Khilafat, an institution challenged after the defeat of the Ottoman empire in the First World War.[2]

Gandhi's universalist definition of the Indian nation echoed that of the man he regarded as his guru in politics, Gopal Krishna Gokhale (1866–1915), and, more generally speaking, of the first generation of Congress leaders. For the founders of Congress, the Indian nation was to be defined according to the territorial criterion, not on the basis of cultural features: it encompassed all those who happened to live within the borders of British India. Therefore, it was not perceived as being within Congress's purview to deal with religious issues which, in fact, were often social issues—such as child marriage and widow re-marriage—all such issues being those that came under the personal laws of different denominations. Moreover, the early Congress had started for

---

[1] See C. Jaffrelot, 'Opposing Gandhi: Hindu Nationalism and Political Violence', in D. Vidal, G. Tarabout, and E. Meyer, eds, *Violence/Non-Violence. Some Hindu Perspectives* (Delhi: Manohar-CSH, 2003), pp. 299–324. On Tilak, see R. Cashman, *The Myth of the Lokmanya* (Berkeley: University of California Press, 1975).

[2] See Gail Minault, *The Khilafat Movement: Religious Symbolism and Political Mobilization in India* (New York: Columbia University Press, 1982).

this latter purpose a National Social Conference which met at the same time and in the same place as Congress did, during its annual session, but as a separate body. In contrast with the founders of Congress, Gandhi acknowledged religious identities in the public sphere, even as he viewed the nation as an amalgamation of many different communities. In the 1920s and after, however, the legacy of the first-generation Congress leaders was still pursued and deepened by major Congress Party figures: the Nehrus, i.e. Motilal Nehru (1861–1931) and his son, Jawaharlal Nehru (1889–1964), who advocated a liberal nation-building process based on individuals, not groups. For Motilal, who was elected president of the Congress in 1919 and 1928, and for Jawaharlal, who—before independence—occupied the same post in 1929, 1936, and 1946, and who was to become Gandhi's spiritual son, the construction of the Indian nation could only be rooted in secular, individual identities. The Nehrus represented a variant of the universalist standpoint, quite different from that embodied by Gandhi.

Hindu nationalism, like Muslim separatism (a movement which in India was formed around the same time), rejected both versions of the universalist view of nationalism articulated by Congress.[3] This ideology assumed that India's national identity was summarized by Hinduism, the dominant creed which, according to the British census, represented about 70 per cent of the population. Indian culture was to be defined as Hindu culture, and the minorities were to be assimilated by their paying allegiance to the symbols and mainstays of the majority as those of the nation. For Congressmen like Nehru this ideology—like that of the Muslim League or of Sikh separatists—had nothing to do with nationalism. They branded it with the derogatory term 'communalism'. But in fact the doctrine that was to become known by the name 'Hindutva' fulfilled the criteria of ethnic nationalism.[4] Its motto, 'Hindu, Hindi, Hindustan', echoed many other European nationalisms based on religious identity, a common language, or even racial feeling.

All the same, the essential characteristics of Hinduism scarcely lent themselves to such an 'ism'. This is, first, because Hinduism has no

---

[3] On this typology, see Gyanendra Pandey, *The Construction of Communalism in Colonial North India* (Delhi: Oxford University Press, 1990).

[4] I have made this argument in *The Hindu Nationalist Movement and Indian Politics* (New Delhi: Penguin, 1999).

'book' which can truly be said to serve as a common reference point. As Louis Renou points out, in Hinduism 'religious books can be described as books written for the use of a sect.'[5] Moreover, Hinduism has often been described not as a religion but as a 'conglomeration of sects'.[6] In fact the term 'Hindu' derives from the name of a river, the Indus; it was used successively by the Achaemenids, the Greeks, and the Muslims to denote the population living beyond that river,[7] but till the medieval period it was not appropriated by the people themselves.[8] A 'Hindu' consciousness apparently found its first expression in the seventeenth and eighteenth centuries in the empire of Shivaji, and then in the Maratha confederacy. But the conquests of the Marathas in the direction of the Gangetic plain 'did not imply the existence of a sense of the religious war based on ethnic or communal consciousness';[9] they resulted from a motivation that was ritual in character— to restore to the Hindus certain holy places, such as Varanasi, which were revered throughout India. The development of Hindu nationalism is therefore a modern phenomenon that has developed on the basis of strategies of ideology-building, and *despite* the original characteristics of a diverse set of practices clubbed under the rubric of Hinduism.

An Ideological Reaction to the Other: From Reform to Revivalism in the Nineteenth Century

The first expression of Hindu mobilization emerged in the nineteenth century as an ideological reaction to European domination and gave

[5] L. Renou, *Religions of Ancient India* (New Delhi: Munshiram Manoharlal, 1972), 2nd edn, p. 50.

[6] R. Thapar, 'Imagined Religious Communities? Ancient History and the Modern Search for a Hindu Identity', *Modern Asian Studies*, vol. 23, no. 2, 1989, p. 216.

[7] R.E. Frykenberg, 'The Emergence of Modern Hinduism as a Concept and as an Institution: A Reappraisal with Special Reference to South India', in G.D. Sontheimer and H. Kulke, eds, *Hinduism Reconsidered* (Delhi: Manohar Publications, 1989), p. 30.

[8] See, for instance, J.T. O'Connell, 'The Word "Hindu" in Gaudiya Vaishnava Texts', *Journal of the American Oriental Society*, vol. 93, no. 3, 1973, pp. 340–4.

[9] C.A. Bayly, 'The Pre-History of "Communalism"? Religious Conflict in India 1700–1800', *Modern Asian Studies*, vol. 19, no. 2, 1985, p. 187.

birth to what came to be known as 'neo-Hinduism'.[10] To begin with, Europeans fascinated the local intelligentsia. In Bengal, where the British first settled, the East India Company used the services not only of *compradores* but also of the local literati, who came from the Hindu upper castes—these *bhadralok*, who were mostly Brahmins and, as a result, a new elite of upper-caste British-trained white-collar workers took shape.[11] This intelligentsia often admired Britain for its remarkable scientific, technical, legal, and social achievements.

Yet most members of this intelligentsia also regarded the West as a threat. They were inclined to reform their traditions along modern lines but not to the extent that they would abandon or even disown them; in fact they often wanted to reform these traditions in order to save them. Reformists, therefore, became revivalists by pretending that, in emulating the West, they were only restoring to pristine purity their own traditions via eliminating later accretions.

Within the Hindu milieu this transition from reform to revivalism took place in the course of the nineteenth century. This is well illustrated by the contrast between the Brahmo Samaj and a later—but not un-related—organization, the Arya Samaj. The former was founded in 1828 by Ram Mohan Roy (1772–1833), the renowned Bengali Brahmin who had been employed by the East India Company and who looked at the British presence in India as a providential development.[12] Roy supported Western reformist ideas, including the abolition of sati. At the same time, he was very critical of the proselytizing work of Western missionaries. He steadfastly vindicated Hinduism against Christian expansionism, though in the reformist way. He admitted that missionaries were right when they stigmatized polytheism, the caste system and the condition of Hindu women. But he argued that these retrograde practices were latter accretions in Hinduism, that in its original form Hinduism did not lay itself open to such opprobrium.

[10] On neo-Hinduism see K. Jones, *Socio-Religious Reform Movements in British India* (Cambridge: Cambridge University Press, 1989); and A. Copley, ed., *Gurus and their Followers: New Religious Reform Movements in Colonial India* (Delhi: Oxford University Press, 2000).

[11] On this peculiar category, see J.H. Broomfield, *Elite Conflict in a Plural Society: Twentieth-century Bengal* (Berkeley: University of California Press, 1968).

[12] S.D. Collet, *The Life and Letters of Raja Ram Mohan Roy* (Calcutta: Sadharan Brahmo Samaj, 1962).

It had ignored idol worship—in fact it was even more monotheistic than Christianity, which admitted the Trinity—and it was an egalitarian creed emphasizing unmediated access between the individual and God. Roy argued that he had discovered all these virtues in the Upanishads—a late addition to Vedanta, the most recent part of the Veda.[13] He suggested that, according to these sacred texts, each man is endowed with an *atma*, which is nothing other than a part of Brahma—the divine substance that supports the world. Therefore, the Vedic religion relied on an unmediated relation between man and God. He fought with Unitarian missionaries to hammer home this point during long public debates. The notion of a Vedic 'golden age' when Hinduism was superior to Christianity can be seen to crystallize at this time.[14] This idea was embodied in the doctrine of the Brahmo Samaj (Society of Brahma), the organization he founded in 1828 and which survived Roy's death in 1833 (in London, where he had travelled as the first major Hindu reformer).[15]

The Brahmo Samaj attracted Hindu reformists from various regions, including the Bombay Presidency. This was the region from which Swami Dayananda Saraswati came. Dayananda was a Gujarati Brahmin who had embraced *sanyas* (asceticism). He travelled to Calcutta in 1873, meeting Keshab Chandra Sen—the most famous Brahmo Samaji leader of the time—who had just returned from England and was especially critical of the moral decay of that otherwise modern country.[16] Sen promoted the idea that India was technically less advanced but spiritually superior.[17]

[13] See B.C. Robertson, *Raja Rammohan Ray: The Father of Modern India* (Delhi: Oxford University Press, 1995).

[14] See H.C. Sarkar, ed., *English Works of Raja Rammohun Roy*, vol. 1 (Calcutta: Brahmo Samaj Centenary Committee, 1928).

[15] On the Brahmo Samaj, see D. Kopf, *British Orientalism and the Bengal Renaissance* (Calcutta: Firma K.L. Mukhopadhyay, 1969) and idem, *The Brahmo Samaj and the Shaping of the Modern Indian Mind* (Princeton: Princeton University Press, 1979).

[16] See M. Borthwick, *Keshub Chandra Sen: A Search for Cultural Synthesis* (Calcutta: Minerva Associates, 1977).

[17] This aspect of neo-Hinduism is scrutinized in T. Raychaudhuri, *Europe Reconsidered: Perceptions of the West in Nineteenth-Century Bengal* (Delhi: Oxford University Press, 1988).

Dayananda Saraswati capitalized on the intellectual legacy of Roy and Sen in the 1870s, but he also took it several steps further, and in a somewhat different direction. While the Brahmo Samajis focused on the religious dimension of the Vedic 'golden age', Dayananda argued that, in addition to its spiritual glory, Indian antiquity was imbued with cultural and social greatness. The Vedic epoch was in his construction no longer embodied only in spirituality but also in a people—in its culture and its land. Dayananda maintained that the 'Aryas' of the Vedas formed the autochthonous people of Bharat, the sacred land below the Himalayas. They had been endowed by their god with the most perfect language, Sanskrit, the mother of all languages. This claim was strengthened by British Orientalism, whose most famous eighteenth-century exponent William Jones argued that it was the fount of an Indo-European family of languages. The idea that Europe's languages originated in Sanskrit had by this time become widespread.[18] Last, but not least, Dayananda depicted Aryan society as endowed with robust egalitarian values. He did not ignore the caste system, but he reinterpreted it, arguing that, to begin with, this social system did not rely on hereditary hierarchical relations but on a merit-based division of labour, each *varna* fulfilling complementary functions. In the original Aryan society, for Dayananda, children were assigned to different *varnas* by their gurus according to their aptitude and inclination, a novel idea which reflected the influence upon him of Western individualism.

In fact, Dayananda's revivalism inaugurated a specific combination of stigmatization and emulation of the threatening 'Other'. In contrast to the old reformists *à la* Ram Mohan Roy, Dayananda did not look upon British colonialism as a providential development but rather as posing a threat to Hindu civilization, including its caste system. In order to defuse this threat Dayananda recommended some emulation of the West. In this respect he followed Roy. His idea of reform was not to make India like the West, but to make its standards acceptably Western. His effort was to dissuade the British from changing Hindu

[18] See P.J. Marshall, ed., *The British Discovery of Hinduism in the Eighteenth Century* (Cambridge: Cambridge University Press, 1970), and W. Halbfass, *India and Europe: An Essay in Philosophical Understanding* (New York: State University of New York, 1988).

customs by law, as well as to dissuade Hindus from admiring the West and/or converting to Christianity. This was best done by arguing that what fascinated Hindus about the West existed already, deeply buried, in their own ancestral traditions. Dayananda's interest was thus to emulate the West in order to more effectively resist its influence.

It followed that the conversion of Hindus—including the Untouchables—to Christianity was perceived by Dayananda as a challenge to Hinduism. By the end of his life he introduced a ritual of reconversion—something no one could find in the Hindu scriptures as having previously existed. For this purpose he adapted the old ceremony of *shuddhi*, by which upper-caste Hindus who had been defiled could reintegrate with their caste. Shuddhi was therefore a purification procedure which Dayananda transformed into a reconversion technique, drawing inspiration from Christianity.[19] Dayananda presided over the 'shuddhization' of a few Christian converts who wished to return to Hinduism during his lifetime, but even at that time, and more so after his death, the prime target of the Shuddhi movement's disciples were Muslims and Sikhs.[20]

Dayananda founded the Arya Samaj in 1875, in Punjab, the province where Hindus, more than anywhere else, felt a strong sense of vulnerability because of their demographic weakness *vis-à-vis* Muslims (51 per cent of the local population) and Sikhs (7.5 per cent). After Dayananda's death the Arya Samaj continued to develop in Punjab and became politicized.[21]

The Political Turn: The Hindu Sabhas Movement

In Punjab the Arya Samaj attracted upper-caste notables who were involved in trade and commerce. This social milieu appreciated the

[19] R.K. Ghai, *Shuddhi Movement in India* (New Delhi: Commonwealth Publishers, 1990).

[20] K. Jones, 'Ham Hindu Nahin: Arya–Sikh Relations, 1877–1905', *Journal of Asian Studies*, vol. 32, no. 3, May 1973.

[21] On the Arya Samaj, the best source remains, K. Jones, *Arya Dharm— Hindu Consciousness in Nineteenth-Century Punjab* (Berkeley: University of California Press, 1976). See also Lajpat Rai, *The Arya Samaj: An Account of its Aims, Doctrine and Activities, with a Biographical Sketch of the Founder* (New

sect's reformist creed because it did not recognize any sort of supremacy by Brahmins—on the contrary it denied the role of Brahmins as intermediaries between man and God. Hitherto, Brahmins had here claimed to occupy the upper rungs of society, even though the merchant castes had, in fact, become the dominant force in society.

The merchant castes had indeed become so powerful that they played the role of moneylenders for the entire Punjab peasantry. When debtors failed to pay their dues, as often happened, merchant castes bought their land. This phenomenon accelerated by the late nineteenth century to such an extent that the British—who wanted to protect rural society as it had supported their rule—introduced in 1901 the Punjab Alienation of Land Act, a piece of legislation protecting 'rural tribes' from such transfer of property.[22] The British further antagonized the Hindu elite in 1906 when Lord Minto promised a Muslim delegation—which was to spawn the Muslim League by the end of the year—that the Muslim minority of India would be granted a separate electorate. This announcement did not materialize all over British India until 1909, in the framework of the Morley–Minto constitutional reforms, but in Punjab it led the Hindu urban elite to organize as early as 1907: Hindu Sabhas (Hindu associations) were formed throughout the province, mostly under the impulse of Arya Samaj leaders, including Lal Chand, who formulated the standard expression of Hindu anxiety regarding British policy in 1909, in a series of articles in *The Panjabee*.[23]

While Arya Samajis, thus far, did not view themselves as 'Hindus' but as followers of the Vedas—so much so that they did not declare themselves 'Hindus' in the census—British policy convinced them to give up this claim and join hands with the other streams of Hinduism,

Delhi, D.A.V. College, 1914); S.K. Gupta, *Arya Samaj and the* Raj (New Delhi: Gitanjali Publishing House, 1991); D. Vable, *The Arya Samaj: Hindu without Hinduism* (New Delhi: Vikas, 1983); Saraswati Pandit, *A Critical Study of the Contribution of the Arya Samaj to Indian Education* (Delhi: Sarvadeshik Arya Pratinidhi Sabha, 1975); and V. Dua, *The Arya Samaj in Punjab Politics* (New Delhi: Picus Books, 1999).

[22] N.G. Barrier, *The Punjab Alienation of Land Bill of 1900* (Durham: Duke University Press, 1966).

[23] Lajpat Rai, *A History of the Arya Samaj* (Bombay: Orient Longman, 1967).

including the orthodox, who paid allegiance to Sanatan Dharma (the Eternal Dharma), which had criticized the reformist zeal of Arya Samajis against idol worship, the caste system, and Brahmin priesthood.[24]

The Sanatanis had developed major strongholds in the United Provinces (the region rechristened Uttar Pradesh after independence), this being the crucible of Hindu orthodoxy and home to holy cities such as Haridwar and Varanasi, where the Arya Samaj only had substantial pockets of influence in the western areas. Sanatanis were therefore primarily responsible for the formation of the Hindu Sabha of the United Provinces in the mid-1910s, which happened as a reaction against the extension of a separate electorate in favour of Muslims at the municipal level. The leader of this Hindu Sabha, Madan Mohan Malaviya, was a well-known Sanatani, famous for his orthodoxy and his interest in educational matters.[25] Malaviya is indeed best remembered as having initiated the foundation of the Banaras Hindu University (BHU) in 1916.[26]

The Hindu Sabha movement spread beyond Punjab and the United Provinces into Bihar, Bengal, the Central Provinces and Berar, and into the Bombay Presidency. Some of these regional branches sent delegates to Haridwar for the founding of an All India Hindu Sabha, or Hindu Mahasabha, in 1915. But this intended umbrella organization was still-born, not only because of persisting difficulties between Arya Samajis and Sanatanis over social reform, but also over British rule: the latter continued to pay allegiance to the British in spite of everything, while Arya Samajis resented their politics and even indulged, sometimes, in radical forms of resistance.

The Hindu Sangathan Movement: Hindu Nationalism Crystallizes

The Hindu Mahasabha was rekindled in the 1920s. At this time the ideology of Hindu nationalism was codified and acquired its distinctive

[24] See Lal Chand, *Sanatana Dharma: An Advanced Text Book of Hindu Religion and Ethics* (Benares: Central Hindu College, 1904), 2nd edn.

[25] See the 1000-page-long biography of Malaviya by Parmanand, *Mahamana Madan Mohan Malaviya. An Historical Biography* (Varanasi: BHU, 1985), 2 vols.

[26] S.L. Dar and S. Somaskandan, *History of the Benares Hindu University* (Banaras: BHU, 1966).

features. This development followed the same logic as the initial stages of socio-religious reform movements: Hindu nationalism crystallized in reaction to a threat subjectively felt if not concretely experienced. This time the threatening Other was neither Christian missionaries nor colonial bureaucrats, but Muslims, not only because of their special equation with the British—as evident from the separate electorates issue—but also because of their mobilization during the Khilafat movement.

This movement had developed in the wake of World War I as a sequel to the peace treaties which abolished the Muslim Khilafat—a word deriving from the title 'Khalifa' (Caliph), held till then by the Ottoman sultan, one of the defeated rulers. In India, Muslims demonstrated against the British, who had naturally taken part in the post-War negotiations. But their mobilization also affected Hindus, who were a more accessible target, and with whom they sometimes happened to be locked in socio-economic conflicts locally. In the early 1920s riots multiplied, including in South India, where inter-communal relations had been traditionally much less tense. In fact the first large riot occurred in what is now Kerala, caused by economic frustrations among the Mappilas or Moplahs (Muslim peasants) *vis-à-vis* Hindu landlords.[27]

The wave of riots which spread over India in the early 1920s fostered a Hindu reaction that resulted in a relaunching of the Hindu Mahasabha. While the movement had stopped organizing regular sessions after 1919, it met again at Haridwar in 1921 and became the crucible of the collaboration between Arya Samajis and Sanatanis, who now agreed that Muslims were posing such a threat to Hindus that they could not afford to fight each other any more. This convergence found expression in the collaboration between Malaviya and Lajpat Rai, the latter being one of the most important Arya Samaji leaders in Punjab.

Hindu Sabhaites then emphasized the need for an organization (*sangathan*) for the majority community. However, for the Arya Samajis sangathan meant something more than it did to Sanatanis. For Swami Shraddhananda, for instance, the Shuddhi movement needed to be revived and directed more towards Untouchables to make them feel

---

[27] R.L. Hardgrave, Jr., 'The Mappilla Rebellion, 1921: Peasant Revolt in Malabar', *Modern Asian Studies*, vol. 11, no. 1, 1977.

better integrated in society once they had been 'purified'. This was something Sanatanis continued to accept reluctantly, as a temporary response to Muslim militancy.[28]

The Hindu Mahasabha was not a party in its own right but a sub-group of Congress members. It worked as a lobby within Congress.[29] Such a position weakened its general stand—especially after Gandhi rose to power in Congress—introduced a more centralized decision-making process, and made it embody a broad-based Hindu brand of politics. Because his style and programme were based on a universalist and reformist Hinduism, Gandhi did not leave the Hindu Sabhaites much room for manoeuvre in Congress and, more generally, in the Indian public sphere. Eventually, therefore, the Hindu Mahasabha had to part company with Congress. It became a full-fledged party in the late 1930s under the leadership of V.D. Savarkar, who made its ideology so radical that Congress leaders like Nehru were not prepared to cohabit with what they saw as a communal and fundamentalist variety of politics. Savarkar was a Maharashtrian Brahmin from Nasik; but even before he took over as president of the Hindu Mahasabha, the centre of gravity had shifted from North to Central India, more especially to the Central Provinces and Berar, and to the Bombay Presidency.

The Maharashtrian Crucible of Hindu Nationalism

Hindu nationalism as we know it today was born in Maharashtra in the 1920s, in the context of reaction to the Khilafat movement. Its ideology was codified by Savarkar much before he joined the Hindu Mahasabha. A former anti-British revolutionary, Savarkar wrote *Hindutva: Who is a Hindu?* in the early 1920s while still a prisoner of the British at Ratnagiri in Maharashtra. His book was the first attempt at endowing what he called the Hindu Rashtra (the Hindu nation) with a clear-cut identity: namely Hindutva, a word coined by Savarkar

[28] G.R. Thursby, 'Aspects of Hindu–Muslim Relations in British India: A Study of Arya Samaj Activities, Government of India Politics, and Communal Conflicts in the Period 1923–1928', PhD dissertation, Duke University, 1972.

[29] R. Gordon, 'The Hindu Mahasabha and the Indian National Congress 1915 to 1926', *Modern Asian Studies*, vol. 9, no. 2, 1975.

and which, according to him does not coincide with Hinduism. Declaring himself an atheist, Savarkar argued that religion was only one aspect of Hindu identity, and not even the most important. In fact he draws his definition of Hindu identity out of Western theories of the nation. The first criterion of the Hindu nation, for him, is the sacred territory of Aryavarta as described in the Vedas, and by Dayananda, whose book *Satyarth Prakash* Savarkar read extensively.[30] Then comes race: for Savarkar the Hindus are the descendants of 'Vedic fathers' who occupied this geographical area since antiquity. In addition to religion, land and race, Savarkar mentions language as a pillar of Hindu identity. When doing so he refers to Sanskrit but also to Hindi: hence the equation he finally established between Hindutva and the triptych: 'Hindu, Hindi, Hindustan'. Hindu nationalism appears for the first time as resulting from the superimposition of a religion, a culture, a language, and a sacred territory—the perfect recipe for ethnic nationalism.

For Savarkar, who invented this new doctrine in the wake of revivalists *à la* Dayananda, Hindu Sabhaites, and Sangathanists, the Indian identity is epitomized by Hindutva: the majority community is supposed to embody the nation, not only because it is the largest but also because it is the oldest. Hindus are the autochthonous people of India, whereas the religious minorities are outsiders who must adhere to Hindutva culture, which is the national culture. In the private sphere they may worship their gods and follow their rituals, but in the public domain they must pay allegiance to Hindu symbols. This applies especially to Muslims and Christians, the proponents, in his view, of truly un-Indian religions. Buddhists, Jains, and Sikhs are not considered non-Hindus by Savarkar—they are followers of sects closely linked to Hinduism.

Because Savarkar wrote *Hindutva* in reaction to the pan-Islamic mobilization of the Khilafat movement, most of his thought derives from his deep-rooted hostility to Islam and its followers. For Savarkar the Muslims of India constituted fifth-columnists whose allegiance was to Mecca and Istanbul (the political capital of the Umma until the

[30] While in England in 1906–10 Savarkar stayed at India House, a guesthouse founded by Shyamji Krishna Varma, who had been a close disciple of Dayananda. See D. Keer, *Veer Savarkar* (Bombay: Popular Prakashan, 1988), p. 29.

1920s). Though in a minority, Muslims were a threat to Hindus because of their pan-Islamism, and because, being more aggressive and better organized, they could outmanoeuvre Hindus, who remained effete and divided into many castes and sects.

While Savarkar provided Hindu nationalism with an ideology, he did not outline a plan of action by which Hindus ought to react to the Muslim threat, or reform and organize themselves. This task was taken up by another Maharashtrian, Keshav Baliram Hedgewar (1889–1940), who paid a visit to Savarkar in the mid-1920s and then founded the RSS in his home town, Nagpur.[31] This organization—which quickly developed into the largest Hindu nationalist movement—was intended not only to propagate the Hindutva ideology but also to infuse new physical strength into the majority community.

To achieve this twofold objective the RSS adopted a very specific *modus operandi*. Hedgewar decided to work at the grassroots in order to reform Hindu society from below: he created local branches (*shakhas*) of the movement in towns and villages according to a standard pattern. Young Hindu men gathered every morning and every evening on a playground for games with martial connotations and ideological train-ing sessions. The men in charge of the shakhas, called *pracharaks* (preachers), dedicated their whole life to the organization; as a part of RSS cadres they could be sent anywhere in India to develop the orga-nization's network. At the time of India's independence there were also about 600,000 *swayamsevaks* (volunteers).[32] The RSS soon became the most powerful Hindu nationalist movement, but it did not have much impact on public life in India simply because it remained out of politics. M.S. Golwalkar, who succeeded Hedgewar as *Sarsanghchalak* (head) of the organization in 1940, had made apoliticism a rule. Savar-kar, who revived the Hindu Mahasabha after being released by the British in 1937, asked Golwalkar for support at a critical juncture—when the Mahasabha left Congress and became a full-fledged party—but in vain.[33]

[31] B.V. Deshpande and S.R. Ramaswamy, *Dr Hedgewar the Epoch Maker* (Bangalore: Sahitya Sindhu, 1981).
[32] J.A. Curran, *Militant Hinduism in Indian Politics—A Study of the RSS* (N.P.: Institute of Pacific Relations, 1951).
[33] W. Andersen and S.D. Damle, *The Brotherhood in Saffron—The Rashtriya*

However, soon after independence, the RSS leaders realized they could not remain out of politics. In January 1948 Mahatma Gandhi was killed by a former RSS swayamsevak, Nathuram Godse, and Prime Minister Jawaharlal Nehru immediately imposed a ban on the organization, whose leaders then realized that they could not expect help from any party in the political arena. A section of the movement's leaders who were already favourably inclined towards involving the RSS in politics now argued that this state of things justified the launching of a party of its own by the RSS. Though reluctant, Golwalkar allowed them to discuss the matter with Shyama Prasad Mookerjee, who had been president of the Hindu Mahasabha. These negotiations resulted in the creation of the Bharatiya Jana Sangh (forerunner of the present Bharatiya Janata Party or BJP) in 1951, on the eve of the first general elections.

The Sangh Parivar Takes Shape

At its inception, the Jana Sangh was Janus-faced, with former Hindu Sabhaites like Mookerjee and RSS members like Deendayal Upadhyaya at its helm.[34] After the untimely death of the former in 1953, Upadhyaya took over the party organization and eliminated the Hindu Sabhaites. Upadhyaya, however, was not only an organization man: he was first and foremost an ideologue, probably the last major Hindu nationalist ideologue. In the 1960s his doctrine of 'Integral Humanism' became the official platform of the Jana Sangh. Not only did Upadhyaya draw inspiration from the Hindutva ideology of Savarkar, his eulogy of the organic unity of the varna system harked back to Dayananda: a century of ideology-building then culminated in Upadhyaya's conservative thought.

The xenophobic dimensions of the Jana Sangh were, however, more evident in the writings of Balraj Madhok, president of the Jana Sangh

---

Swayamsevak Sangh and Hindu Revivalism (New Delhi: Vistaar Publications, 1987).

[34] B. Graham, *Hindu Nationalism and Indian Politics: The Origins and Development of the Bharatiya Jana Sangh* (Cambridge: Cambridge University Press, 1990).

in the late 1960s. Madhok's views echoed those of Savarkar and Golwalkar inasmuch he exhorted minorities to 'Indianize'—meaning they
should adopt Hindu cultural features and assimilate into a 'Hindian'
nation.[35]

The Jana Sangh was only one of the front organizations set up by
the RSS, the latter's aim no longer being merely to penetrate society
only through shakhas but also to establish organizations working within
specific social categories. Thus in 1948 RSS cadres based in Delhi
founded the Akhil Bharatiya Vidyarthi Parishad (ABVP—Indian Students' Association), a student union whose primary aim was to combat
the communist influence on university campuses. (The ABVP currently
ranks first among student unions in terms of membership.) In 1955
the RSS gave itself a workers' union, the Bharatiya Mazdoor Sangh
(BMS—Indian Workers' Association) whose primary mission was also
to counter the 'red unions' in the name of Hindu nationalist ideology,
this being a doctrine that also sought to promote social cohesion over
class struggle. (In the 1990s the BMS became India's largest trade
union.)

In addition to these unions the RSS developed more targeted organizations. In 1952 it founded a tribal movement, the Vanavasi Kalyan
Ashram (VKA—Centre for Tribal Welfare),[36] which aimed above all
to counter the influence of Christian movements among the aboriginals
of India, proselytism and priestly social work having resulted in
numerous conversions. The VKA applied itself to imitating missionary
methods and thus achieved a number of 'reconversions'.

---

[35] On this notion, see R.G. Fox, 'Gandhian Socialism and Hindu Nationalism: Cultural Domination in the World System', *The Journal of Commonwealth
and Comparative Politics*, vol. 25, no. 3, November 1987; and R.E. Frykenberg,
'The Concept of "Majority" as a Devilish Force in the Politics of Modern Asia',
The Journal of Commonwealth and Comparative Politics, vol. 15, no. 3, November
1987.

[36] Hindu nationalists translate 'indigenous peoples' as 'vanavasi', literally,
'those who live in the forest', instead of the more commonly used term throughout India, 'adivasi', in other words 'those who were there first'. From the Hindu
nationalist ideological standpoint the initial inhabitants of the country were
'Aryans' and not aboriginals: the latter they argue were driven away or conquered
by Aryan invasions.

In 1964, in association with Hindu clerics, the RSS set up the Vishva Hindu Parishad (VHP—World Council of Hindus), a movement responsible for grouping the heads of various Hindu sects in order to lend this hitherto unorganized religion a sort of centralized structure. Here too, Hindu nationalists took Christianity, particularly the notion of 'consistory', as a model. For a long time the VHP only attracted gurus who had founded their own ashrams. Such gurus used the VHP as a soapbox, even a form of legitimacy, with the main sect leaders remaining purposefully at a distance.[37]

Another subsidiary, Vidya Bharati (Indian Knowledge), was established in 1977 to coordinate a network of schools first developed by the RSS in the 1950s on the basis of local initiatives. Lastly, in 1979 the RSS founded Seva Bharati (Indian Service) to penetrate India's slums through social activities (free schools, low-cost medicines, etc.). Taken together, these bridgeheads are presented by the mother organization as forming the 'Sangh Parivar', or 'the family of the Sangh', that is, of the RSS.[38]

Hindu Nationalism and Political Strategy

The Jana Sangh always wavered between two strategies: one, moderate, involved positioning itself as a patriotic party on behalf of national unity, as the protector of both the poor and of small privately-owned businesses, deploying a populist vein. The other line, more militant, was based on the promotion of an aggressive form of 'Hinduness', symbolized by the campaign to raise Hindi to the level of India's national language and protecting of cows (by banning cow slaughter), the cow being sacred for Hindus but not for Muslims. The latter were in fact the implicit target of an agitation against slaughtering cows set off in 1966, in the context of the fourth general elections campaign.

---

[37] C. Jaffrelot, 'The Vishva Hindu Parishad: A Nationalist but Mimetic Attempt at Federating the Hindu Sects', in Vasudha Dalmia, Angelika Malinar, and Martin Christof, eds, *Charisma and Canon: Essays on the Religious History of the Indian Subcontinent* (Delhi: Oxford University Press, 2001).

[38] For more details, see C. Jaffrelot, ed., *The Sangh Parivar: A Reader* (Delhi: Oxford University Press, 2005).

Although the militant strategy was more in keeping with RSS wishes and the feelings of its activists, it ran up against India's constitutional rules of secularism and prevented the Jana Sangh from broadening its base and striking up alliances with other parties. This strategy changed in the 1970s. In 1977 the Jana Sangh resigned itself to following a moderate line and merged with the Janata Party, which had just defeated Indira Gandhi's Congress Party. However, the former Jana Sangh had not broken with the RSS, to the great displeasure of some of its new partners in power, particularly the socialists. This latter group, associated with the government's second-in-command Charan Singh (who sought to destabilize Prime Minister Morarji Desai—all the better to take his place), drew their argument from an upsurge in Hindu–Muslim riots within which RSS activists were involved, to demand that the former Jana Sanghis break with the RSS. The Jana Sanghis' refusal precipitated the break-up of the Janata Party, paving the way for Indira Gandhi's return.

In 1980 the former Jana Sangh leaders started a new party, the Bharatiya Janata Party (BJP), which remained faithful to the moderate strategy. The BJP, which had Atal Behari Vajpayee as its first president, diluted the original ideology of the Jana Sangh in order to become more acceptable in the Indian party system and to find allies in this arena. This more moderate approach to politics was considerably resented by the rest of the Sangh Parivar.

The RSS kept its distance from the BJP and made greater use of the VHP to rekindle ethno-religious political activism. This more militant strategy found its main expression in the launching of the Ayodhya movement in the mid-1980s. Ayodhya, a town in Uttar Pradesh, is described in the Hindu tradition as the birthplace and capital of the god-king Lord Rama. The site was supposedly once occupied by a Rama temple until destroyed in the sixteenth century on the orders of Babur, the first Mughal emperor, and replaced by mosque, the 'Babri Masjid'. In 1984 the VHP called for this site to be returned to the Hindus. In 1989, throughout the entire summer, with the logistical support of the RSS, the VHP organized Rama Shila Pujan festivals, which involved worshipping bricks (*shila*) printed with Rama's name. These holy bricks were to be used to rebuild the Ayodhya temple.

The BJP rallied to the call of this ethno-religious mobilization strategy and even participated in the processions which took place all over

India: the agitation contributed to its success at the polls, taking it from 2 to 88 parliamentary seats and from 7.4 to 11.6 per cent of the votes cast. In 1990, while the party was a major component of the co-alition in power that had just ousted the Congress Party, its president, L.K. Advani, went on a 10,000 km 'chariot-journey' or Rath Yatra that was to culminate in the construction of the Ayodhya temple. Advani was stopped before entering Uttar Pradesh and during the re-pression of activists who attacked the mosque some dozen were left dead. This episode reinforced the champion-of-Hinduism image that the BJP had been trying to acquire among the majority community. The 1991 general elections actually enabled the party to win 20.08 per cent of the vote and 120 seats in the Lok Sabha. Paradoxically, its success in Uttar Pradesh, where the BJP was able to form the state gov-ernment, did not enable it to solve the Ayodhya issue.

Hindu nationalist militants put an end to this deadlock by demo-lishing the mosque on 6 December 1992. This operation and the en-suing Hindu–Muslim riots—1200 dead within a few days—prompted New Delhi to take a number of repressive measures, including the dissolution of assemblies in states where the BJP was in power (Uttar Pradesh, Madhya Pradesh, Himachal Pradesh, and Rajasthan), and a ban on the RSS and the VHP. These proved temporary measures and did not affect the Sangh Parivar.

By the mid-1990s the BJP reverted to its moderate line, discarding the manipulation of religious symbols for political ends in favour of touting more legitimate issues such as national unity and economic independence. This was not only because it had lost elections in UP, MP, and HP in 1993—the voters obviously punishing the party for violent excesses related to the Ayodhya affair—but also because Sangh Parivar leaders admitted they could not acquire power unless the BJP formed political alliances with regional parties. Moreover, Advani, the party's president, allowed Vajpayee to take the forefront once again because Vajpayee was less marked by Hindu nationalist activism.

The BJP was able to build a coalition of more than fifteen parties in the late 1990s. This 'National Democratic Alliance' enabled Vajpayee to form a government after the 1998 and 1999 elections. The arrange-ment forced the BJP to put on the backburner contentious issues—such as the construction of a temple in Ayodhya; restrict Article 30 of the Indian constitution guaranteeing the right of religious and linguistic minorities to establish educational institutions; abolish Article 370 of the constitution granting a partially autonomous status to Jammu and Kashmir; promulgate a uniform civil code, primarily to put an end to the possibility given to Muslims to follow Islamic law (*sharia*).

Once in office, the BJP implemented some of the traditional items of the Hindu nationalist programme. Vajpayee's first major decision was the nuclear test of May 1998. The policy of the minister for human resources and development, Murli Manohar Joshi, was also well in tune with Hindu nationalist leanings: he appointed personalities who had been close to the Sangh Parivar as heads of the directive body of the Indian Council of Historical Research (ICHR),[39] the Indian Council of Social Science Research (ICSSR), and the search committee for faculty appointments in the National Council for Educational Research and Training (NCERT) which was entrusted with the task of designing a new school curriculum. One of Joshi's priorities was to create new textbooks—including those dealing with Indian history—rewritten in a vein more in line with Hindu nationalist ideology.

But the BJP distanced itself from several other traditional mainstays of its ideology, such as economic nationalism—a notion encapsulated by the word 'swadeshi'. The government in fact opened new sectors to foreign investment. This new, sympathetic approach of 'liberalization' caused some concern within the Sangh Parivar. The Swadeshi Jagaran Manch—a newly created offshoot of RSS—and the Bharatiya Mazdoor Sangh complained to the RSS, whose governing body, the Akhil Bharatiya Pratinidhi Sabha, passed a resolution in March 2000 supporting an 'India-centric and need-specific' model of development.[40]

In May 2004, during the parliamentary elections, the NDA government led by the BJP was surprisingly defeated and replaced by a Congress-led coalition. The defeat was considered by most components of the Sangh Parivar to be that of the Vajpayee moderate line. The VHP leaders were especially vocal. For them the BJP-led government

---

[39] In February 2000 the ICHR 'suspended' two volumes of its series called 'Towards Freedom', namely those edited by Sumit Sarkar and K.N. Panikkar, both known for being highly critical of the Sangh Parivar.

[40] For more details on the Vajpayee government policies, see T. Hansen and C. Jaffrelot, eds, *The BJP and the Compulsions of Politics in India* (Delhi: Oxford University Press, 2001), 2nd edn.

had betrayed the Hindus by not building the Rama temple they longed for in Ayodhya. The compulsions of coalition politics had stymied the Hindutva agenda. Former socialists and other self-proclaimed secularist allies of the BJP-led coalition would not allow Hindutva-oriented objectives such as the building of a Rama Mandir in Ayodhya.[41] The BJP had become adept at coalition-making, to stay in power, but the rules of the coalition game had diluted the agenda.

As a result, Hindutva forces are today deeply divided. The BJP leaders consider that any return to a radical brand of Hindu nationalist politics by the party will alienate its allies and postpone *sine die* its comeback to the helm of political affairs in the country. The RSS and VHP leaders assume that the BJP lost the 2004 elections because the Vajpayee government had disappointed too many Hindus. They fear that any further dilution of the ideology of the party would widen the gap between the BJP and the rest of the Sangh Parivar. When such differences emerge between the political sector of the Sangh Parivar and the rest, the political wing eventually falls in line. In the late 1980s, for instance, Advani succeeded Vajpayee for the second time and took the party towards the Hindutva direction, as desired by the RSS. Undoubtedly, Advani departure as president of the BJP on the eve of new year's day 2006 was largely perceived as being at the behest of the RSS. The tensions between the RSS and the BJP cannot be taken lightly anyway. They affect two mainstays of the self-perception—and indeed the identity—of the Hindutva movement. First, while the Sangh Parivar claims to form a 'family', with its members playing complementary parts, the RSS and the BJP (and the VHP and the BJP) appear to be at cross purposes.[42]

Second, the experiment of the Vajpayee government has shown that the RSS could not really exert the influence it wanted over power, even when the BJP was in office. This failure, once again, puts into question a key element of the Sangh Parivar's identity. Certainly, the

[41] See C. Jaffrelot, 'The BJP and the 2004 Elections: Dimensions, Causes and Implications of an Unexpected Defeat', in Katharine Adney and Lawrence Saez, eds, *Coalition Politics and Hindu Nationalism* (New York: Routledge, 2005).

[42] C. Jaffrelot, *The Sangh Parivar: A Reader* (New Delhi: Oxford University Press, 2005).

RSS aspires to reshape society in its own image at the grassroots level, in a long-term perspective. But it also wants to the 'Raj guru', the mentor of goverment.[43] The Vajpayee government episode has demonstrated that such an objective is very difficult to achieve. This realization may force the Sangh Parivar to change its functioning.

The present reader is divided into two parts. The first is intended to build upon the foregoing summary of the history of Hindu nationalism from the standpoint of ideology formation. Here I take into consideration a wide spectrum of thinkers, ranging from Dayananda to Upadhyaya, in order to analyse the different phases and modalities of this process. Such an exercise enables us to identify the continuities, recurrences, and discrepancies of Hindu nationalism. Indeed, this section makes it clear that the Hindutva doctrine resulted from an ambivalent reaction to the West and Islam. Hindu nationalists imitated features of the Other—to whom they attributed superiority—in order to resist the Other more effectively rather than become like the Other. Hindu nationalism also offers a conservative ideology imbued with Brahminical values at a time when the rise of plebeian groups—especially Dalits—are challenging upper-caste domination. As a result, social organicism is a part of this ideology which fulfills the criteria of ethnic nationalism—as reading the pages which follow should make clear.

The selection of the political thinkers, or ideologues, included in this anthology has been determined by a very simple consideration: those who have played a role in organized Hindu nationalist movements have been systematically preferred to individuals who have never been mentors to institutionalized socio-political associations. As a result, Sri Aurobindo and Swami Vivekananda—whose thought processes had affinities with Hindu nationalism—have been omitted.[44]

[43] For more details, see C. Jaffrelot, *The Hindu Nationalist Movement*, op. cit., ch. 3.

[44] On the ideology of Aurobindo and Vivekananda, see D. Dalton, *Indian Idea of Freedom. Political Thought of Vivekananda, Aurobindo Ghose, Rabindranath Tagore and Mahatma Gandhi* (Gurgaon: The Academic Press, 1982). Two recent anthologies centred on, respectively, Aurobindo and Vivekananda, also

The second part of this book focuses on issues which occupy major positions within Hindu nationalism. These issues, ranging from language to conversion, are central to the Hindutva movement's activities. Some of these issues have transformed themselves over a long span of time without losing their salience. This part of the book, by selecting about a dozen such issues, is therefore intended to assess the continuity of Hindu nationalist ideology over a century and more.

In order to contextualize the items that comprise this reader, they are all prefaced by short introductions giving information on respective authors and explaining the issues at stake.

The book ends with a detailed bibliography.

---

argue that such thinkers cannot really be appropriated, without distortion, by Hindu nationalism. See Peter Heehs, ed., *Sri Aurobindo: Nationalism, Religion, and Beyond* (Delhi: Permanent Black, 2005); and Amiya P. Sen, ed., *The Indispensable Vivekananda* (Delhi: Permanent Black, 2006).

PART 2

The Making and Reshaping of Hindu Nationalist Ideology

1

Swami Dayananda Saraswati

Swami Dayananda (1824–83), originally from Gujarat, began his public career as a monk (*sannyasin*) of the Dandi order founded by Shankara.[1] His guru, Swami Virjananda, had fought—in the spirit of Shankara—against the division of Hinduism into sectarian groups and for a return to the Vedas.[2] Dayananda pursued this goal too, but in a more militant manner, after his meeting with Brahmos—including Keshab Chandra Sen and Debendranath Tagore—in Calcutta, where he went in 1873. He founded the Arya Samaj in 1875 in Punjab.[3] (The Bengali elite had already established the Brahmo Samaj.[4]) The Arya Samaj marked the transition of neo-Hinduism from reformism to revivalism, as is evident from Dayananda's book, *Satyarth Prakash* (*The Light of Truth*), which was published in 1875, in Benares. This book, mostly written in the form of a dialogue, was translated from Hindi—the language Dayananda had chosen to use, though his mother tongue was Gujarati—into English in 1908. This version was revised in the 1940s by Pandit Ganga Prasad Upadhyaya and a new edition was published in 1946—the one from which the following excerpts are taken.

[1] K.C. Yadav, ed., *Autobiography of Swami Dayanand Saraswati* (New Delhi: Manohar, 1976), p. 21.

[2] J.T.F. Jordens, *Dayananda Saraswati—His Life and Ideas* (Delhi: Oxford University Press, 1978), p. 37.

[3] On the Arya Samaj in Punjab, the best source remains K. Jones, *Arya Dharm—Consciousness in Nineteenth-Century Punjab* (Berkeley: University of California Press, 1976).

[4] K. Jones, 'The Bengali Elite in Post-Annexation Punjab: An Example of Inter-Regional Influence in Nineteenth-Century India', *The Indian Economic and Social History Review*, vol. 3, no. 4, December 1966.

The extracts make it clear that Dayananda favoured a degree of Western-inspired social reform. While he criticized the Indian intelligentsia's copying of European dress and manners, he admits that 'The Europeans are very dutiful and well disciplined' and that 'these qualifications and deeds have contributed to their advancement . . .'.[5] Dayananda accepted Western criticism of Hindu forms of worship and the role of Brahmins as intermediaries between man and god, but he argued that in the Vedic era Hinduism had been free of the blemishes for which it was now being condemned (idolatrous polytheism, caste-based social hierarchy, etc.). According to him, in that period the deity was worshipped in the form of an abstract Absolute—something that Arya Samaj ritual tried to restore—and, above all, no system of hereditary endogamous castes, or *jatis*, was admitted. Society recognized only varnas by which children were to be classified by gurus according to their individual qualities. Therefore Dayananda rejected the social system (by which he meant jati) that British observers had represented as backward, urging that it be replaced by the 'traditional' varna system, and emphasizing its compatibility with the individualistic values of Europeans. This was his way of seeking to make Hindus regain their self-esteem. His reinterpretation, in fact, enabled him to rehabilitate a social system of ritual hierarchy in the guise of the so-called ancestral varna system. Even though he considered Brahmins responsible for superstition and the decline of Hindu society, the alternative social model he proposed was based largely on the traditional—mainly Brahminical—worldview, as his recommendations relating to the strict endogamy of the varnas indicate. He considered, within his organicist perspective, that such an arrangement 'will maintain the integrity of each *varna* as well as good relations'.

Dayananda goes one step further than the Brahmos here since he not only outlines an idealized, monotheist version of Hinduism but also an idealized version of Hindu *society*. He is then in a position to invent his Vedic golden age. The Aryans of the Vedic era are therefore described as the chosen people to whom 'the formless God revealed perfect knowledge of the Veda'. Some time after the Creation, they

---

[5] Swami Dayananda, *The Light of Truth*, English translation of *Satyarth Prakash* by Pandit Ganga Prasad Upadhyaya, 1875; revised edn, 1946 (Allahabad: Dr Ratna Kumari Svadhyaya Samsthana, 2nd edn, 1981), p. 484.

apparently came down from Tibet into Aryavarta—virgin territory between the Himalayas and Vindhya mountains, the Indus and the Brahmaputra—and then became the 'sovereign lords of the earth', whose inhabitants they instructed in Sanskrit, the 'mother of all languages',[6] before falling into a decadent state characterized by the basest superstitions and idolatry. The proto-nationalist ethnic pride inherent in Arya Samajist ideology was combined with an overt stigmatization of the Others, whom the Arya Samaj nonetheless emulated, principally in order to resist them more efficiently, as evident from the last two chapters of *The Light of Truth*, which Dayananda devoted to a critical study of the Bible and the Koran. He dislikes the idolatry of the Old Testament,[7] and the weakness of the Prophet—'that God', he says, 'is not omniscient'.[8] All this notwithstanding, Dayananda was not a proponent of *Hindu* nationalism. Arya Samaj members, until the beginning of the twentieth century, preferred to stress their specificity and distinction from Hinduism, which they saw as a degraded form of the Vedic religion. In 1891 the movement's leadership in the Punjab called on its members to declare themselves 'Aryas' and not Hindus, during the census.[9]

Two Extracts from *The Light of Truth* (*Satyarth Prakash*)[10]

66. Q.—In whose minds and when were the Vedas revealed? [. . .]

A.—To the heart of Brahma it was transmitted by Agni and others. Look at what Manu says: 'Agni-vayu-ravibhyastu trayam brahma sanatanam. Dudoha yajna siddhyarthamrg-yajuh-sama laksanam' (Manusmrti, I.23).

In the beginning of the Universe, God first created men and then

---

[6] Cf. *The Light of Truth*, pp. 248, 277–9 and 341–5.

[7] See, for instance, ibid., p. 623.

[8] Ibid., p. 681.

[9] K. Jones, 'Religious Identity and the Indian Census', in N.G. Barrier, ed., *The Census in British India* (New Delhi: Manohar, 1981), p. 87.

[10] First extract from Chapter VII: 'God and the Vedas', *Satyarth Prakash* (*The Light of Truth*), English translation from the Hindi by Ganga Prasad Upadhyaya (Allahabad: Dr Ratnakumari Svadhyaya Samsthana, 1981), 2nd edn, pp. 246–53; second extract from Chapter VIII: 'Creation', ibid., pp. 276–9.

revealed the four Vedas to Agni, Vayu, Aditya and Angiras. These sages transmitted the Vedas to Brahma. Thus Brahma learnt (literally milked) the Vedas from Agni, Vayu, Aditya, and Angiras.

67. Q.—Why did He reveal the Vedas only to these four? Why not to others? This makes God partial.

A.—These four were the purest of all men, none else were like them. Therefore, the sacred Word was revealed to these only.

68. Q.—Why were the Vedas revealed in Sanskrta? Why not in the language of some one country?

A.—If God had sent this revelation in the language of some one country, He would have been guilty of being partial, as the learning of the Vedas would have been easier to the people of that country and more difficult to others. Therefore, the revelation was made in Sanskrita which belongs to no country. Besides, the Vedic language is the source of all languages. In that very language were the Vedas revealed. Just as the earth and all other creations of God are meant for all countries and their people and are equally the source of their art and craft, similarly the language of God's teaching should also be the same so that people of all countries have equal difficulty in acquiring the knowledge of the revelation and God may have no charge of partiality against Him.

69. Q.—How do you prove the Vedas to be God-revealed and not man-composed?

A.—God is holy, all-knowing, pure in nature and just, merciful, etc. in quality. The book that describes God exactly as He is, is God's not others [sic]. That book is God's in which there is nothing against laws of nature, or evidences such as perception, authority etc. God's knowledge is infallible and therefore, the teachings of God's book should also be equally infallible. In God's book there should be the same order of things as exists in nature, the same description of God, soul, creation, its cause etc. as they actually are. The Vedas are such books. There is nothing in them which might be contradictory to the laws of nature or invalid according to the laws of logic. The Bible and the Qoran do not stand this test and are not therefore, God's books . . .

70. Q.—What is the need of positing that the Vedas are from God? Men increase their knowledge step by step and in the long run succeed in composing books.

A.—They can never do so. There can be no effect without a cause. The men living in jungles cannot be learned by mere observation of nature. They can be learned only when someone gives them education. Even in these days nobody becomes learned without receiving education. In the same way, had not God taught the sages the Vedas, and they to others, there would have been no educated man today. If anybody is put in a secluded place in the midst of the ignorant or of animals, he will remain ignorant like his associates. Bhils and other forest tribes corroborate our statement. So long as education was not introduced by the people of India, Egypt, Greece and Europe were quite ignorant. Similarly so long as Europeans like Columbus had not gone to America, the Americans too were devoid of education for hundreds and thousands of years; when they got education, they become learned, similarly in the beginning of the universe men got knowledge from God and in due course raised their qualifications step by step.

Sa purvesamapi guruh kalenanavacchedat (Yoga Sutra, Samadhipada Sutra, XXVI).

Just as we, these days, acquire knowledge by reading with our teachers, similarly, God is the teacher of those, Agni and other sages who were born in the beginning of the universe. The soul becomes unconscious during Dissolution and sound sleep, God does not. His knowledge is imperishable. It follows, therefore, that no effect is possible without a cause.

71. Q.—The Vedas were revealed in Sanskrta. Agni etc. did not know that language. How did they then understand the Vedas?

A.—It was the Supreme Being who made it known to them. And whenever virtuous men, yogins, sages, etc. went into communion with God, expressed an eagerness to understand the Vedas, God helped them to do so. When the Vedas became known to many, those sages wrote commentaries and historical books. These books came to be known as the Brahmanas or notes on Brahma, i.e., Vedas . . .

73. Q.—Which books are called the Vedas?

A.—The Rg, the Yajur, the Sama, the Atharva—only the mantra portion (collections of the mantra).

Q.—Are the Vedas eternal or non-eternal?

A.—Eternal. God being eternal, His knowledge is also eternal. Eternal substances have eternal qualities, activities and nature. Non-eternal things have non-eternal qualities etc.

76. Q.—Are these books also eternal?

A.—No. A book is made of paper, ink etc. How can it be eternal?

But words and their relation with the things they stand for are eternal.

Q.—God might have given knowledge to those sages and they might have composed the Vedas.

A.—There is no knowledge without the knowable. There is none except the omniscient God who might have the ability of composing Gayatri and other verses having Gayatri and other metres and accents such as sadja long, short or balanced notes.

77. The rishis have composed books on grammar, philosophy, prosody etc., after having read the Vedas. If God had not revealed the Vedas, nobody could have composed anything. Therefore, the Vedas are the books of God. All persons should act according to their injunctions. If anybody asks them what religion they belong to they should say their religion is Vedic.

78. So much has been said about God and the Vedas. In the next chapter we shall deal with creation.

43. Q.—Were men and other creatures born young, grown up or old in the beginning of the Universe?

A.—Fully grown-up.

Had they been born young, they should have required parents to bring them up. If they had been created old, sexual intercourse being impossible, there would have been no reproduction.

44. Q.—Has this universe any beginning or not?

A.—No. Just as night precedes day and day precedes night, or day follows night and night follows day, just so dissolution precedes creation and creation precedes dissolution, or dissolution follows creation and creation follows dissolution. This cycle has been going on from eternity. It has neither beginning nor end. But as you see the beginning and end both, of every day and every night, similarly every creation and every dissolution has its beginning and its end. God, soul and materia-radica, these three are eternal by themselves (i.e., individually). But the creation and life of the universe are cyclically eternal. By cyclical eternity, we mean stream-like continuity. The stream of a river is ever continuous. It may dry up in the summer but in the rainy season it again begins flowing. Just as attributes, activities and nature of God are beginningless, so are the creation, sustenances and dissolution of His world. Just as there is no beginning or end of God's attributes, activities and nature, similarly there is no beginning or end of the actions, which, of necessity, emanate from Him.

45. Q.—God has given some souls the life of man; some cruel bodies of lions etc.; some, those of deer, cow, and other animals; some, those of trees, insects, worms, moths etc. This imputes partiality of God.

A.—No. This inequality is due to the inequality of action in the previous cycle of creation. If God had given them these lives irrespective of their actions, God would have been partial.

46. Q.—Which is the place where man was first created.

A.—In Trivistapa, which is now known as Tibet.

Q.—In the beginning was there one caste (class) or many?

A.—Only one-man-class. Later on, according to the saying of Rgveda (1, 51, 8) 'Vijani hyaryyan ye ca dasyavah' (distinguish the Aryas from those who are Dasyus), there became two classes, Arya, i.e., learned and virtuous and Dasyus, i.e., evil doers and the ignorant. According to the Atharvaveda (uta sudra utarye) the Aryas were divided into four classes, Brahmana, Ksattriya, Vaisya, and Sudra. The twice-born or educated persons came to be known as Aryas and the ignorant as Sudra or anadi (=anarya or non-Arya).

47. Q.—How did they then come here?

A.—There arose constant quarrels between the Devas or Aryas who were educated, and Asuras or Dasyus who were uncultured When troubles increased, the Aryas selected this part of the globe as the most excellent and settled in it. Since then it is called by the name Aryyavartta.

48. Q.—What are the geographical boundaries of the Aryyavartta?

. . . 1. The Himalayas in the north, the Vindhya in the south; and ocean on the east and the west.

2. Or in the west the Sarasvati (river Attak or Sindh), in the east, the Drsadvati (Brahmaputra) which rises in the eastern hills of Nepal and flowing in the east of Bengal and Assam, and in the west of Burmah falls into the southern sea (Bay of Bengal). The Aryyavartta is the name of the country lying between the northern mountains called Himalayas and the southern mountains called Vindhyas stretching right up to Ramesvaram in the south. This Aryyavartta was colonized

by the devas or Aryas, i.e., cultured and was called Aryyavartta because the Aryas or cultured people dwelt herein.

49. Q.—What was its previous name and who dwelt here?

A.—No name at all. Nor there lived any people here before the Aryas. The Aryas came to this country direct from Tibet shortly after the dawn of the creation.

50. Q.—Some say that these people came from Iran (Persia) and therefore, they were called Aryas. Previously here lived aborigines called Asuras and Raksasas. The Aryas called themselves Devas (gods). When there arose wars between them, these wars came to be known as Devasura-Sangrama or god-demon-wars in folklore.

A.—It is absolutely wrong.

Vijanihyaryanye ca dasyavo barhismate randhaya sasad avratan (Rgveda, 1, 51, 8). Uta sudra utarye (Atharvaveda, IX, 62.1). We have already written that 'Arya' is the name of virtuous, cultured and reliable persons, and 'Dasyu' of those who were just the reverse, thieves, vicious, unrighteous and uncultured. The Brahmanas, Ksattriyas, and Vaisyas (who are twice-born educated) are called Arya and the Sudras or un-educated as Anarya or non-Arya (ignorant). When the Vedas say so, how can we accept the idle talks of the foreigners? In the hilly tracts of the Himalayas there was war between the Aryas and Asuras or Mlecchas. In this war the Kings of the Aryyavattra, such as Arjuna and Dasaratha came to the help of the Aryas and contributed to their victory over the Asuras. It that outside the boundaries of the Aryyavartta the tracts lying East, East-South, South, South-West, and North-West, North, and North-East were inhabited by the Asuras and whenever these people fought with the Aryas, the royal families of the Aryyavartta proceeded to their succour. The war between Rama and Ravana which took place in the south is not called Devasura Sangrama. It is called the war between the Aryas and the Raksasas. No Sanskrta work writes that the Aryas came from Iran, and after defeating and driving out the aborigines became the rulers of this country. How can we, then, accept the statements of foreigners?

51.—Mleccha-vacas-caryavacah sarve te dasyavah smrtah (Manu-smrti. X.45).

Mlecchadesastu atah parah (Manusmrti. II.23).

The countries outside that Aryyavartta are called Dasyu-desa or Mleccha-desa. This is another testimony to the fact that Dasyu, Mleccha or Asura is the name of the people living outside the Aryyavartta towards the East, North-East, North, North-West, and West, and Raksasa the name of those who lived in the South-West, South and South-East. Even now the Abyssinians have frightful shapes as those imputed to the then Raksasas in the books. The people of the country just down the Aryyavartta on the other side of the globe were called Nagas and their country was called 'Patalas' because they were, so to speak, below the feet of the Aryas. They were called Nagas because they were the descendants of some ancestor of the name Naga. Ulopi, the wife of Arjuna, was the daughter of one of the kings of this dynasty. From Iksvaku to the times of the Kauravas and the Pandavas we find Arya dynasties ruling over the whole world, and the Vedic religion partially prevailing in all the countries outside the Aryyavartta. It is proved by the fact that Virata was the son of Brahma, Manu of Virata, Marici etc. ten sons of Manu, and Svayambhava etc. seven kings were the descendants of this dynasty. Iksvaku was a descendant of these. These were the early kings who colonized the Aryyavartta. Now due to ill-luck and idleness, vanity, as well as mutual animosities, the Aryas have come to such a pass, that, not to speak of ruling over foreign countries, they do not enjoy at present the indivisible, independent, free and fearless sway even over their own homes. Whatever little is left is also downtrodden by the outsiders. Very few rulers are independent. When evil days come country-men have to suffer all sorts of troubles. Whatever one may do, indigenous rule is always the best. Foreign government cannot be perfectly beneficial even when it is free from religious bias, race-prejudice, and imbued with parental justice and mercy. It is very hard to shake off linguistic differences, cultural angularities, and estrangement due to customs and manners . . .

2

R.B. Lal Chand

Dayananda founded the Arya Samaj in Punjab, and of all the Indian provinces Punjab remained for years the most receptive to his message. This state of things resulted from several factors. As mentioned earlier, the Brahmos of Bengal had prepared the grounds for this development in Punjab. Second, the anti-Brahminic dimension of Dayananda's discourse—though only one aspect of his perspective— was well in tune with the social context of a province where the merchant castes (Khatris, Aroras, etc.) were ascendant yet lacked the social status of Brahmins—hence their simmering resentment and interest in a more egalitarian creed. Third, Dayananda's discourse was meritocratic. His emphasis on merit struck a chord with the value system of the merchant castes, who believed in the entrepreneurial ethos. Finally, Hindus were in a minority in Punjab, comprising 40.7 per cent of the population, against 51.3 per cent Muslims and 7.5 per cent Sikhs (according to the 1881 census). The Arya Samaj's militant Hinduism thus exerted a peculiar appeal over the Hindu urban intelligentsia who saw their interests put in jeopardy because they were a minority.

The movement's recruits soon entered the political arena and shaped the first blueprint of *Hindu*—not 'Vedic' or 'Arya'—nationalism. Local Arya Samajis initiated the first Hindu political body, the Hindu Sabha (Hindu Association) when the pro-Muslim bias of the British administration was gradually translated into the granting of various important concessions, one of which was the setting up of separate electorates in 1909. Before that, the British had also decided to recruit a greater number of Muslims in the administration to promote the socio-economic status of a community that remained, in their eyes, backward.[1]

---

[1] N.G. Barrier, 'The Punjab Government and Communal Politics, 1870–1900', *Journal of Asian Studies*, vol. 17, no. 3, May 1968, pp. 523–39; and

The Hindu intelligentsia was also affected, at the same time, by the British policy defending the interests of rural Punjab *vis-à-vis* the urban merchants' community. A major expression of the policy was the Punjab Land Alienation Act (1901), which drastically restricted the possibility of those not classified among the 'Agricultural Tribes' from buying land.[2] This discrimination awakened in certain Hindus, especially within the Arya Samaj, a feeling of vulnerability, and of the need for a new Hindu solidarity, which precipitated the formation of a new pan-Hindu consciousness. The text below is very revealing of this ideological transformation.

Its author, Lal Chand (1852–1912), had been among Dayananda's first followers. He was responsible for formulating the plans for the Dayananda Anglo-Vedic (DAV) College, one of the first independent educational undertakings launched by Indians. The college was to become a major institution in Lahore and spawned many branches over North India. Lal Chand was the college's first president and occupied the position for twenty years, from 1884 till 1904. A lawyer by profession, he was also associated with the creation of the Punjab National Bank, the first bank established by Indians.[3]

Self-Abnegation in Politics appeared first as a series of articles in *The Punjabee* of Lahore in 1909. These articles, and the pamphlet which emerged from them, were published anonymously because of the risks the author would have taken by signing them. Lal Chand wrote that 'patriotism ought to be communal and not merely geographical',[4] an idea in direct opposition to the view of the Congress Party, which defined the Indian nation as consisting of all individuals of all communities living within the British-Indian realm. Lal Chand's ideas made a strong impact on the Hindus of Punjab: in fact his analysis underpinned the foundation by Arya Samajis of the Hindu Sabha in the

---

idem, 'The Arya Samaj and Congress Politics in the Punjab 1894–1908', *The Journal of Asian Studies*, vol. 26, no. 3, May 1967.

[2] N.G. Barrier, *The Punjab Alienation of Land Bill of 1900* (Durham: Duke University Press, 1966).

[3] P. Tandon, *A Punjabi Century* (Berkeley: University of California Press, 1968).

[4] Lal Chand, *Self-Abnegation in Politics* (Lahore: Central Hindu Yuvak Sabha, 1938), p. 103.

Punjab by the end of the first decade of the twentieth century. Lal Chand was elected president of the Reception Committee of the first meeting of the Hindu Sabha in 1911. Soon after, in the 1911 census, the Arya Samajis of Punjab declared themselves not as 'Aryas', as they had previously, but as 'Hindus'—a highly significant development.[5]

Extract from *Self-Abnegation in Politics*[6]

. . . In replying to the Mohammadan Deputation Lord Morley said: 'I know very well that any injustice, or suspicion that we are capable of being unjust to Mohammadans in India, would certainly have a *severe and injurious reaction* in Constantinople.' The italics are mine: that seems to me to form the crux of the whole situation. Mohammadans have Constantinople behind their back, not to speak of other Mohammadan independent states with which more or less British statesmanship have to deal. It is only but recently, under the new Turkish regime, that the British Government has been able to regain the lost ground of cordiality with Turkey, and it is nothing but natural that under the circumstances British statesmanship should be very anxious not to give any offence to Muslim claims, whether fancied or real. British statesmen, therefore, not only desire to conciliate Muslim opinion, but are seriously nervous lest they should give any offence to it. This frame of mind of British policy is now fully known to, and is understood by, the Indian Mohammadans, and they have seized the opportunity to press their demands. Their attitude, under the circumstances, far from being suppliant, is dictatorial, knowing full well as they do the complacent disposition of the Government. This is further evident from the growing impudence of the tone of demands which the Mohammadans have made during the last three years. And now they do not care to conceal their arrogance. On the least semblance even of a check to, or fancied attack upon, what they consider to be their vested rights they begin to utter threats.

---

[5] For more details, see C. Jaffrelot, 'The Genesis and Development of Hindu Nationalism in the Punjab: From the Arya Samaj to the Hindu Sabha (1875–1910)', *Indo-British Review*, vol. 21, no. 1, pp. 3–40.

[6] R.B. Lal Chand, *Self-Abnegation in Politics*, op. cit., pp. 1–13.

The events of the last three years amply justify this presumptuous attitude on the part of the Mohammadans. They have all along succeeded, and sometimes, beyond their own expectations. On the other hand, the Hindus have to fall back on their gullibility. They have no independent State to support their cause not even to cheer them with sympathy for their grievances. They are circumscribed within the four walls of Hindustan and have no outside assistance to influence the attitude of their rulers. They might cry themselves hoarse over this Charter and that Proclamation, but words and protests do not make up for the inherent weakness of their position. Their only weapon is talk. They might talk discontent or loyalty, but neither materially influences the situation. If they talk discontent and sedition it would only require a stronger and more numerous recruitment of police and especially of Mohammadan police, and the passing of a few more repressive laws. But their discontent does not inspire the same awe or desire to conciliate as does the regard for Constantinople. While if the Hindus sing loyalty, they are taken to be either hypocrites or devoid of the manly qualities of a race which deserves respect.

To add to this natural misfortune the Hindus have got a self-inflicted one in what is called and known as the Congress. This has proved a veritable source of weakness for purely Hindu interests. If there is one thing which is strictly forbidden within the precincts of the Congress it is the term 'Hindu'. Resolution may be passed to favour purely Mohammadan interests but the Hindu is tabooed there. I am not drawing simply on imagination. A special resolution was passed in the Congress respecting Mohammadan grievances with regard to the law of endowments. It did not, of course, affect the Hindus in any manner, but I give it as an instance of sectarian resolution. In the 2nd Congress which was held at Lahore a resolution was strongly supported by the Congress leaders, demanding special concessions to Mohammadans in the matter of education, but it was dropped owing to strong opposition by the delegates. On the other hand, a resolution relating to the Land Alienation Act could not be put forward because it was objected to by one Mohammadan delegate and might possibly give offence to Mohammadans outside the Congress. And what is the result of that piece of class legislation? The Hindu middle class, which, as past history shows, is the real backbone of the community has now been driven away from one legitimate source of livelihood, namely, the land. In the

absence of any effective opposition the state of affairs has gone from
bad to worse. Even the little which was left under the original Land
Alienation Act has, it is said for the sake of consistency, been taken
away under the Land Alienation Amendment Act. And mark the difference again here so far as the Government is concerned. There were
two Acts at the same time for disposal before the Punjab Legislature,
one relating to the Chenab Colonies and the second for amending the
Land Alienation Act. The former was objected to by Mohammadans
equally with Hindus as it encroached on their interests also, and it was
finally vetoed. The latter, which was objected to by the Hindus only,
was passed in spite of strong Hindu discontent at the time. Not only
this, but the Hindus received a good thrashing at the same time to put
them on their good behaviour. A number of men regarded as their
'leaders' were prosecuted on criminal charges, and one deported. And
yet a Hindu must be *non est* as a Hindu in the Congress. Nay, he has
no place even in the public press. Taking its cue from the Congress
Pandal the Hindu press has accepted as one of the cardinal maxims of
its creed not to utter or use the word 'Hindu'. Whenever there is a
Hindu grievance it must be agitated as an 'Indian' grievance, or not at
all. It is indeed a very dangerous sentimentality which chokes the
Hindu press. The Hindu press is afraid and feels ashamed to ventilate
a pure Hindu grievance, with the result that neither the Government
nor anyone else ever hears that there is any such thing as a Hindu
grievance.

Take another instance in this province, namely the public service.
There is no doubt that there is a considerable amount of discontent
among the Hindu middle class with regard to their position in relation
to Government service. Being driven away from their livelihood on
the land, they are also being gradually ousted from Government service
as a means of living. And, barring law and medicine, the only remaining
source left is trade and industry where they are making a struggle. But
the Hindu press is afraid by its self-inflicted creed to take up the pure
Hindu cause. We may say things in disguise or in a round-about manner, but not directly, because we are afraid of being twitted with taking
up a sectarian cause. That privilege, with great magnanimity, is left for
the Muslim press. While therefore the Mohammadan press may go on
sapping the very foundations of Hindu interests, the Hindu press

must look on with generosity and see the fire consuming their own houses. It is afraid of being charged with sectarianism, as if sectarianism even under pressure of competition were loathsome to touch. The highest ideal of conduct, no doubt, is universal brotherhood, provided there were no such things as race and nation. If these two terms could be expunged from the human dictionary [we would arrive at the] millennium, but evidently it is an impossible ideal to attain. It is a high ideal again, no doubt, to have a united nation. But it looks to me the very height of folly and absurdity to go on crying for a united nation when one important community, by its words and actions, makes it persistently and absolutely clear that they do not desire nor seek for union. The remedy when such evil exists is not to say we are one, but to declare emphatically that we are two. The generosity under such circumstances is taken for weakness and only aggravates the disease. It helps to add to the aggressive and presumptuous attitude of the other party. The moral ideal, that when slapped on one cheek you should offer the other for a slap, has no place in politics. Here the maxim is just the reverse. If you are slapped, give proper return, and you would at once find a desire by the other side to make friends. The method of offering the other cheek for being slapped has now been tried for over twenty years. There has been enough of coaxing and fawning, which by giving undue importance to the other community has begotten only insolence and impudence. May we not now try the counter method and see its result? At least this is a method equally worth trying, and I am sure we shall not thereby be worse off than we are. This method seems to have been very recently tried, and tried with great success, in a railway carriage, though in a different sphere of life. A Dogra Hindu Rajput entered a railway carriage at night time at a certain station, and finding a berth occupied by a British soldier who was lying at his ease and no other room, he took his seat just at the end of the berth occupied by the soldier. The latter stretched out his legs and gave a gentle push. The Rajput bore it with meekness and removed himself a little further to the end. This, however, did not satisfy the son of Mars. He gave a second and a more violent push with his feet. This naturally exasperated the Dogra Rajput, and the latter at once gave a slap, which being returned, the soldier was in a minute down on the floor of the carriage with the Rajput's hands on his throat. This at once brought humility and reconciliation, and the soldier left the carriage at the next station.

I do not for a moment say and urge that the Hindus ought to be offensive and aggressive, or take up quarrels with other communities. They ought to try to live on the best possible peaceful terms with neighbours, and true to their charitable instincts, even occasionally make a sacrifice for reconciliation as the Rajput did. But a purely and persistent aggressive attitude ought to be met by an equally aggressive attitude. In war this is one of the elementary principles of tactics, and it ought to have an equally important place in politics. When Hindu interests are threatened at the very foundations, these should not only be safeguarded but protected effectively. And my own impression is that if such policy is pursued a favourable change will soon be visible in the mode of thinking and conduct and behaviour of our Muslim brethren. But what is the result at present? The Hindus have no outside friends and sympathisers to look after or press their claims. Inside India they are helpless between the police and repressive measures, even if they give utterance to their grievances. The Congress, the only political machinery in the country, will not take up their cause because from the very commencement it has assumed to itself a sentimental ideal and is now afraid to climb down, happen what may even though the situation may result in disaster to the Hindus. The Hindu press is wedded to the Congress cry and is equally hesitant to advocate purely Hindu interests. What is to be done then? Are the Hindus then simply to remain as spectators of their own ruin? I shall attempt to answer this question in another communication.

II

In my letter under the heading 'Self-Abnegation in Politics' printed in the *Punjabee* of 23rd ultimo, I referred to the imbecility of the Hindus in protecting their own interests and the dangerous predicament they were placed in owing to their self-imposed attempt at unification. I further alluded to the fact that, while their cause lacked support, both from within and without, their political rivals were busy heart and soul in pushing forward their communal nationality and making the gulf between the two communities as wide as it may be. The result was that Hindu nationality and Hindu sentiments were being gradually obliterated and thrown in the background if not pushed out of existence. The view I took hardly stood in need of any support, but by a strange coincidence it has received ample vindication even at the hands of your local Mohammadan contemporary in a very recent issue.

There is one little question which at present is troubling the self-jubilant serenity of the Muslim mind, viz. the claims of Urdu against the Punjabee language and literature, and the writer in that issue takes the opportunity to read a sermon to Hindus on the futility of their Vedantic doctrines. He points out forcibly that Vedantism, as preached by Guru Nanak has failed to make one religion in India, it has failed to achieve political union when proclaimed by Congress, and it must equally fail when pressed in service for the unification of language and letters. This is a very clear exposition of the relative attitude of the two communities, not only in religion but also in politics and daily intercourse, and should the Hindus still remain immersed in pseudo-Vedantism and regard the whole world as Maya or unreality and Hindus and Mussalmans as a united Indian nation? If they do so, it will not be the fault of their ancestors. For the latter worked out not an incomplete philosophy. While they doubtless expiated on the One Cause for the universe, they were at the same time careful to lay the foundations of the Nyaya Shastra. Should not then the logic of events arouse the Hindus from their political sleep, for even Kumbh Karna used to awake at least once in six months or a year? It seems to me as if we are seized with sleeping sickness of a very dangerous type. Wrapped up in fantastic reveries of imagination like an opium-eater we continue to act the part in life of a Sheikh Chilly, and to revolve on ideas of a 'united Indian nation', the rights of a 'British citizen', colonial form of government, and other nonsense of the same genus and nature. And the wonder is that even the rudest shocks, threats and pricks do not avail to awaken us from our intense slumber.

Our rulers politely but plainly tell us that we ought not to amuse ourselves with any such musings, and that it is pure folly and madness to ask for concessions which even have a semblance of encroaching upon the complete maintenance and integrity of the sovereign rights of the ruling race. And yet we obdurately persist in talking of and demanding what we choose to call a 'peaceful revolution'. Not only that, but we actually imagine as if the mirage is within our easy grasp, and begin to dance merrily and with loud hallelujahs proceed to congratulate ourselves for receiving and our rulers for granting the boon. Verily the writer in the *Observer* is right in saying that we are Vedantists not only in religion, but in our political creed also.

Our nextdoor neighbours, the Mohammadans, never miss an opportunity to remind us that Hindu and Muslim are two inconsistent and even in great many respects antagonistic terms. This was also very forcibly pointed out in the address delivered by the chairman of the Conference at Amritsar. And yet we go on crying for unity. Blow after blow is administered and yet the *Andh Tam Vislrit Maya* cannot be knocked out of the Hindu brains. Here is an object lesson given by the Mohammadan community. They feel or pretend to feel that the Urdoo-Punjabee question in this province touches them vitally. And in giving vent to their feelings they have not hesitated to shower abuse on the head of a most prominent member of the Hindu community and even to accuse the rulers of Irish proclivities for sympathising with the Indian Nationalists. They have, moreover, declared in the clearest possible manner that even though every minute they speak the common language, yet their linguistic ideal is not identical with ours, but different, and must imbibe inspiration from countries beyond the confines of India. Again take another instance of Mohammadan *amour propre.* H.H. the Agha Khan, who is in no small degree fed and maintained by the offerings of his Hindu votaries, when interviewed on the question of the appointment of a member to the Council of the Viceroy of India, would rather not have the appointment made at all if a Hindu alone would receive the appointment. It is clear as day-light that the appointment is not intended for a Hindu alone, and that a Mohammadan is sure to get his chance in the alternative—knowing what we know of the action of the Government in other matters and yet His Highness cannot brook the idea of a Hindu being the sole member in the Viceroy's Council for the space of two years. His Highness, it will be remembered, is one of the leading members of the Mohammadan community and one of the main pillars and supporters of Aligarh Custantania.

In my previous letter I have given some instances of Government leanings in favour of Mohammadans, and if His Highness could but check his volubility for a while from giving vent to his inner rancorous feelings, he would have found the solace laid to his heart even in this matter at any early opportunity. It appears to me necessary to support my position by a few more instances in the same direction before proceeding further. And let us begin with the highest, the Secretary of State's own Council. Two members have been appointed to the Council, one a Hindu and another a Mohammadan. One feels tempted to question on what principle the two appointments were made. Were they made on the basis of numerical proportion? If so at least three Hindus to one Mohammadan ought to have been appointed. Were they made on the basis of fitness and qualifications? If so, could not two Hindus or two Mohammadans of similar qualifications be secured in the country to join the Council? Was it necessary to have class representation? If so, why not have in the Council representatives of Sikhs, Jains, Eurasians and Native Christians, and Parsees as well? The Secretary of State, in his reply to the Mohammadan Deputation headed by Mr Amir Ali, emphatically repudiated the idea that there is any need of class representation on the Executive Council of the Viceroy. On what principle, then, one is driven to ask the question, did the Secretary of State select one Hindu and one Mohammadan for his own Council? The mischief was once for all committed when the selection was made not on the simple principle that the nominees were qualified, but also on the ground that one was a Hindu and the other a Mohammadan by religion. There cannot be any manner of doubt that a second Hindu of even better claims could have been secured. But this was not done in due deference to Mohammadan feelings and sentiments. A principle of equal division and importance was conceded with all the ruinous results which must follow from it. It was an act of brave and glaring injustice to the Hindu community. For whether on the basis of numerical ratio or importance in matter of qualifications, influence and affluence, the Hindus were entitled to have three seats to one appointment of a Mohammadan. But who would speak for Hindu interests? Not the Congress, that slavishly follows the heels of a Parsee knight and which is even more afraid to give offence to Mohammadan sentiments than the Secretary of State himself, for the sake of a few Mohammadan delegates in borrowed *choghas*, as Bakhshi Tek Chand has rightly pointed out in his able and well-considered letter. Not the Hindu press, which must *nolens volens* echo the Congress tune.

Take, again, another instance, the next best in rank and nearer home, viz., the appointments to High Courts in India. Within the last two years four Mohammadan judges have been appointed to the High Courts (including Chief Courts) and the proportion at present for all India is four Mohammadans against five Hindus. Is this a right proportion in justice to Hindu interests? In Madras Presidency, according to the figures given by the Secretary of State, the Hindus are 89 per cent against 6 per cent of Mohammadans. In the United Provinces the proportion is 85 per cent against 15. In Bengal the ratio is 57 to 38, and in the whole of India the ratio is 75 to 25 per cent. And yet in spite of these figures the proportion of appointments is 5 to 4, and appointments in equal number have been made in Bengal, Madras and the United Provinces. It would appear as if Mohammadan legal talent has sprung up all of a sudden into obtrusive existence. In a speech in reply to a Mohammadan deputation the Governor of Bombay was reported to have remarked that legal talent is not an accident of birth. But His Excellency evidently overlooked that there is a natural birth as well as an artificial birth, and that the latter can be *forced* into creation and service by the mere accident of heat supplied by the warmth of State patronage.

It is true that the Madras appointment was first offered to a Hindu outside the Presidency who declined. But could it not be offered to an equally qualified Hindu inside the Presidency or another Hindu outside who would have agreed to it, when the numerical proportion of the two communities in that Presidency is 89 to 6? The Secretary of State speaks of the importance of Mohammadans as a community in the United Provinces in spite of their minor numerical strength, but he takes it for granted that the Hindu minority in the Punjab is of no importance against the Mohammadan majority so that according to the Secretary of State where the Mohammadans form a majority they must get a lion's share as a matter of course; and where they are in a minority, they will get it on the basis of their supposed importance. Was this then the basis on which the first appointment in the United Provinces was conferred on Mr Justice Mahmud over the heads of men like Pandits Bishambhar Nath and Ajudhia Nath? It appears as if the figures become elastic according as they meet or not the Moham-madan interests. When these various appointments were made, not a word was said that they were partial and displayed bias in favour of one religious community, not a word was uttered that they unjustly encroached upon the Hindu interests. The Congress and press were equally dumb because the process, it was imagined, united the nation—a very desirable end to achieve even by self-immolation. I believe the unification would very well and easily be expedited if the Hindus were one morning to embrace Islam in a body; or if that were to prove too much a 'strain' for Mr Gokhale and his Society, then if they were to retire altogether from the arena of public life, leaving the field to other communities and themselves taking to pursuits such as hewing wood and carrying water. I am not sure whether this even will be held to be satisfactory. But it will at least lead to unification by a process of eli-mination. Both in theory and in practice the Hindus have already been reduced to a position as if they formed 50 per cent of the popu-lation. They will soon be reduced to a position of one-third as another community of one kith and creed with the rulers is rapidly rising. Where we shall be in the end in this process of self-abnegation and self-immolation under a desire to form a united nation it is not very difficult to imagine. I shall attempt to support my view by a few more concrete instances in my next.

3

Har Bilas Sarda

B y the turn of the twentieth century the Arya Samajist version of Hindu nationalism, which had been taken up by the Hindu Sabha movement, reached canonical dimensions, not only because its ideologues had no hesitation comparing their civilization with others in order to claim its superiority, but also because this 'ism' now relied on strictly codified principles: the grandeur of Hinduism harked back to a Vedic golden age which was characterized by (1) a perfectly harmonious social system where caste was not a handicap but a functional tool towards a form of non-individualist, organic unity; (2) an ancient language, Sanskrit, which was the mother of all the world's languages; (3) a universal significance—especially in spiritual terms, as the resounding success of Vivekananda's participation in the World Congress of Religions at Chicago had shown in 1897—deriving from the putative spiritual and cultural domination that India exerted over the world in ancient times. Mostly this argument was supported by invoking Western authors who had indeed been responsible for identifying the Indo-European family of languages,[1] a notion from which some of them had deduced the idea of a superior Aryan race.[2] Obviously, citing Western writers enhanced the credibility of the discourse of Hindu ideologues in their own eyes, even though they remained highly critical of everything Western. This paradox is perhaps most blatant in parts of Har Bilas Sarda's book, *Hindu Superiority,*

---

[1] P.J. Marshall, ed., *The British Discovery of Hinduism in the Eighteenth Century* (Cambridge: Cambridge University Press, 1970).

[2] C. Jaffrelot, 'The Idea of the Hindu Race in the Writings of Hindu Nationalist Ideologues in the 1920s and 1930s: A Concept between Two Cultures', in Peter Robb, ed., *The Concept of Race in South Asia* (Delhi: Oxford University Press, 1995), pp. 327–54.

reproduced below. The British colonial administrators Todd and Elphinstone are repeatedly resorted to as scientific authorities, and the text is largely made of quotations (Sarda cites 550 books in all).

H.B. Sarda (1867–1955) belonged to the second generation of Arya Samajis. He may never have met Dayananda.[3] He joined the Arya Samaj in 1888 and became one of its main leaders in Rajputana, having been born in Ajmer (Rajasthan) and educated in Calcutta. A civil servant, he was well versed in literary work, to the extent that he wrote a biography of Dayananda and edited the Swami Dayananda Commemoration Volume in 1933.[4] He was also known for his reform-ist views because of his activity, as a member of the Central Legislative Assembly in 1924–34, against child marriages.[5] Elected to the assembly after retirement in 1924, he sponsored the Child Marriage Restraint Act in 1925: this was popularly known as the 'Sarda Act'. His reformist discourse, however, was typically Arya Samajist in the sense that within it some issues—such as inter-caste marriages—remained taboo. As a politician he was a key figure in the Hindu Mahasabha of Rajasthan over the two decades before independence. *Hindu Superiority* was published for the first time in English in 1906, and reprinted in 1917 and 1975.

Two Chapters from *Hindu Superiority: An Attempt to Determine the Position of the Hindu Race in the Scale of Nations*[6]

SOCIAL SYSTEM

Hail, social life! into the pleasing bounds
Again I come to pay the common stock
My share of service, and, in glad return
To taste the comforts, thy protected joys.

—Thomson: *Agamemnon*

---

[3] Sarda is known to have attended a lecture by Dayananda when he was eight years old.

[4] H.B. Sarda, *Life of Dayanand Saraswati* (Ajmer: n.p. 1968).

[5] For his many speeches in the assembly on this issue, see Har Bilas Sarda, *Speeches and Writings* (Ajmer: Vedic Yantralaya, 1935).

[6] Har Bilas Sarda, *Hindu Superiority: An Attempt to Determine the Position of the Hindu Race in the Scale of Nations* (New Delhi: R.T. Bhatia, 1975), 3rd edn, ch. 3, pp. 27–31; ch. 9, pp. 97–102.

The Hindus perfected society. The social organization of the people was based on scientific principles, and was well calculated to ensure progress without party strife. There was no accumulation of wealth in one portion of the community, leaving the other portion in destitute poverty; no social forces stimulating the increase of the wealth of the one and the poverty of the other, as is the tendency of the modern civilization. The keynote of the system, however, was *national service*. It afforded to every member of the social body, opportunities and means to develop fully his powers and capacities, and to use them for the advancement of the common weal. Everyone was to serve the nation in the sphere in which he was best fitted to act, which, being congenial to his individual genius, was conducive to the highest development of his faculties and powers.

There was thus a wise and statesmanlike classification which procured a general distribution of wealth, expelled misery and want from the land, promoted mental and moral progress, ensured national efficiency, and, above all, made tranquillity compatible with advancement; in one word, dropped *manna* all round and made life doubly sweet by securing external peace with national efficiency and social happiness— a condition of affairs nowhere else so fully realized.

This classification—this principle of social organization—was the *Varnashrama*. Mankind were divided into two classes, (1) the Aryas and (2) the Dasyus, or the civilized and the savage. The Aryas were subdivided into:

1. Brahmanas, who devoted themselves to learning and acquiring wisdom and following the liberal arts and sciences.
2. Kshatriyas, who devoted themselves to the theory and practice of war, and to whom the executive government of the people was entrusted.
3. Vaishyas, who devoted themselves to trade and the professions.
4. Sudras (men of low capacities), who served and helped the other three classes.

This classification is a necessary one in all civilized countries in some form or other. It was the glory of ancient Aryavarta that this classification existed there in its perfect form and was based on scientific principles—on the principle of heredity (which has not yet been fully appreciated by European thinkers), the conservation of energy, economy of labour, facility of development, and specialization of faculties. Literary men, soldiers, doctors, lawyers, clergymen, traders, and servants are to be found in England, France, America, and in every other civilized country of modern times, as they were in Ancient India. The only difference is that in one case the division was perfect and the working of its marvellous mechanism regular, while in the other the classification is imperfect and its working irregular and haphazard.

The *Varnashrama* was not the same as the caste system of the present day—a travesty of its ancient original. No one was a brahman by blood nor a sudra by birth, but everyone was such as his merits fitted him to be. 'The people,' says Col. Olcott, 'were not, as now, irrevocably walled in by castes, but they were free to rise to the highest social dignities or sink to the lowest positions, according to the inherent qualities they might possess.'

The son of a brahman sometimes became a kshatriya, sometimes a vaishya, and sometimes a sudra. At the same time, a sudra as certainly became a brahman or a kshatriya. Shanker Dig Vijaya says:

जन्ममना जायते शूद्रः संस्कारद्द्विज उच्यते ।
वेद पाठी भवेद्विप्रः ब्रह्म जानाति ब्राह्मणः ।।

'By birth all are Sudra, by actions men becomes *dwija* (twice-born). By reading the Vedas one becomes *vipra* and becomes *brahman* by gaining a knowledge of God.'

A passage in the Vanparva of the *Mahabharata* runs thus: 'He in whom the qualities of truth, munificence, forgiveness, gentleness, abstinence from cruel deeds, contemplation, benevolence are observed, is called a Brahman in the Smriti. A man is not a Sudra by being a Sudra nor a Brahman by being a Brahman.' The *Mahabharata* (Santiparva) says:

न विशेषोऽस्ति वर्णानां सर्वं ब्राह्ममिदं जगत् ।
ब्रह्मणा पूर्व सृष्टं हि कर्मभिर्वर्णतां गतम् ।।

'There are no distinctions of caste. Thus, a world which, as created by Brahma, was at first entirely brahmanic has become divided into classes, in consequence of men's actions.'

In his paper 'Sanskrit as a Living Language in India', read before the International Congress of Orientalists at Berlin, on the 14 September 1881, Mr Shyamji Krishnavarma said: 'We read in the Aitareya Brahmana (II.3.19), for example, that Kavasha Ailusha, who was a sudra and son of a low woman, was greatly respected for his literary attainments, and admitted into the class of Rishis. Perhaps the most remarkable feature of his life is that he, sudra as he was, distinguished himself as the rishi of some of the hymns of the Rig Veda (Rig, X.30–4). It is distinctly stated in the Chandogyopanishad that Jabala, who is otherwise called Satyakama, had no gotra, or family name whatever (Chan-Upa, IV.4); all that we know about his parentage is that he was the son of a woman named Jabala, and that he is called after his mother. Though born of unknown parents, Jabala is said to have been the founder of a school of the Yajur Veda. Even in the Apastamba Sutra (II.5–10) and the Manusmriti (X.65), we find that a sudra can become a brahman and a brahman can become a sudra, according to their good or bad deeds. Panini mentions the name of a celebrated grammarian called Cakravarmana in the sixth chapter of his Ashtadhyayi (p. VI.1.130); now Cakravarmana was a kshatriya by birth, since he has the prescribed Kshatriya termination at the end of his name, which is a patronymic of Cakravarmana.'

Who were Visvamitra and Valmiki but sudras. Even so late as the time of the Greek invasion of India, the caste system had not become petrified into its present state. The Greeks describe four castes. Megasthenes says that a Hindu of any caste may become a Sophist (brahman). Arrian counts seven classes: Sophists, agriculturists, herdsmen, handicrafts and artizens [sic], warriors, inspectors and councillors. (See Strabo, Lib XV.)

Colonel Tod says: 'In the early ages of these Solar and Lunar dynasties, the priestly office was not hereditary in families; it was a profession, and the genealogies exhibit frequent instances of branches of these races terminating their martial career in the commencement of a religious sect or "gotra" and of their descendants reassuming their warlike occupations.'[7]

---

[7] Manusmriti, II, 158 says: 'As liberality to a fool is fruitless, so is a Brahman useless if he read not the Holy Texts; or again, he is no better than an elephant made of wood or an antelope made of leather.'

There was no hereditary caste. The people enjoyed the advantages of hereditary genius without the serious drawbacks of a rigid system of caste based on birth.

'The one great object which the promoters of the hereditary system seem to have had in view was to secure to each class a high degree of efficiency in its own sphere.' 'Hereditary genius' is now a subject of serious enquiry amongst the enlightened men of Europe and America, and the evolution theory as applied to sociology, when fully worked out, will fully show the merits of the system. In fact the India of the time of Manu will appear to have reached a stage of civilization of which the brilliant 'modern European civilization' only gives us glimpses.

Even the system in its present form has not been an unmitigated evil. It has been the great conservative principle of the constitution of Hindu society, though originally it was a conservative as well as a progressive one. It is this principle of the Hindu social constitution which has enabled the nation to sustain, without being shattered to pieces, the tremendous shocks given by the numerous political convulsions and religious upheavals that have occurred during the last thousand years. 'The system of caste,' says Sir Henry Cotton, 'far from being the source of all troubles which can be traced in Hindu society, has rendered most important service in the past, and still continues to sustain order and solidarity.'

As regards its importance from a European point of view, Mr Sidney Low in his recent book, *A Vision of India*, says: 'There is no doubt that it is the main cause of the fundamental stability and contentment by which Indian society has been braced for centuries against the shocks of politics and the cataclysms of Nature. It provides every man with his place, his career, his occupation, his circle of friends. It makes him at the outset, a member of a corporate body; it protects him through life from the canker of social jealousy and unfulfilled aspirations; it ensures him companionship and a sense of community with others in like case with himself. The caste organization is to the Hindu his club, his trade-union, his benefit society, his philanthropic society. There are no work-houses in India, and none are as yet needed. The obligation to provide for kinsfolk and friends in distress is universally acknowledged; nor can it be questioned that this is due to the recognition of the strength of family ties and of the bonds created by associations and common pursuits which is fostered by the caste principle. An India without caste, as things stand at present, it is not quite easy to imagine.'

FOREIGN RELATIONS

In the theatre of the world.
The people are actors all.
One doth the sovereign monarch play;
And him the rest okay.

—Calderon

When such brilliant national character combines with such happy social organization of the people as to excite the admiration of all who study it, one can easily conceive what noble achievements of peace and war the ancient Hindus must have accomplished. It is true, 'peace hath her victories no less renowned than war'; still a peculiar halo of glory attaches to military achievements. The achievements of the Hindus in philosophy, poetry, sciences and art prove their peaceful victories. But their military achievements were equally great, as will appear from their mastery of the science of war.

Their civilizing missions covered the globe, and Hindu civilization still flows like an undercurrent in the countless social institutions of the world.

In the Aitereya Brahmana, Emperor Sudas is stated to have completely conquered the whole world, with its different countries.

That the Hindus were quite capable of accomplishing this feat, is clear from the remarkable article that appeared in the *Contemporary Review* from the pen of Mr Townsend. He says: 'If the Prussian conscription were applied in India, we should, without counting reserves or landwehr or any force not summoned in time of peace, have two-and-a-half millions of soldiers actually in barracks, with 800,000 recruits coming up every year—a force with which not only Asia but the world might be subdued.'

General Sir Ian Hamilton, in his scrap book on the first part of the Russo–Japanese War, says: 'Why there is material in the North of

India and in Nepaul sufficient and fit, under good leadership, to shake the artificial society of Europe to its foundations.'

The territorial strength of India in ancient and even in mediaeval times, was greater than it has ever been during the last thousand years. Pururawa is said to have possessed thirteen islands of the ocean. See *Mahabharata* Adiparva, 3143, '*Trisdasa samudra ya dwipa asnan Pururawah*', etc.

That the Hindus were a great naval power in ancient times is clear from the fact that one of the ancestors of Rama was 'Sagara, emphatically called the Sea-king, whose sixty thousand sons were so many mariners.'

Pliny, indeed, states that 'some consider the four satrapies of Gedeosia, Arachosia, Aria and Paropamisus to belong to India.' 'This would include,' says Mr Elphinstone, 'about two thirds of Persia.'

Strabo mentions a large part of Persia to have been abandoned to the Hindus by the Macedonians.

Colonel Tod says: 'The annals of the Yadus of Jaisalmer state that long anterior to Vicrama, they held dominion from Ghazni to Samarkand, that they established themselves in those regions after the *Mahabharata*, and were again impelled on the rise of Islamism within the Indus.' He adds: 'A multiplicity of scattered facts and geographical distinctions fully warrants our assent to the general truth of these records, which prove that the Yadu race had dominion in Central Asia.' He also says: 'One thing is now proved that princes of the Hindu faith ruled over all these regions in the first ages of Islamism, and made frequent attempts for centuries after to reconquer them. Of these, Babur gives us a most striking instance in his description of Ghazni; or, as he writes, Ghazni, when he relates how the Rai of Hind besieged Subakhtagin in Ghazni, Subakhtagin ordered flesh of kine to be thrown into the fountain, which made the Hindus retire.' The celebrated Balabhi was reduced by the same stratagem.

'Bappa, the ancestor of the Ranas of Mewar, abandoned Central India after establishing his line in Chitor, and retired to Khorasan. All this proves that Hinduism prevailed in those distant regions, and that the intercourse was unrestricted between Central Asia and India.'

'The Bhatti Chronicle calls the Langas in one page Pathan and in another Rajput, which are perfectly reconcilable, and by no means indicative that the Pathan or Afghan of that early period or even in the time of Rai Sehra was Mohamedan. The title of Rai is a sufficient proof that they were even then Hindus.' Colonel Tod adds: 'Khan is by no means indicative of the Mohamedan faith.'

Eminent Greek writers—eye-witnesses of the splendour of India—bear testimony to the prosperity of the country, which, even in her decline, was sufficiently great to dazzle their imagination. The Indian court was the happy seat to which Greek politicians repaired as ambassadors, and they all speak of it in glowing terms.

Mr Weber says: 'Thus Megasthenes was sent by Seleucus to Chandergupta, Deimachus again by Antiochus and Dionysius, and most probably Basilis by Ptolemy II to Amritaghata, son of Chandergupta.'

Antiochus the Great concluded an alliance with Sobhagsen about 210 BC, but was eventually defeated and slain by him. Colonel Tod says: 'The obscure legends of the encounters of the Yadus with the allied Syrian and Bactrian kings would have seemed altogether illusory did not evidence exist that Antiochus the Great was slain in these very regions by the Hindu king Sobhagsen.'

The Greek king, Seleucus, even gave Chandergupta his daughter to wife. Professor Weber says: 'In the retinue of this Greek princess there of course came to Patliputra, Greek damsels as her waiting-maids, and these must have found particular favour in the eyes of the Indians, especially of their princes. For not only are . . . mentioned as articles of traffic for India, but in Indian inscriptions also, we find Yavan girls specified as tribute; while in Indian literature, and especially in Kalidasa, we are informed that Indian princes were waited upon by Yavanis (Greek damsels) . . .

The Persian Emperor, Nausherawan the Just, gave his daughter in marriage to the then Maharana of Chittor. Even *Ramayana* says that in Ayodhia, ambassadors from different countries resided. According to Justin, the monarch of Ujjain (Malwa) held a correspondence with Augustus. Augustus received at Samos an embassy from India. The ambassadors brought elephants, pearls and precious stones. There was a second embassy from India sent to Emperor Claudius, of which Pliny gives an account. He received from the ambassadors, who were four in number, the information about Ceylon which he has embodied his *Natural History*. Two other embassies from Hindu princes to

Rome were sent before the third century AC [presumably 'After Christ'—Ed.] one to Trajan (107 AC) and another to Antonius Pius. These relations continued as late as the time of Justinian (530 AC).

Strabo mentions an ambassador from King Pandion to Augustus, who met him in Syria. It appears from Periplus and Ptolemy that Pandion was the hereditary title of the descendants of Pandya, who founded the kingdom in the fifth century BC. A brahmin followed this ambassador to Athens, where he burnt himself alive.

'In one of Ashoka's inscriptions, five Greek princes appear.—(1) Antiochus of Syria, (2) Ptolemy, Philadelphos of Egypt, (3) Antigonos Gonatos of Macedon, (4) Magas of Kerene, (5) Alexander II of Epirus.' 'Great intercourse,' says a writer, 'formerly subsisted between the Hindus and the nations of the West.'

Thus, when even in those days, India was so great as to exact the homage of all who saw her, though her grand political and social institutions had lost their pristine purity and vigour, and those mighty forces which worked for her welfare and greatness were disappearing, when even in her fall she was the idol of foreign nations, how mighty must she have been when she was at the height of her power, at the zenith of her glory! Her constitution still stands like some tall ancient oak in a forest shorn of foliage, but still defying the discordant elements that rage round it, still looking down, with a majesty and dignity all its own, upon the new-sprung, prosperous young trees growing round it in happy ignorance of the storms and gusts in store.

It is curious to learn that even in her decline, India was sufficiently strong to defy the great conquerors of the old world. It was threatened by the prosperous empire of Assyria, then at the meridian of her power under the celebrated queen Semiramis. She used the entire resources of the empire in preparations to invade India, and collected a considerable army. 'After three years spent in these extraordinary preparations, she sent forward her armies, which some writers describe as amounting to several millions of combatants, but the narrative of Ctesias estimates them at three hundred thousand foot, five hundred thousand horse, while two thousand boats and a great number of mock elephants were conveyed on the backs of camels.' But what was the result? 'The army was utterly routed and Semiramis brought back scarcely a third of her host; some authors even maintain that she herself perished in the expedition.'

> Horrid suggestion! I thinkest thou then the gods
> Take care of men who came to burn their altars,
> Profane their rites, and trample on their laws?
> Will they reward the bad? It cannot be.

> —Sophocles: *Antigone*

In later times, the Yadu king, Gaj Singh, who founded Gajni (Ghazni), single-handed 'defeated the combined armies of Shah Secunder Roomi and Shah Mamraiz.'

4

Madan Mohan Malaviya and Lala Lajpat Rai

Although the first Hindu Sabha took shape in Punjab in the early 1910s, a network of similar sabhas developed soon afterwards elsewhere in North India. The first region to follow Punjab was the United Provinces (today's Uttar Pradesh). There the movement took shape, as it had done in Punjab, in reaction to the granting of special concessions to the Muslim minority. The turning point occurred in 1916 when Muslims were awarded a separate electorate at the municipal level. However, in this region the ideological overtone of the Hindu Sabhaites was generally more conservative. Not only was the Ganges belt a stronghold of Hindu orthodoxy (in part because of the holy cities of Benares, Haridwar, and Prayag or Allahabad), but also because the upper castes here exerted a commanding influence on account of their hold over land, administration, and trade, as well as their sheer numbers: they represented one-fifth of society, 10 per cent of them being Brahmins. The United Provinces was also the stronghold of the Sanatan Dharma Sabha (Association for [the Defence] of the Eternal Religion), which arose in reaction to the reformist zeal of the Arya Samaj but which was responsible, eventually, for the expansion of the Hindu Sabha in the region.

The key figure in all these developments was Madan Mohan Malaviya (1861–1946), a pandit from Allahabad whose family was highly respected for its orthodoxy and command of the sacred texts of Hinduism.[1] A lawyer by training, Malaviya became a member of the Congress upon its inception, and was a professional politician: he was appointed

[1] S. Chaturvedi, *Madan Mohan Malaviya* (Delhi: Government of India, 1972), pp. 1–3.

president of Congress in 1909 and in 1918 got himself first elected to
the Municipal Council of Allahabad and then to the Provincial Legislative Council without interruption for decades.[2] He constantly defended moderate positions on the British presence in India, as well as
conservative views of social reform. He was the archetypal orthodox
Brahmin.[3] He would not accept food from people who were not of his
own jati.[4] He started the Hindu Samaj (Hindu Society) in 1880 to
defend the region's Hindu festivals, in particular the yearly Magh
Mela, which he felt was under threat on account of missionaries.[5]
Soon afterwards, he launched plans for a Hindu university. This was
to become the Benares Hindu University (BHU) in 1916. The idea
was to preserve Hindu tradition, including a hereditary caste system.[6]
Soon after the opening of BHU, in 1922 Malaviya was instrumental
in reviving the Hindu Mahasabha within Congress.

This was made possible because Sanatanists of the United Provinces
à la Malaviya, and Arya Samajis from Punjab, joined hands. From
among the latter, Lala Lajpat Rai (1865–1928) played a major role.
Lajpat Rai had been attracted by the Brahmo Samaj before turning to
the Arya Samaj.[7] A lawyer by training, like most of his colleagues, he
worked as a journalist—he also founded *The Punjabee*—before embracing a political career. As a Congressman he belonged to the Extre-
mists, a group which advocated more radical anticolonial protest action

[2] S.L. Gupta, *Pandit Madan Mohan Malaviya* (Allahabad: Chugh Publications, 1978), pp. 5–6.

[3] N.C. Kelkar, 'Malaviyaji: His Personality and Work', in *Malaviya Commemoration Volume* (Benares: Benares Hindu University, 1932), p. 1031.

[4] Nand Lal Singh, ed., *Mahamana Malaviyaji Birth Centenary Volume*
(Benares: Benares Hindu University, 1961), p. 26.

[5] *Speeches and Writings of Pandit Madan Mohan Malaviya* (Madras: G.A.
Natesan, 1919), p. 3.

[6] V.A. Sundaram, ed., *Benares Hindu University, 1916–1942* (Benares: 1942),
p. viii. See also J. Lütt, 'The Movement for the Foundation of the Benares
Hindu University', in *German Scholars in India* (New Delhi: Cultural Department of the Embassy of Federal Republic of Germany), vol. 2; and S.L. Dar
and S. Somaskandan, *History of the Benares Hindu University* (Benares: BHU,
1966).

[7] Lala Lajpat Rai, *Autobiographical Writings* (Delhi/Jullundur: University
Publishers, 1965), p. 26.

than that initiated by the Congress founders, and which the Moderates, including Malaviya, wanted to follow. As a result Lajpat Rai took part in demonstrations and his radicalism landed him in Mandalay Jail in 1907.

In the early 1920s Malaviya and Lajpat Rai worked together at the helm of the Hindu Mahasabha, the national confederation of local Hindu sabhas that had been formed in 1915.[8] Their collaboration had been precipitated by a mobilization on the part of the Muslims within the framework of the Khilafat movement.[9] As noted earlier, this was the agitation which degenerated in some instances into anti-Hindu riots. In 1921, during a peasant uprising against landlords on the Malabar coast of Kerala, the Mapillas—descendants of Arab merchants who had settled there from the eighth century—established a Khilafat king and attacked Hindus, some of whom were converted by force.[10] These violent episodes marked the beginning of inter-communal riots, especially in North India,[11] which culminated in reinforcing a sense of vulnerability among the majority community. The Hindu Mahasabha leaders kindled their organization within the framework of a movement they called the Hindu Sangathan (Hindu Organisation for Unity), and on a firmer ideological base than before. One of the declared objectives of the Hindu Sangathan movement was the integration of Untouchables into Hindu society, with a view to dissuading them from converting to other religions. In 1923 the Hindu Mahasabha voted in favour of resolutions calling for Untouchables to enjoy full access to roads, schools, wells, and even temples.[12] At the time, the Hindu Mahasabha functioned as a pressure group within Congress,

---

[8] R. Gordon, 'The Hindu Mahasabha and the Indian National Congress 1915 to 1926', *Modern Asian Studies*, vol. 9, no. 2 (1975), pp. 145–203.

[9] G. Minault, *The Khilafat Movement: Religious Symbolism and Political Mobilization in India* (New York: Columbia University Press, 1982), pp. 121–9.

[10] R.L. Hardgrave, Jr., 'The Mapilla Rebellion, 1921: Peasant Revolt in Malabar', *Modern Asian Stdies*, vol. 11, no. 1 (1977), p. 82; and C. Wood, *The Moplah Rebellion and its Genesis* (New Delhi: People's Publishing House, 1987).

[11] D. Page, *Prelude to Partition: The Indian Muslims and the Imperial System of Control* (New Delhi: Oxford University Press), 1982, p. 74.

[12] *Indian Annual Register*, 1923, vol. 1, p. 139.

aiming to influence the party leadership, which continued to entertain a non-ethnic conception of the nation.

Presidential Addresses at two Hindu Mahasabha Annual Meetings[13]

Madan Mohan Malaviya: Presidential Address, as Reported (1923)

Pt Malaviya began his address with Veda path (recitation of Vedic mantras) and heartily thanked the audience for electing him president. He laid emphasis on the greatness of hoary Hindu civilisation, the four varnas (castes) and four ashramas (stages) of Hindu society. Paying respects to Buddha he said Lord Buddha, the thrice greatest benefactor of mankind, is worshipped by Hindus as one of the ten incarnations of God. The ten Buddhistic commandments exactly tally with Manu's rules about 'achar' and there is no difference between Hindus and Buddhists. He said that the ashrama system of Hindu society was un-paralleled in its perfection, which divided life into four parts of brahma-charya, grehastha, vanaprastha and sanyasa. Ancient great men and sages, Ram and Krishna, Bhishma, Drona, Yudhistira, Arjuna, Vasishta, Gautama and others were seers of the Hindu civilisation. Tolerance and forgiveness were characteristics of the Hindu society and even in the later age Prithvi Raj captured Mohammad Ghori and set him free. The Hindu ideal is never to hurt or be aggressive to anybody, but at the same time Hindus wished that they should not also be hurt or attacked by others.

The Hindu religion sustained many attacks. Hindus never cared so much for rajya as for dharma. We had fallen down and before the Bri-tish advent anarchy and chaos reigned supreme in India. Hindus and Mahomedans both had fallen down and were fighting one another. The British came to India and ruled over India, of course with a selfish motive and interest, but some common advantages have been deriv-ed by us. People of different and farthest corners have been brought nearer and together due to railways and telegraphs and on account of

---

[13] Presidential addresses by M.M. Malaviya and Lala Lajpat Rai at two Hindu Mahasabha annual meetings, *Indian Annual Register*, 1923, pp. 127–40 and *The Indian Quarterly Register*, vol. I, January–June 1925, pp. 377–85, respectively.

a common language and common laws, mutual relations have increased and they have ample facility for coming together. From 1885 to 1915 the Congress strove its utmost and worked hard for India's uplift, although the Mahomedans as a community kept themselves aloof, except a few liberal-minded statesmen. In 1916 all of us joined and drew up a scheme for reform. Something was given, but it was insufficient and incomplete. Since then our condition has been worse. The greatest of Indians and the saint of the world, Mahatma Gandhi (cheers), was most unjustly imprisoned by the Government (Shame) and we have not yet been able to get him released—our weakness and helplessness cannot be greater than this, that we have not yet been able to effect his release. The heart of India is most pained at this Government attitude and explosives are collecting [*sic*] which may one day prove very dangerous. Besides this, our trade and commerce are destroyed. Traders and merchants are impoverished. Government is increasing taxation and our condition and status are pitiable. Formerly the Government had some fear of us, but since Mahatma Gandhi's preachings of non-violence the Government's attitude had completely changed. We have now to consider what is our duty in the present circumstances, what relations we have to maintain towards the Government, Mahomedans, Parsis and other Indian communities.

Hindu–Muslim Problem: Referring to relations with Mahomedans the Pandit said that it was an unhappy, a painful episode. The relations between Hindus and Mahomedans have not been as happy and cordial as they ought to be. During the Bengal Partition days the Government were inciting Mahomedans to attack Hindus. In 1916 in Eastern Bengal inhuman, brutal, unparalleled atrocities were perpetrated on Hindus. Hindu women were outraged by fanatic Mahomedans and many Hindu women had to take shelter in rivers and tanks to protect their honour. Then came the Great War in 1914. In 1914 in the frontier districts, particularly Muzaffarnagar, Hindu houses were regularly looted and Hindu women dishonoured, but Indian patriots preached not to heed them. By Mahatma Gandhi's advice Hindus worked with Mahomedans and helped them in the Khilafat cause, not because the former wanted something in return, but because they were for the liberty and freedom of every nation and also because of their sympathy for fellow Muslim brothers. The speaker emphasised that he did not attribute such inhuman attacks to good and gentle Mahomedans but to rogues, vagabonds and bad elements of the Muslim society. Again in 1920 brutal and inhuman atrocities were perpetrated on Hindus by Moplahs in Malabar. Hindu houses were looted, women were outraged, male and female butchered with the greatest cruelty for refusing to embrace Islam and many were forced into Islam at the point of the sword. The speaker pathetically and movingly said that it is better to die than to be beaten and oppressed anywhere and everywhere, than to see women's modesty outraged, temples attacked and burnt and idols broken. The whole of India was severely pained and afflicted at these horrible inhumanities. Due to tolerance we patiently bore all this and drank the bitter dose simply with anxiety and desire that no ill-feeling and differences be created between the two sister communities. The Amritsar episode is not out of memory. At Multan temples were burnt down and women's chastity was outraged and latter [sic] on burnt Geeta and Granth Saheb and broken temple idols were found. Next an appeal was issued to maintain unity and peace on Bakrid day, but riots occurred at several places, although not so many as were expected. Our ladies do not consider they are as safe as 50 years ago. Amritsar Hindu women do not come out of houses so frequently and abruptly as they used to do formerly. Every moment they fear of being dishonoured. Everybody knows what happened at Panipat and at Ajmer. Temples were broken and burnt and idols destroyed.

In such circumstances it is our individual and social duty to increase our strength and be on terms of love and good-will with Muslims. It is most deplorable that Hindus are so fallen that a handful of foreigners can be ruling over us. Fie on the Hindus who live to see the breaking of temples and the outrage of women. Miss Ellis was kidnapped and the vibration pervaded the whole British Empire. Behind English girls and women there is national strength which protects them wherever they go. So also with Mahomedan women. There was a time when Hindu ladies had also such national backings behind them. Unless we have such strength, we cannot continue among strong nations of the world. Whatever steps we adopt, we should see that we may not harm others and put hindrance to national unity. The main reason of the present disunity is that Hindus are comparatively weak and cannot protect their religion and women. Unity and good-will can exist only between two equally strong parties. When the irresponsible element of Muslims will realise that we can react to the policy of tit for tat they would never venture to attack us.

The Pandit continued: 'I solemnly affirm before God I never mean to hurt Muslims or have the supremacy of Hindus over Muslims. If that be the sentiment in me, God may give me the greatest punishment, but I wish that my Hindu brethren be wiped off this earth if they cannot protect their sisters, daughters and others, cannot save the honour of our religion. We are responsible for our weakness. We have forgotten our duty. We should not fight shy of being called Hindus. When Hindus are oppressed we should approach Muslim leaders to devise means to settle disputes. In case riots occur we should settle matters in consultation with leaders of both communities.'

Pandit Malaviya then emphasised on girls' education. He laid great emphasis on the importance and necessity of brahmacharya, physical strength and exercise and urged the establishment of wrestling places (Akharas) in every quarter, every town and village. He next urged economy in social functions such as marriages, upanayan and others. He denounced dowry and urged its wholesale stoppage. Regarding untouchability the Pandit spoke very feelingly and tears were trickling down his cheeks when he referred to the untouchables. He said the Hindu Sabha comprises all sects of Hindus. Our untouchables follow the Hindu religion, worship Rama, Krishna and other Hindu gods, take their meal after bath, and if wealthy, even build temples. (Swami Shraddhanand interrupted: But then they are not allowed to enter those temples and worship there.) With tears in his eyes the Pandit then took out the turban from his head and said: 'Why should I not place my turban at the feet of my untouchable brother who follows the Hindu religion? Why should I not allow my untouchable brother to have darshan in temples? Full of sins as I am, what right have I to stop my untouchable brother from entering temples?'

Addressing the orthodox pandits, he then said with folded hands: 'Oh, learned Pandits, for God's sake do not prevent these brothers from having darshan in temples'.

Referring to permission to untouchables for drawing water from wells the president said that Christians and Mahomedans are asking untouchables to embrace their religion, for so long as they remain

Hindus they are not allowed to draw water from wells and if they accept their faith, they will not be so outcasted [*sic*], insulted and disallowed. This exactly happened at Panipat. But this is to be remembered that these untouchables who are so outcasted [*sic*] by high caste people were the first to come to defend the Hindu temple at Panipat when it was attacked by Mahomedans. Quoting the story of Raja Rantideva, the Pandit said that this Raja after starvation for 48 days got something to eat. A brahman beggar went to him and he fed him with that food and then successively came two untouchable beggars with dogs to whom Rantideva gave all that he had with the greatest respect and affection. Pertinently remarked Pandit Malaviya: 'An untouchable comes under the hottest sun from your labour and is extremely thirsty. I ask what true Hindu is there who will so cruelly prevent these untouchables from drawing water from wells while they do not object untouchables' entry in houses when their services are required. Teach them to be clean. When they travel with us in trains, when they sit with us in schools, we do not object because this has been forced upon us by the Government.'

Re-conversion: Referring to the Shuddhi movement Pandit Malaviya said there are forty-eight crores of Muslims in India of whom not more than fifty lakhs are those who might have come from outside. The rest were converted from Hinduism. Theirs is a proselytising religion while our religion has closed the doors for those who wish to come in our fold. Mullas have recently prepared an expansive scheme for reconversion of Hindus on a grand active scale in their private very confidential meeting and have scrupulously given no publication to this resolution and they have also collected fifty lakhs, but you will be surprised to know that it has not been scrupulously kept secret. Hindus are converted by dupes. In Gujrat some Mussalmans with notices bearing prints of 'Om preach Kalauki incarnation is H.H. Aga Khan' say that they should join that sect. Within three years one lakh of Hindus have been converted by Khojas. He asked: 'Is there no prayashchitta for those who unknowingly took anything touched by non-Hindus. Malkanas ought to be taken into Hinduism. He asked: What Hindu is there who has this right to say that some particular man has no right to offer prayers after coming into the Hindu fold?

The President then referred to a verse in *Dharmshastra Mahaprabandha* which lays down that those who had been converted to other religion either by force or willingly can be taken back to the Hindu religion if they so desire. He asked the audience to decide this question. Replying to those who say that we should not care for our numerical strength and that those who have already been converted should not be taken into Hinduism, the Pandit said: 'When now we are so badly treated with a numerical strength of 22 crores, what would be our condition in future with a much reduced Hindu population, if we allow this rate of conversion from Hinduism and do not allow reconversion into Hinduism?

Lala Lajpat Rai's Presidential Address, as Reported (1925)

Lala Lajpat Rai in the course of his Presidential Address said:

'The Hindus have no political aims of their own separate from those of their countrymen of other faiths. There was a time when good many of the Hindu leaders wanted the Hindus to abstain from all political activity and to engage only in religious exercises. That class has now almost disappeared. But another class has come to the front who hold out that Hindu leaders have injured the Hindu community by taking to too much anti-government political activities and by raising the standard of Swaraj, and that it is time that we should make up with the Government and give up all anti-government activities. I am afraid I cannot agree with them. I am not at all sorry for the part the Hindu leaders have so far played in the development of the movement of freedom. The future historian of India will I hope, give them credit for their activities in this direction. It must be understood that no living nation can avoid politics. Politics is the very breath of associated life and political activities of a healthy kind are absolutely necessary for social progress and national prosperity. In this respect the following quotation from the *Maha-Bharata* ought to be very carefully borne in mind by such Hindu leaders as preach to us political inactivity:

> When Politics become lifeless, the triple Veda sinks, all the Dharmas (i.e., the basis of civilization) (howsoever) developed, completely decay.
>
> When traditional State-Ethics are departed from, all the divisions of individual life are shattered,

In Politics are realised all the forms of renunciation, in Politics are united all Sacraments, in Politics are combined all knowledge; in Politics are centred all the Worlds'. *Maha Bharata* Shantiparva—63-28-29.

Political activities are of two kinds—anti-government and pro-government. It will be foolish to oppose Government for the sake of opposition. It will be equally foolish to support Government with the object of individual or communal gain. The Hindus have so far followed a National policy and, I think, they must stick to that. They will be stultifying themselves if they replace their nationalism by communism. Yet we can not ignore the fact that there are some communities in India who want to take undue advantage of our nationalism and are pushing forward their communalism to such an extent as is injurious to the interests of the whole nation and certainly disastrous to those of the Hindu community. Such communalism we are bound to oppose as, in our judgment, it can only lead to permanent slavery, permanent disunity and a state of perpetual dependence.

Hindus do not Want a Hindu Raj: 'There is some apprehension in the mind of a certain section of our Muslim countrymen that the Hindus are working for a Hindu Raj. It is to be deplored that some Hindus, too, should have taken to that line of argument in retaliation to the Mohammedan cry for Muslim Raj. We know that all Mohammedans do not want a Muslim Raj, and we also know as a fact that the bulk of the Hindus do not want a Hindu Raj. What the latter are striving after is a National Government founded on justice to all communities, all classes and all interests. In my judgment, the cry of a Hindu Raj or a Muslim Raj is purely mischievous and ought to be discouraged.

'Some time ago I had the occasion to read in one of the Muslim papers an article on Muslim Raj. The writer dismissed the idea of establishing Muslim Raj by the help of foreign Mohammedan states, such as Kabul and Turkey. And he also dismissed the idea of establishing a Muslim Raj by deceiving the Hindus into a unity for turning out the British and then establishing a Muslim Raj. But he actually advocated the policy of co-operation with the Government which might in the course of time lead that Government to hand over their power to the Muslims as the best organised and the most powerful body of men fit to rule. It seems to me that the writer has done great injustice to the Mohammedans by this line of argument as his conclusion seems to be more in the interests of Anglo-India than of the Muslim community. I am confident that this conclusion is not shared by the whole Mohammedan community, though unfortunately the utterances and actions of some of the foremost Muslim leaders do lend colour to it. Anyway, I am clear in my mind that neither a Hindu Raj nor a Muslim Raja is in the realm of possibility. The correct thing for us to do is to strive for a democratic Raj in which the Hindus, Muslims and the other communities of India may participate as Indians and not as followers of any particular religion.

So far as Politics are concerned, the Hindu Mahasabha has no special political functions except to define the position of the community in relation to other communities. The Hindus as a community are opposed to communal representation as such in any shape or form. The preponderance of opinion seems to be that the Lucknow Pact was a mistake but it is wrong to represent, as has been done by Mr M.A. Jinnah recently at Aligarh, that the Hindus are altogether opposed to any revision or reconsideration of the Lucknow Pact. In conversations at Delhi, the position of the Hindu representatives was that they would accept any uniform principle of representation applicable to the whole of India subject to *one* consideration that the electorates in all cases should be mixed and that the principle of communal representation shall not be extended beyond the legislature. In face of this to say that the Hindus as such are opposed to any compromise is not true. I do not consider that an understanding between the Hindus and the Mohammedans is impossible, but it must be clearly understood that the Hindus will not submit to any coercion whatsoever in arriving at some settlement. No amount of riots and disturbances will make them enter into any agreement which they do not consider fair and just.

The Problem of North-West Frontier—The Fear of Invasion: It is said that the Hindus are very much obsessed by a fear of the Indian Mohammedans making a common cause with the Mohammedan Powers beyond the North West Frontier to establish Mohammedan dominions in India. In this connection we have been assured by some Mohammedan leaders that the apprehension is absolutely unfounded, and is in fact a reflection on their patriotism. They are as much interested in the independence of India of any foreign control, be it a Mohammedan or a non-Mohammedan, as the Hindus. I have no doubt that this assurance is perfectly *bona fide* and sincere as far as it goes. But there is no guarantee that the Mohammedans of the North West Frontier Province, the Punjab and Sindh, are likely to take the same view if any such situation arises. If anything, the indications are to the contrary. We have several evidences of the mentality of the Frontier Moham-medans in this respect. Some Mohammedans have already suggested that all the territories which lie between Peshawar and Agra should be handed over to the Mohammedans in which they might establish Mohammedan Government as a member of the Mohammedan League of Nations. At the last session of the Muslim League held at Bombay, M. Mohammad Ali actually suggested that the Mohammedans of the Frontier Province should have the right of self-determination to chose between an affiliation with India or with Kabul. He also quoted a certain Englishman who had said that if a straight line be drawn from Constantinople to Delhi, it will disclose a Mohammedan corridor right up to Saharanpur. But the most important evidence of this menta-lity is to be found in the statement of a very important Mohammedan leader made by him before the Frontier Enquiry Committee in 1923. The name of this gentleman is Sardar Mohammad Gul Khan who appeared before the Committee as a witness in the capacity of President of Islamia Anjuman, D.I. Khan. We take the following from the Minute of dissent by Mr N.M. Samarth on page 122 of the Report of the said Enquiry Committee. 'This witness', says Mr Samarth, 'was asked by me: "Now, suppose the Civil Government of the Frontier Province is so modelled as to be on the same basis as in Sindh, then this Province will be part and parcel of the Punjab, as Sindh is of the Bombay Presi-dency. What have you to say to it?" ' He gave me, in course of his reply, the following straight answer: 'As far as Islam is concerned and the Mohammedan idea of the League of Nations goes, I am against it.' On this answer, I asked him some further questions to which he gave me frank, outspoken replies without mincing matters. I extract the per-tinent portions below:

> Q.—The idea at the back of your Anjuman is a Pan-Islamic idea, that Islam is a League of Nations, and as such amalgamating this Province with the Punjab will be detrimental, will be prejudicial to that idea. That is the dominant idea at the back of those who think with you. Is it so?

A.—It is so, but I have to add something. Their idea is that the Hindu–Muslim unity will never become a fact, it will never become a *fait accompli*, and they think that this Province should remain separate and a link between Islam and the Britannic Commonwealth. In fact, when I am asked what my opinion is—I, as a member of the Anjuman, am expressing this opinion—we would much rather see the separation of Hindus and Mohammedans, 23 crores of Hindus to the South, and 8 crores of Muslims to the North. Give the whole portion from Raskumari to Agra to Hindus and from Agra to Peshawar to Mohammedans, I mean transmigration from one place to the other. This is an idea of exchange. It is not an idea of annihilation. Bolshevism at present does away with the possession of private property. It nationalises the whole thing and this is an idea which of course pertains to only exchange. This is of course impracticable. But if it were practicable, we would rather want this than the other.

Q.—That is the dominant idea which compels you not to have amalgamation with the Punjab?

A.—Exactly.

Q.—When you referred to the Islamic League of Nations, I believe you had the religious side of it more prominently in your mind than the political side?

A.—Of course, political; Anjuman is a political thing. Initially, of course, anything Mohammedan is religious, but of course Anjuman is a political association.

Q.—I am not referring to your Anjuman but I am referring to the Mussalmans. I want to know what the Mussalmans think of this Islamic League of Nations, what have they most prominently in mind, is it the religious side or the political side?

A.—Islam, as you know, is both religious and political.

Q.—Therefore politics and religion are intermingled?

A.—Yes, certainly.

'Now I have reasons to believe that this opinion is shared by a large number of Mohammedans in the Frontier Province and the Punjab and Sindh. In the light of this evidence, the Hindu apprehension cannot be dismissed as entirely unfounded. The question of the Frontier is very important to the whole of India and it specially concerns the safety and security of the Hindu community. It is not right to say that the territories beyond Indus were taken possession of by the British Government from the Mahomedans. Just like Alsace-Lorraine, the territories between the Indus and Peshawar have continuously been changing hands in the historical period and have been a bone of contention between the Government of India and other Governments situated beyond Peshawar. Speaking historicially, they have been for a larger part of the historical period a portion of the Indian territories than otherwise. There was a time when all the territories between Indus and the eastern boundary of Persia proper formed part of the Indian province of the Iranian Empire. Then came the Empire of the Hindu Morians which included all these territories as a part of the Indian Empire. On the rise of Islam, the Moslem Generals of the Khalifa conquered these territories from the Hindus and the several sovereigns of the Ghazni families fought pitched battles with the Hindus on the North West Frontier side to Peshawar. Since then the territories comprising the North West Frontier Province have often been changing hands. They have several times been in the possession of Afghans, at others, formed part of the Indian Empire. The Sikhs held possession of these territories as a part of their Empire, and the British Government took possession of these provinces from the Sikhs. So far as Hindus are concerned, the question is one of pure Frontier defence and should be judged purely on its merits as such. The Hindus do not desire any domination over the Mohammedan population. What they want is the safeguarding of their interests and that of India generally.

I have nothing more to say about politics. Real politics must be left to political associations like the Congress and the Liberal League. The Hindus must not on any account give up the Congress. That would be prejudicial to the best interests of the country, and the Hindu Sabhas should make no encroachment on the province of the Congress, except so far as purely communal questions are concerned.

Sangathan: The Hindu community is being furiously attacked on all sides on account of the Sangathan movement. I can see no justification in these attacks. Every religious community is trying to unify itself and organise itself in different ways. It is true that the Hindus have so far neglected that work, but if they have learnt the lesson from the example of other communities and are doing the right thing towards their own community, no one has a right to find fault with them on that ground. Looking at the history of Hindu Sangathan movement, it is not a new movement at all though it has taken a more tangible shape now and for obvious reasons. It is the duty of the Hindus to organise themselves and bring about unity of action in their relations with other communities and the Government. The Hindu Mahasabha stands for this unity of action and I appeal to all the different sections of the Hindu community to lay aside their difference and unite under the flag of the Hindu Mahasabha. We must recognise the common dangers, both internal and external. The external dangers I have already referred to. The internal dangers are still more formidable. We are too much dis-united on account of the divisions and sub-divisions of the community into so many creeds and castes. Now I have no intention of finding fault with any creed or caste. But we must recognise the necessity of all-round fusion for the purpose of meeting common dangers and performing common duties. The community must realise the absolute necessity of internal consolidation for the purpose of getting sufficiently strong to live its own life and not lag behind other communities in progress and in numbers. We cannot afford to lose very many of our people. The old game of throwing out people on very small pretences must be given up and occasions must be sought to bring people back into our fold without injuring anybody's scruples.

Depressed Classes: I will take the Depressed Classes first. The Depressed Classes, it is said, number about six or seven crores, but these numbers are unreliable. The figures have been swelled either intentionally or unintentionally. There are many classes included under this heading who are not untouchables anyway. Again there are some classes who are untouchables in one province and not so in another. If we were to take the figures of those who are untouchables in all provinces, the number will dwindle down to a very small figure. Now I beg of the Hindu community to remove the untouchability of all because it is wrong to consider any human being as untouchable, particularly when he belongs to one's own religion; in any case there ought to be no untouchability in relation to those classes who are not uniformly untouchables throughout India. There is a great deal of controversy between the orthodox people and those who favour the entire removal of untouchability about the extent to which untouchability should be removed. Personally I am in favour of untouchability being removed altogether. Personally I will go much farther than the minimum laid down by the Hindu Mahasabha at its Special Session held at Allahabad.

But with the object of conciliating my orthodox brothers, I will not urge upon the Mahasabha to go farther. I think it should be left to the Provincial Sabhas to consult Hindu opinion in their Provinces with regard to the actual steps they would sanction for the removal of untouchability and the uplift of the Depressed Classes. This should satisfy the orthodox opinion because they can do what they think best in their spheres of influence with regard to this matter. But there is a great danger in our continual neglect of these classes. There are other people out to absorb them who have greater secular influence and larger resources to take them into their own folds. For the Hindus at this stage to neglect the Depressed Classes will be simply suicidal and I will beg of them to take a broader view of the question than they may be inclined to do on the ground of their religious scruples. One glory of Hinduism consists in its adaptability to the circumstances of the times, and but for this the Hindus would have been nowhere by this time. They would have been absorbed by other communities and would have disappeared. The crying need of the time is to adapt ourselves to the exigencies of the present. We can at least all join together in providing education and economic facilities for the uplift of the Depressed Classes. In this respect all credit is due to those Hindu philanthropists who with great sacrifice and labour are working in this cause.

5

Swami Shraddhananda

S wami Shraddhananda (1857–1926) exemplifies a peculiar Arya Samajist tradition, combining asceticism and social activism.[1] Born in a village of Jullundur district, the life of Munshi Ram—Shraddhananda's name before his initiation to spiritual life—was transformed in the 1880s after he read *Satyarth Prakash* and later met Guru Dutt (1864–90), Dayananda's most religious disciple.[2] He became a *vanaprastha* (voluntary exile in the forest) in 1902 and then a *sannyasi* in 1917, when he changed his name. Alongside these spiritual inclinations, Shraddhananda remained true to Arya Samaj ideology. He claimed that 'the plateau of Thibet was the first to come out of water and therefore the revelation of the Vedas was imparted to early humanity at the sacred soil. Mankind was then divided into the good or virtuous and the bad or vicious. The first were named "Aryas" and the latter "Dasyus" in the Veda itself.'[3]

Also true to the Arya Samaj worldview, Shraddhananda believed Hindus underwent a steady decline since the Vedic golden age and that foreign invasions—the Muslim ones to begin with—but also a constant degradation of culture and society, were responsible for this state of decadence. The slow death of the Hindus was, he believed,

---

[1] The best biography of Swami Shraddhananda remains the book by J.T.F. Jordens, *Swami Shraddhananda—His Life and Causes* (Oxford: Oxford University Press, 1981).

[2] See M.R. Jambunathan, ed., *Swami Shraddhananda* [Autobiography] (Bombay: Vidya Bhavan, 1961).

[3] Swami Shraddhananda, *Hindu Sangathan. Saviour of the Dying Race* (Delhi: Arjun Press, 1926), p. 71.

measured in the census figures that the British had produced every ten years since 1871 (and more thoroughly since 1881) because they bore testimony to a steady erosion of the population share of the majority community. Ergo, Hindus were bound to be turned into a minority in the foreseeable future. As P.K. Datta demonstrates, this obsession with figures has been long associated with the Hindu's cultural and physical features in Hindu nationalist writings: the Hindus are here seen as weak notably because of their division into castes, whereas social classes in England are seen as bonded by common sentiments, 'such as those provided by sports, defence requirements and church activities . . . Islam too had produced a sense of commonness through masjid congregations.'[4] Discourses like Shraddhananda's gave birth to what Datta calls 'the production of Hindu communal common sense', a process through which communal stereotypes tended to form a routinized discourse stressing the need for a Hindu nationalist reaction.

For Shraddhananda the making of the Hindu nation implied seriously implementing the agenda of the Hindu Sangathan movement. Here, social reform was the cornerstone of the desired unity among Hindus. He showed the way himself by having his daughter married to an Arora (he was from a Khatri family himself).[5] More importantly, Shraddhananda fought untouchability. He did this by resorting to the old Arya Samajist recipe of Shuddhi.[6] This ritual formula, which was traditionally used by upper-caste Hindus who happened to be polluted by some hypothetically impure contact, had as we saw been reinterpreted by Dayananda and his followers to 'purify' converts to other religions who wanted to return to the Hindu fold. Shraddhananda systematized this technique in order to integrate Untouchables into mainstream Hindu society. This radical method of social change alienated the Hindu Sabhaites of Sanatanist obedience to such an extent that, eventually, Swami Shraddhananda left the Hindu Mahasabha.

[4] P.K. Datta, 'Dying Hindus—Production of Hindu Communal Common Sense in Early Twentieth Century Bengal', *Economic and Political Weekly*, 19 June 1993, p. 1307.

[5] R.S. Pareek, *Contributions of Arya Samaj in the Making of Modern India 1875–1947* (New Delhi: Sarvadeshik Arya Pratinidhi Sabha, 1973), p. 132.

[6] See J.F. Seunarine, *Reconversion to Hinduism through Shuddhi* (Madras: The Christian Literature Society, 1977).

Extract from *Hindu Sangathan: Saviour of the Dying Race*[7]

The Hindu Sabha has also resolved that those non-Hindus who have faith in Hindu Samskars and Hindu Dharma should be taken within the fold of the Hindu Dharma. This means that every non-Hindu has a right to be absorbed in Hinduism if he has faith in the Hindu religion and culture, in short it means that every Christian, Muhammadan, Jew & c., can be converted to the Hindu Dharma without any hindrance according to the dictum of the Hindu Mahasabha. Thus moral sanction of the Hindu community as a whole is with the reformers in this respect. But the task is uphill. Without sufficient funds and enthusiastic workers the work is languishing. Therefore, the first remedy is to make the Bhartiya Hindu Shuddhi Sabha a living body, to collect lakhs of rupees for pushing on work in all directions and to induce selfless men of pure intents to go about persuading Hindus to take back to their bosom their strayed brethren.

The second remedy is to revivify the ancient Ashram Dharma and to place it on a sound basis. The Hindu Sabha has laid down the minimum marriageable age at 18 years in the case of males and of 12 years in the case of girls. This reform by doles won't do. Let the minimum marriageable age be fixed at 25 for males and 16 for females and let Hindu society become strict in the enforcement of this scientific rule. Then no widower of the three higher Varnas ought to be allowed to marry a virgin. If, after the death of the first wife, the widower cannot lead a life of Brahmacharya let him marry a widow. If he is compelled to succumb to animal passions let him climb down to the position of a Shudra. Then, polygamy in the North and polyandry in the South should also be unequivocally condemned. And in order to protect and educate Hindus properly separate Gurukulas for boys and girls ought to be opened in all parts of the country.

But the Hindu Samaj has already sinned for more them ten centuries by introducing child marriage for its cowardly safety. Therefore—

The third remedy lies in allowing all the unconsummated child widows, who have the desire, to remarry. It is only Apaddharma आपद्धर्म.

[7] Swami Shraddhananda, *Hindu Sangathan: Saviour of the Dying Race* (Delhi: Arjun Press, 1926), pp. 130–41.

If a Hindu commits a sin or neglects to act according to a virtuous dictum he must expiate for it. Proper prayashchit alone can wash away the fruits of a sin in the case of individuals as well as of nations. The orthodox Hindu professes to believe in the Vedas, the Smritis as well as the Puranas. The Vedas lay down the Eternal Dharma which is true for all ages. The Veda is the original source of Dharma.

वेदो ऽ खिलो धर्म मूलम् ।।

But the Smritis, which are not opposed to the teachings of the Vedas, should also be followed. These Smritis lay down the rules to be followed in times of extreme distress or calamity and such rules constitute what is called आपद्धर्म Apaddharma.

Apart from the Vedas, there is a consensus of authority, in the Smritis, sanctioning the remarriage of unconsummated child widows. The Smritis also hold that if a virgin is forcibly carried away and violated she does not lose the position of a virgin if she has not willingly gone through marriage rites with her ravisher. Out of a hundred or more Smriti texts the following few will suffice to prove the position I have taken up:

या पत्या वा परित्यक्ता विधवा वा स्वेच्छया,
उत्पादयेत् पुनर्भूत्व, लपौनर्वभव उच्यते ।
साचेदक्षतयोनि; स्याद्, गत प्रत्या गतापि वा,
पौनर्भवेन मर्त्रा सा पुन. संस्कार महिति ।।
(मनु अ॰ 6, श्लोक 171, 176)

If a woman abandoned by her husband or a widow having accepted another as a husband begets a child, it is named Punurbhu. If that woman has not been consummated by the first husband she can be legally married to a second husband.

कन्यैवा क्षत योनिर्वा याणि गृहण ठृषिता ।
पुनर्भु: प्रथमा प्रोक्ता पुनः संस्कार महिति ।।
(नारद अ॰ 12, श्लोक 46)

A woman whose marriage rites alone are performed—whether she is a virgin or an unconsummated widow—is called first Punurbhu and is fit to be legally married.

पाणि प्रहे मृने बाला केवल मंत्र संस्कृता ।
सचे दक्षत योनः स्यात पुनः संस्कारमर्हति ।।
(वशिए स्मृति अ॰ 17)

If the husband of a married girl dies at the end of the marriage Samskar and she is unconsummated she is entitled to be married again.

बलाश्च्चेन प्रह्ता कन्या मंत्रैर्य दिन संस्कृता ।
अन्यस्मै विधिवद्देया, यथा कन्या तथैव सा ।।
निसष्टायां छुते घापि यस्यै भर्त्ता म्रियतः सः ।
साचेदक्षत तोनिः स्याद् गत प्रत्या गतालती ।
पौनर्भवेन विधिना पुनः संस्कार मर्हति ।।
(बौधामन धर्मशास्त्र, अ॰ 1, श्लो॰ 15, 16)

(i) If a girl has been forcibly carried away and her marriage has not been lawfully performed she can be married to another according to law because she is like a virgin.

(ii) And one whose husband dies after marriage and she is unconsummated—even if she has been to her husband's home—is fit to be lawfully married a second time.

उद्वाहिता चया कन्या न संप्राप्ता च मैथुनम ।
भर्त्तारं पुनर भ्येति यथा कन्या तथैव सा ।।
समुद् धृत्य तुनां कन्या साचे दक्षत बोनिका ।
कुल शाल घते दधा दिति शाततापोऽब्रवीत ।।

A girl who has been married but remains unconsummated can again be given to a second husband because she is like a virgin.

That girl, if she is unconsummated, can be given in marriage to a man of character belonging to a noble family—so says Shatatap.

The fourth remedy lies in the revival of Varnadharma of the Ancient Aryans. Down with the caste system! that is the dictum of every true son of Mother India. The present day unnatural, immovable division into a hundred castes and thousands of subcastes must go, if the Hindu community is to be rescued from total extinction.

In the first place all distinctions of sub-castes must cease, and no non-caste sects among Hindus should be recognized. I realize the difficulty in remodelling the Hindu Samaj according to the ancient

Varnadharma at once. But there should be no difficulty in all the sub-castes, and even non-castes consisting of the so-called untouchables, being absorbed in the four principal castes. The Brahman caste must be self-contained in the sense that no sub-division into Panchgauras, Panchdravidas, Bhumihars, Tagas &c. should be recognized. The Kshatriya caste should include Rajputs, Khatris, Jats, Gujars &c. and should be one recognized society of protectors of the nation. All the castes and sub-castes engaged in trade and agriculture should be included in the Vaishya caste. And the rest should constitute the Shudra caste and serve society. There should be free marriage relations, to begin with, within the castes and Anuloma marriages should not be interfered with. Then gradually Pratiloma marriages ought to be intro-duced. And lastly (गुण कर्म) character and conduct should become the determining factors in fixing the Varna of a Hindu.

But interdining among all the castes should be commenced at once—not promiscuous eating out of the same cup and dish like Muhamma-dans, but partaking of food in seperate cups and dishes, cooked and served by decent Shudras. This alone can solve the problem of untouch-ability and exclusiveness among the Hindus.

The Hindu Mahasabha has passed a lengthy resolution purporting to deal with the problem of untouchability, but it has resulted in confounding confusion worse. It all depends upon the local Hindus whether the so-called untouchables are to be allowed to draw water from common wells which are not prohibited to Muhammadans and Christians. And then if a devout untouchable goes to worship the image of his favourite deity in a Hindu temple the priest has the op-tion of allowing or not allowing him to approach the place where Muhammadan prostitutes are asked to dance accompanied by Muham-madan players on [sic] music. As regards allowing admission to the children of the so-called untouchables in public Schools and Colleges, the less said the better. But the climax is reached when, after allowing all the abovementioned ambiguous privileges, the Hindu Mahasabha lays down the authoritative dogma that 'initiating the untouchables with sacred thread, teaching them the Vedas and to interdine with them is against the Shastras and custom (लोकमर्यादा) according to Sanatan Dharma.'

To get rid of all this rigmarole and to root out the curse of unseeability, unapproachability, untouchability and exclusiveness, there is only one sovereign remedy—and that is the resuscitation of the Ancient Aryan 'Varna-dharma'.

Basis for Hindu Sangathan: The above fourfold remedies in my humble opinion, constitute the basis of real Hindu Sangathan: the success of all the minor resolutions passed by the Hindu Mahasabha depend upon the right application of these remedies.

It is true that protection of the cow (गोरक्षा) is a powerful factor not only in giving the Hindu community a common plane for joint action but in contributing to the physical development and strength of its several members. But if the drain upon the depressed classes continues and they go on leaving their ancestral religion on account of the social tyramy [*sic*] of their co-religionists and the onrush of Hindu widows towards prostitution and Muhammadanism, on account of the brutal treatment of [*sic*] their relations, is not stopped by allowing them to remarry in their own community, the number of beef-eaters will increase and Gauraksha will remain only a dream of unpractical sentimentalists.

And what would the Hindu Raksha Sangham be able to accomplish against the inroads of non-Hindu Gundas, if their own house is not in order? The best way to avoid conflict with Muhammadans is to take care of your own women and children.

The introduction of uniform Devanagar [*sic*] script and Hindi lingua franca throughout is absolutely necessary, because a common language brings all the individuals speaking that language nearer one another in thought and action, but unless caste and sectarian prejudices vanish there is no likelihood of a common language and literature being evolved.

The salvation of the community depends upon common action taken by the Hindu Samaj as a whole, but individual salvation is the lookout of individuals. Theoretical Dharma is connected with individual salvation and, therefore, there is room for Theists, Pantheists, Henotheists and even Atheists in the broad lap of the organized Hindu Samaj. But the code of practical Dharma has to do with the community as a whole and, therefore here the plea of individual Dharma should not be allowed to prevail nor should it hamper the efforts of the organized Hindu Samaj towards national salvation.

The First Step: The question naturally arises—What is the first step to be taken in our advance towards Hindu Sangathan? In my tour throughout India I have seen educated Hindus reluctant to mix with each other. It is only on rare occasions that they meet to discuss common social problems. The reason is that they have no common meeting place. Their sectarian temples have not sufficient space where even a hundred or two could sit together. In Delhi, besides the Juma and Fatehpuri mosques which can accommodate big audiences consisting of 25 to 30 thousands of Muhammadans, there are several old mosques which can serve as meeting places for thousands. But for Hindus, the only enclosed meeting place is Lakshmi Narayana's Dharamshala which can hardly accommodate some 8 hundred, with this difference that while the Muhammadan meetings are free from all noise, the hubbub of voices from travellers in the Dharamshala hardly allows the speakers to be distinctly heard.

The first step which I propose is to build one Hindu Rashtra Mandir at least in every city and important town, with a compound which could contain an audience of 25 thousands [*sic*] and a hall in which Katha from Bhagavad Gita, the Upanishads and the great epics of Ramayana and Mahabharat could be daily recited. The Rashtra Mandir will be in charge of the local Hindu Sabha which will manage to have Akharas for wrestling and gatka &c. plays in the same compound. While the sectarian Hindu temples are dominated by their own individual deities, the Catholic Hindu Mandir should be devoted to the worship of the three mother-spirits (मातृशक्ति) the Gau-mata, the Saraswati-mata and the Bhumi-mata. Let some living cows be there to represent plenty, let 'Savitri' (गायत्री मन्त्रम्) be inscribed over the gate of the hall to remind every Hindu of his duty to expel all ignorance and let a life-like map of Mother-Bharat be constructed in a prominent place, giving all its characteristics in vivid colours so that every child of the Matri-Bhumi may daily bow before the Mother and renew his pledge to restore her to the ancient pinnacle of glory from which she has fallen!

If a beginning, on lines proposed by me in all humility and love, is made with faith, I hope that all the necessary reforms will follow, as night is followed by the day, and the progeny of the ancient Aryans will once more step forward to give salvation to humanity.

6

Vinayak Damodar Savarkar

With Vinayak Damodar Savarkar (1883–1966), a Maharashtrian Brahmin, the centre of gravity of Hindu nationalism shifts from Punjab and the United Provinces to Maharashtra, where old Congressmen from the Extremist fold, such as B.G. Tilak, had prepared the ground for such an ideology. Savarkar was at first himself an Extremist who did not hesitate to resort to violent methods against the British.[1] Arrested in London, where he had taken part in the assassination plot of Curzon-Wyllie, an associate of the Secretary of State, between 1910 and 1937 he spent twenty-seven years in jail, first in the Andamans and then in Ratnagiri (Maharashtra). This is where he wrote *Hindutva: Who is a Hindu?*, first published anonymously at Nagpur in 1923. This book is the real charter of Hindu nationalism, the ideology which has become precisely equated with the word 'Hindutva'.

Savarkar wrote this book in prison, after he had come in contact with Khilafatists whose attitude apparently convinced him—a revolutionary till then—that Muslims were the real enemies, not the British.[2] Savarkar's book rests on the assumption that Hindus are weak compared to Muslims. The latter are a closely-knit community that entertain pan-Islamic rather than nationalist sympathies. According to him,

---

[1] See V.S. Anand, *Savarkar—A Study in the Evolution of Indian Nationalism* (London: Woolf, 1967); H. Srivasthava, *Five Stormy Years: Savarkar in London* (New Delhi: Allied Publishers, 1983); Chitragupta, *Life of Barrister Savarkar* (Bombay: Acharya Balarao Savarkar, 1987). On the revolutionary movement in Maharashtra, see H.M. Ghodke, *Revolutionary Nationalism in Western India* (New Delhi: Classical Publishing Company, 1990).

[2] D. Keer, *Veer Savarkar* (Bombay: Popular Prakashan, 1988), p. 161.

they pose a threat to the real nation, namely Hindu Rashtra. Drawing some of his inspiration from Dayananda and his followers, Savarkar defines the nation primarily along ethnic categories. For him, the Hindus descend from the Aryas, who settled in India at the dawn of history and who already formed a nation at that time. However, in Savarkar's writings, ethnic bonds are not the only criteria of Hindutva. National identity rests for him on three pillars: geographical unity, racial features, and a common culture. Savarkar minimizes the importance of religion in his definition of a Hindu by claiming that Hinduism is only one of the attributes of 'Hinduness'.[3] This stand reflects the fact that, like most ethno-religious nationalists, Savarkar was not himself a believer.[4] Doubtless, Christians and Muslims represented for Savarkar an Otherness of a threatening nature, but, by defining them as part of a race within which they became converts only a few generations earlier, he suggests that they can be reintegrated into Hindu society provided they pay allegiance to Hindu culture. The third criterion of Hindutva— a 'common culture'—reflects for Savarkar the crucial importance of rituals, social rules, and language in Hinduism. Sanskrit is cited by him as the common reference point for all Indian languages and as 'language par excellence'.[5] Any political programme based on Hindu nationalist ideology has after Savarkar demanded recognition of Sanskrit or Hindi—the vernacular language closest to it—as the national idiom.

There is finally a territorial dimension in this ethnic brand of nationalism. To Savarkar a Hindu is first and foremost someone who lives in the area beyond the Indus river, between the Himalayas and the Indian Ocean, 'so strongly entrenched that no other country in the world is so perfectly designed by the fingers of nature as a geographical unit'.[6] This is why the first Aryans in the Vedic era 'developed a sense of nationality'.[7] Here a shift to an ethnic rationale is expressed for the enclaved nature of what Savarkar calls 'Hindustan', the land of the Hindus,

[3] According to Savarkar, 'a man can be as truly a Hindu as any without believing in the Vedas as an independent religious authority'. *Hindutva*, p. 81.

[4] D. Keer, *Veer Savarkar*, p. 201. On that point, see the typology developed by Ashis Nandy, 'An Anti-Secularist Manifesto', *Seminar*, October 1985, p. 15.

[5] *Hindutva*, p. 95.

[6] Ibid., p. 82.

[7] Ibid., p. 5.

which is described as a decisive factor in the unity of the population on account of intermarriage: 'All Hindus claim to have in their veins the blood of the mighty race incorporated with and descended from the Vedic fathers.'[8] In Savarkar's mind territory and ethnic unity are inseparable.

Extract from *Hindutva: Who is a Hindu*?[9]

What is a Hindu? Although it would be hazardous at the present stage of oriental research to state definitely the period when the foremost band of the intrepid Aryans made it their home and lighted their first sacrificial fire on the banks of the Sindhu, the Indus, yet certain it is that long before the ancient Egyptians, and Babylonians had built their magnificent civilization, the holy waters of the Indus were daily witnessing the lucid and curling columns of the scented sacrificial smokes and the valleys resounding with the chants of Vedic hymns— the spiritual fervour that animated their souls. The adventurous valour that propelled their intrepid enterprises, the sublime heights to which their thoughts rose all these had marked them out as a people destined to lay the foundation of a great and enduring civilization. By the time they had definitely cut themselves aloof from their cognate and neighbouring people especially the Persians, the Aryans had spread out to the farthest of the seven rivers, Sapta Sindhus, and not only had they developed a sense of nationality but had already succeeded in giving it 'a local habitation and a name!' Out of their gratitude to the genial and perennial network of waterways that ran through the land like a system of nerve-threads and wove them into a Being, they very naturally took to themselves the name of Sapta Sindhus an epithet that was applied to the whole of Vedic India in the oldest records of the world, the *Rigveda* itself. About Aryans, or the cultivators, as they essentially were, we can well understand the divine love and homage they bore to these seven rivers presided over by the River, 'the Sindhu', which to them were but a visible symbol of the common nationality and culture. इमा आपः शिबतमा इमा राष्ट्रस्य भेषजी । इमा राष्ट्रस्य वर्धनीरिमा राष्ट्रभूतोपमाः ।।

[8] Ibid., p. 85.

[9] V.D. Savarkar, *Hindutva: Who is a Hindu*? (1923; rpnt. New Delhi: Bharatiya Sahitya Sadan, 1989), pp. 4–12, 42–6, 90–2, 113–15.

The Indians in their forward march had to meet many a river as genial and as fertilizing as these but never could they forget the attachment they felt and the homage they paid to the Sapta Sindhus which had welded them into a nation and furnished the name which enabled their forefathers to voice forth their sense of national and cultural unity. Down to this day a Sindhu—a Hindu—wherever he may happen to be, will gratefully remember and symbolically invoke the presence of these rivers that they may refresh and purify his soul.

इमं मे गंगे यमुने सरस्वति शतद्रु स्तोमं सचता परुष्ण्या ।
असिवन्यामरुद्वृधे वितस्तयार्जीकीय श्रृणुह्या सुषोमया ।।
गंगे च यमुने चैव गोदाबरि सरस्वति ।
नर्मदे सिन्धु कावेरि जलेऽस्मिन् श्रत्रिधिं कुरु ।।

Not only had these people been known to themselves as 'Sindhus' but we have definite records to show that they were known to their surrounding nations—at any rate to one of them—by that very name, 'Sapta Sindhu'. The letter 's' in Sanskrit is at times changed into 'h' in some of the Prakrit languages, both Indian and non-Indian. For example, the word Sapta has become Hapta not only in Indian Prakrits but also in the European languages too; we have Hapta i.e., week, in India and 'Heptarchy' in Europe, Kesari in Sanskrit becomes Kehari in old Hindi, Saraswati becomes Harhvati in Persian and Asur becomes Ahur. And then we actually find that the Vedic name of our nation Sapta Sindhu had been mentioned as Hapta Hindu in the Avesta by the ancient Persian people. Thus in the very dawn of history we find ourselves belonging to the nation of the Sindhus or Hindus and this fact was well known to our learned men even in the Puranic period. In expounding the doctrine that many of the Mlechha tongues had been but the mere offshoots of the Sanskrit language the Bhavishya Puran clearly cites this fact and says—

संस्कृतस्यैव वाणी तु भारतं वर्षमुह्यताम् ।
अन्ये खंडे गता सैव म्लेच्छा ह्यानंदिनोऽभवन् ।।
पितृ पैतरभ्राता च बादरः पतिरेव च ।
सेति सा यावनी भाषा ह्यश्वश्चास्यस्तथा पुनः ।।
जानुस्थाने जैनशब्दः सप्तसिन्धुस्तयैव च ।
हप्तहिन्दुर्यावनी च पुनर्ज्ञेयागु गुरुण्डिका ।। (प्रतिसगंपवं अ॰ 5)

Thus knowing for certain that the Persians used to designate the Vedic Aryans as Hindus and knowing also the fact that we generally call a foreign and unknown people by the term by which they are known to those through whom we come to know them, we can safely conclude that most of the remoter nations that flourished then must have applied the same epithet 'Hindu' to our land and people as the ancient Persians did. Not only that but even in the very region of the Sapta Sindhus the thinly scattered native tribes too, must have been knowing the Aryans as Hindus in the local dialects in accordance with the same linguistic law. Further on, as the Vedic Sanskrit began to give birth to the Indian Prakrits which became the spoken tongues of the majority of the descendants of these very Sindhus as well as the assimilated and the crossborn castes, these too might have called themselves as Hindus without any influence from the foreign people. For the Sanskrit S changes into H as often in Indian Prakrits as in the non-Indian ones. Therefore, so far as definite records are concerned, it is indisputably clear that the first and almost the cradle name chosen by the patriarchs of our race to designate our nation and our people, is Sapta Sindhu or Hapta Hindu and that almost all nations of the then known world seemed to have known us by this very epithet, Sindhus or Hindus.

Name Older Still: So far we have been treading on solid ground of recorded facts, but now we cannot refrain ourselves from making an occasional excursion into the borderland of conjecture. So far we have not pinned our faith to any theory about the original home of the Aryans. But if the most widely accepted theory of their entrance into India be relied on, then a natural curiosity arises as to the origin of the names by which they called the new scenes of their adopted home. Did they coin all those names from their own tongue? Could they have done so? Is it not generally true that when we meet a new scene or enter a new country we call them by the very names—maybe in a slightly changed form so as to suit our vocal ability or taste—by which they are known to the native people there? Of course, at times we love to call new scenes by names redolent with the memory of the clear old ones—especially when new colonies are being established in a virgin and thinly populated continent. But this explanation could only be satisfactory when it is proved that the name given to the new place already existed in the old country and even then it could not be denied that the other process of calling new scenes by the names which they already bear is more universally followed. Now we know it for certain that the region of the Sapta Sindhus was, though very thinly, populated by scattered tribes. Some of them seem to have been friendly towards the newcomers and it is almost certain that many an individual had served the Aryans as guides and introduced them to the names and nature of the new scenes to which the Aryans could not be but local strangers. The Vidyadharas, Apsaras, Yakshas, Rakshasas, Gandharvas and Kinnaras were not all or altogether inimical to the Aryans as at times they are mentioned as being benevolent and good-natured folks. Thus it is probable that many names given to these great rivers by the original inhabitants of the soil may have been sanskritised and adopted by the Aryans. We have numerous proofs of this nature in the assimil-ative expansion of those people and their tongues; witness the words Shalankantakata, Malaya, Milind, Alasada (Alexandria), Suluva (Selu-cus), etc. If this be true then it is quite probable that the great Indus was known as Hindu to the original inhabitants of our land and owing to vocal peculiarity of the Aryans it got changed into Sindhu when they adopted it by the operation of the same rule that S is the sanskritised equivalent of H. Thus Hindu would be the name that this land and the people that inhabited it bore from time so immemorial that even the Vedic name Sindhu is but a later and secondary form of it. If the epithet Sindhu dates its antiquity in the glimmering twilight of history then the word Hindu dates its antiquity from a period so remoter than the first that even mythology fails to penetrate—to trace it to its source.

Hindus, a Nation: The activities of so intrepid a people as the Sindhus or Hindus could no longer be kept cooped or cabined within the narrow compass of the Panchanad or the Punjab. The vast and fertile plains farther off stood out inviting the efforts of some strong and vigorous race. Tribe after tribe of the Hindus issued forth from the land of their nursery and, led by the consciousness of a great mission and their Sacrificial Fire that was the symbol thereof, they soon re-claimed the vast, waste and very-thinly populated lands. Forests were felled, agriculture flourished, cities rose, kingdoms thrived—the touch of the human hand changed the hole face of the wild and unkempt nature. But while these great deeds were being achieved the Aryans had developed to suit their individualistic tendencies and the demands of their new environments a policy that was but loosely centralised. As time passed on, the distances of their new colonies increased, and different peoples of other highly developed types began to be incorporated into their culture, the different settlements began to lead life politically very much centred in themselves. The new attachments thus formed, though they could not efface the old ones, grew more and more pronounced and powerful until the ancient generalizations and names gave way to the new. Some called themselves Kurus, others Kashis or Videhas or Magadhas while the old generic name of the Sindhus or Hindus was first overshadowed and then almost forgotten. Not that the conception of a national and cultural unity vanished, but it assumed other names and other forms, the politically most important of them being the institution of a Chakravartin. At least the great mission which the Sindhus had undertaken of founding a nation and a country, found and reached its geographical limit when the valorous Prince of Ayodhya made a triumphant entry in Ceylon and actually brought the whole land from the Himalayas to the Seas under one sovereign sway. The day when the Horse of Viceroy returned to Ayodhya unchallenged and unchallengeable, the great white Umbrella of Sovereignty was unfurled over that Imperial throne of Ramachandra, the brave, Ramachandra the good, and a loving allegiance to him was sworn, not only by the Princes of Aryan blood but Hanuman, Sugriva, Bibhishana from the south—that day was the real birth-day of our Hindu people. It was truly our national day; for Aryans and Anaryans knitting themselves into a people were born as a nation. It summed up and politically crowned the efforts of all the generations that preceded it and it handed down a new and common mission, a common banner, a common cause which all the generations after it had consciously or unconsciously fought and died to defend.

Foreign Invaders: But as it often happens in history this very undisturbed enjoyment of peace and plenty lulled our Sindhusthan, in a sense of false security and bred a habit of living in the land of dreams. At last she was rudely awakened on the day when Mohammad of Gazni crossed the Indus, the frontier line of Sindhusthan and invaded her. That day the conflict of life and death began. Nothing makes Self conscious of itself so much as a conflict with non-self. Nothing can weld peoples into a nation and nations into a state as the pressure of a common foe. Hatred separates as well as unites. Never had Sindhus-than a better chance and a more powerful stimulus to be herself forged into an indivisible whole as on that dire day, when the great iconoclast crossed the Indus. The Mohammedans had crossed that stream even under Kasim, but it was a wound only skin-deep, for the heart of our people was not hurt and was not even aimed at. The contest began in grim earnestness with Mohammad and ended, shall we say, with Abdalli? From year to year, decade to decade, century to century, the contest continued. Arabia ceased to be what Arabia was; Iran annihi-lated; Egypt, Syria, Afghanistan, Baluchistan, Tartary—from Granada to Gazni—nations and civilizations fell in heaps before the sword of Islam of Peace!! But here for the first time the sword succeeded in striking but not in killing. It grew blunter each time it struck, each time it cut deep but as it was lifted up to strike again the wound stood healed. Vitality of the victim proved stronger than the vitality of the victor. The contrast was not only grim but it was monstrously unequal. It was not a race, a nation of a people India had to struggle with. It was nearly all Asia, quickly to be followed by nearly all Europe. The Arabs had entered Sindh and single-handed they could do little else. They soon failed to defend their own independence in their homeland and as a people we hear nothing further about them. But here India alone had to face Arabs, Persians, Pathans, Baluchis, Tartars, Turks, Moguls—a veritable human Sahara whirling and columning up bodily in a furi-ous world storm! Religion is a mighty motive force. So is rapine. But where religion is goaded on by rapine and rapine serves as a handmaiden to religion, the propelling force that is generated by these together is only equalled by the profundity of human misery and devastation they leave behind them in their march. Heaven and hell making a common cause—such were the forces, overwhelmingly furious, that took India by surprise the day Mohammad crossed the Indus and in-vaded her. Day after day, decade after decade, century after century, the ghastly conflict continued and India single-handed kept up the flight morally and militarily. The moral victory was won when Akbar came to the throne and Darashukoh was born. The frantic efforts of Aurangzeb to retrieve their fortunes lost in the moral field only hastened the loss of the military fortunes on the battlefield as well. At last Bhau, as if symbolically, hammered the ceiling of the Imperial Seat of the

Moghals to pieces. The day of Panipat rose, the Hindus lost the battle, but won the war. Never again had an Afghan dared to penetrate to Delhi, while the triumphant Hindu banner that our Marathas had carried to Attock was taken up by our Sikhs and carried across the Indus to the banks of the Kabul.

Hindutva at Work: In this prolonged furious conflict our people became intensely conscious of ourselves as Hindus and were welded into a nation to an extent unknown in our history. It must not be forgotten that we have all along referred to the progress of the Hindu movement as a whole and not to that of any particular creed or religious section thereof—of Hindutva and not Hinduism only. Sanatanists, Satnamis, Sikhs, Aryas, Anaryas, Marathas and Madrasis, Brahmins and Panchamas—all suffered as Hindus and triumphed as Hindus. Both friends and foes contributed equally to enable the words Hindu and Hindusthan to supersede all other designations of our land and our people. Aryavartha and Daxinapatha, Jambudweep and Bharatvarsha, none could give so eloquent an expression to the main political and cultural point at issue as the word Hindusthan could do. All those on this side of the Indus who claimed the land from Sindhu to Sindhu, from the Indus to the seas, as the land of their birth, felt that they were directly mentioned by that one single expression, Hindusthan. The enemies hated us as Hindus and the whole family of peoples and races, of sects and creeds that flourished from Attock to Cuttack was suddenly individualised into a single Being. We cannot help dropping the remark that no one has up to this time taken the whole field of Hindu activities from AD 1300 to 1800 into survey from this point of view, mastering the details of the various now parallel, now correlated movements from Kashmir to Ceylon and from Sindh to Bengal and yet rising higher above them all to visualise the whole scene in its proportion as an integral whole. For it was the one great issue to defend the honour and independence of Hindusthan and maintain the cultural unity and civic life of Hindutva and not Hinduism alone, but Hindutva, i.e. Hindudharma that was being fought out on the hundred fields of battle as well as on the floor of the chambers of diplomacy. This one word, Hindutva, ran like a vital spinal cord through our whole body politic and made the Nayars of Malabar weep over the sufferings of the Brahmins of Kashmir. Our bards bewailed the fall of Hindus, our seers roused the feelings of Hindus, our heroes fought the battles of Hindus, our saints blessed the efforts of Hindus, our statesmen moulded the fate of Hindus, our mothers wept over the wounds and gloried over the triumphs of Hindus . . . no people in the world can more justly claim to get recognized as a racial unit than the Hindus and perhaps the Jews. A Hindu marrying a Hindu may lose his caste but not his Hindutva. A Hindu believing in any theoretical or philosophical or social system, orthodox or heterodox, provided it is unquestionably indigenous and founded by a Hindu may lose his sect but not his Hindutva—his Hinduness—because the most important essential which determines it is the inheritance of the Hindu blood. Therefore all those who love the land that stretches from Sindhu to Sindhu from the Indus to the Seas, as their fatherland consequently claim to inherit the blood of the race that has evolved, by incorporation and adaptation, from the ancient Suptasindhus can be said to possess two of the most essential requisites of Hindutva.

Common Culture: But only two; because a moment's consideration would show that these two qualifications of one nation and one race—of a common fatherland and therefore of a common blood—cannot exhaust all the requisites of Hindutva. The majority of the Indian Mohammedans may, if free from the prejudices born of ignorance, come to love our land as their fatherland, as the patriotic and noble-minded amongst them have always been doing. The story of their conversions, forcible in millions of cases, is too recent to make them forget, even if they like to do so, that they inherit Hindu blood in their veins. But can we, who here are concerned with investigating into facts as they are and not as they should be, recognize these Mohamme-dans as Hindus? Many a Mohammedan community in Kashmir and other parts of India as well as the Christians in South India observe our caste rules to such an extent as to marry generally within the pale of their castes alone; yet, it is clear that though their original Hindu blood is thus almost unaffected by an alien adulteration, yet they cannot be called Hindus in the sense in which that term is actually understood, because, we Hindus are bound together not only by the tie of the love we bear to a common fatherland and by the common blood that courses through our veins and keeps our hearts throbbing and our affections warm, but also by the tie of the common homage we pay to our great civilization—our Hindu culture, which could not be better rendered than by the word Sanskrit suggestive as it is of that language, Sanskrit, which has been the chosen means of expression and preservation of that culture, of all that was best and worth preserving in the history of our race. We are one because we are a nation, a race and own a common Sanskriti (civilization) in the case of some of our Mohammedan or Christian countrymen who had originally been forcibly converted to a non-Hindu religion and who consequently have inherited along with Hindus, a common Fatherland and a greater part of the wealth of a common culture—language, law, customs, folklore and history—are not and cannot be recognized as Hindus. For though Hindusthan to them is Fatherland as to any other Hindu yet it is not to them a Holyland too. Their Holyland is far off in Arabia or Palestine. Their mythology and Godmen, ideas and heroes are not the children of this soil. Consequently their names and their outlook smack of a foreign origin. Their love is divided. Nay, if some of them be really believing what they profess to do, then there can be no choice—they must, to a man, set their Holyland above their Fatherland in their love and allegiance. That is but natural. We are not condemning nor are we lamenting. We are simply telling facts as they stand. We have tried to determine the essentials of Hindutva and in doing so we have discovered that the Bohras and such other Mohammedan or Christian communities possess all the essential qualifications of Hindutva but one, and that is that they do not look upon India as their Holyland.

It is not a question of embracing any doctrine propounding any new theory of the interpretation of God, Soul and Man, for we honestly believe that the Hindu Thought—we are not speaking of any religion which is dogma—has exhausted the very possibilities of human specu-lation as to the nature of the Unknown—if not the Unknowable, or the nature of the relation between *that* and *thou*. Are you a monist—a monotheist—a pantheist—an atheist—an agnostic? Here is ample room, O soul! Whatever thou art, to love and grow to thy fullest height and satisfaction in this Temple of temples, that stands on no personal foundation of Truth. 'Why goest then to fill thy little pitcher to wells far off, when thou standest on the banks of the crystal-streamed Ganges herself? Does not the blood in your veins, O brother of our common forefathers, cry aloud with the recollections of the dear old scenes and ties from which they were so cruelly snatched away at the point of the sword? Then come ye back to the fold of your brothers and sisters who with arms extended are standing at the open gate to welcome you—their long lost kith and kin. Where can you find more freedom of worship than in this land where a Charvak could preach atheism from the steps of the temple of Mahakal—more freedom of social organisation than in the Hindu society where from the Patnas of Orissa to the Pandits of Benares, from the Santalas to the Sadhus, each can develop a distinct social type of polity or organize a new one? Verily, whatever could be found in the world is found here too. And if anything is not found here it could be found nowhere. Ye, who by race, by blood, by culture, by nationality possess almost all the essentials of Hindutva and had been forcibly snatched out of our ancestral home by the hand of violence—ye, have only to render wholehearted love to our common Mother and recognize her not only as Fatherland (Pitri-bhu) but even as a Holyland (Punyabhu); and ye would be most welcome to the Hindu fold.

This is a choice which our countrymen and our old kith and kin, the Bohras, Khojas, Memons and other Mohammedan and Christian communities are free to make—a choice again which must be a choice of love. But as long as they are not minded thus, so long they cannot be recognized as Hindus.

$$\frac{7}{}$$

M.S. Golwalkar

Madhav Sadashiv Golwalkar (1906–1973) was born in a Maharashtrian Brahmin family in Nagpur. Like Dayananda and Shraddhananda, he had been attracted to monastic life during his youth and had joined an ashram in Bengal.[1] On the campus of the Benares Hindu University, where he taught zoology, his long hair and sannyasin-like robes earned him the nickname 'Guruji', which he retained all his life. It is there, at BHU, that K.B. Hedgewar convinced him in 1931 to join the RSS, the movement he had founded in 1925.

Keshav Baliram Hedgewar (1889–1940) had, as we saw, founded the RSS after visiting Savarkar in Ratnagiri. The movement has developed into a considerable Hindu nationalist organization, inheriting most of its ideology from the author of *Hindutva*. However, Golwalkar, who succeeded Hedgewar at the head of the RSS in 1940, gave the movement its ideological charter only in 1938 with *We or Our Nationhood Defined*. This document, and other writings by Golwalkar reproduced below, gave a definition of Hindu Rashtra even more rigid than the one found in Savarkar's works.

Like Savarkar, Golwalkar requests religious minorities to pledge allegiance to Hindu symbols of identity, assuming that these epitomise Indian national identity: Indian identity is equated with Hindu culture, and religious minorities are enjoined to keep expressions of community particularism to the private sphere. Golwalkar actually labelled members of these minorities, as well as foreigners—namely 'those who do not subscribe to the social laws dictated by the Hindu Religion and

[1] R. Kohli, *Political Ideas of M.S. Golwalkar* (New Delhi: Deep and Deep, 1993).

Culture'—as *mlecchas* (barbarians), this being in keeping with the traditional usage of this term.[2] In ancient India a mleccha was someone at the fringe of the caste system dominated by the values of the Brahmin.[3] The characterization of Hindu nationalism as 'upper-caste racism' by the historian Gyanendra Pandey is perfectly relevant in this case.[4]

In contrast with Savarkar, Golwalkar pays no attention to the territorial dimension of nationalism. He repeatedly indicts Congress for 'the amazing theory that the nation is composed of all those who, for one reason or the other happen to live at the time in the country'.[5] In contrast with Savarkar, again, Golwalkar claims that the racial factor 'is by far the important ingredient of a nation'.[6] In this area Golwalkar claims inspiration from Hitler's ideology. He applies this nationalist ethnic reasoning to India's Muslim minority, which he believed posed a threat not only because it enjoyed the backing of a whole series of Islamic states but also because it was a 'foreign body' lodged in Hindu society. Golwalkar considers India's Christians and communists as anti-national elements too.

Extracts from *We or Our Nationhood Defined*[7]

Chapter II: 'What is the notion of the Democratic states about Nation?' Is it the same haphazard bundle of friend and foe, master and thief, as we in Hindusthan understand it to mean? Or do the political thinkers of the democratic West think otherwise?

We believe that our notions today about the Nation concept are erroneous. They are not in conformity with those of the Western Political Scientists we think we are imitating. It is but proper, therefore, at

[2] M.S. Golwalkar, *We or Our Nationhood Defined* (1939; rpnt Nagpur: Bharat Prakashan, M.N. Kale, 1947), 4th edn, p. 62.

[3] Romila Thapar explains that this exclusion is not based on any racial criterion; it is social and ritual in nature and can thus be overcome through acculturation and recognition of the Brahmin's superiority. See R. Thapar, *Ancient Indian History* (New Delhi: Orient Longman, 1978), pp. 165, 169, 179.

[4] G. Pandey, 'Which of us are Hindus?', in G. Pandey, ed., *Hindus and Others—The Question of Identity in India Today* (New Delhi: Viking, 1993), p. 252.

[5] M.S. Golwalkar, *We or Our Nationhood Defined*, p. 59.

[6] Ibid., p. 23.

[7] Ibid., pp. 21–52.

this stage to understand what the Western Scholars state as the Universal Nation-idea and correct ourselves. With this end in view, we shall now proceed with stating and analysing the World's accepted Nation-concept.

The word 'nation' denotes a compound idea. It consists of certain distinct notions fused indissolubly into a whole, which stands so long as its components exist in unison. The various political philosophers have expressed the idea in different words but always conveying the same sense. Modern dictionaries, too, give the same meaning. Fowler defines the word 'Nation' to mean 'a people or race distinguished by community of descent, language, history, or political institutions.' The definitions given by the various Political Scientists are more comprehensive and more to the point. We will quote a few, though a large number of the authors can easily be cited, and examine them to find out what, in essence, they in common subscribe to.

According to Prof Hole-Combe [Arthur N. Holcombe], 'It (Nationality) is a corporate sentiment, a kind of fellow-feeling or mutual sympathy relating to a definite home country. It springs from a common heritage of memories, whether of great achievement and glory, or of "disaster and suffering".' With Burgess, Nation means 'a population having a common language and literature, common customs and common consciousness of rights and wrongs, inhabiting a territory of a geographical unity.' Bluntsley [Johann Kaspar Bluntschli], the famous German writer on politics, defines Nation thus—'It is a union of masses of men of different occupations and social states, in a hereditary society of common spirit, feeling and race bound together especially by a language and customs in a common civilization which gives them a sense of unity and distinction from all foreigners, *quite apart from the bond of state.*'[8] Getel [Raymond Garfield Gettell] is very clear in his expression of the concept when in his 'Introduction to Political Science' he says that 'Nationality is to denote a population having common bonds, of race, language, religion, tradition and history. These influences create the consciousness of unity that binds individuals into a nationality.'

Gumplovic [Gumplowicz] is brief but most significant in defining 'Nation' as a 'community of civilization'. Our own writer on politics

[8] Author's italics.

Mr Kale says in his 'Indian Administration', 'A Nation is a community, members of which are bound to one another by racial, ethnological, religious and linguistic ties.'

It is needless to multiply quotations. Let us see what we obtain as the gist of the idea. That 'a definite home country', a territory of a 'geographical unity' is essential for a nation is evident, though every one may not have explicitly expressed its absolute necessity, to [sic] so many words. The next point which comes up as [being] of the essence of the concept is 'Race'—'hereditary Society', 'Religious idea', 'common civilization', expressed also as 'Common heritage of memories,' 'Linguistic unity'—these are the three other factors most prominently present in the Nation-concept as understood by the learned political thinkers of the world. In fine, the idea contained in the word Nation is the compound of five distinct factors fused into one indissoluble whole. The famous five 'Unities'—Geographical (country), Racial (race), Religious (religion), Cultural (culture) and Linguistic (language). We will take each severally and examine its place in the concept.

COUNTRY—That for any race to live the life of a Nation it is essential that it should have a territory of its own, delimited if possible, by natural geographical boundaries, is an unquestionable truth. Indeed such a piece of land is the physical basis of any National life. A Nation without its country is unthinkable. It is only when a race inhabits a definite territory as its own possession and develops therein, that blossoming forth into its peculiar culture, it attains to the resultant nationhood. History records abundant proofs of races acquiring a country, shaping themselves into Nations in course of time. It may be said that even the USA in which a number of European peoples settled and amalgamated themselves into homogeneous whole, have achieved independent nationhood as a result merely of a separate country; otherwise there is nothing to distinguish the parent stocks from their American offspring. At the same time it is an illustration in point to show how an independent life in a separate country produces varying interest and, in time, stands the mother race with a distinct new culture, giving rise to a new Nation. History also records notable examples of ancient Nations being deprived of nationality as a consequence of their losing their mother-land. Take for example the Jews. The Jews were a prosperous nation. But times changed. The nation was conquered and subjected to a tyrannous rule under the Romans. A number of Jews, finding it difficult to live in those conditions maintaining their own religion and culture, left their country Palestine and came to Hindusthan— the purest stock of the children of Israel—and to this day they are inhabiting the country of the Hindus (Ben Israel of Bombay Presidency). Later, the engines of destruction let loose under the name of Islam, completely destroyed their power and the Jews, in order to save what was most dear to them—their religion and culture, fled from the country and scattered, all the world over, naturalising themselves in various parts of the globe. Thus scattered they still live and with them live their religion, culture, and language. They are all still the same old Jews. With them nothing has changed except that they are exiles from their country and have no place to call their own and they are all without exception a rich and advanced people. But they are a people in name and are not a nation, as the whole world knows. The recent attempts to rehabitating [*sic*] Palestine with its ancient population of the Jews is nothing more than an effort to reconstruct the broken edifice and revitalize the practically dead Hebrew National Life. Another example is of the Parsis. The same old tale of Islamic invasion, with its attendant massacres, devastation, destruction, loot and arson, violating all sacred places, desecration of religion and culture, and forced conversion to the faith of the ready executioner, and everything else that ever went hand in hand with the spread of Islam, was then repeated in all its hideousness in Iran. A number of staunch Parsis decided to trust the harsh elements of nature rather than the unparalled cruelty of Islam, took with them their sacred fire and set sail for anywhere away from Iran and from the murderers who enthroned themselves in that fair land. They happened to land in Hindusthan, the land of the generous Hindus, who extended to them the hand of fraternal love and gave them succour and protection. And in this new country they have lived and prospered and are today a wealthy class with their religion and culture intact. But the Parsis are not a Nation. No one can say that the Iranean [*sic*] Nation of Parsis is extant today. Why? Because they lost their own country, because they have no geographical unit of a territory to call their own, wherein to live in undisputed possession and develop according to their own natural tendencies, their traditions and their culture. But let these two notable examples suffice, for no one can seriously dispute the fact that for a people to be and to live as a Nation, a hereditory [*sic*] territory, a definite home country, relating to which it has certain indissoluble bonds of community, is essential.

RACE—It is superfluous to emphasize the importance of Racial Unity in the Nation idea. A Race is a 'hereditory [*sic*] Society having common customs, common language, common memories of glory or disaster; in short, it is a population with a common origin under one culture. Such a race is by far the most important ingredient of a Nation. Even if there be people of a foreign origin, they must have become assimilated into the body of the mother race and inextricably fused into it. They should have become one with the original national race not only in its economic and political life, but also in its religion, culture and language, for otherwise such foreign races may be considered, under certain circumstances at best members of a common state for political purposes; but they can never form part and parcel of the National body. If the mother race is destroyed either by destruction of the persons composing it or by loss of the principles of its existence, its religion and culture, the nation itself comes to an end. We will not seek to prove this axiomatic truth, that the Race is the body of the Nation, and that with its fall, the Nation ceases to exist.

RELIGION AND CULTURE—Where religion forms the very life-breath of a people, where it governs every action of the individual as well as of the society as a whole, where in short, it forms the only incentive to all action, worldly and spiritual, it is difficult to distinguish these two factors clearly. They become one, as it were. Culture being the cumulative effect of age-long customs, traditions, historical and other conditions and most particularly of religious beliefs and their attendant philosophy (where there is such a philosophy) on the Social mind, creating the peculiar Race spirit (which it is difficult to explain), it is plainly a result mainly of that religion and philosophy, which controls the social life and shapes it, generation after generation, planting on the Race consciousness its own particular stamp. But ordinarily, where religion is a mere matter of form, or worse still, a toy luxury to play with, it is culture which is the important factor, and can be easily distinguished from Religion. For example in Europe, except Turkey and modern Russia, the whole continent professes Christianity, but this religion, not having permeated into the life of the people, remains practically an ornament, without moulding the minds of the people. As such, each Nation, while being Christian in common with the others, has developed its own peculiar culture, and evolution of the Race spirit of its pre-Christian ancestors. And every Nation is proud of this distinctive feature and guards it most zealously. For, where religion does not form a distinguishing factor, culture together with the other necessary constituents of the Nation idea, becomes the crucid [sic] point in the making up of individual Nationality. On the other hand in Hindusthan, Religion is an all-absorbing entity. Based as it is on the unshakable foundations of a sound philosophy of life (as indeed Religion ought to be) it has become eternally woven into the life of the Race, and forms, as it were its very soul. With us every action in life, individual, social, or political, is a command of Religion. We make war or peace, engage in arts and crafts, amass wealth and give it away, indeed we are born and we die—all in accord with religious injunctions. Naturally, therefore, we are what our great Religion has made us. Our Race-Spirit is a child of our Religion, and so with us culture is but a product of our all-comprehensive Religion, a part of its body and not distinguishable from it.

But whether the two, Religion and Culture, can be shown in distinction or not, whether the one forms an appendage of the other, every unit which we call a Nation, does profess and maintain a National Religion and Culture, these being necessary to complete the Nation idea.

At the present, however, there is a general tendency to affirm that Religion is an individual question and should have no place in public and political life. This tendency is based upon a misconception of Religion, and has its origin in those, who have, as a people, no religion worth the name. And yet it will not be unprofitable to consider this problem at this stage. If Religion concerns itself merely with matters other-worldly, if there be another world, so the sceptic will say, then surely it should have no place in affairs of this world. Then only will it surely be a question to be solved by each in his own individual way, in the privacy of his life. In Europe, in practically the whole of the world except Hindusthan, Religion means not more than a few opinions, dogmatically forced down the throats of one and all, without any consideration for individual aptitudes or the fact that the teachings therein do not accord with modern knowledge. It is just the only way for all—a square hole for balls of all shapes and sizes to fit in. And at its best it is an attempt to establish a relationship between the individual and God, for the spiritual benefit of the former. With this view of Religion, even at its best, it is natural to affirm that it should have no place in Politics. But then, this is but a fractional part of Religion. Religion in its essence is that which by regulating society in all its functions, makes room for all individual idiosyncrasies, and provides suitable ways and means for all sorts of mental frames to adopt, and evolve, and which at the same time raises the whole society as such, from the material, through the moral to the spiritual plane. As many minds, so many ways—that is the spiritual rule of true Religion. On the worldly or material plane, too, it affords opportunities for the development of each to the fullest stature of his manhood, not for a moment, however, desisting from pointing out and leading on the way to the attainment of the highest spiritual life and Bliss Infinite. Such Religion—and nothing else deserves that name—cannot be ignored in individual or public life. It must have a place in proportion to its vast importance in politics as well. To give it a go-by or even to assign it an insignificant place, would mean degeneration on all hands. Indeed politics itself becomes, in the case of such a Religion, a small factor, to be considered and followed solely as one of the commands of Religion and in accord with such commands. We in Hindusthan have been living such a Religion. For us individual, social and political prosperity is the first stage to be attainded towards achievement of real life in its fullness. We cannot give up religion in our National life, as it would mean our stopping short on the lowest rung of the ladder, when we have the whole way clear before us, as it would mean that we have turned faithless to our Race-Spirit, to the ideal and mission for which we have lived for ages inspite of greater calamities than what sufficed to annihilate Babylon and Misar and Iran and a number of the ancient civilizations.

Apart from this, and taking that Europe has a religion (those who have raised this cry of no-religion being all European) it is small wonder that they should have said so. Europe has been the scene of much bloodshed in the name of Religion. Although they are all Christian Nations, from an ill-placed pride in a particular form of worship in the minds of the ruling classes, they shed much innocent blood and acquired such notoriety, that for the general peace it was considered profitable to assume a more tolerant attitude towards the various sects and religious persuasions and leave the individual to choose whichever he liked, provided only, he did not, in following his beliefs, become a nuisance to his neighbours. To ban religion altogether from all public and political life is but one step forward and a natural one.

There is yet another and much more important consideration. Sects, forms of worships, are only parts of a religion, followed by a group of persons or by individuals; they [sic] are not so many Religions. Europe, therefore, has but one Religion all over. Naturally, Religion does not form there a distinguishing factor of Nationality. And so in the conflict of Nations religious zeal does not form an incentive to any act of war or peace. Under such conditions National differences arise solely out of the country, race, culture and possibly the language being different. Such is the state of affairs obtaining in Europe since long. And most of the modern thinkers on Political Science being Europeans and having before them the problem of the Christian countries only, they found the religion factor superfluous in their political life. Hence the proposition that religion has no place in politics.

And yet, as we shall soon see, religion, though thus cried down, has been still zealously maintained as an essential ingredient, expressly or implicitly in the Nationhood of most of the European Nations themselves. So also with culture. If there be but one culture throughout and one religion, country and race with the difference of language, if such difference exists, will be sufficient to constitute distinct Nationalities. Not that under such conditions the two shall not be factors in the nation idea, only they will not be manifest, for then they shall have no need to be so. This fact should be borne in mind, as it will have to be referred to again, when we will study our old conception of 'Rashtra'.

There is one more question. The modern Socialistic doctrine denies religion altogether. We reserve this question for a later page. In passing we shall only state that Socialism, in whatever form is the 'theory of the State' and takes no account of Nationality and at present is beyond our scope. We will, therefore, for the time being let it be.

LANGUAGE—Every Race, living in its own country evolves a language of its own, reflecting its culture, its religion, its history and traditions:

supplanting it with another is dangerous. It is an expression of the Race spirit, a manifestation of the National web of life. Every word, every turn of expression depicts the Nation's life. It is all so intertwined into the very being of the race that the two cannot be severed without fatal results.

Take away from a nation its ancient language—its whole literature goes with it—and the Nation as such ceases to be. It is not for nothing that the English long tried, even by the force of arms, to force down their language on the Irish and to suppress their mother tongue. It is also not for nothing that not only the Irish fought hard and preserved their sacred language but the little Welshmen also in these modern times of glorious political life as a part of Great Britain, are striving hard to stem the tide supplanting their tongue with the 'foreign' language, not without success. For these all know that loss of their ancient language would for ever kill out their dear national sentiment, and with it wipe out any possibility of their building up independent healthy national life. One of the best evidences of an enslaved people is their adoption of the language and customs of their conquerors. Language, therefore, being intricably [sic] woven in the all-round life of a race is an ingredient of great importance in its nationality. Without it the nation concept is incomplete.

Ordinarily in every nation, these three, religion, culture and language form a compound factor. In the modern nations it is only latterly that they can be seen in their separateness. We shall, therefore, illustrate the importance of these factors in unison. Take the example of Afghanistan. It was once Gandhar, a province of the Hindu Nation. It changed its form of faith by embracing Buddhism and gradually had the hold of religion upon it progressively weakened, till at last, with the advent of the Muslims, it fell an easy prey to the invaders and was deprived of its religion and with it, its Hindu culture and language. The country is there, the ancient race, too, is there, but it no longer is the same old nation that it used to be. Gandhar is no more. Similarly with Baluchistan. Palestine became Arab, a large number of Hebrew nations in Palestine changed faith and culture and language and the Hebrew nation in Palestine died a natural death. Where is the Parsi Nation today? Their land is there, still inhabited by the descendants of the old Parsis, but is there the Parsi Nation in their home country, Iran? It has ceased to be with the destruction in its country, of the three essentials, Religion, Culture, and to a less extent, language. But let us not multiply examples. These few, though merely indicative, suffice for our present purpose.

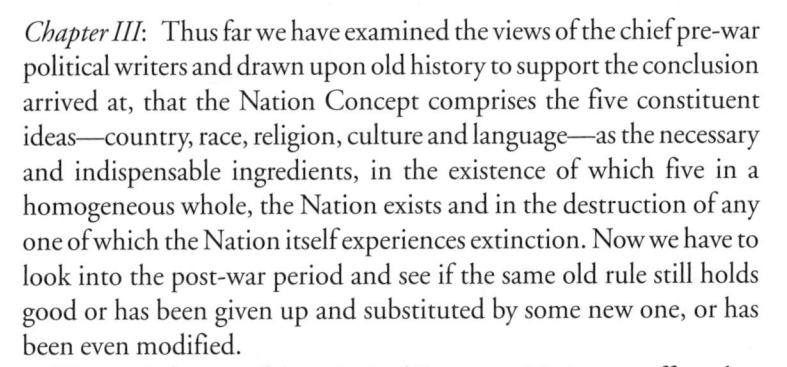

Chapter III: Thus far we have examined the views of the chief pre-war political writers and drawn upon old history to support the conclusion arrived at, that the Nation Concept comprises the five constituent ideas—country, race, religion, culture and language—as the necessary and indispensable ingredients, in the existence of which five in a homogeneous whole, the Nation exists and in the destruction of any one of which the Nation itself experiences extinction. Now we have to look into the post-war period and see if the same old rule still holds good or has been given up and substituted by some new one, or has been even modified.

The war left most of the principal European Nations unaffected so far as their constitutions went. Germany changed from a monarchist state to a Republican one but its national life did not alter with the change in the form of Government. So also with Russia. But a number of small states were created out of the remains of the old Nations, together with the territories despoiled from the vanquished nations. These new states were thus composed of the original national race with an incorporation in its body politic of a people racially, culturally and linguistically different. It was, therefore, necessary to frame certain standard rules in order to establish peaceful governments in these states. The League of Nations supervised over all these changes and reorganized and formulated the now famous 'Minority Treatises' whereby the rights of the national and foreign races could be equitably adjusted and due protection granted to the minorities in such states. If indeed, the world were of opinion that Nationality was only another name for political unity and Race, Religion, Culture, and Language had nothing to do with politics, there would have been no trouble, for then there could be no class of people to demand special privileges and protection. But the League of Nations, composed of the best political brains of practically all the Nations of the world, thinks otherwise and does not seem to countenance the view endorsed by raw political agitators. The very definition of the word 'Minority' as a 'class of people incorporated in the body of a Nation', 'citizens who differ from the majority of the population in Race, Religion and Language (culture also is implicitly there) [*sic*].' To discuss the problem of minorities is though very useful for a proper understanding of our problem today, not within scope of this book. We shall only state in one small sentence that for such a foreign race to claim preferential treatment at the hands of the Nation, it should not be an upstart, a new, voluntary settlement, and it should not be below 20 per cent of the total population of the state.

To return to our subject, the post-war statesmen, though not speaking of Religion, Culture and Language as essential constituents of the Nation concept, have tacitly acknowledged that they are so, and have even gone to the length of emphasising the necessary nature of the Race factor, as for the Geographical unity, since every state with which they had to deal, did not live in the air, but inhabited a properly delimited territory possessed by the national Race, from the very beginning of its national life, there arose no reason to express 'country' as an essential factor for National life. This however, was made express, when in order to confer their lost Nationality upon the exiled Jews, the British with the help of the League of Nations, began to rehabilitate the old Hebrew country, Palestine, with its long-lost children. The Jews had maintained their race, religion, culture and language; and all they wanted was their natural territory to complete their Nationality. The reconstruction of the Hebrew Nation in Palestine is just an affirmation of the fact that Country, Race, Religion, Culture and Language must exist unavoidably together to form a full Nation idea. Thus it is evident that the war and its resultant adjustments have not affected the old conception and that as of yore, the world, the western world especially, still holds firm to the statement that for the Nation to manifest itself and live, it must be composed of the five constituent 'Unities', Geographical, Racial, Religious, Cultural, and Linguistic, and of all these five, without exception.

Latterly some thinkers, thinking it wise to drop the words Religion, Culture and Language altogether from the Nation idea, have defined 'Nation' to mean a race living in a hereditary territory and possessed of common traditions and common aspirations. It is considered that this definition satisfies those who are impatient of the maintenance of

Religion in politics. It is thought that by adopting this new outlook on Nationality, all problems arising out of religious, cultural and linguistic differences shall cease and the world be blessed with smooth running states. That the states should run without the least friction amongst those who live under their sway, we also heartily wish, but we fail to see how this change of words in expressing the Nation idea can bring about this desirable state of affairs. Indeed has the understanding of the Nation concept undergone a change in its expression? At least we do not see that this new definition alters the old conception in the least, far less supersedes it, for, to any person, with average intelligence, it will be evident that this 'New' definition acknowledges the two first constituents Country and Race in so many words, but substitutes the other by 'common traditions and common aspirations'. 'What are Common Traditions'? Is not the tradition of a race the sum-total [*sic*] of its religious, cultural and political life? And is not the distinctive language of every race the result of its own peculiar traditions? In fact the one word 'Traditions' is expressive of all the three factors, Religion, Culture, and Language, as it embraces the whole past life of the Race in all its aspects. Thus far we have nothing more than a play of words, calculated to blind-fold the unwary tramp on the road to an under-standing of the Nation idea. Thus far this 'New' definition has been merely stated in another garb, what the old thinkers right up to the League of Nations, have emphasised as the essence of the concept. The only 'change' which now remains to be considered is in the additional words 'Common Aspirations'. The aspirations of the individual, as also of the Race, are conditioned by its mental frame. As is the mould in which the Racial mind is thrown—of course by its age-long tradi-tions, so are its desires—its aspirations. It is the Race Consciousness awakening to march further on, but it must tread the road into which its past traditional way has led it. It cannot abandon its fixed groove without seriously upsetting the whole fabric of its existence and en-dangering its life. Indeed it cannot help moving along the path which tradition has opened out for it. Look at Italy, the old Roman Race consciousness [*sic*] of conquering the whole territory round the Medi-terranean Sea, so long dormant, has roused itself, and shaped the Racial–National aspirations accordingly. The ancient Race spirit which prompted the Germanic tribes to over-run the whole of Europe, has re-risen in modern Germany. With the result that the Nation perforce follows aspirations, predetermined by the traditions left by its depredatory ancestors. Even so with us: our Race spirit has once again roused itself as is evidenced by the race of spiritual giants we have produced, and who today stalk [*sic*] the world in serene majesty. Thus the words 'common aspirations' add nothing material to our old tested definition; they only seem to confer on every Race the indisputable right of excommunicating from its Nationality all those who, having been of the Nation, for ends of their own, turned traitors and entertained aspirations contravening or differing from those of the National Race as a whole.

Accordingly, we state that our proposition stands unchallenged. Indeed it is based on such scientific understanding of the question, that it could not be otherwise. Thus the conclusion at which after so much discussion we arrive is that for the Nation concept to exist and be manifest, it must have as its indissoluble component parts the famous five unities, 'Geographical (country), Racial (race), Religious (religion), Cultural (culture) and Linguistic (language)', that the loss or destruction of any one of these means the end of the Nation as a Nation. This is the unassailable position on the view of Nationality, subscribed to by the world's Political notaries, ancient and modern.

Having thus far studied what in essence the word 'Nation' ought to mean, we shall go into the present condition of some important modern states and see how far the 'Ought' accords with what 'Is'. Theory and practice are not always in agreement and the theory which can find no place in practical life, deserves to be discarded. Whether our theoretical conception of the Nation arrived at above is one of these dead theories, or stands the test of practical life, has now to be seen.

The Nation, with which to-day we are most in contact, is England and we will take it first in our study. So far as Country and Race are concerned they are so patent facts [*sic*] that no one questions their importance in the Nation concept. Culture, too, belongs to the same category, it being notorious how each nation jealously guards it and keeps it at its best. The knotty point is Religion and to a certain extent Language. Especially today, when democratic states boast of having washed their hands clean of it, Religion deserves careful scrutiny. Does England believe in a state Religion? The answer is plainly in the affirmative, for, otherwise, why should it be an essential condition that the king of England must be of the Protestant persuasion? [*sic*] Why should the whole galaxy of priests of the Church of England be paid out of the State treasury? More notably, why should there be a Bishop of that Church appointed at Calcutta, at State expense? Does not the English Nation, openly or clandestinely, help the missionary activities in Hindusthan and other places? If it is but Religious toleration [*sic*], why are not the Hindu priests of the most important holy places paid by the British Government? And why is not the Bishop of Calcutta left to his own resources to live upon the charity of his flock? There is but one answer. England has a State Religion, the Protestant form of the Christian faith, and believes in maintaining and strengthening it, as in its strength that of the Nation is preserved. As for language, the English attempts at killing out the indigenous languages and forcing upon the conquered races the 'National' English tongue are notorious. Wherever the English went—Ireland, Wales, Hindusthan—in all such places they have tried to supplant the original language by English. Indeed, such is the Englishman's pride in his 'National' language that he tries his best to make it the world's Lingua Franca. With England, then, theory fully accords with practice regarding the Nation idea.

The other Nation most in the eye of the world today is Germany. This Nation affords a very striking example. Modern Germany strove, and has to a great extent achieved what she strove for, to once again bring under one sway the whole of the territory, hereditarily possessed by the Germans but which, as a result of political disputes, had been portioned off as different countries under different states. Austria for example, was merely a province, on par with Prussia, Bavaria and other principalities, which made the Germanic Empire. Logically Austria should not be an independent kingdom, but be one with the rest of Germany. So also with those portions inhabited by Germans, which had been included, after the War, in the new State of Czechoslovakia. German pride in their Fatherland for a definite home country, for which the race has certain traditional attachments as a necessary concomitant of the true Nation concept, awoke and ran the risk of starting a fresh World-conflagration, in order to establish one, unparalleled, undisputed, German Empire over all this 'hereditary territory'. This natural and logical aspiration of Germany has almost been fulfilled and the great importance of the 'country factor' has been once

again vindicated even in the living present. Come we next to the next
ingredient of the Nation idea—Race, with which Culture and language
are inseparably connected, where Religion is not the all-absorbing
force that it should be. German race pride has now become the topic
of the day. To deep up the purity of the Race and its culture, Germany
shocked the world by her purging the country of the semitic Races—
the Jews. Race pride at its highest has been manifested here. Germany
has also shown how well-nigh impossible it is for Races and cultures,
having differences going to the root, to be assimilated into one united
whole, a good lesson for use in Hindusthan to learn and profit by.
Then the state language is German, and the foreign races living in the
Country as minorities, though they have freedom to use their respective
languages among themselves, must deal in the nation's language in
their public life. The factor of religion, too, is not to be ignored. The
president, if any, of the Republic has to take an oath, which in its nature is purely religious. The state holidays are mostly the Christian
holidays, according to the Roman Catholic sect. To be brief, all the
five constituents of the Nation idea have been boldly vindicated in
modern Germany and that too, today in the actual present, when we
can for ourselves see and study them, as they manifest themselves in
their relative importance.

Another notable example is that of Russia. We had reserved this
'Nation' as it professes no particular religious creed. And yet, howsoever
it may have changed since the War, it still conforms fully to the complete
Nation concept. In the beginning, when the new doctrine of Socialism,
in the Communistic form, was in full swing in Russia, the slogan was
'Workers and peasants of the world, unite.' It seemed as if the people
had burst the bounds of nationality and set out for Internationalism,
with the whole of humanity as its field of work. But the rest of the
world and even most of the people in Russia itself, were not ready to
grasp such a broad ideal. Human mind is what it is and unless it takes
up a high philosophical attitude, it cannot even conceive of the oneness
of the world. As a natural consequence Russian Internationalism is no
more and today we find that Russia is a more orthodox Nation probably
than any other in the world. It is now not the old kind of nation, that
is all. But that it is a Nation all the same is evident. There is as of old
the Country and its old Race with its Russian language. So far nothing

has altered. The only change is that the Nation has given up its old Religion and Culture and built up new ones in their place. In Russia now we have the new religion known as Socialism—and the new culture that of the workers, evolved out of their materialistic culture of Russia; they may, however, feel surprised at our statement that Socialism is modern Russia's Religion. But there is nothing to be surprised at. To most, religion means a set of opinions to be dogmatically followed, for the good of the individual and of the society and for the attainment of God. Here we have a religion which does not believe in God. It is a Godless religion but a religion none the less. For the Russians, their prophet is Karl Marx and his opinions are their Testament. Even in other parts of the world there have been Godless religions in the past. The Russian religion is the modern form of those ancient ones. The socialists are veritably the descendants of Virochana and Charwak. But it does not profit us to discuss the beliefs to which the Russian Nation adheres with religious fervour. These beliefs are sacred to them and they are intolerant of all who differ from them or hold other or contradictory views. There is but another example of Semitic religious intolerance, which has, in this form, once again bathed the world in blood. We rest satisfied with pointing out that Russia has its country, race, its materialistic godless religion, with its resultant culture and its language and stands out before the world a Nation in its complete Nationhood, shorn of its borrowed feathers of Inter Nationalism [sic].

We shall take only one more example, that of Czechoslovakia, as it is very instructive to us. This was a state formed after the Great War, of portions of Germany, Austria, Hungary and Poland, joined to the Czech rule, to serve as a buffer state against Germany. The League of Nations adjusted and balanced the rights of the Nation—the Czech with those of the minorities, among them the Sudeten Germans. Under the direct supervision of the League was made this distinction within the state, of the Nation supreme in the state and minorities living under the protection of the Nation and owing a number of duties to it, in return for the right of the state citizenship. Czech language, Czech religion, the state language and all without exception had to deal in that language and denationalisation (which could result only by giving up one's religion and culture and consequently race, situated as Czechoslovakia is, or by political opposition to the establishment) was declared on offence and the offenders liable to be penalized. Here was implicitly an avowal by the League of Nations, that 'Nation' and 'State' are not synonymous, that in the 'State', the 'Nation' should be supreme and its components Country, Race, Religion, Culture and Language should be respected and where possible followed by all the foreign races living in the state as minorities. And yet inspite of the most scruplous care taken, to bring about harmony, inspite of the vigilance of the League, all unnational [*sic*] elements in the Czech state have fallen out and justified the fears of many political scholars, regarding the wisdom of heaping together in one State, elements conflicting with the National life. But of this later.

No need multiplying examples. Those interested may first purge their minds of any preconceived notions and look into the constitution of the various nations of the world and convince themselves, how everywhere National existence is entirely dependent upon the co-ordinated existence of the five elements constituting the Nation idea— Country, Race, Religion, Culture and Language. That is the final incontrovertible verdict of theoretical discussions and their practical application to the world conditions past and present.

Chapter IV: Now we shall proceed to understand our Nationhood in the light of this Scientific concept. Here is our vast country, Hindusthan, the land of Hindus, their home country hereditary territory, a definite geographical unity, delimited naturally by the sublime Himalayas on the North side, the limitless ocean on the other three sides, an ideal piece of land, deserving in every respect to be called a Country, fulfilling all that the word should imply in the Nation idea. Living in this Country since pre-historic times is the ancient Race—the Hindu Race, united together by common traditions, by memories of Common glory and disaster, by similar historical, political, social, religious and other experiences, living under the same influences, and evolving a common culture, a common mother language, common customs, common aspirations. This great Hindu Race professes its illustrious Hindu Religion, the only Religion in the world worthy of being so denominated, which in its varity [*sic*] is still an organic whole, capable of feeding the noble aspirations of all men, of all stages, of all grades, aptitudes and capacities, enriched by the noblest philosophy of life in all its functions, and hallowed by an unbroken, interminable succession of divine spiritual geniuses, a religion of which any sane man may be justly proud. Guided by this Religion in all walks of life, individual, social, political, the Race evolved a culture, which despite the degenerating contact with the debased 'civilizations' of the Musalmans and the Europeans, for the last ten centuries, is still the noblest in the world. The fruit proves the worth of the tree and the common mind of a people the value of its culture. The spirit of broad Catholicism, generosity, toleration [*sic*], truth, sacrifice and love for all life, which characterises the average Hindu mind, not wholly vitiated by Western influence, bears eloquent testimony to the greatness of Hindu culture. And even those, spoiled by contamination with foreign influences do not but compare favourably with the best in the rest of the world. Not only has this culture been most markedly effective in moulding man after the picture of God, but in the field of learning (we distinguish learning and knowledge [*sic*]) also, it has produced, to the immortal glory of the Race, intellectual giants, outshining the greatest savants of the modern Scientific world. Great mathematicians like Bhaskaracharya, great chemists and physicians like the authors of the Charak Samhita, Bhavaprakash and Sushruta, great artists and sculptors, whose works like the Taj, the Ajanta paintings, the Werool (Ellora) Caves, and numerous others well known to the world still delight and charm the people of the world, great politicians and diplomats like Arya Chanakya, Amatya Rakshasa, great economists like Kautilya, great warriors and Emperors like the Hero of the Ramayana, Chandragupta, Harsha, Pulakeshi, Pratap, Shivaji, Chhatrasal, the godly Sikh Gurus— all these and many more—succeeded in our times by their worthy offspring, Ramanujam, Sir C.V. Raman, Sir Jagdish Chandra Bose, Dr B. Sahni, Dr Bhattacharya, Kaviraj N.N. Sen, Raja Ravi Varma, the painters—Tagore and others; Gokhale, Lala Lajpat Rai, Bipin Chandra Pal, Lok Tilak, C.R. Das, Shastri, V.G. Kale, the heroes of 1857, Tatya Tope, Kunwar Singh, the warrior queen Laxmibai of Jhansi, great poets and dramatists of old—Kalidas, Bhavabhuti, Magh and countless others represented today through the medieval Ramprasad, Tulsidas, Surdas, Jnaneshwar, Ramdas, Tukaram, by Rabindra Nath

Tagore, Sharatchandra Chakrawarti, Rameshchandra Dutt, Babu Premchandra, N.C. Kelkar, V.D. Savarkar and many more—the whole line of luminaries in every branch of learning, all these and many more, unnamed for want of space, are the glorious fruit of this ancient culture and bear unimpeachable testimony to its greatness. More glorious still is the succession of Religious, spiritual philosophers, from the Vedic sages down to the seers of our own day—Swami Vivekananda, Swami Ramtirth, Maharshi Ramana, too numerous to name. Europe may boast of a few (she is, however, ashamed of them today) St Francis, St Theresa, St Paul, Luther, Max Müller, Paul Duessen, Romain Rolland, but here are countless such even today, who, in their divinity, vie with the 'Master' of the European saints. No race is endowed with a nobler and more fruitful culture surely. No Race is more fortunate in being given a Religion, which could produce such a culture. In a nutshell such are the religious and cultural complements of this Nation. The last, language, seems to present some difficulties, for in this country every province has its own language. It appears as if the Linguistic unity is wanting, and there are not one but many 'Nations', separated from each other by linguistic differences. But in fact that is not so. There is but one language, Sanskrit, of which these many 'languages' are mere offshoots, the children of the mother language, Sanskrit, the dialect of the Gods, is common to all from the Himalayas to the ocean in the South, from East to West and all the modern sister languages are through it so much inter-related as to be practically one. It needs but little labour to acquire a going acquaintance [sic] with any tongue. And even among the modern languages Hindi is the most commonly understood and used as a medium of expression between persons of different provinces. We have no hesitation in saying that though the vastness of our country has had the necessary consequence of giving birth to different dialects in the various localities, still all these local tongues are naturally united in their great parent, the Sanskrit, and are essentially one. There is thus no doubt regarding the existence in us of the fifth component of the Nation idea—language. Thus applying the modern understanding of 'Nation' to our present conditions, the conclusion is unquestionably forced upon us that in this country, Hindusthan, the Hindu race with its Hindu Religion, Hindu Culture and Hindu Language (the natural family of Sanskrit and her offsprings) complete the Nation concept; that, in fine [*sic*], in Hindusthan exists and must needs exist the ancient Hindu nation and nought else but the Hindu Nation. All those not belonging to the national i.e. Hindu Race, Religion, Culture and Language, naturally fall out of the pale of real 'National' life.

We repeat: in Hindusthan, the land of the Hindus, lives and should live the Hindu Nation—satisfying all the five essential requirements of the scientific nation concept of the modern world. Consequently only those movements are truly 'National' as aim at re-building, revitalizing, and emancipating from its present stupor, the Hindu Nation. Those only are nationalist patriots, who with the aspiration to glorify the Hindu race and Nation next to their heart, are prompted into activity and strive to achieve that goal. All others, posing to be patriots and wilfully indulging in a course of action detrimental to the Hindu Nation are traitors and enemies to the National Cause or to take a more charitable view if unintentionally and unwillingly led into such a course, mere simpletons, misguided ignorant fools.

Extracts from *Bunch of Thoughts*[9]

Internal Threats

The Muslims: It has been the tragic lesson of the history of many a country in the world that the hostile elements within the country pose a far greater menace to national security than aggressors from outside. Unfortunately, this first lesson of national security has been the one thing which has been consistently ignored in our country ever since the British left this land. Wishful thinking born out of lack of courage to face realities, mouthing of high-sounding slogans by the persons at the helm of affairs to cover up the tragedies overtaking us one after another, and opportunistic alliances of parties and groups with the hostile elements to further their narrow self-interests, have all combined to make the threat of internal subversion to our national freedom and security very acute and real.

[9] M.S. Golwalkar, *Bunch of Thoughts* (1966; rpnt Bangalore, Jagarana Prakashana, 2nd edn, revised & enlarged, 1980), pp. 232–65.

First, let us take the case of Muslims.

Even to this day, there are so many who say, 'Now there is no Muslim problem at all. All those riotous elements who supported Pakistan have gone away once and for all. The remaining Muslims are devoted to our country. After all, they have no other place to go and they are bound to remain loyal.'

Let Facts Speak: But what are the facts? Is it true that all pro-Pakistani elements have gone away to Pakistan? It was the Muslims in Hindu majority provinces led by U.P. who provided the spearhead for the movement for Pakistan right from the beginning. And they have remained solidly here even after Partition. In fact, the Muslims of Punjab, Bengal, Sind and NWFP which [*sic*] went over to Pakistan had totally rejected Muslim League in the 1937 elections. It was only in later years that, because of the wrong policies of our leadership, the Muslims there were pushed into the arms of the Muslim League.

And again, before Partition there were elections for the setting up of the Constituent Assembly. In those elections Muslim League had contested making the creation of Pakistan its election plank. The Congress also had set up some Muslim candidates all over the country. But at almost every such place, Muslims voted for the Muslim League candidates and the Muslim candidates of Congress were utterly routed. NWFP was an exception. It only means that all the crores of Muslims who are here even now, had *en bloc* voted for Pakistan.

Have those who remained here changed at least after that? Has their old hostility and murderous mood, which resulted in widespread riots, looting, arson, raping and all sorts of orgies on an unprecedented scale in 1946–47, come to a halt at least now? It would be suicidal to delude ourselves into believing that they have turned patriots overnight after the creation of Pakistan. On the contrary, the Muslim menace has increased a hundredfold by the creation of Pakistan which has become a springboard for all their future aggressive designs on our country.

Pakistan—A Continuing Aggression: Their aggressive strategy has always been twofold. One is direct aggression. In the pre-independence days, Jinnah called it 'Direct Action'. The first blow got them Pakistan. Our leaders who were a party to the creation of Pakistan may try to whitewash the tragedy by saying that it was a brotherly division of the country and so on. But the naked fact remains that an aggressive Muslim State has been carved out of our own motherland. From the day the so-called Pakistan came into being, we in Sangh have been declaring that it is a clear case of continued Muslim aggression. The Muslim desire, growing ever since they stepped on this land some twelve hundred years ago, to convert and enslave the entire country could not bear fruit, in spite of their political domination for several centuries, because the conquering spirit of the nation rose in the form of great and valiant men from time to time who sounded the death-knell of their kingdoms here. But even though their kingdoms lay shattered, their desire for domination did not break up. In the coming of the British they found an opportunity to fulfil their desire. They played their cards shrewdly, sometimes creating terror and havoc, and ultimately succeeded in brow-beating our leadership into panicky surrender to their sinful demand of Partition.

We of the Sangh have been, in fact, hammering this historical truth for the last so many years. Some time ago, the noted world historian Prof. Arnold Toynbee, came forward to confirm it. He visited our country twice, studied our national development at close quarters, and wrote an article setting forth the correct historical perspective of Partition. Therein he has unequivocally stated that the creation of Pakistan is the first successful step of the Muslims in this 20th century to realise their twelve-hundred-year-old dream of complete subjugation of this country.

Their direct aggression, whetted by their first success, then turned against Kashmir. There too they met with success, though partial. One third of Kashmir continues to be in their clutches even to this day. Now, Pakistan is trying to gobble up the rest of Kashmir also with the help of powerful pro-Pakistani elements inside Kashmir.

Pursuing Jinnah's Dream: The second front of their aggression is increasing their numbers in strategic areas of our country. After Kashmir, Assam is their next target. They have been systematically flooding Assam, Tripura and the rest of Bengal since long. It is not because, as some would like us to believe, East Pakistan is in the grip of famine that people are coming away into Assam and West Bengal. The Pakistani Muslims have been infiltrating into Assam for the past fifteen years. Does it mean then that famine has been stalking East Pakistan all these fifteen years? They are entering Assam surreptitiously and the local Muslims are sheltering them. As a result, the percentage of Muslims there which was only 11 per cent in 1950, has now more than doubled. What else is this but a conspiracy to make Assam a Muslim majority province so that it would automatically fall into the lap of Pakistan in course of time?

In the anti-Bengali riots (1960) that rocked Assam, the Muslim population and the Muslim ministers, as usual, played their treacherous game. They set up Assami Hindu against Bengali Hindu and vice versa as it suited their designs and carried sword and fire into Hindu hearths and homes in their bid to oust the Bengali Hindus. By this, they increased their percentage in relation to the Hindus in that province. Certain things which have happened there are tell-tale [*sic*]. Many were the cases where the house of a Bengali Muslim gentleman was safe but the houses of Bengali Hindus on either side were burnt down. Papers also have reported that some persons were arrested while trying to carry away looted property to East Pakistan. It is a patent fact that Muslims from Pakistan had poured into Assam in truckloads to carry out their designs. When we remember that Kashmir and Assam were to have formed part of the Pakistan of Jinnah's dream, their plan of action becomes clear as daylight.

It would be suicidal on our part to dismiss their plan of realising the dream of Jinnah as mere wishful thinking. And so did we, at one time, dismiss Jinnah's demand for Pakistan as 'fantastic'. But all the same, it is now a stark reality. Their hectic activities of collecting arms and ammunition are going on unabated. Their meetings in masjids and incitement to violence are dangerously on the increase. A few years ago the Police Commissioner of Calcutta had warned that the Nakhoda masjid alone had stored sufficient arms and ammunition to blow up half of Calcutta and unless the masjid was searched and cleared of the dangerous stuff, maintaining public peace in Calcutta was well-nigh impossible. For this courageous warning he was at once transferred from Calcutta! The bomb explosions going on in Delhi and several other places in the country are a glaring proof of their subversive preparations—if proof be needed even after the history of a thousand years of their naked aggression.

They are especially emboldened in their nefarious designs by the fact that the present-day leadership is too weak to put a strong check on them. They remember very well that their acts of violence and bloodshed in Calcutta, Noakhali and Tripura had unnerved our leaders and made them succumb to bartering away the unity of our motherland and handing over a part of the country to them. Even to this day they see that goondaism pays rich dividends at the hands of our present leadership.

An incident happened in the wake of the massacres and mass expulsion of Hindus from East Bengal in 1950. It was precisely at that period that a series of riots broke out in many parts of Bengal, Bihar, Uttar Pradesh and Delhi. Our Government suffers from a strange obsession that wherever there is a 'communal riot' there must be the hand of RSS in it! Accordingly, the U.P. Government clamped some of our workers behind bars. Then I happened to meet Sardar Patel for some other reason. I naturally inquired why our persons were arrested. He replied that the U.P. Government had received reports that the Sangh workers were responsible for all those disturbances. Then I told him, 'If you had observed the position of the areas where the disturbances have taken place, it would have been clear to you that they are the same as those that Jinnah had demanded as a corridor to join West and East Pakistan. Further, these riots have coincided with the mass expulsion of Hindus from East Bengal. The only meaning is that they want to browbeat our Government into yielding to their demand of the corridor.' Sardar Patel remained silent for a minute and then said, 'Yes. There is truth in what you say.' Needless to say, all our workers were released soon after. We were fortunate that we had in Sardar Patel a person with an iron will to face the reality in those days.

The Time-Bomb: Sardar Patel was aware that Western U.P. had continued to be as powerful a Muslim pocket as before. He did not want that it should be linked to West Pakistan by a continuous Muslim belt. Hence he had taken due precautions to see that the Muslims driven out of East Punjab after Partition did not resettle anywhere near West Punjab so as to form a continuous Muslim chain from West Pakistan to U.P. But, on account of pressure from Acharya Vinoba Bhave, Muslims were allowed to resettle first in Gurgaon district. Now, over four lakh Muslims have resettled in those regions.

There are sure signs that an explosive situation similar to that of 1946–47 is fast brewing and there is no knowing when it will blow up. Right from Delhi to Rampur and Lucknow, the Muslims are busy hatching a dangerous plot, piling up arms and mobilising their men and probably biding their time to strike from within when Pakistan decides upon an armed conflict with our country. And when they do strike, it is very likely that even Delhi may be rocked to its foundations unless we wake up in time to nip the mischief in the bud. Not that our leaders do not know it. The secret intelligence reports reach them all right. But it seems they have in view only elections. Elections mean vote catching, which means appeasing certain sections of people having a solid bloc of votes. And the Muslims are one such solid bloc. Therein lies the root of all this appeasement and consequent disastrous effects.

Forgetting Nothing, Learning Nothing: Muslim League has again raised its ugly head in the South. The creation of Pakistan woke up the Hindus in the North, at least for the time being, to the danger of Muslim League. So the League leaders shifted their headquarters to the South. Now they have come out with the statement that they have been carrying on their activities all these years in secret. The mass agitation in Kerala which brought down the Communist Government, gave them a golden opportunity to come out in the open. The elections that followed proved to be a windfall for them. The Congress, learning nothing from its past experience of placating the Muslim League which had landed our country in the calamity of Partition, once again stretched its arms to embrace that treacherous party during elections. And in order to justify their blatantly anti-national move, Pandit Jawaharlal Nehru gave the Muslim League a clean chit of patriotism saying that it was not the old Muslim League but a new patriotic party devoted to their community and religion! What a marvellous definition of patriotism! But to his misfortune, on the very next day, the All-India President of the Muslim League came out with the statement that theirs was the same old party with not a shadow of change! Now in Kerala, they openly propagate for an independent 'Moplaland'.

In these developments, one almost sees over half-a-century-old happenings coming to life once again. During the twenties, in a bid to win friendship of Muslims, our leaders had called upon the Hindus to take up the Khilafat movement (a movement against the British who had dethroned the king in Turkey) as their own. In Kerala too, Hindus came forward with men and money to help the movement. But the Muslim wrath against the British soon developed into a jehad against the Hindu 'kafirs' carrying with it all the usual atrocities of Muslim barbarism like killing, burning, molesting, looting and forcible con-versions. When the news of these hair-raising atrocities reached and shocked other parts of the country, an eminent leader came out in open appreciation of those heinous Muslim criminals, calling them 'brave Moplas'! Let us just compare those words with the words of the present leaders speaking of them as 'patriotic' and we will get an idea of the long suicidal stupor which has deadened all our faculties of national alertness and security.

Everywhere the Muslims are being abetted in their separatist and subversive activities by our own Government, our leaders and political parties. Take the case of Calcutta riots which occurred in the wake of the holocaust of Hindus in Khulna, Narayanganj and Dacca areas of East Pakistan in 1963. Our men in power tried to paint it as a reaction to those East Bengal riots. But what are the facts? It was the Muslims in Calcutta who first started the attack on a peaceful procession of stu-dents. It was again they who set fire to the grand exhibition pandal erected in connection with the Swami Vivekananda centenary cele-brations and destroyed the precious exhibits. Can anyone in his senses believe that the Hindus of Calcutta could have destroyed a pandal containing Swami Vivekananda's exhibits? It was only after the Muslims began perpetrating such vandalism that the Hindus rose to defend themselves. Thus the Calcutta riots were, beyond a shadow of doubt, only an extension of—and not a reaction to—the riots in East Bengal.

But our Government, as usual, following in the footsteps of their erstwhile British masters, came down upon the Hindus with a heavy hand and shot them indiscriminately. One of our Central Ministers even declared, 'Every Muslim life is sacred to us,' whereas every life ought to be a sacred trust with any Government worth the name. He even boasted that more Hindus were killed in police firing than Muslims. By this statement he had only betrayed the real mind of the Government in the matter. That, in fine [sic], is how things are going on in our own country.

Countless 'Miniature Pakistans': In fact, all over the country wherever there is a masjid or a Muslim mohalla, the Muslims feel that it is their own independent territory. If there is a procession of Hindus with music and singing, they get enraged saying that their religious suscept-ibilities are wounded. If there religious feelings have become so sensitive as to be irritated by sweet music then why don't they shift their masjids to forests and pray there in silence? Why should they insist on planting a stone on the roadside, whitewash it, call it a prayer spot and then raise a hue and cry that their prayers are disturbed if music is played?

Some years back, an Arab Muslim moulvi who was on a visit to our country was requested to recite Quran as they do in their country. To that he replied, 'There we sing to the accompaniment of harmonium, tabor and such other musical instruments. Here if I do that, the local idiotic Muslims will cut me to pieces!' Is it not obvious that the so-called religious susceptibility of the Muslims here regarding music has nothing to do with religion or prayer but is solely motivated with a view to picking up quarrel with the Hindus and establishing their own little independent cells?

How is it that they dare to carry on these offensive and anti-national practices openly? It is because our Government too overtly and covertly supports them. Though the High Courts have upheld the fundamental right of the citizens to go in procession with band in all public roads, the Government, under the cover of discretionary powers vested in the executive for regulating processions in the interest of peace and order, often prevents the Hindus altogether from taking out processions in streets where masjids happen to be situated. That could set the premium on those who want to violate peace. And peaceful citizens, in the enjoyment of their inherent rights as citizens, are the prey of such violations. The law-abiding citizens are told to restrict themselves, and those who are out to indulge in violence are given a free hand to do what they like. This is in a way admitting, though indirectly, that within the country there are so many Muslim pockets, i.e., so many 'miniature Pakistans', where the general law of the land is to be enforced only with certain modifications and the whims of the miscreants have to be given the final say. This acceptance, indirect though it may be, implies a very dangerous theory fraught with possibilities of destruction of our national life altogether. Such 'pockets' have verily become centres of a widespread network of pro-Pakistani elements in this land.

Instances Galore: To cite an example, there was a riot in Malegaon (1963) in Maharashtra. The idol of Ganesha was being taken in procession for immersion. The Muslims attacked it. There was a skirmish. The Government, as usual, came forward to establish law and order, and took into custody scores of leading Hindu gentlemen as though they were responsible for the outbreak of lawlessness! Later, I had occasion to meet one important high-up in that State. I said to him, 'This incident took place at about 9 or 10 o'clock in the night. The very next morning the Pakistan radio broadcast that there had been "a great genocide of Muslims" in that particular town! How did Pakistan come to know about the affair within these few hours? There must be some pro-Pakistani gentleman with a transmitter and he must be in constant touch with Pakistan.' He said, 'Yes, that is the only possibility.' Then I asked him, 'Do you know that the reports of even the in-camera conferences that go on in the Prime Minister's house which are supposed to be very confidential often go to Peking and Rawalpindi the very same night?' He said, 'Yes, I am aware of it.'

The conclusion is that, in practically every place, there are Muslims who are in constant touch with Pakistan over the transmitter enjoying not only the rights of an average citizen but also some extra privileges and extra favour because they are 'minorities'! Our C.I.D. department seems to be more concerned about patriotic persons than about such elements as are trying to undermine our very national existence!

Some time back an M.L.A. threw a challenge in the U.P. Assembly that several transmitters were active in Lucknow City alone and that he would guide the police—if they dared—to trace them. So far the Government does not seem to have heard him at all! No wonder the enemy agents carry on their nefarious schemes merrily as if the Government itself is on their side! Such elements may be there even in positions of high responsibility and strategic importance. We are sitting as if on a volcano, feeling that all is well with our 'secular world'.

The Great 'Nationalist Muslims': Let us now at least wake up, look around and understand the true significance of the words and actions of even the very eminent Muslims. Their own statements have exposed the greatest of the so-called 'nationalist Muslims' in their true colours today.

Maulana Mohammad Ali, the right hand man of Mahatma Gandhi in the early days of the freedom struggle, had announced in public, not once but repeatedly, that the worst sinner and debauchee among the Muslims was, in his eyes, far superior to even Mahatma Gandhi!

I had once an opportunity to talk to a great scholar of the Sufi sect in our country. He said that the only way to meet the challenge of the godless philosophy of Communism was to mobilise and bring together all men having faith in God to whatever sect or religion they might belong. I asked him, 'What is that common plank on which all can come together?' Without a moment's hesitation he replied, 'Islam'! That is how the minds of even their so-called scholars and philosophers work!

The greatest 'nationalist Muslim' of our times, Maulana Azad too in his last days gave out his mind in the book *India Wins Freedom* in unmistakable terms. Firstly the whole of the book, from start to finish, is an unabashed egocentric narration which depicts all other leaders including Gandhiji, Nehru etc., as simpletons and Patel as a communalist. Secondly, he has not a single word of censure for the heinous massacres and atrocities committed by Muslims on Hindus in various places like Calcutta, Noakhali, etc. More than all, the entire burden of his opposition to the creation of Pakistan was that it would be against the interests of Muslims! In effect, Azad says, the Muslims were fools in following Jinnah, as thereby they got only a fraction of the land, whereas if they had followed his advice they would have had a decisive voice in the affairs of the entire country in addition to all the benefits of Pakistan! Sri Mehrchand Mahajan, Ex-Chief Justice of the Supreme Court, has come out with the same comments about that book. For instance, he says, 'The Maulana was more shrewd than Mr Jinnah. Left to him, India would become virtually a Muslim-dominated country.'

Face Reality: Even today, Muslims, whether in high positions of the Government or outside, participate openly in rabidly anti-national conferences. Their speeches carry the ring of open defiance and rebellion. A Muslim Minister at the Centre, speaking from the platform of one such conference, warned that unless the Muslim interest was well protected the story of Spain would be repeated here also, meaning thereby that they would rise in armed revolt.

They have now been emboldened to such an extent that they are not only contesting elections in the name of the Muslim League in several provinces but are invariably raising the slogan 'Pakistan Zindabad' in their public meetings and processions. For them, only those areas in which their unbridled sway is established are '*Pak*', i.e., holy, and the rest of Bharat where they are living and flourishing is '*na-Pak*', i.e., unholy. Can any son, however debased and depraved he may be, ever call his mother unholy and sinful? And still, we are asked to believe that such elements are the sons of this soil!

It is strange that the creators of Pakistan should have chosen to name that state in that fashion. Calling that territory alone as *pak*, i.e. holy, amounts to lessening the holiness of even Mecca and Madina. Because even they would be *na-pak* when compared to Pakistan!

Let us cry a halt, before it is too late, to this long and suicidal spell of wishful thinking and come to grips with the cruel realities of the situation keeping the interests of national security and integrity as the one supreme consideration.

The Christians

So far as the Christians are concerned, to a superficial observer they appear not only quite harmless but as the very embodiment of compassion and love for humanity! Their speeches abound in words like 'service' and 'human salvation' as though they are specially deputed by the Almighty to uplift humanity! They run schools and colleges, hospitals and orphanages. The people of our country, simple and innocent as they are, are taken in by all these things. But what is the real and ulterior motive of Christians in pouring crores of rupees in all these activities?

The Claw Bared: Our late President, Dr Rajendra Prasad, had once gone to Assam. He visited the schools and hospitals established by the Christian missionaries in those hilly regions and expressed his appreciation. But he also advised them at the end, 'You have no doubt done very good work. But do not exploit all these things for the purpose of proselytisation.' But the missionary who spoke next bluntly said, 'If we had been prompted to do all this by mere humanitarian considerations, why should we have come all the way here? Why should we have spent so much money? We are here for only one reason and that is to increase the number of followers of our Lord Jesus Christ.' They are very clear about it.

Towards that end they feel that any tactic, however foul, is fair. The various surreptitious and mean tactics they employ for conversion are all too well known. There is the case of a village where, in the last census, the Christian missionaries got the whole population entered as Christians. When the mischief was known and the people there protested, the Christian missionaries told them, 'Nothing can be done now. You have been registered as Christians in Government records. So you have to behave hereafter only as Christians.' The poor Hindu villagers, cut off from the support and succour of the indifferent Hindu Society, believed in their words and embraced Christianity. It is through such tactics that they are swelling their numbers day in and day out.

Many leading Christian missionaries have often declared unequivocally that their one single aim is to make this country 'a province of the Kingdom of Christ'. The Archbishop of Madurai has said, as reported in *Vedanta Kesari* of Madras, that their sole aim is to fly the flag of Christ over the whole of Bharat. Even during the recent 'Eucharistic Congress' at Bombay, Cardinal Gracias bewailed that after centuries of proselytising in Bharat the Catholics were only six million and the overwhelming majority remained Hindus. He exhorted his followers that every one of them should hereafter feel himself a missionary in the cause of proselytisation. What does all this mean? It means that all the people in this country should be converted to Christianity. That is, there hereditary religion, philosophy, culture and way of life should be demolished and they should become absorbed in a world federation of Christianity.

Religion or Politics? The way they are behaving towards other people forces us to conclude that the modern proselytising religions have very little of true religion in them. In the name of God, Prophet and religion, they are only trying to further their political ambitions. In true religion there need be no proselytisation, no change in the way of worship. Our religious missionaries who reached distant lands in ancient times did not force their religion on other people. On the contrary, without negating their mode of worship, our great teachers tried to make it more sublime by fortifying it with an all-comprehensive philosophy, to inculcate in them noble and chaste qualities of head and heart and make them better devotees in their own form of worship. That was real *dharma*.

The concept of religion as propagated by the Christian missionaries is really amazing. Once I met a missionary. He gave me a book written by an Archbishop in England and told me that the book would make the nature of their work clear to me. I read it. When I returned it to him, he asked me with quite an interest, 'How is the book?' I replied,

'If such is your Archbishop, what about you?' That startled him. I pointed out to him some passages in that book which said that to attain God it is enough if one prays twice a day and attends the church on Sundays and that during the rest of the time there is no harm in indulging in any kind of physical pleasures and enjoyments. These words are, in fact, totally opposed to the sublime teachings of that great seer, Jesus Christ.

Even St Paul, the great disciple of Christ, has said, as quoted by Lokmanya Tilak in his *Gita Rahasya*, 'How can it be a sin if by uttering falsehood I add to Your (God's) Glory?' No wonder, the present Christian missionaries have made full use of that statement to further their nefarious designs. Truly has it been said, 'There was but one true Christian, and he died on the Cross!'

The Impartial Verdict: Their activities are not merely irreligious, they are also anti-national. Once I asked a Christian missionary why they abused our sacred scriptures, gods and goddesses. He said frankly, 'Our aim is to knock out the faith from the heart of the Hindu. When his faith is shattered, his nationalism is also destroyed. A void will be created in his mind. Then it becomes easy for us to fill that void with Christianity.'

Some years ago, the Madhya Pradesh Government appointed a committee to report on the activities of these Christian missionaries. The Chairman of the committee, Sri Niyogi, was a highly respectable retired High Court Judge, not belonging to any group or party. The Committee members toured the whole of Madhya Pradesh and met the converted Christians, missionaries and other people. They also visited many churches. On the basis of all these personal investigations, the Committee prepared a lengthy report. The substance of that report is: 'All the philanthropic acts of the missionaries are simply a mask for carrying on proselytising activities, sometimes by intimidating and sometimes by tempting the simple folk. At the root of the activities is their ambition to carve out a separate Christian State for themselves on the strength of their numbers. They are spending crores of rupees for that single purpose.'

For a 'Padrestan': The creation in Assam of 'Nagaland' is a glaring example in point. That the open rebellion going on in the Naga Hills

is all engineered by the Christian missionaries was accepted even by
Pandit Nehru. But our Government is never tired of telling the country
time and again that 'peace' has been established there, only to be followed on the next day by the news that some train was looted, some
bridge was blown up or some of our army men were ambushed and
killed! When it was asked in Parliament how the rebels had come in
possession of such large quantities of arms and ammunition, the reply
given was that, during the last war, when the Japanese were fleeing,
being unable to carry the load of arms, they threw them away in the
jungles and the Nagas took possession of them. But a report had appeared in the press that during one of the clashes with our military
some rebels were killed and their arms captured. The arms were of the
latest American make with an imprint of the year of manufacture. It
was 1955 and 1956! And we are asked by our leaders to believe that the
Nagas had secured those American arms made in 1955 and 1956, as
far back as 1944! It is reported that the Nagas are in possession of even
anti-aircraft guns of the latest model. It is also evident how these arms
must have come into their possession. The American arms which
come to Pakistan are handed over to the Christian missionaries in
Assam.

Thus the revolt has continued and for the time being our leaders
have partly accepted their demand and set up Nagaland. The ominous
feature about it is that it is under the direct charge of the Foreign
Ministry and not of the Home Ministry which governs all other States
in our country today. The pressure under which this concession was
made is still continuing. This pressure is of two types. One is the internal rebellion which is still continuing and gaining momentum in view
of the partial success they have achieved. Even after the decision to
form Nagaland, one of our planes was shot down. The second type of
pressure is international. We know that Phizo, the rebel Naga leader,
disappeared from our country with the help of Pakistan and some
other countries and went to England. He was given asylum by a noted
Christian missionary, Michael Scott, who abetted him in making various statements damaging our reputation. Our leaders, who are over-
sensitive with regard to their international reputation—whatever it
may be!—thought it better to give a Nagaland than stake their reputation as peacemakers in the world. And now they have started 'peace

talks' with the Naga rebels with a view to giving them greater autonomy, and included that gentleman Michael Scott in the 'peace mission'. To show themselves off as peacemakers, partition of the country seems to be a very cheap price for our leaders. Since that international pressure is also mounting, it will be little wonder if at no distant date Nagaland is separated and formed into an independent State ridden and dominated by the Christian fanatics.

Agents of World Strategy: There is already the demand for another separate Hill State round about Shillong in Assam inspired by the Christian missionaries. They are also carrying on agitation for a separate 'Jharkhand' in Bihar. Of course, our leaders have categorically stated that their demands are fantastic and cannot be met. But we cannot be sure of what will happen in future. Because our experience tells us that whenever our leaders vehemently denounce a particular demand as fantastic, anti-national and so on, then it is a sure indication that they have already made up their mind to accede to it! That has been our uniform experience right from Partition down to the formation of Nagaland.

Then in Kerala, during the people's agitation against the Communist Ministry, the Christian leaders used to say that it was a life and death struggle for the Christian Missions in Kerala. They also went to the extent of saying, 'Kerala shall be ruled either by the Catholics or by the Communists. And WE want to rule.'

In a pamphlet circulated at an international gathering of Christian Fathers in Europe some years ago, a detailed plan was put forth to start centres of Christian influence all along our coast and right across the country through the Vindhyas and the Satpuras. That was the first stage of the plan—to surround the Southern peninsula and make it Christian-dominated. Then the whole of the Himalayan belt was to be captured in the second sweep.

Some time back, news had leaked out in papers that an agreement had been reached between the Christian missions in our country and the Muslim League that the two should join together and between themselves partition the country, the whole of the Gangetic plain between Punjab and Manipur going to the Muslims and the Peninsula and the Himalayas to the Christians.

A few years ago, there was an All-India Conference of Christians wherein they were called upon to pledge themselves to establish Christian Empire in Bharat. And one of our Central Ministers was present there to bless the proceedings.

Such is the role of Christian gentlemen residing in our land today, out to demolish not only the religious and social fabric of our life but also to establish political domination in various pockets and if possible all over the land. Such has been, in fact, their role wherever they have stepped—all under the alluring garb of bringing peace and brotherhood to mankind under the angelic wings of Jesus Christ. Jesus had called upon his followers to give their all to the poor, the ignorant and the downtrodden. But what have his followers done in practice? Wherever they have gone, they have proved to be not 'blood-givers' but 'blood-suckers'! What is the fate of all those lands colonised by these so-called disciples of Christ? Wherever they have stepped, they have drenched those lands with the blood and tears of the natives and liquidated whole races. Do we not know the heart-rending stories of how they annihilated the natives in America, Australia and Africa? Why go so far? Are we not aware of the atrocious history of Christian missionaries in our own country, of how they carried sword and fire in Goa and elsewhere?

There is the story of 'Saint' Xavier, who used to experience the highest joy of his life when he used to see the new converts trampling upon their former gods and goddesses, razing their temples to the ground and insulting their own parents and elders who remained Hindus. And even as recently as during the Congress rule (a *de facto* Christian rule!) in Kerala after the quitting of the British, hundreds of ancient and sacred Hindu temples, including the famous one at Shabarimalai, were desecrated and their idols broken by the Christian vandals. It is the same Christian fanatics who smashed the Vivekananda Memorial Tablet on the Vivekananda Rock at Kanyakumari. Such are the men who come to us to preach that Christianity would shower bliss of peace and milk of human kindness on humanity!

So long as the Christian here indulge in such activities and consider themselves as agents of the international movement for the spread of Christianity, and refuse to offer their first loyalty to the land of their birth and behave as true children of the heritage and culture of their ancestors, they will remain here as hostiles and will have to be treated as such.

The Communists

After the British quit this land and we became free to shape our future national set-up, the discussion of various theories and 'isms' has become a live issue for us. No doubt we have opted for the Western type of democratic set-up. But have we been able to reap its beneficial fruits after all these years of experimentation? Instead of symbolising the collective will of the people, it has given rise to all sorts of unhealthy rivalries and forces of selfishness and fission.

Preparing Ground for Communism: A serious failure of democracy in our country is the growing menace of Communism which is a sworn enemy of democratic procedure. In a bid not to be left behind the Communists in their economic appeal to the masses, our leaders are only making Communism more respectable by themselves taking up the Communist jargon and the Communist programmes. If the leaders imagine that they will be able to take away the wind out of the Communist sail by such tactics, they are sadly mistaken.

They also feel that economic development is the only defence against Communism. It is the constant dinning into the ears of the masses of the promise of 'higher standards of life', thus raising their expectations at a time when they cannot possibly be satisfied, that is aggravating the sense of frustration and paving the way for popular discontent and chaos. Nowhere do we find the appeal to higher sentiments like patriotism, character and knowledge; nor is there any stress on cultural, intellectual and moral development. It is only in such imbecile and despairing minds that the seeds of Communism strike root.

Adding Fuel to the Fire: The approach of the Western countries to the menace of Communism is contributing its own share in giving a fillip to the spread of Communism here. America believes that dollar aid will solve the problem of Communism. As experience has shown in the case of China and now Viet Nam, such aid will be of little avail without a corresponding building up of national character and morale.

The countrywide propaganda that accompanies each one of their economic aids is only aggravating the 'economic consciousness' of the masses to the exclusion of those aspects which form the real backbone of a free and democratic life.

The Westerners also suffer from a strange hallucination that the 'old Hinduism' must go if our country is to be saved from Communism. They feel that Christianity alone can stem the tide of Communism. Once, Arnold Toynbee had truly described Communism as a 'Christian heresy' and strangely enough it is he who has now come forward to say that Christianity is the one answer to Communism. How can Christianity solve a problem which came up as a reaction due to its own deficiencies? Those who think Christianity alone can save this 'heathen country' should pause and ponder why Russia, the most orthodox country of Christendom, disowned Christ. In our own country, is it not significant that the province where the Christian population and influence is the greatest, Kerala, is also the biggest Communist pocket? If the Westerners believe that by pouring men and money to convert Hindus to Christianity they will save this country from Communism, they are only labouring under a suicidal self-deception. Because, the spread of Christianity shatters the ancient faith and nationalism of the people, and Communism takes root only where faith is shattered. That has been the major psychological factor in the growth of Communism.

When Faith goes Communism Comes: Man does not live by bread alone. He must have a faith to live by and die for. Without such a faith life loses its direction and meaning, and man begins to drift. He feels lost. It is an impossible state of being. Till the rise of science, Christianity provided the necessary faith for European life. But science made mincemeat of Christianity. It blasted the Christian concept of time, space, life and the world. However, Europe lost one sheet-anchor but gained another. It lost its faith in religion but gained a new faith in science. Indeed, science became its new religion. Then people believed science to be omniscient and omnipotent as any God thought of in any religion.

However, within a course of some centuries, science began disproving itself. The scientists began to confess their ignorance of the Universe. Einstein, than whom there has been no greater scientist in recent times, admitted the existence of a Reality beyond the reach of physical sciences. Thus, from the omniscient mood of the Victorian Era, the scientists felt themselves no more than picking pebbles on the shore with a whole ocean of knowledge lying unexplored before them. This collapse of faith in science left the Western man rudderless on an unexplored sea. The old faiths were dead and no new faiths were in sight. It was in this situation of vacuity of faith that some specious faiths came to fill the gap. One such faith was Communism.

So any attempt, from whatever quarter, to uproot our ancient and life-giving faith, a faith which has sustained us and produced the finest flowers of human culture, is bound to bring about sure national disaster.

Danger of Reactionary Approach: Various are the attempts going on to neutralise the appeal of Communism in our country. Some people feel that the Bhoodan movement launched by Vinobaji will take away the appeal of Communism. On the contrary, with its Communistic slogan of 'land to the tiller' and with threats by some of his shortsighted followers like, 'If you do not give of your own accord, Communists are bound to come up and take away your all by force' it will only give rise to an impression in the mass mind that after all Communism is correct and is inevitable. It will be an indirect sanction for Communism. Further, the masses will have a suspicious feeling that all such movements which come up in the name of their uplift are only half-hearted and deceptive. They may very well say, 'Now that the Communists are making headway, you want to come forward with all these reforms and promises! We would rather prefer the blunt Communists. They are at least honest and bold. They mean what they say and we can believe them.' Thus, contrary to expectations, this movement may pave the way for Communists. In fact, to work merely with a view to counteracting Communism is always dangerous. It is only the inculcation of a right and positive faith that can make the masses rise above the base appeal of Communism.

There are some who feel that the growth of Communism is inevitable so long as economic disparity persists. But the fact is, economic disparity is not the real cause for mutual hatred on which the Communists thrive. The idea of dignity of labour is not properly imbibed by our people. For example, a rikshawala who makes a daily earning of 3 to

4 rupees is addressed as 'a fellow' and a clerk getting but Rs 60 a month is addressed as 'Babuji'. It is this disparity in outlook in all walks of our life which creates hatred. This is a recent perversion that has entered our life. In our philosophy, there is no distinction of high or low in one's *karma*, i.e., duty. Every work is the worship of the same Almighty in the form of society. This spirit has to be revived once again.

'Socialism by Ballot': The threat of Communism has become real from another quarter in our country. And that is by the present policy of our Government who have declared 'Socialism' (same in content as Communism and differing only in the method of achievement) as their goal. In the first place, our leaders say that they will achieve Socialism by the ballot-box, and not by the bullet as was done in Russia and China. That only means that there is a difference between the people in Russia and China, and the people in our country. In Russia and China, probably the people were alive and kicking and therefore they had to be cowed down by the bullet. Here our people are docile hero-worshippers. If the hero comes and says, 'My dear friend, come on, bend forward, I want to behead you,' our people will certainly bend forward and offer to be beheaded! With such docile people, why is the bullet required? A ballot-box is sufficient. If the leader says, 'Vote for Socialism,' the people will vote for it. If tomorrow they find that having voted for Socialism their independence is gone, and as individuals they have become only dead parts of a machine, they will take it as an ordinance of fate and submit to it.

Our people submitted to the Muslim rule for more than a thousand years, to the extent that even today we find people saying that Muslims were great and godly persons! Some have even gone to the extent of saying that we must erect statues of Hyder who jailed his Hindu king and usurped his throne, and of his son Tippu who forcibly converted countless people to Islam, demolished many temples and molested a number of women! To this extent the infatuation still remains. When the British came, some persons said, 'They have been sent from heaven.' Some even said, 'In the *Bhavishya Purana*, it has already been prophesied that our country would be ruled by a queen named Vikateshwari and she is none other than Queen Victoria herself.' With such a docile people a little propaganda is enough.

In John Bunyan's *The Pilgrim's Progress*, the Pilgrim is caught by the Giant. The Giant wants to murder him straightaway but on advice from his wife tries to persuade him to commit suicide. The Giant says, 'Why are you undergoing all the troubles of life? Nothing is sweeter than suicide. Choose whatever you like, knife, halter or poison, make an end of your miserable life and be relieved forever.' He so convinces the Pilgrim that the latter gets ready to commit suicide. Just then a friend counsels the Pilgrim and prevents him from falling into that trap. The moral is, for innocent docile people, a little persuasion does the work of a bullet.

The Writing on the Wall: Under the garb of Socialism, what is it that is actually taking place? We find that all the measures being undertaken here are only an improved carbon copy of what has happened in China. The only difference is that these developments were brought about by brutal violence in China whereas here the same things are being done through polished propaganda. This will be quite clear to us if we compare the governmental measures of both countries. When the present Communist Government in China first came to power, they did not want any challenge to their absolute power. So they liquidated the old nobles, chiefs and industrialists and nationalised all industries. They liquidated the landholders and ultimately the smaller zamindars and farmers.

Here also, landlords were liquidated. Now the 17th Amendment has come by which even the smaller farmer, having even half an acre of land, is considered an estate-holder, and the Government is empowered to take away his property practically without any compensation. Co-operative farming, collective farming, nationalisation of banks and industries and such socialistic doctrines are in the air. All this is, in a way, following the Chinese line step by step. Let us try to see the close parallel and read the writing on the wall. And before we are reduced to mere slaves and tools, beware!

Further, Socialism is not a product of this soil. It is not in our blood and tradition. It has absolutely nothing to do with the traditions and ideals of thousands of years of our national life. It is a thought alien to crores of our people here. As such it does not have the power to thrill our hearts, and inspire us to a life of dedication and character. Thus we see that it does not possess even the primary qualification to serve as an ideal for our national life.

Unfit on All Counts

And finally, as we have already seen, Socialism (the same as Communism in its original form, as even Russia calls itself a Socialist State) was born as a reaction steeped in the theory of class conflict and has failed to deliver the goods in Russia itself. As a theory it was exploded long back and now it has been exploded in practice also.

Nowadays our leaders are trying to cover up the fatal defect of Socialism, i.e., the wiping out of the individual as a living entity, by coining new slogans like 'Democratic Socialism', 'Socialistic Democracy' and so on. As a matter of fact, the two concepts of Democracy and Socialism are mutually contradictory. Socialism cannot be democratic and Democracy cannot be socialistic. For, individual freedom, as we have seen, is the first faith with Democracy, whereas it is the first victim of Socialism. In Democracy, the majesty of the individual is held high, whereas, in Socialism, he is only a cog in the wheel, just a lifeless screw in the colossal machine called State.

Revive National Genius: Thus, after the quitting of the British, we find ourselves in a confused state of affairs trying to catch at something of each of the foreign theories and 'isms'. This is highly humiliating to a country which has given rise to an all-comprehensive philosophy, capable of furnishing the true and abiding basis for reconstruction of national life on political, economic, social and all other planes. It would be sheer bankruptcy of our intellect and originality if we believe that human intelligence has reached its zenith with the present theories and 'isms' of the West. Let us therefore evolve our own way of life based on the eternal truths discovered by our ancient seers and tested on the touchstone of reason, experience and history.

8

Deendayal Upadhyaya

The RSS never considered the state as a major institution in relation to society. Golwalkar's view was: 'The ultimate vision of our work . . . is a perfectly organised state of society wherein each individual has been moulded into a model of ideal Hindu manhood and made into the living limb of the corporate personality of society.'[1]

This long-term agenda took little account of the state because it was deemed an artificial agency that did little to help in the making of 'the new man', an undertaking which included the reshaping of individual psyches through man-to-man contact. Only a long-term—even millenarial—work could produce a new, organic society whose members would be aware that they together form a harmonious nation. This Hindu Rashtra was to be different from the Hindu Raj promoted by politicians of the Hindu Mahasabha. It had little to do with the state, at least with a form of the state based on the notion of social contract: Hindu Rashtra was not an artefact but a natural, latent reality; its members had simply to awake and become aware of it. Deendayal Upadhyaya (1916–68) was one of the most articulate spokespersons of this vision.

Born into a Brahmin family of the village Nagla Chandrabhan (Mathura district), Upadhyaya had abandoned his studies—after completing the first year of an MA in English Literature—in order to dedicate himself entirely to the RSS, which he first joined while in college at Kanpur, in 1937.[2] He worked for the organization first as

---

[1] M.S. Golwalkar, *Bunch of Thoughts*, p. 88.
[2] S. Raje, ed., *Pt Deendayal Upadhyaya—A Profile* (New Delhi: Deendayal Research Institute, 1972).

pracharak in Lakhimpur district in the United Provinces, and then, between 1947 and 1951, as joint pracharak for the whole region (*prant*). He was the first non-Maharashtrian prant pracharak of the RSS.

In the eyes of his peers and those in charge in Nagpur, Deendayal Upadhyaya represented the 'ideal *swayamsevak*'.[3] This was because he had devoted his whole life to the RSS, to the extent of refusing marriage, and also because, in the opinion of RSS veterans, 'his discourse reflected the pure thought-current of the Sangh'.[4] As a result, in the early 1950s he was endowed with the task of launching a weekly publication, *Panchjanya*, which was to become the most important 'India-wise' mouthpiece of the RSS in Hindi.

When the Jana Sangh took over from the RSS, Golwalkar seconded Upadhyaya to the party and asked him to transform it into a genuine component of the nascent Sangh Parivar. He was asked to give the Jana Sangh a doctrine of its own. This doctrine found its main expression in *Integral Humanism* (1965), a text which provided the bases of the Jana Sangh's 'Principles and Policies' in 1965. As in Upadhyaya's first text, *Two Plans*, which targeted Nehru's economic policy, the salient point of *Integral Humanism* lies in its promotion of society *vis-à-vis* the state which, by comparison, is shown to be a secondary institution. This approach was in conformity with RSS ideology, which focused on groundwork at the local level, but paradoxical in the case of a political party whose vocation was, in theory at least, the conquest of power. Upadhyaya advocated decentralization of power to the village level and the rehabilitation of the old varna system in an organic vein, so much so that his thought had some affinities with Gandhian notions.

Though he ran for office only once during a by-election, Deendayal Upadhyaya remained the Jana Sangh's general secretary from 1953 to 1967. He then became party president but was mysteriously assassinated in 1968. In the 1970s the RSS named its think tank, the Deendayal Research Institute, after Upadhyaya and he has remained a reference point for the official programme of the Jana Sangh, and later the BJP—as is evident from the frequent deployment of *Integral Humanism* in the election manifestos of these parties.

[3] He was described thus on his death by Bhaurao Deoras, *Organiser*, 25 February 1968, p. 3.

[4] Babasaheb Apte, 'Panditji had a Cool Head and a Warm Heart', *Organiser*, 10 March 1968, p. 5.

Two Extracts from *Integral Humanism*[5]

Bharatiya Culture is Integrated

The first characteristic of Bharatiya culture is that it looks upon life as an integrated whole. It has an integrated view point. To think of parts may be proper for a specialist but it is not useful from the practical standpoint. The confusion in the West arises primarily from its tendency to think of life in sections and then to attempt to put them together by patch work. We do admit that there is diversity and plurality in life but we have always attempted to discover the unity behind them. This attempt is thoroughly scientific. The scientists always attempt to discover order in the apparent disorder in the universe, to find out the principles governing the universe and frame practical rules on the basis of these principles. Chemists discovered that a few elements comprise the entire physical world. Physicists went one step further and showed that even these elements consist only of energy. Today we know that the entire universe is only a form of energy.

Philosophers are also basically scientists. The Western philosophers reached up to the principle of duality; Hegel put forward the principle of thesis, anti-thesis and synthesis; Karl Marx used this principle as a basis and presented his analysis of history and economics. Darwin considered the principle of survival of the fittest as the sole basis of life. But we in this country saw the basic unity of all life. Even the dualists have believed the nature and the spirit to be complementary to each other than conflicting. The diversity in life is merely an expression of the internal unity. There is complementarity underlying the diversity. The unit of seed finds expression in various forms—the roots, the trunk, the branches, the leaves, the flowers and the fruits of the tree. All these have different forms and colours and even to some extent different properties. Still we recognise their relation of unity with each other through the seed . . . It is a simple truth that society is a group of men. But how did society come into being? Many views have been put forward by philosophers. Those propounded in the West and on which the western socio-political structure is based can be broadly summarised as 'society is a group of individuals brought into being by

[5] Deendayal Upadhyaya, *Integral Humanism* (New Delhi: Bharatiya Jana Sangh, 1965), pp. 18–30, 31–9.

the individuals by an agreement among themselves.' This view is known as 'Social Contract Theory'. Individual is given greater importance in this view. If there are differences in different western views, these pertain only to the questions, namely, 'If the individual produced a society, then in whom the residual power remains vested, in the society or in the individual? Does the individual have the right to change the society? Can the society impose a variety of regulations on the individual and claim a right to the allegiance of the individual to itself? Or the individual is free as regards these questions?'

Individual versus Society

There is a controversy in the West on this question. Some have opted for the society as supreme and from this a conflict has arisen. The truth is that the view that individuals have brought society into being, is fundamentally incorrect. It is true that the society is composed of a number of individuals. Yet it is not made by people, nor does it come into being by mere coming together of a number of individuals.

In our view society is self-born. Like an individual, society comes into existence in an organic way. People do not produce society. It is not a sort of club, or some joint stock company, or a registered co-operative society. In reality, society is an entity with its own 'SELF', its own life; it is a sovereign being like an individual; it is an organic entity. We have not accepted the view that society is some arbitrary association. It has its own life. Society too has its body, mind, intellect and soul. Some western psychologists are beginning to accept this truth. McDougal has produced a new branch of psychology called group mind. He has accepted that the group has its own mind, its own psychology, its own methods of thinking and action.

Group has its feelings too. These are not exactly similar to the individual's feelings. Group feelings cannot be considered a mere arithmetic addition of individual feelings. Group strength too is not a mere sum of individuals' strength. The intellect, emotions and energies, strength of a group, are fundamentally different from those of an individual. Therefore, at times it is experienced that even a weakling, despite his individual weak physique, turns out to be a heroic member of the society. Sometimes an individual may be ready to put up with an affront to his person, but is unwilling to tolerate an insult to his society. A person may be ready to forgive and forget a personal abuse to him, but the same man loses his temper if you abuse his society. It is possible that a person who is of a high character in his personal life, is unscrupulous as a member of the society. Similarly an individual can be good in society but not so in his individual life. This is a very important point.

Let me give you an illustration. Once during a conversation between Shri Vinobaji and the Sar Sanghachalak of Rashtriya Swayamsevak Sangh, Shri Guruji, a question arose as to where the modes of thinking of Hindus and Muslims differ. Guruji said to Vinobaji that there are good and bad people in every society. There can be found honest and good people in Hindus as well as in Muslims. Similarly rascals can be seen in both the societies. No particular society has a monopoly of goodness. However, it is observed that Hindus even if they are rascals in individual life, when they come together in a group, they always think of good things. On the other hand when two Muslims come together, they propose and approve of things which they themselves in their individual capacity would not even think of. They start thinking in an altogether different way. This is an everyday experience. Vinobaji admitted that there was truth in this observation but had no reasons to explain it.

If we analyse this situation, we shall discover that the modes of thinking of an individual and of a society are always different. These two do not bear an arithmetic relation. If a thousand good men gather together, it cannot be said for certain that they will think similarly of good things.

An average Indian student at present, is a mild and meek young man. Compared to an average student of twenty years ago, he is weaker and milder in every way. But when a score of such students get together, the situation becomes difficult. Then they indulge in all sorts of irresponsible actions. Thus a single student appears disciplined but a group of students become indisciplined. We shall have to consider why this change comes about. This is known as mob-mentality as distinct from individual mentality. This mob-mentality is a small aspect of mind. When a group of persons collect for a short time, the collective mentality obtained in that group is known as mob-mentality. But society and social mentality evolves over a much longer period. There is a thesis that when a group of people live together for a long time, by historical tradition and association, by continued intercourse, they begin to think similarly and have similar customs. It is true that some uniformity is brought about by staying together. Friendship arises between two persons of similar inclination. However a nation or a society does not spring up from mere co-habitation.

Why Mighty Nations of Antiquity Perished

It is known that some ancient nations disappeared. The ancient Greek nation came to end. Egyptian civilization similarly disappeared. Babilonian [*sic*] and Syrian civilisations are a matter of history. Cynthians perished. Was there ever a time when the citizens of those nations stopped living together? It was only the fact that there were wide differences among people that led to the downfall of these nations.

The Greece in the past produced Alexander and Heredotes [*sic*], Ulysis [*sic*] and Aristotle, Socrates and Plato, and the present day Greece is inhabited by people of the same hereditary stock. There was no interruption in their heredity, because there never was a time when the whole of Greece was devoid of human population and when a new race inhabited that country. Such a thing never happened. Father and son tradition of old Greece was never interrupted. It is possible to trace the ancestry of present day Greeks to the old Greeks, some 250 to 500 generations back. Despite all this the old Greek Nation is nonexistent. So also the old Egyptian Nation is no longer there. New nations have arisen in those places. How did this happen? This simple fact is indisputable, that nations do not come into existence by a mere co-habitation. There was never a time in the lives of the citizens of these decadent nations, when they stopped living in a group. On the other hand Israeli Jews lived for centuries with other peoples scattered far and wide, yet they did not get annihilated in the societies in which they lived because of co-habitation. It is clear, therefore, that the source of national feeling is not in staying on a particular piece of land, but is in something else.

What is a Nation?

That source is in the goal which is put before the people. *When a group of persons lives with a goal, an ideal, a mission, and looks upon a particular piece of land as motherland, this group constitutes a nation.*[6] If either of the two—an ideal and a motherland—is not there, then there is no nation. There is a 'Self' in the body, the essence of the individual; upon the severance of its relation with the body, a person is said to die. Similarly there is this Idea, Ideal, or fundamental principle, of a nation, its soul. Although it is believed that man takes birth again and again, yet the reborn person is a different individual. They are treated as two separate beings. The same soul leaves one body and enters another, but the previous and the latter are two different individuals. The end of a person is nothing but the departure of his soul from his body. The other components of the body also undergo change. From childhood to old age, there is a drastic change! The biologists tell us that in the course of a few years, every cell of our body is replaced by a new one. A variety of changes takes place. Because the soul resides in the body without interruption, the body continues its existence. Such a relation is known as 'the law of identity' in logic. It is due to this identity that we admit the continued existence of any entity. In this connection a nice illustration of a barber's razor is sometimes advanced.

Once while shaving a customer, a barber prided in his razor being 60 years old. His father too had worked with the same razor. The customer was surprised especially because the handle was quite shiny and new in appearance. 'Why the handle is quite shiny? How have you preserved the brightness for sixty years?' he asked. Barber too was amused with this. 'Is it possible to preserve the handle in a brand new appearance for sixty years? It has been replaced only six months ago'. He replied naturally. The customer was curious, 'and how old is the steel?' 'Three years', was the reply. In brief, the handle was replaced, the steel was also replaced, but the razor remained old! Its identity was intact. Similarly a nation too has a soul. There is a technical name for it. In the 'Principles and Policies' adopted by the Jana Sangh, this name is mentioned. The word is Chiti. According to McDougal, it is the innate nature of a group. Every group of persons has an innate nature. Similarly every society has an innate nature, which is inborn, and is not the result of historical circumstances.

A human being is born with a soul. Human personality, soul, and character are all distinct from one another. Personality results from a

---

[6] Author's italics. Ed.

cumulative effect of all the actions, thoughts and impressions of an individual. But soul is unaffected by this history. Similarly national culture is continuously modified and enlarged by the historic reasons and circumstances. Culture does include all those things which, by the association, endeavours, and the history of the society, have come to be held up as good and commendable, but these are not added on to Chiti. Chiti is fundamental and is central to the nation from its very beginning. Chiti determines the direction in which the nation is to advance culturally. Whatever is in accordance with Chiti, is included in culture.

Chiti,—Culture,—Dharma

By way of an illustration consider the story of Mahabharat. Kauravas were defeated, and Pandavas won. Why did we hold up the conduct of Pandavas as Dharma? Or why this battle was not considered just a battle for a kingdom? The praise for Yudhisthir and the dishonour heaped on Duryodhana are not a result of political causes. Krishna killed his uncle Kansa, the established king of the times. Instead of branding this as a revolt, we consider Krishna as an Avatar of God, and Kansa as an Asura.

Rama was assisted in his invasion of Lanka by Vibhishana, brother of Ravana. Such conduct of Vibhishana, instead of being branded as treason, is considered good and exemplary. He betrayed his brother and his king, even as Jaichand had done later on. He might be branded as a 'quisling'. But Vibhishana is not called 'quisling' by anyone. On the contrary he is highly praised for his conduct, and Ravana's actions are disapproved. Why so? The reason behind this is not political.

If there is any standard for determining the merits and demerits of a particular action, it is this Chiti; from nature whatever is in accordance with 'Chiti', is approved and added on to culture. These things are to be cultivated. Whatever is against 'Chiti' is discarded as perversion, undesirable, is to be avoided. 'Chiti' is the touch-stone, on which each action, each attitude is tested, and determined to be acceptable or otherwise. 'Chiti' is the soul of the nation. On the strength of this 'Chiti', a nation arises, strong and virile if it is this 'Chiti' that is demonstrated in the actions of every great man of a nation.

An individual is also an instrument in bringing forth the soul of the nation, 'Chiti'. Thus apart from his own self, an individual also represents his nation. Not only that, but he also mans the various institutions that are created for the fulfilment of the national goal. Therefore he represents these too. The groups larger than nation such as 'mankind' are also represented by him. In short, an individual has a multitude of aspects, but they are not conflicting; there is co-operation, unity and harmony in them. A system based on the recognition of this mutually complementary nature of the different ideals of mankind, their essential harmony, a system which devises laws, which removes the disharmony and enhances their mutual usefulness and co-operation, alone can bring peace and happiness to mankind; can ensure steady development.

'Institution'—A Means to Fulfill National Needs

According to Darwin's theory, living beings develop various organs as per the requirements dictated by the circumstances. In our shastras, it was stated slightly differently, that the soul constructs, using the strength of 'Prana', various organs as the need is felt, for the purpose of continuing life. Just as the soul produced these different organs in the body, so also in the nation many different organs are produced as instruments to achieve national goals. Like various departments in a factory, buildings, machinery, sales, production, maintenance etc. nations also produce different departments, which are called institutions. These institutions are created to fulfil the needs of a nation. Family, castes, guilds (which are now known as trade unions) etc., are such institutions. Property, marriage are also institutions. Formerly there were no marriages. Later on some Rishi established this practice of marriage. He produced the institution of marriage. Similarly Gurukul and Rishikul were institutions. In the same way, the state is also an institution. The Nation creates it. A lot of trouble in the West is due to the fact that they confused the state with the nation, they considered the state synonymous with the nation. Truly speaking, nation and state are not the same. In our country, the state was produced as per the social contract theory. Formerly there was no king. Mahabharat describes that in Krityuga, there was no state, or king. Society was sustained and protected mutually by practising Dharma.

Later on interruption and disorganisation came into existence. Greed and anger dominated. Dharma was on the decline and the rule 'might is right' prevailed. The Rishis were perturbed over the developments. They all went to Brahma to seek counsel. Brahma gave them a treatise on 'Law and the Functions of the State', which he had himself written. At the same time he asked Manu to become the first King. Manu declined saying that a king will have to punish other persons, put them in jail and so on; he was not prepared to commit all these sins. Thereupon Brahma said, 'Your actions in the capacity of a king will not constitute sin, as long as they are aimed at securing conditions under which the society can live peacefully and according to Dharma. This will be your duty, your Dharma. Not only that but you will also have a share of the Karma of your subjects, whereby you will gain Dharma considerably if your subjects maintain conduct according to Dharma.' Although it is not explicitly stated here, but I believe that if the society under any king committed sin, a part of that too must automatically go to the account of the king. It is not proper if only good things are shared by the king and not the bad ones; both must be shared in the same proportion. Thus state came into existence as a contract. *This contract theory can be applied to the state, but not to the nation.* In the West, it was exactly opposite. Society as a nation, according to them, was a contract, but the king claimed a divine right and proclaimed himself the sole representative of God. This is wrong. In our country, the king may have been first recognised in antiquity but the society as a nation is considered self-born. State is only an institution.

Similarly other institutions, like the state, are created from time to time as the need is felt. Every individual is a limb of one or more of these institutions. A person is a member of his family, as well as his community; he may also be a member of some association of his fellow professionals, if he pursues a profession. Above all he is a member of the nation and society. If we consider even larger spheres he is a member of the whole of mankind, and then the entire universe. Truly speaking an individual is not merely a single entity, but a plural entity. He is a part of not just one, but a member of many institutions. He lives a variety of lives. The most important aspect is that despite this multiple-personality, he can and should behave in a way which does not bring different aspects of his life into mutual conflict but which is mutually sustaining, complementary and unifying. This quality is inherent in man.

A person who uses this quality properly, becomes happy, and on the other hand one who does not do so reaps unhappiness. Such a person will not have balanced development in life. As an illustration, a man is son of his mother, husband of his wife, brother of his sister, and father of his son. A single individual is a father and is also a son, he is brother and also husband, he has to maintain all these relations with intelligence, understanding and tact. Where a person fails to do so, there is conflict. If he sides with one party the other feels wronged. The conflicts between his wife and his sisters, his wife and mother, result from his inability to behave properly. Thereupon some of his relations are strained. He is pained because his duties towards his mother and towards his wife clash. When he can resolve this conflict, and fulfill all his obligations properly, it can be said that his development will be integrated.

Society and Individual not Conflicting

We do not accept the view that there is any permanent inevitable conflict among the multifarious personality of an individual, and different institutions of the society. If a conflict does exist, it is a sign of decadence, perversion and not of nature or culture. The error in western thinking lies in that some people there believe that human progress is a result of this fundamental conflict. Therefore they consider the conflict between the individual and the state as a natural occurrence, on the same basis they also theorised on the class conflict.

Classes do exist in a society. Here too, there were castes, but we had never accepted conflict between one caste and another as a fundamental concept behind it. In our concept of four castes, they are thought of as analogous to the different limbs of Virat-Purusha. It was suggested that from the head of the Virat-Purusha Brahmins were created, Kshatriyas from hands, Vaishyas from his abdomen and Shudras from legs. If we analyse this concept we are faced with the question whether there can arise any conflict among the head, arms, stomach and legs of the same Virat Purusha. If conflict is fundamental, the body cannot be maintained. There cannot be any conflict in the different parts of the

same body. On the contrary 'one man' prevails. These limbs are not
only complementary to one another, but even further, there is individuality, unity. There is a complete identity of interest, identity of
belonging. The origin of the caste system was on the above basis. If
this idea is not kept alive, the castes, instead of being complementary,
can produce conflict. But then this is distortion. It is not a systematic
arrangement, rather it is absence of any plan, any arrangement. This
is indeed the present condition of our society.

This process of deterioration can set in within the various institutions
of a society, due to a variety of reasons. If the soul of the society weakens, then all the different limbs of the society will grow feeble and
ineffective. Any particular institution may be rendered useless or even
harmful. Besides the need and the usefulness of any particular
institution may change with time, place and circumstances. While
examining the present state of an institution, we ought, at the same
time, to think of what it should be like; mutual [sic] complementary
and a sense of unity, alone can be the standards of proper conduct.
Family, Community, Trade Union, Grampanchayat, Janapada, State
and such other institutions are various limbs of the nation and even of
mankind. They are interdependent, mutually complementary. There
should be a sense of unity through all of them. For this very reason,
there should be a tendency toward mutual accommodation in them,
instead of conflict or opposition.

State is one of the several institutions, an important one, but it is
not above all others (सर्वोपरि). One of the major reasons for the problems
of the present day world is that almost everyone thinks of the state to
be synonymous with the society. At least in practice, they consider the
state as the sole representative of the society. Other institutions have
declined in their effectiveness while the state has become dominant to
such an extent that all the powers are gradually being centralised in the
state.

We had not considered the state to be the sole representative of the
nation. Our national life continued uninterruptedly even after the
state went in the hands of foreigners. The Persian nation came to an
end with their loss of independence. In our country, there were foreign
rules now and then in various parts of the country. At sometime [sic]
the Pathans seized the throne of Delhi, and then the Turks, the Mughals,

and the British too established their rules. Despite all this, our national life went on, because the state was not its centre. If we had considered state as the centre, we would have been finished as a nation long time ago. In some tales for children, it is described that an evil spirit resided in some parrot and to kill the evil spirit one had to kill that parrot. Those nations whose life centred in the state, were finished with the end of the state. On the other hand, where state was not believed central to its life, the nation survived the transfer of political power.

This had its bad effects also. Late Dr Ambedkar had said that our Gram Panchayats were so strong that we neglected the throne of Delhi. We did not remain alert as regards the state, as much as we ought to have done, thinking that the nation's life did not depend on the state. We forget that, though it may not be central, the state is definitely an important institution serving some needs of the nation just as a limb of the body. It is possible to pluck a hair without much harm, but along with the hair, if some skin is also removed, and a little further, if the head too is cut off, then there will be great loss for the body. Therefore the body must be protected. Although the various limbs of the body are not absolutely indispensable, yet each of them serves an important purpose. From the same standpoint, state, too, should have been deemed important in the life of a nation. There were persons who attended to this aspect. It was for this reason that the great teacher of Shivaji, Samarth Ramdas Swami, directed him to establish his kingdom. Dharma wields its own power, Dharma is important in life. Shri Ramdas would as well have preached to Shivaji to become a mendicant and spread Dharma following his own example. But on the contrary, he inspired Shivaji to extend his rule, because state too, is an important institution of the society. However, to consider something important is different from saying that it is supreme (सर्वोपरि). The state is not supreme. The question arises, then, that if the state is not of fundamental importance, what is it that is absolutely important. Let us consider this question.

Dharma Sustains the Society

We shall have to examine the reasons why the state was established. No one will dispute that the state must have some specific aim, some

ideal. Then this aim, or ideal must be considered of highest importance
rather than the state which is created to fulfil this ideal. A watchman
is not deemed greater than the treasure he is supposed to protect, nor
is a treasurer. The state is brought into existence to protect the nation;
produce and maintain conditions in which the ideals of the nation can
be translated into reality. The ideals of the nation constitute 'Chiti',
which is analogous to the soul of an individual. It requires some effort
to comprehend Chiti. The laws that help manifest and maintain Chiti
of a nation are termed Dharma of that nation. Hence it is this 'Dharma'
that is supreme. Dharma is the repository of the nation's soul. If Dharma
is destroyed, the Nation perishes. Anyone who abandons Dharma,
betrays the nation.

Dharma is not confined to temples or mosques. Worship of God is
only a part of Dharma. Dharma is much wider. In the past, temples
have served as effective medium to educate people in their Dharma.
However, just as schools themselves do not constitute Dharma. A
child may attend school regularly and yet may remain uneducated.
So also, it is possible that a person may visit temple or mosque without break and yet he may not know his Dharma. To attend temple or
mosque constitutes a part of religion, sect, creed, but not necessarily
'Dharma'. Many misconceptions that originated from faulty English
translations, include this most harmful confusion of Dharma with
religion [. . .]

There are a number of norms of behaviour which are not found in
any statute book, yet they do exist. At times they are even stronger and
more binding than any statutory law. The precept that one should respect one's parents is not written in any law. The present day governments
which are turning out variety of laws, day in and day out, have not
passed a law to this effect. Still, people respect their parents. Those
who do not are criticized. If tomorrow there arises a discussion, even
in a court, it will be generally accepted that as long as a person does not
attain majority, he should accept his parents' decisions and should
respect them.

Thus the fundamental law of human nature is the standard for
deciding the propriety of behaviour in various situations. We have
termed this very law as 'Dharma'. The nearest equivalent English term
for Dharma can be 'Innate law', which, however, does not express the

full meaning of Dharma. Since 'Dharma' is supreme, our ideal of the state has been 'Dharma Rajya'. The king is supposed to protect Dharma. In olden times at the coronation ceremony the king used to recite three times: 'There is no authority which can punish me.' (Similar claim was made by kings in the western countries, i.e., it was said, 'King can do no wrong', and hence there too, nobody could punish the king.) Upon this, the Purohit used to strike the king on his back with a staff saying, 'No, you are subject to the rule of Dharma. You are not sovereign.' The king used to run around the sacred fire and the Purohit would follow him striking him with the staff. Thus after completing three rounds, the ceremony would come to an end. Thereby the king was unambiguously told that he was not an unpunishable sovereign. Dharma was above him, that even he was subject to Dharma. Can the people do whatever they please? It may be contended that democracy means just that. The people can do what they please. But in our country, even if people wish, they are not free to act contrary to Dharma. Once a priest was asked: 'If God is omnipotent, can he act contrary to Dharma?' 'If He can't, he is not omnipotent.' This was a dilemma. Can God practice Adharma or is he not omnipotent? Actually God cannot act contrary to Dharma. If he does, then he is not omnipotent. Adharma is a characteristic of weakness, not of strength. If fire instead of emitting heat, dies out, it is no longer strong. Strength lies not in unrestrained behaviour, but in well regulated action. Therefore God who is omnipotent is also self-regulated and consequently fully in tune with Dharma. God descends in human body to destroy Adharma and re-establish Dharma, not to act on passing whims and fancies. Hence even God can do everything but cannot act contrary to Dharma. But for the risk of being misunderstood, one can say that Dharma is even greater than God. The universe is sustained because He acts according to Dharma. The king was supposed to be a symbol of Vishnu, in as much as he was the chief protector of Dharma Rajya.

Dharma Rajya does not mean a theocratic state. Let us be very clear on this point. Where a particular sect and its prophet or Guru, rule supreme, that is a theocratic state. All the rights are enjoyed by the followers of this particular sect. Others either cannot live in that country or at best enjoy a slave-like, secondary citizen's status. Holy Roman empire had this basis. The same concept was existing behind 'Khilafat'.

The Muslim kings world over used to rule in the name of Khalifa. After the First World War, this came to an end. Now efforts are afoot to revive it. Pakistan is the most recent theocratic state. They call themselves an Islamic State. There, apart from Muslims, all the rest are second class citizens. Apart from this difference there is no other sign of Islam in Pakistan's administration. Quran, Masjid, Roja, Id, Namaz etc. are same both in Bharat as well as in Pakistan. There is no need to tie up state and religion. By such a tie-up, there is no increase in an individual's capacity to worship God. The only result is that the state slips in its duty. This does not happen in a Dharma Rajya. Rather there is freedom to worship according to one's religion. In a theocratic state one religion has all the rights and advantages, and there are direct or indirect restrictions on all other religions. Dharma Rajya accepts the importance of religion in the peace, happiness and progress of an individual. Therefore the state has the responsibility to maintain an atmosphere in which every individual can follow the religion of his choice and live in peace. The freedom to follow one's own religion necessarily requires tolerance for other religions. We know that every kind of freedom has its inherent limits. I have the freedom to swing my hand, but as soon as there is conflict between my hand and someone else's nose, my freedom has to be restricted. I have no freedom to swing my hand so as to hit another person's nose. Where other person's freedom is likely to be encroached upon, my freedom ends. The freedom of both parties has to be ensured. Similarly every religion has the freedom to exist. But this freedom extends only as far as it does not encroach upon the religion of others. If such encroachment is carried on, it will have to be condemned as misuse of freedom and will have to be ended. Such limitations will be required in all aspects of life. Dharma Rajya ensures religious freedom, and is not a theocratic state.

Nowadays the word 'secular state' is being used as opposed to a theocratic state. The adoption of this word is mere imitation of the western thought pattern. We had no need to import it. We called it a secular state to contrast it with Pakistan. There is some misunderstanding arising out of this. Religion was equated with Dharma, and then secular state was meant to be a state without Dharma. Some said ours is a निर्धर्मी state (without Dharma), whereas others trying to find a better sounding word, called it धर्मनिरपेक्ष (indifferent to Dharma) State.

But all these words are fundamentally erroneous. For a state can neither be without dharma nor can it be indifferent to Dharma just as fire cannot be without heat. If fire loses heat, it does not remain fire any longer. State which exists fundamentally to maintain Dharma, to maintain law and order can neither be निधर्मी nor धर्मनिरपेक्ष. If it is निधर्मी, it will be a lawless state, and where there is lawlessness, where is the question of the existence of any state. In other words the concepts of धर्मनिरपेक्षता (attitude of indifference towards Dharma) and state are self-contradictory. State can only be धर्मराज्य (rule of Dharma), nothing else. Any other definition will conflict with the reason of its very existence.

In a Dharma Rajya, the state is not absolutely powerful. It is subject to Dharma. We have always vested sovereignty in Dharma. Presently there has arisen a controversy. Parliament is sovereign or the Supreme Court? Legislature is higher or Judiciary? This quarrel is like a quarrel whether left hand is more important or right hand. Both are limbs of the state, the Legislature as well as Judiciary. Both have distinct functions to perform. In their individual sphere each is supreme. To consider either one above the other would be a mistake. Yet the Legislators say, 'we are higher'. On the other hand members of the Judiciary assert that they have a higher authority, since they interpret the laws which the Legislature makes. The Legislature claims to have given powers to the Judiciary. If necessary, Legislature can change the constitution. Hence it claims sovereignty. Now since powers are bestowed by constitution, they are talking of amendments to the constitution. But I believe that even if by a majority the constitution is amended, it will be against Dharma. In reality both the Legislature and the Judiciary are on an equal plane. Neither the Legislature is higher nor the Judiciary. Dharma is higher than both. The Legislature will have to act according to Dharma and the Judiciary too will have to act according to Dharma. Dharma will specify limits of both. The Legislature, the Judiciary or the people, none of these is supreme, Some will say, 'Why! People are sovereign. They elect.' But even the people are not sovereign because people too have no right to act against Dharma. If an elected government allows people to go against Dharma and does not punish, then that government is in reality a government of thieves. Even the general will cannot go against Dharma. Imagine the situation, if by some manoeuvring, thieves gain a majority in the government and send one of their ranks as an executive! What will be the duty of the minority if the majority is of thieves and elects a thief to rule? The duty clearly will be to remove the representative elected by the majority.

During the Second World War when Hitler attacked France, the French army could not stall the onward march of Nazi troops. The then Prime Minister of France, Marshall Petain decided to surrender. The French public supported the decision, but De Gaulle escaped to London where he declared that he did not accept the surrender. France is independent and will remain so. From London, he formed a Government of France in Exile and eventually liberated France. Now if the majority rule is to be considered supreme, then De Gaulle's action will have to be condemned. He had no right to fight in the name of independence. De Gaulle derived his right from the fact that the French nation was above the majority public opinion. The national Dharma is above all. Independence is Dharma of every nation. To preserve independence, and to strive for regaining it when lost is the duty of every citizen.

Even in our country a majority had not risen against the Britishers; only a few had. Some revolutionaries arose, some brave people arose and fought. Lokmanya declared 'Freedom is my Birthright'. He did not declare this birthright with the support of a majority or by a referendum from the public. Nowadays people advocate that the merger of Goa should be decided by referendum, that there should be plebiscite in Kashmir etc. This is wrong. National unity is our Dharma. Decision concerning this cannot be made by plebiscite. This type of a decision has already been taken by the nature [sic]. Elections and majority can decide as to who will form the government. The truth cannot be decided by the majority. What the government will do will be decided by Dharma.

You all know that in the USA where they swear by democracy, at one time Lincoln did not accept wrong public opinion. On the question of the abolition of slavery, when the Southern states declared their intention to secede, Lincoln stood firm and told them: 'You have no right to secede even in a democracy.' He fought against this and did not allow them to secede. Nor did he tolerate slavery. He did not show readiness for a compromise whereby there may continue partial slavery to accommodate southern states. He did not accept the principle of meeting halfway. He categorically declared that the system of slavery was against tradition, the Dharma, the principles which were at the basis of American nation. Therefore the system of slavery had to be abolished. When the Southerners decided to secede he told them 'You cannot secede'. On this point there was a civil war and Lincoln did not compromise with Adharma.

Here in our country the situation in this regard is very much like the old Hindu marriages where a married couple could not divorce even if both the parties wished. The principle was that their behaviour should be regulated not by their sweet will but by Dharma. The same is the case with the nation. If the four million people of Kashmir say that they want to secede, if the people of Goa say they want to secede, some say they want the Portuguese to return, all this is against Dharma. Of the 45 million people of India, even if 449,999,999 opt for something which is against Dharma, even then this does not become truth. On the other hand, even if a person stands for something which is according to Dharma, that constitutes truth because truth resides with Dharma. It is the duty of this one person that he tread the path of truth and change people. It is from this basis that person derives the right to proceed according to Dharma.

Let us understand very clearly that Dharma is not necessarily with the majority or with the people. Dharma is eternal. Therefore, in the definition of democracy, to say that it is a government of the people, it is not enough; it has to be for the good of the people. What constitutes the good of the people, Dharma alone can decide. Therefore, a democratic Government 'Jana Rajya' must also be rooted in Dharma i.e. a 'Dharma Rajya' must also be rooted in Dharma i.e. a 'Dharma Rajya'. In the definition of 'Democracy' viz. 'government of the people, by the people and for the people', 'of' stands for independence, 'by' stands for democracy, and 'for' indicates Dharma. Therefore the true democracy is only where there is freedom as well as Dharma. धर्मराज्य encompasses all these concepts.

9

Balraj Madhok

Proponents of Hindu nationalism have always claimed that Indian civilization is represented by Hindu civilization. For them this equation harks back to the autochthonous quality of the Hindu people: being sons of this soil, they embody the national ethos. As a result, paradoxically—and in contrast to the Hindu Mahasabha—the Sangh Parivar has tended to shun the epithet 'Hindu' in the names it has given to its component. Except for the Hindu Vishva Parishad, these components are all 'rashtriya' or 'bharatiya', that is, 'national' (in Hindi and Sanskrit).

This qualification was especially important for the Bharatiya Jana Sangh (BJS) because the party tried hard to project itself as pan-Indian. Nomenclature did not however make any difference to the ideological content of its programme: what the party meant by 'Indianization' was in fact 'Hinduization'. The minorities—especially Muslims and Christians—were requested to pay allegiance to Hindu symbols of identity and adopt Hindu cultural habits and customs in order to forsake their 'non-national' origins. This is evident from the Indianization charter that Balraj Madhok gave to his party, the Jana Sangh, in the late 1960s and early 1970s.

Madhok was born in an Arya Samajist family in Jammu within the then princely state of Jammu & Kashmir. He joined the DAV College in Lahore in the 1930s and then—after attending some communist meetings—became a member of the RSS in 1938.[1] Back in Jammu, he launched a political party, the Praja Parishad, for the defence of Hindus

---

[1] B. Madhok, *RSS and Politics* (New Delhi: Hindu World Publications, rpnt, 1986), p. 24.

in the state, but was expelled from Jammu & Kashmir in 1948. Settled in Delhi, he launched the student union of the Sangh Parivar, namely the Akhil Bharatiya Vidyarthi Parishad, the same year, and took part in the making of the BJS in 1951. He was appointed party president in 1966–7 and tried, at that time, to transform the BJS into the focal point of a loose coalition of rightist forces—like the Swatantra Party—that opposed Indira Gandhi's brand of socialism. In 1969 he viewed the split of the Congress Party as a new step in this direction, which might prepare the ground for bipartisanship. However, A.B. Vajpayee, the rising star of the BJS, objected to this conservative option, believing that Indira Gandhi should be challenged on her own ground—that of populism. Upadhyaya and then Vajpayee replaced Madhok as party president in the late 1960, and early 1970s. Madhok immediately denounced the 'leftist' leanings of the party as well as the influence that the RSS exerted over the party.[2] L.K. Advani, who succeeded Vajpayee at the helm of the BJS in 1973, suspended Madhok from the party for three years. The quick marginalization of Madhok showed that the organization prevailed over men, and more specifically that it was impossible for a Jana Sangh leader to stand against the RSS. Madhok tried to launch another party but never managed to attract much support.

He set forth his arguments for the necessary 'Indianization' of the minorities, for the first time, at a conference in Patna in December 1969.

Extracts from *Indianization?*
What, Why and How[3]

[. . .] The fact is that Muslim problem as it has emerged in India today is entirely the creation of the ruling Congress Party, particularly its present leadership, which has developed a vested interest in Muslim communalism for Muslim support in the elections just as the British had developed a vested interest in Muslim communalism for using it

---

[2] M.R. Varshney, *Jana Sangh, RSS and Balraj Madhok* (Aligarh: Varshney College, no date).

[3] Balraj Madhok, *Indianisation? What, Why and How* (New Delhi: S. Chand, 1970), pp. 678–9, 90–5, 98–9, 100–3.

against the nationalist forces led by the Indian National Congress before 1947. Had this leadership learnt the lessons of partition and had it been serious about solving this problem for good, it would have taken concerted steps right from 1947 to wean away the Muslim masses from the communal leadership of Muslim League and its allies who became Congressmen overnight by changing their caps.

It could have built up a really patriotic leadership among Muslims and brought them into the national mainstream with little effort. But it did quite the opposite. It systematically worked up in their minds imaginary fear of nationalist parties like the Jana Sangh and tried to keep them tied to the apron strings of the Congress by offering them baits like continuation of polygamy among them and going out of the way to reconstruct Aligarh Muslim University without changing its communal and anti-national character. By doing so it prevented modernisation of Islam which is an essential pre-requisite for its Indianisation.

The campaign against communalism that has of late been started by the Congress and Communist Parties is primarily aimed at strengthening and mobilising Muslim communalism in favour of these parties. It has nothing whatsoever to do with eradication of communalism as such. Its main aim as Mr Frank Moraes, Chief Editor of *Indian Express*, who himself is a Christian by religion, has pointed out in a recent article (*Indian Express*, May 18, 1970) is to exploit the minorities for political ends. 'Who has created and revitalised this image of majority and minority?' he asks and then adds, 'Let it be said frankly, none other than the Prime Minister of India.'

Therefore, the first thing to be done to eradicate communalism which is a real and growing danger to India's very existence as a nation is to take it out of the party politics. The lead in this matter must come from the ruling party. Let all political parties declare and swear that they will not work up and exploit communalism for party ends. Let the Government remove the wide-spread impression that it has double standards and that it has been trying to appease the Muslims at the cost of others as is clear from its refusal to extend the common civil code in regard to monogamy to Muslims to secure their votes in the elections.

This policy of appeasement of Muslim communalism is reminiscent of the similar Congress policy in pre-partition days and its disastrous results. It is important that leaders of Muslim League and Majlis-e-Mushawarat are made to realise that separatism and communalism will not pay. So long as they feel that a policy of separatism and communal instransigence yields rich dividends, they cannot be expected to give it up. Unfortunately the history of the past fifty years has created a feeling in this leadership in India as also in the rulers of Pakistan that an aggressive policy towards Hindus and India is a wise policy. [. . .]

[. . .] Urdu is once again becoming a symbol of Muslim separatism. This is neither good for Urdu nor for Muslims. Urdu will flourish in India because of its literature in the making of which non-Muslims have played an equally important role and not because of Muslims. But it will have to take to Dev Nagri script progressively.

It is wrong to bind any language with a particular script. All the European languages, though quite different from one another, are written in the same script. This is a great help to learning of different European languages and in creating a common European outlook. Dev Nagri is already the common script of India. It happens to be the most scientific script too. *Dewan-i-Ghalib*, a great Urdu classic, written in Dev Nagri script, has been sold in lakhs while that written in Persian script has few buyers. Therefore, introduction of a common script and discouragement to any language getting bound with any religious community is very important for Indian unity. And this can be best done through a correct policy about education.

History plays a great part in shaping the minds of men. It is a great vehicle for building up national feeling as well. India has a long and chequered history. It has its share of glory and decay, victories and defeats, heroes and traitors. But with all this it is one whole which gives us a panoramic view of India's growth from Vedic past to the present day.

Proper approach to history is to treat facts as sacred and interpret them to suit the social needs of the day. But what is being done in India is quite different.

In the name of secularism, historical facts are being distorted or whitewashed to suit the ideological or political convenience of the powers that be. For example Aurangzeb is sought to be presented as a liberal ruler and therefore Jaziya is explained to be just a tax which all governments have to levy to keep themselves going. This kind of distortion is having quite the opposite effect on the younger generation which anyway knows the glaring facts of our history even without reading the text-books.

This tampering with history and removal of references to India's traditional heroes and heroines from the text-books in the name of secularism and eradication of communalism is most impolitic and may have the opposite effect. Historical memories cannot be effaced by whitewashing the history. They have become part of the country's heritage and got stuck to the race mind. The proper thing is to let the rising generation know about these things. It is the job of the teachers and leaders to create admiration for right things and revulsion for wrong things irrespective of the creed of the person or persons who might have done them. That is the approach to history adopted in all countries of the world except those under the control of Communists for whom regimentation of mind on a particular pattern is essential for maintaining their authoritarian regimes. In Britain, for example, never has attempt been made to hide the fact of Queen Mary having burnt Sir Thomas More and hundreds of other Protestants on the stakes. But the Indian secularists want the Indian people not to know the misdeeds of Aurangzeb and martyrdom of Guru Teg Bahadur and many other saints and patriots at his hands. If they want to create respect for an Indianised Akbar they must condemn the un-Indian and inhuman conduct of Aurangzeb.

The same is true in regard to places of worship. Indianisation demands that places of worship of all creeds should be respected. But the so-called secularists and opponents of Indianisation who raised such a hue and cry against the arson in Al Aqsa mosque in Jerusalem by a lunatic have not a word to say against desecration and demolition of temples and other places of worship by past and present fanatics. Even a Muslim like Kamal Pasha found it difficult to reconcile himself to the use of the Church of Saint Sophia in Constantinople as a mosque. As a via media he converted it into a museum. But here in India some of the holiest places of the country like the birthplaces of Shri Ram and Shri Krishna are still in the hands of Muslims. It is true they did not demolish these temples and built mosques in their places. That was the work of barbarians like Aurangzeb. But has the conscience of any so-called 'nationalist' Muslim or their secularist patrons been ever pricked by such ghastly sights which continue to be the greatest barrier in the way of emotional integration of our people? Truly Indianised Muslims will offer these places to those whom they belonged voluntarily and I am sure that this gesture will be reciprocated by construction of new mosques for them nearby.

It is the job of education and educationists to create this kind of atmosphere and consciousness in the country. I know it for certain that there are many Muslims in India who hold the same views. But they are afraid of speaking out their mind for fear of victimisation at the hands of those for whom Aurangzeb is an ideal Muslim King and Akbar a heretic.

Indianisation of educational system in general to suit Indian conditions and make it a vehicle for creating consciousness and pride of being an Indian is, therefore, very essential for Indianisation of the Indian classes. The masses so far have remained generally untouched by the de-Indianising effects of education. But education has to reach them too sooner or later. Therefore, reform in the educational system, induction of moral and national content in it and use of Hindi and other national languages as media of instruction up to the highest state with a planned effort to make every Indian know Bhasha Bharti and Dev Nagri script is most urgent. The name 'Bhasha Bharti' instead of Hindi for the common language of the country should be popularised. This Bhasha Bharti will have as many shades as the linguistic regions of our vast country. Bhasha Bharti spoken and used in North Western parts of India will have more words of Persian and Turkish origin and the Bhasha Bharti . . . of Tamil Nadu will have more of Tamil influence on it. It must draw upon the current words and technical terms in all the Indian languages and fall back to Sanskrit where no current word is available. Some of the current English words will also have to be Indianised and incorporated in Bhasha Bharti.

National fairs and festivals play a great role in moulding the minds of men in any country. India is in a very happy position in this respect. It has a number of festivals which are celebrated all over the country in one form or the other. Most of such festivals are connected with seasons though they have come to have some mythical or historical association as well. Most important of such festivals are Onam, Vasant, Holi, Baisakhi, Deepawali and Dussehra. Onam which is called Makar Sankaranti and Maghi in some parts of the country marks the movement of the Sun from Dakshinayan to Uttarayan and, therefore, marks the climax of winter and beginning of the new year. This is celebrated all over the country. 'Gur' and 'til' are specially used in all parts of the country in this festival.

Vasant ushers in the spring and as such is a purely seasonal festival. It has also come to be treated as festival of students who worship the goddess of learning—Saraswati—on that day. Association of goddess Saraswati with Vasant and students is not confined to India alone. Saraswati is specially adored by students in Japan and elsewhere as well.

Holi is the May-pole day of India. It is a festival of gaiety and abandon in which all social barriers are broken. As such it is a festival of social cohesion as well. It is particularly the festival of the common people, symbolised by Kisan, the sturdy peasant of India.

Dussehra or Vijay Dashmi is the army day of India since ages past. It is the day of victory of good over evil. It is also the day for adoration of arms and armed men who are as much essential for the existence of a nation as the farmers and others. It is a festival of 'Jawans' par excellence. Jai Jawan and Jai Kisan go together. There will be no victory (Jai) for Bharat without Jai for Jawan and Kisan.

Deepawali which traditionally marks the homecoming of Shri Ram after the conquest of Lanka also marks the end of summer and beginning of autumn. It marks the end of harvesting of summer crops and beginning of sowing of the winter crops. As such it marks the traditional beginning of the new financial year in India. It is why it has become specially associated with the business class and the worship of Lakshmi, the goddess of wealth. All over India traders of all religions start their new ledgers on this day.

Till recently these festivals were observed in common by all Indians irrespective of caste and creed. Akbar, though a Muslim, patronised them officially. It is a well-known historical fact that when the envoy of the Amir of Afghanistan in the court of Maharaja Ranjit Singh begged to be excused from taking part in Holi because he was a Muslim, the lion of Punjab reminded him that it was the festival of India and not of any religious community and then himself threw coloured water on him.

These festivals have to be distinguished from denominational festivals like Janam Ashtami, Shivaratri, Buddha Purnima, Gur-Parav, Rishi Bodh Utsav, Id, Muharram and Christmas which cannot be treated as national festivals. They are the festivals of different religious communities and are connected with the lives of the founders of the different religious sects and paths of worship prevailing in India. They naturally have sectarian character and sectarian appeal even though it would be in the fitness of things and in keeping with Indian tradition if people of all faiths participate in them too.

But so far as national festivals are concerned, they are a class apart. They should not be mixed up with the festivals of different religious groups. The State should take the initiative in celebrating these festivals in a really national way. If that is done, these national festivals can become a very big factor for national integration and Indianisation of the people.

With the development of modern means of communication distance is being eliminated and there is greater mixing up of people from different parts of the country than was possible in the past. This process has been further accelerated by the coming up of huge administrative and industrial complexes in different parts of the country where workers coming from all parts of the country live together. The armed forces and cantonments or military stations in which they live provide the best example of community living where men from different castes and religious groups meet with a common purpose.

All these can be utilised for fostering a spirit of nationalism and Indianness in the people with a little effort. A good job in this respect is being done by the Defence Forces. Their example can be usefully emulated by other organisations which provide for joint working and living of large number of diverse people at one place.

∼

Annexure I: Jana Sangh on Indianisation—I

The resolution on Indianisation passed by Bharatiya Jana Sangh, at its Plenary Session held at Kanpur, in December, 1952, under the Presidentship of Late Dr Shyama Prasad Mukerji.

It is the considered view of the Jana Sangh which is borne out by the history of other countries as well that geographical unity alone cannot sustain nationalism. So long as the people of India shared a common national outlook and owned a common culture, its unity and nationalism were preserved in spite of its being divided into a number of states. It was only when the foreign rulers of this country for their selfish political ends ignored and denigrated Indian way of life and culture and tried to impose foreign mode of life and culture on it, that Indian nationalism got undermined. As a result in spite of loud declaration about India being one nation, the two nation theory reflecting Muslim communalism triumphed, the country was partitioned and it was made impossible for non-Muslims to live in the areas included in Pakistan. On the other hand the mentality behind the two nation theory continues to get sustenance in truncated India by the policy of the bolstering up of Muslim separatism through encouragement and support to the stand that Muslims have a separate culture. This has become the greatest hurdle in the way of national reconstruction and natural unity.

Therefore, Jana Sangh resolves that in the interest of proper evolution of Indian nationalism and a national outlook it is essential that the concept of the whole of India and all its people irrespective of their way of worship, sect or region being one nation with one culture be stressed and propagated among the people. To achieve that end the people and Government must act on the following lines:

1. Education should be based on national culture and tradition. Knowledge about Upanishads, Bhagvad Geeta, Ramayana, Mahabharata and the literature and literary figures of the modern Indian languages who have contributed towards revival and preservation of Indian cultural traditions be disseminated and efforts should be made to bring that day nearer when knowledge about this common cultural stream will be considered essential by people of all parts of the country.

2. Birthdays of national heroes and other national days be celebrated in a national way in which all people irrespective of caste, creed or religion should participate and the Government should extend its administrative and monetary co-operation for such celebrations.

3. The major festivals of the country like Holi, Diwali, Raksha Bandhan and Vijay Dashmi be treated as national festivals and celebrated as such.

4. Special attention should be paid to development of national and regional language and their use in all fields of activity so that the Indian life may develop on the basis of national culture and genius.

5. Sanskrit language should be revived and its knowledge be made compulsory for all votaries of higher learning. At the same time Devnagri script should be popularised and accepted as the common script for all the Indian languages.

6. Indian History should be so re-written that it may become the record of the Indian people and not merely of foreign invaders and conquerors. The division of history into periods should be based not on the names of foreign invaders but on the basis of social movements and revolutions which have played a vital part in the evolution of the Indian society. The story of expansion of Indian thought and culture outside India should have a special place in the text books on Indian history.

7. It is essential for the cultural uplift and national unity that Hindu society removes its internal weaknesses. Particular attention should be paid by it to the removal of social disparities and creation of a sense of oneness in all sections of Hindu society by uplifting the backward sections and removing the feeling of high and low on the basis of caste. To that end it is essential that social and religious festivals be celebrated in a collective and disciplined way and co-operation of all strata of society be received in such celebration.

Along with this internal reform it is the duty of the Hindu society to make concerted efforts to Indianise those sections of the Indian society which have been cut off from the national mainstream because of the influence of foreign invaders and foreign missionaries or have remained cut off from it for other reasons.

Annexure II: Jana Sangh on Indianisation—II

Resolution of Bharatiya Jana Sangh Passed at Plenary Session at Patna on 30th December, 1969:

168 HINDU NATIONALISM: A READER

The spate of communal riots, rapid erosion of the rule of law, determined attempts to disrupt the unity of the country and subvert democracy and constitutional government in different parts has created an explosive situation which if not tackled quickly and effectively may have dangerous repercussions.

The communal riots, of which those at Ahmedabad, Jagatdal and Varanasi are the latest examples, have a set pattern. They are invariably started by that section of the Indian Muslims which has stuck to the ideology which led to the partition of the Motherland in 1947, with the direct or indirect help and abetment of the CPI, CPM, and a section of the Congress Party which have developed vested interest in perpetuating communalism and separatism among the Muslims and keeping them away from the mainstream of Indian life so that they may have the monopoly of their votes in the elections.

Government's failure to prevent the outbreak of disturbances, and later to control them once they got started, has made the situation more serious. Rioters, to whatever community they may belong, ought to be dealt with sternly under the law.

The communally motivated West Asian Policy of the Government of India which impelled it to gate-crash into Islamic Conference at Rabat and invite insult and humiliation of the whole country, its policy of lionising Al-Fatah saboteurs and the planned working up of a communal frenzy all over the country in the name of protest against arson in Al-Aksa Mosque in Jerusalem have further roused and strengthened extra-territorial loyalties among a section of the Indian Muslims. Pakistan and her agents are taking advantage of this situation to egg them on to adopt aggressive postures resulting in riots which add grist to Pakistan's propaganda mills against India. That Pakistan is striving for another partition of India has become clear from the recent writings of Mr Bhutto, Maulana Bhashani, and the memorandum submitted by a number of Muslim organisations to the High Commissioner of India at London. The continued infiltration of Pakistani Muslims in the border states of Assam, West Bengal, Bihar, and Jammu and Kashmir which has been intensified of late points to the same designs of Pakistan on Indian territory.

The dependence of Mrs Indira Gandhi's government on the Muslim League and support of other elements susceptible to communal and sectional appeals of Mr Fakhr-ud-Din Ali Ahmed and Mr Jagjivan Ram has given a new import to the communal problem which cannot be ignored by any nationalist.

The Communist Parties which never made any secret of their determination to wreck the constitution, subvert democracy and disrupt the unity of India are exploiting this situation to serve their ends. They have forged an alliance with Muslim League and pro-Pakistan elements all over the country which has already replaced the Congress–Muslim alliance in the states like West Bengal, Assam and Kerala.

Formation of Mallapuram district in Kerala, the audacity and intransigence of anti-India elements in Jammu and Kashmir and friendliness of Chief Minister Sadiq towards them and the reign of terror let loose by CPM in West Bengal are some of the fruits of this anti-national alliance.

The growing feeling of regionalism and sub-regionalism partly born out of imbalances in economic development has become another major threat to peace and unity of the country. With the weakening of the Central Government attempts are being made to develop and project the personality of different states even at the cost of the personality of the country. The state boundaries have begun to be treated as more sacrosanct than the boundaries of the country which have been steadily shrinking. The formation of sub-State of Meghalaya in Assam has given encouragement to protagonists of sub-regional States in other parts of the country.

The general economic unrest in the country with growing unemployment and frustration among the youth is being further aggravated by the false hopes aroused by Indira Government coupled with policies which are actually retarding production and curtailing employment opportunities. This has created a situation which is ideally suited to the operation of Communist technique of creating lawlessness and anarchy in the country as a prelude to taking over of the State apparatus by them with the help of indoctrinated minority. The forcible occupation of land by them in West Bengal and Kerala and their terrorist activities which have created a general sense of fear and insecurity give a clear inkling of their plans and designs. Naxalites are outdoing them in this regard. They have extended their activities to Kerala, Bihar, Andhra Pradesh, Orissa and other states. Their emergence as an all India Party with open commitment to violence and Maoism has added new dimensions to the Communist menace.

This situation demands urgent attention and concerted effort on the part of all patriotic parties and elements irrespective of their differences in regard to other matters.

The Jana Sangh takes serious note of the increasing interference of foreign powers. Broadcasts relayed by Moscow Radio and Radio Peace and Progress and reports appearing in Russia's government-controlled press regarding happenings in India cannot but be regarded as gross interference in our internal matters.

Western countries also have been exerting to exploit India's illiteracy and poverty by using their economic aid measure, their cheap and provocative literature, and, above all, their missionaries as instruments for a campaign of mass conversion. Jana Sangh strongly condemns their activities as well. We want to warn these foreign powers not to indulge in activities that violate India's sovereignty and independence and demand that the Government of India take stern measures to curb them.

Bharatiya Jana Sangh being the champion of Indian nationalism and committed to preservation and strengthening of Indian unity feels particularly concerned over this state of affairs, and demands that:

1. Every effort should be made to revive and strengthen the sense of nationalism which is the sum total of cohesive forces in any country. This requires a clear understanding of the concept of nationalism and its main-springs.

2. Indianisation—by which we mean the subordination of all narrow loyalties like those of religion, caste, region, language or dogma to the overriding loyalty to the nation of all fissiparous elements, especially of those with extra-territorial loyalties or allegiance, overt or covert, to the two-nation theory.

3. A permanent tribunal should be set up to tackle interstate disputes of all types. The decision of such a Commission should be binding on the parties concerned.

4. Immediate steps should be taken to extend the Constitution of India to the Jammu and Kashmir State to bring it in line with

other States and also to implement fully the recommendations of Gajendragadkar Commission in regard to separate development boards for the Kashmir Valley, Jammu and Ladakh with a clear division of development funds between these three regions.

5. A high powered commission should be set up to look into regional and sub-regional economic imbalance and backwardness and suggest remedies to remove the same.

6. With the lapse of Preventive Detention Act, the need for enacting a law of treason has become an imperative necessity. This law should define treason and treasonable activities and lay down deterrent punishment for all persons and parties indulging in such activities.

PART 3
Hindu Nationalist Issues

10

The RSS and Politics

S ome professional Sangh Parivar politicians, ranging from Balraj
Madhok in the 1960s and 1970s to BJP leaders today, have
complained about the RSS's interference in BJP party politics.
Ironically, Hindu nationalists who believed that the Sangh should
actually play a part in politics failed to draw the RSS into the political
arena until the 1950s. Savarkar, for instance, was not able to convince
Hedgewar or Golwalkar to join hands with the Hindu Mahasabha.

Golwalkar changed his mind very slowly after independence, under
pressure from fellow swayamsevaks, and in very peculiar circumstances.
In 1948 the assassination of Mahatma Gandhi by a former RSS member
resulted in a ban on the organization and the arrest of 20,000 swayamsevaks. Those who had gone underground then discovered that no
major political force was prepared to advocate the cause of the RSS in
parliament or elsewhere. Such people, who had emancipated themselves
from the RSS hierarchy after the first wave of arrests, recommended
that their movement become involved in politics. One of them was
K.R. Malkani, who wrote in 1949: 'Sangh must take part in politics
not only to protect itself against the greedy design of politicians, but
to stop the un-Bharatiya and anti-Bharatiya policies of the Government
and to advance and expedite the cause of Bharatiya through state
machinery side by side with official effort in the same direction . . .
Sangh must continue as it is, an "ashram" for the national cultural
education of the entire citizenry, but it must develop a political wing
for the more effective and early achievement of its ideals.'[1]

[1] *The Organiser*, 1 December 1949, pp. 7–14.

Kewalram Ratanmal Malkani (1921–2003), who was born in Hyderabad (Sindh) into a Congress family—his elder brother, N.R. Malkani was a lieutenant of Gandhi—joined the RSS in 1941. He had moved to Delhi after Partition to become sub-editor of *The Hindustan Times* in 1948. The RSS leadership asked him to revive the English weekly of the movement, *The Organiser*, in 1949. He worked for thirty-four years as editor of this publication, and of *The Motherland* for five years, from 1971 to 1975. He was also Vice President of the Deendayal Research Institute from 1983 to 1990. When the BJP gained momentum he benefited, like many in the RSS cadres, from various sinecures: he was elected to the upper house of Parliament in 1994 and ended his career as governor of Pondicherry, a post he assumed in 2002.[2]

Golwalkar approved of the views of Malkani and others regarding the formation of a new party in 1950, after the demise of Sardar Patel who, in his opinion, could have transformed the Congress by emphasizing its affinities with Hindu nationalism.[3] Obviously, Jawaharlal Nehru was now, post-Patel, strong enough to impose his anti-communal line within his party. Therefore, Golwalkar met S.P. Mookerjee in Nagpur. He recalled that: 'I had to warn him that the RSS could not be drawn into politics, that it could not play second fiddle to any political or other party since no organization devoted to the wholesale regeneration of the real, i.e. cultural life, of the Nation could ever function successfully if it tried to be used as a handmaid of political parties.'[4]

Golwalkar settled for seconding senior swayamsevaks to the newly-formed Jana Sangh—including Deendayal Upadhyaya, Balraj Madhok

[2] Seshadri Chari, 'Doyen of Hindutva School Departs', ibid., 9 November 2003, p. 3.

[3] In January 1948—three weeks before Gandhi's murder—Patel had made a speech in Lucknow inviting the Hindu Mahasabha and the RSS to change their heart and join Congress: 'In the Congress, those who are in power feel that by the virtue of authority they will be able to crush the RSS. You cannot crush an organisation by using the *danda* [stick]. The *danda* is meant for thieves and dacoits. They are patriots who love their country. Only their trend of thought is diverted. They are to be won over by Congressmen, by love.' *Hindustan Times*, 8 January 1948, pp. 1, 8.

[4] *The Organiser*, 25 June 1956, p. 5.

and Atal Behari Vajpayee. These men, who took their orders in Nagpur, took over power in the party after Mookerjee's demise.

Golwalkar's successor, Balasaheb Deoras, got much more deeply involved in politics than any earlier RSS sarsanghchalak. For this reason, he exemplified that specific brand of swayamsevaks known as 'activists'.[5] A Maharashtrian Brahmin, like most of Hedgewar's early disciples, Madhukar Dattaraya (alias Balasaheb) Deoras—and his brother, Murlidar Dattaraya alias Baurao—joined the RSS in Nagpur. He obtained his LLB at the University of Nagpur and became secretary of the local unit of the RSS. He was the first pracharak sent to Bengal, but then returned to the movement's headquarters to direct the publication of *Tarun Bharat* (Young India), a Marathi daily, and then *Yugadharma* (Religious War), a Hindi daily. He became general secretary of the RSS in 1965. During the same year he addressed the annual meeting of the Jana Sangh, an unprecedented move by an RSS dignitary which reflected his strong interest in politics and his will to make the movement play a larger part in the public sphere. He became sarsanghchalak in 1973, after Golwalkar's death, having been designated his heir. The following year Deoras gave expression to his activist leanings by having the RSS support the 'JP Movement'—the anti-Indira Gandhi movement led by Jayaprakash Narayan. Deoras remained at the helm of the RSS till Rajendra Singh took over from him.

The Jana Sangh was never like other Indian political parties. As soon as RSS men took over the Jana Sangh, Hindu traditionalists who had joined the party because of S.P. Mookerjee were sidelined. The organization was then restructured to such an extent that the pillars of the party apparatus were *sangathan mantris* (organization secretaries) who all came—at the district or state level—from the RSS. The party also drew from the RSS a millenarian view of its mission. Its ultimate objective was the reform of society in the long run—not the conquest of power, since the state was not viewed as a prominent institution. Therefore the Jana Sangh was very reluctant to enter into any alliance not fully in tune with its ideology. In 1962 Upadhyaya justified this

[5] W. Andersen and S. Damle, *The Brotherhood in Saffron: The Rashtriya Swayamsevak Sangh and Hindu Revivalism* (New Delhi: Vistaar Publications, 1987), p. 114.

approach by arguing that coalitions were bound to 'degenerate into a struggle for power by opportunist elements coming together in the interest of expediency'.[6] He wanted to build the Jana Sangh as an alternative party to the Congress and considered elections an 'opportunity to educate the people on political issues and to challenge the right of the Congress to be in power.'[7] This indifference *vis-à-vis* party politics and power was on a par with lack of interest in the state and the desire to make it weaker, or at least more decentralized. For the Jana Sangh the basic units of the administration were the villages and the *janapadas*, groupings of districts which, in contrast with the states of the union (which are much larger) would not coincide with linguistic areas: the Jana Sangh, like all Hindu nationalists, was against linguistic states because they entertained regionalist or even sub-national identities.

The Jana Sangh doctrine started being diluted in the late 1960s— when the party made alliances and became part of the anti-Congress coalitions—and even more in the 1970s when it became part of the 1971 Grand Alliance and then merged with the Janata Party in 1977. For ex-Jana Sanghis this submersion of their initial identity was a major turning point. However, other components of the Janata denounced the allegiance they continued to pay to the RSS. This 'dual membership' controversy ended with the reluctant secession of ex-Jana Sanghis, who could not resign themselves to questioning their affiliation with the RSS.

Yet, the party they created in 1980, the Bharatiya Janata Party, was meant to be heir to the Janata Party—it was not meant to go back to square one, i.e. the Hindu nationalist identity and the Jana Sangh constituency. The dilution of its ideology, which was evident from its new slogans promoted by the party president, A.B. Vajpayee—slogans such as 'Gandhian socialism' and 'positive secularism', was not to the liking of the RSS, which decided to support the Congress in some Indian states—to create a new party in Tamil Nadu, the Hindu Munnani, and to support another of its offshoots, the VHP, to launch an ethno-religious mobilization on the Ayodhya issue. The BJP gradually rallied around this campaign after L.K. Advani replaced Vajpayee as

[6] D. Upadhyaya, 'Jana Sangh', *Seminar*, no. 29, January 1962, p. 20.
[7] Ibid.

party president in 1986. This shift was officially recognized at the Palampur session of 1989.

The instrumentalization of the Ayodhya issue and the related communal riots that polarized the electorate along religious lines helped the BJP make progress election after election. However, the BJP realized in the mid-1990s that, before long, it would not be in a position to form the government on its own. Therefore, it adopted a more moderate approach to politics in order to make allies. In 1998 it built a majority coalition in the Lok Sabha and was able to do the same in 1999 after the mid-term elections.

The RSS and other components of the Sangh Parivar, while they appreciated some of the measures taken by the Vajpayee government, such as the testing of a nuclear bomb, were rather disappointed by its overall performance. The VHP resented the fact that no concrete step had been taken towards building the Ram temple in Ayodhya. The BMS objected to the liberalization policy of the government. Along with the RSS, they all believed the BJP leaders had been victims of their thirst for power: they had preferred to compromise to remain in office instead of sticking to their principles. In April 2005 K. Sudarshan (who took over from Rajendra Singh in 2000), echoed their views and suggested—in the course of a TV interview!—that A.B. Vajpayee and L.K. Advani should make room for new faces so that new faced could emerge and reach the BJP's high commons! L.K. Advani, who had been the hatchet man of the RSS against Madhok, objected, saying the RSS should not interfere that way in the party affairs, but resigned from the BJP's presidentship in December 2005.

Extract from K.R. Malkani, *The RSS Story*[8]

. . . Dr Hedgewar and his friends were active, militant Congressmen before they formed the RSS. Congress was a very different and a very superior thing before Independence. Even though Dr Hedgewar felt that it was not a good enough instrument, either for fighting the British or for rebuilding an India of our dreams, he found that politics is a game of power and not the instrument of nation-building and

[8] K.R. Malkani, *The RSS Story* (New Delhi: Impex India, 1980), pp. 113–21.

character-building. And so even while very much interesting itself in national issues—on the eve of 1957 and 1962 elections, Shri Guruji even advised the electorate on how they may vote—RSS has always been above and beyond politics.

Shri Guruji also thought poorly of politics and politicians. In fact, he felt the adverse effect of politics in every walk of life—the tendency to look upon political leaders as pillars of society. This had led to a steep fall in moral values and seeping of corruption into every walk of life. This was a topsy-turvy state of affairs, he felt. 'A crow does not become the best bird in the world just because it happens to sit on the top of the spire of a temple,' he once said, alluding to the exaggerated importance given to ruling politicians.

The first political attack on RSS came as early as 1934. The British were trying to pit Muslims against Hindus, non-Brahmins against Brahmins. In CP and Berar they were backing the non-Brahmins against Brahmins, to divide the freedom movement. When people influenced by RSS stood up against this British game, the Government issued a notification warning District Local Board employees not to join RSS, although only half a dozen such employees were attending Shakha at the time. Although RSS was then in its infancy, it was able to mobilise all the nationalist elements in the Provincial Assembly and to get the Government defeated on a cut motion on the subject.

Gandhiji looked upon Jamnalal Bajaj as his son. And Jamnalalji was also Congress Working Committee member and Party Treasurer. When he saw RSS, he liked it so much that he wanted it to be an integral part of the Congress. For this reason he asked Appaji Joshi, PCC Secretary-turned-Sanghachalak of Wardha, to take him to Dr Hedgewar. Shri Appaji knew Doctorji's Sangha point of view thoroughly well. He, therefore, tried to explain to him the futility of his plan. Doctorji wanted to keep the organization completely aloof from politics and party feuds. He therefore told Bajajji that it would be embarrassing for them to go to Doctorji and then get no response. But he could not deter him from his resolve. On the contrary Bajajji thought that Appaji was deliberately avoiding to take him to Doctorji. He therefore arranged to see Doctorji independently. Couple of days later, on January 31, 1934, Jamnalalji, accompanied by Late Shri Ganpatrao Tikekar, an esteemed friend of Doctorji, met him. He requested him to run the organization under the Congress control. By doing this, he assured Doctorji, Sangha would get all sorts of help, there would not be any monetary difficulty and it would attain an All-India status within a short period of time, as contemplated by Doctorji.

Doctorji conceded that Congress was the greatest political organization and that he was a member thereof. But Doctorji said: 'I insist on RSS flourishing independently on its intrinsic organizational strength. It is our experience that plants never grow under gigantic trees. I do not want to produce volunteers for the politicking of politicians. Sangha does not want Swayamsevaks to merely abide by the orders of superiors. My intention is to create Swayamsevaks capable of thinking over all the facets of our national life and leading the nation towards progress, on their own strength. This work cannot be done by any political leader or party of the day. It is self-dependent. Swayamsevaks have to evolve it through their toil and sacrifices. We shall not receive money or any other help from others; that will make us dependent upon them. Independently, we shall stand. That is our determination and so I cannot agree with you.'

Seth Jamnalalji came back rather disappointed.

Shri Appaji Joshi writes: 'Thereafter, Jamnalalji tried to organize different *vyayamshalas* by donating to them band instruments, etc. It was a headache for us for a couple of years. But it bore no fruit. He also realised that it was not a joke to run an 'organization'. Seth Jamnalalji was a noble-hearted and cultured man. Even though he was disappointed by us, he was not angry at all. Till his last, he loved and helped us. But the Congress and its offsprings with varied socialistic tinges began to hate Sangha because of the fact that this great organization could not be exploited for their narrow political ends. Many of them tried to create Dals, Senas and Sanghs on the lines of the RSS, but with no success. Our critics are angry with us not because of any ideological differences but because of the fact that Sangha cannot be exploited for their own ends and it is gaining strength day by day. This is the main reason why people hate Sangha though Sangha never hates anybody.'

If Congress was disappointed, the Hindu Mahasabha was, if anything, even more disappointed. Since both organizations, Mahasabha and RSS, were wedded to Hindutva, the Mahasabha assumed that RSS would back it in the political sphere. The expectation was the greater because Mahasabha leader Dr B.S. Moonje had been like an elder brother to Dr Hedgewar for decades. As long as Dr Moonje was in Congress, there was no problem; but when he came out of Congress, and joined Mahasabha, a serious problem arose. They insisted on RSS support to the Mahasabha against the Congress.

Writes Appaji: 'Sooner or later, a time was bound to come when they were to be told "No" in plain words. When the time came, Doctorji asserted: "Sangha is an organization totally aloof from politics. Hence it will work for no political party. A Sangha Swayamsevak is at liberty to join any political party and work for it. He may participate actively in elections too. But the organization will not follow him. It will be aloof from parties and will not abandon this stand for any reason." '

Due to this frank expression, Mahasabha friends were rather angry. They started a new organization known as 'Ram Sena'. A 'Vanar Sena' (Monkey Brigade) was already there in Nagpur for the Congress party. Two opposition parties (for their own purposes) started brigades in the name of Bhagavan Ram! Afterwards, there were a few clashes between Ram Sena and Sangha. Having seen Doctorji very much pained at this, Appaji went to Dr Moonje, explained the Sangha point of view and tried to appease him as far as possible.

It is clear that even a Hindutvavadi organisation like Hindu Mahasabha which had no differences with regard to aims, objects or policy of Sangha, was opposed to Sangha. The main reason behind it was the fact that the Sangha could not be exploited for their political purposes. Wrote Appaji years later: 'Hindu Sabhaites blame the present Sangha leadership (Shri Guruji) by saying that it was really good of Doctorji that he was a Hindu Sabhaite. But, if you refer to the old issues of "Vandemataram", the then organ of Hindu Mahasabha, you will find that these very people had vomited nothing short of venom against Doctorji through its columns.'

Veer Savarkar, long-time President of Hindu Mahasabha, had also been very unhappy with RSS for not helping his political activities. He once wrote: 'The epitaph on a Sangha Swayamsevak will be: "He was born; he joined RSS; he died"'. It was only years later that he appreciated RSS decision to keep out of politics, as good and right.

RSS had been working for twelve years when Congress came to power in 1937. All this time they had not said a word against RSS; indeed many Congressmen were active workers of Sangha. But now that they were in power, they began to look upon RSS as a possible political rival. Shri E.S. Patwardhan, Secretary CP & Berar PCC, wrote to Dr Hedgewar what were the aims and objects of Sangha and where it stood *vis-à-vis* Congress. After consulting his co-workers, Doctorji wrote to him that RSS was an old enough organisation for every political worker in the province to know what it was. He added that RSS had nothing against Congress and that many active Congressmen were also active Sangha workers.

Patwardhan wrote back that he was 'not satisfied' with the replies. He now sent a long list of questions for the RSS to answer. Dr Hedgewar wrote to him that RSS people had left school long ago and they had lost the habit of answering question papers like that. Soon after, the Congress ministries resigned.

For the next ten years, when the RSS reached every nook and corner of the country, Congress did not utter one word against RSS. But as soon as they came to power in 1946, they again saw a possible potential political rival in the RSS. And so the Congress Working Committee asked the Congress Government to ban RSS. Pandit Nehru even wrote to Dr Gopichand Bhargava, Punjab Chief Minister, to ban RSS and Akali Dal. Obviously the Punjab Government considered discretion the better part of valour and didn't ban either the one or the other. For the next three years while Sardar Patel looked for cooperation between Congress and RSS, Pandit Nehru tried to crush RSS. He once even went so far as to say that if he lost out to pro-RSS forces, he would go abroad and fight these forces from there. He did not seem to realise that that would be an anti-national activity. After Gandhiji's murder, Nehru tried very hard to crush RSS but failed.

In September 1949, the Congress Working Committee decided, on a reference made to it by the Bihar PCC, that RSS workers could join the Congress. (This was nothing surprising. As the Bihar PCC President put it as late as 1974, 'There are more Sanghis in Congress than in Jana Sangha.') Subsequently, addressing Congress workers in Kanpur, Congress President Pattabhi Sitaramayya said: 'The RSS is not the enemy of the Congress. It is not a communal political organisation.'

When the CWC took the above decision, Pandit Nehru was on a long foreign tour. When he returned he said that Congress rules did not permit a member of any volunteer organisation, except that of the

Congress Seva Dal, to join the Congress. He overlooked the facts that Congress Seva Dal existed only in name; that RSS was not a volunteer organisation like Boy Scouts or Seva Dal; and that many Congress leaders were also leaders of Arya Vir Dal etc.

And he would not answer the question why RSS men could not join Congress when even Jamiat-ul-Ulema and Muslim League men could. The funniest part of the whole proceeding was that Nehru's November 20, 1949 Ramlila Maidan meeting was managed by red-uniformed volunteers of Ahrars, a Muslim organisation.

The whole thing was reminiscent of Swami Shraddhananda's experience of Congress double standards. 'On the 13th February 1923, I was called to lead the movement for the reclamation of Malkana Rajputs by their several brotherhoods . . . I found to my astonishment, that while Muhammadan leaders, doing *tabligh* (conversion) work openly, were allowed to guide the policy of the Congress and work as its accredited representatives, those engaged in the work of rescuing the Hindu Samaj from disintegrating were tabooed, and kept out of the Congress executive.'

Sardar Patel was too ill to fight out the issue of Swayamsevaks' membership of Congress. But he did get Purushottamdas Tandon elected Congress President, in the hope that he would be able to bring Congress and RSS together. Indeed it is believed that Socialists left the Congress and formed a separate party on the advice of Nehru who wanted to join them, just in case the Patel group prevailed in the Congress. But in another year Patel died and Nehru promptly threw out Tandon, made himself Congress President and forgot all about the Socialists.

The RSS viewed the scene with some amusement. Commenting on the Congress closing its doors to RSS, Babasaheb Apte of the RSS told Delhi University students: 'Of course we have no doors to close. Why, we don't have any walls either. We play on open grounds.'

Nor was this RSS phobia confined to Nehru. Pakistan shared it in full measure. When East Bengal language riots took place in 1953, 'Dawn' blamed it on 'RSS and Reds'. And when the Huq-Suhrawardy-Mujib alliance routed Muslim League in the 1954 elections in East Pakistan, 'Dawn' published on May 18, 1954 a cartoon showing Fazlul

Huq breaking 'The Wall of Pakistan ideology' and letting the flood waters of 'Fifth Column RSS' rush in, to overwhelm Pakistan!

In 1948, some 17,000 Sangha workers were unjustly detained without trial. Later, over 60,000 Sangha workers offered satyagraha. Thousands went on fast for weeks because of the treatment meted out to them in jail. But while all these excesses were being perpetrated, not one MP nor one MLA anywhere in the country asked one question on the subject. The legislatures were packed with Congressmen and their yes-men bent upon crushing the Sangha. Workers, therefore, began to wonder whether Sangha could work in peace in this political jungle and whether a political protective shield was not necessary. And yet there was no suitable party which they could join. The Nehru Congress was in a sulk. Socialists and Swayamsevaks were on different wavelengths. The CPI was out of the question. And the Hindu Mahasabha was more dead than alive. At this stage Dr Shyama Prasad Mookerji, formerly of the Hindu Mahasabha, quit the Nehru cabinet on the issue of betrayal of East Bengal Hindus. He was also thinking of launching a new party. The two thought currents on the same lines resulted in the birth of Bharatiya Jana Sangha. Dr Mookerji became President and Dr Bhai Mahavir, an RSS leader, General Secretary.

In the very first General Elections, Jana Sangha secured enough votes to be recognised as an All India Party.

As the Bharatiya Jana Sangha grew, some people began to ask questions about its relationship with the RSS. In an article written for 'Organiser' (June 25, 1956), Shri Guruji put the record straight. He said that after Dr Mookerji resigned from the Government, he did not find any existing party suitable. He, therefore, thought of founding a new party. Dr Mookerji met him to seek his counsel and cooperation. 'As a result we met often and discussed all relevant matters. Naturally I had to warn him that the RSS could not be drawn into politics, that it could not play second fiddle to any political or other party, since no organisation, devoted to the wholesale regeneration of the real, that is cultural, life of the Nation, could ever function successfully if it was to be used as a handmaid of political parties.

'He realised this position and agreed that it was correct. At the same time he opined that the new political party also could not be made subservient to any other organisation, which position was evidently the one necessary for its proper growth and evolution. With agreement on these fundamentals as to the relations of the RSS and the proposed party, the other aspect to be considered was the idealism to which the party would be devoted. So far as the RSS is concerned, it has definite, settled ideals and method of work. As such, if the cooperation of any member of this organisation was desired, it was possible only if there was idealism in the political identity of the party also.

'On this point also there was full agreement, to the extent that when on his stating in one of his press conferences that the Hindu Mahasabha was communal in as much as it believed in Hindu Rashtra, I had pointed out to him that we of the RSS had equal, if not more, emphatic belief in the Bharatiya Rashtra being Hindu Rashtra, and as such the RSS would be, for him, equally deserving of being kept at arm's length, and that as a consequence he need no longer count upon my sympathy or the cooperation of such of his colleagues as staunchly believed in, and untiringly worked for, the re-establishment of the Hindu Rashtra idea of the RSS. He acknowledged that he had made an inadvertent remark. He expressed full agreement on the Hindu Rashtra idea, adding that the Constitution had failed to realise and state the Bharatiya Nationhood and that the ideal of re-establishing the Hindu Rashtra in its own glory was not incompatible with the modern concept of a democratic state. The Hindu Rashtra, he said, guaranteed full civic freedom and political, religious and cultural status of equality in the life of the country even to the non-Hindu communities, so long as they did not indulge in any anti-national activities or entertain ambitions to grab power and supplant the Nation from its proper pedestal of supreme glory. He even expressed his eagerness to clarify this fact in the aims and objects of his political party.

'When thus there was complete agreement, I chose some of my colleagues, staunch and tried workers, who could selflessly and unflinchingly shoulder the burden of founding the new party and who had the ability to lay broad, unshakable foundations for its rise to the status of a popular, respectable All-Bharat political party. Thus did Dr Mookerji realise his ambition of founding what is known as the Bharatiya Jana Sangh.'

Shri Guruji went on: 'Having given Dr Mookerji a set of good workers, I, in keeping with our convictions, detached myself wholly from all further activities of the Jana Sangha and concentrated upon the RSS work of building up the cultural organisation of the Hindu people. But from time to time, whenever we had occasion to meet, he would tell me of the progress of the Jana Sangha and of any proposed programmes or movements. I also would seek his help and cooperation in the work of the RSS, and he unstintingly placed himself at the disposal of our workers wherever and whenever needed. A close bond of love, transcending mere comradeship in public life, had sprung up between us and day by day it was becoming stronger. In almost every important step which we took in our respective bodies and fields of activity, we rarely failed to consult each other, though we were always very careful not to meddle in, or interfere with, each other's work, or confuse the two bodies or impose the one upon the other.'

Thus the RSS and Jana Sangha were two entirely different and separate entities. The one was cultural, the other political. The RSS Constitution even provided that nobody who held office in that organisation could hold office in any political party.

The RSS attitude to politics continues to be the same as it was fifty years ago. It is not in politics; and it is not after power. Bhaiyaji Dani, long-time RSS General Secretary, used to reminisce that in the Forties, RSS could have easily captured many Praja Mandals in Central India and automatically come to power in those princely States. But it had refrained from doing so. The RSS is engaged in the task of character-building and nation-building. It is, therefore, very much interested in the country's problems. It ponders deep over these problems and gives its dispassionate and disinterested opinion from time to time.

This is in conformity with the ancient Indian tradition going back to Vyas and Vasisht. In more recent times, Swami Ramdas acted as the mentor of Shivaji. In modern times Gandhiji played this role for the national movement—and Jayaprakash for Janata movement. Even Pandit Nehru regularly called on Acharya Vinoba Bhave for his moral leadership.

The relationship of RSS with the Jana Sangha was of the same kind. Here were two different organisations with their separate aims, objects, leaderships, constitutions, flags, funds, policies and programmes. As and when they felt like, BJS leaders could exchange notes with RSS leaders. But they followed their own line. For example while Shri Guruji was opposed to birth control by artificial means, Jana Sangh was not; Shri Guruji advised all Punjabi Hindus to acknowledge Punjabi as their mother tongue, but many BJS workers were wont to declare Hindi; while Shri Guruji opposed the Indo-Soviet Treaty, the Jana Sangha welcomed it.

As Shri Guruji used to point out: 'Sangha is strongest in Nagpur, but Jana Sangha has never won an election there. That is a measure of the differences in the nature and aims of the two organisations.'

But politicians interested in harassing the RSS and blaming their failure on it, continued to dub it as political—as though it would be some kind of a sin to be political; and as if anything, apart from its own volition, prevented the RSS from entering politics. .

Extract from *Sri Balasaheb Deoras* *Answers Questions*[9]

Q. How would you define the relation between the BJP and the RSS? Or would you totally deny any kind of relationship?

A. A Swayamsevak, just as any other citizen, has a right to join or form any political party. As such, in the RSS constitution, the Swayam-sevak in his individual capacity is allowed to join any political party which does not believe in violence or secrecy, or has no extra-national loyalties or does not encourage communalism. But it is for the other political parties to welcome him. If they don't welcome him, we can't help it. Take the example of Congress. In 1950s, Sardar Patel had got passed in the Congress Working Committee a resolution opening its doors to RSS Swayamsevaks. However, Pandit Nehru, who was abroad at that time, after his return, reversed the decision.

And previous to that, a peculiar situation had developed. When the RSS was founded in 1925 and even later on, there was no discussion about the RSS relationship with political parties. When, however, Gandhiji was murdered in 1948, and the Sangh was banned—and although it was a totally unjustified and uncalled-for ban—not a single Member of Parliament or of any Assembly challenged the unjust ban. Then we launched *Satyagraha* in which one lakh Swayamsevaks courted arrest. At that time also no political leader opened his lips. Some of

[9] Balasaheb Deoras, *Shri Balasaheb Deoras Answers Questions* (rpnt, Bangalore: Sahitya Sindhu, 1984), pp. 36–7.

our Swayamsevaks felt that such an isolation is no good and something must be done. They felt that though RSS may have no politics, some members of the RSS, who have the liking and ability, should take part in politics. That view was shared by Swayamsevaks like Deendayal Upadhyaya, Atal Behari Vajpayee, Lal Krishna Advani, Sundar Singh Bhandari, etc.

In 1951 or so, when Dr Shyama Prasad Mukherjee came forward to start the Jana Sangh, the situation was such that it was the only party which was prepared to welcome the RSS members. Naturally, the Swayamsevaks whom I mentioned now and other like-minded members joined the Jana Sangh. Unfortunately, Dr Shyama Prasad Mukherjee died within two years, and the burden of building up the Jana Sangh as a political party fell on the shoulders of these RSS men. But our stand has always been that RSS and Jana Sangh—now BJP— are totally different bodies; their constitution, their office-bearers, their finances—all these are entirely different from ours.

Only when you go into this historical background can you properly appreciate the relationship between the two.

However, I do want our Swayamsevaks to join different political parties. The reason is, there is 'political casteism' today in our country. Just as there is social casteism, this political casteism is also creating many nasty problems. This barrier of 'casteism' can be broken if RSS people join all political parties. Then, they would be working in different parties, but in the morning or in the evening they would be playing and singing together in the Shakha and imbibing the faith that all are patriots having a common meeting-ground. So I say, let the other political parties welcome the Swayamsevaks without any reservations.

L.K. Advani's Concluding Statement at the National Executive Meeting of the BJP, 18 September 2005

The Bharatiya Janata Party is celebrating 2005 as the year of its Rajat Jayanti (Silver Jubilee). Since its inception in 1980, the BJP has been the beacon of hope for crores of Indians who cherish the ideals of cultural nationalism, national security, democracy and development.

The people of India know that, during the six years of the NDA government at the Centre between 1998 and 2004, we made an earnest effort to take our country forward on the basis of these ideals, an effort in which we succeeded substantially. The NDA government laid the foundation and set direction for India's recognition as an important geo-political power centre of the world.

On the political front, our greatest achievement in the past twenty-five years has been our emergence as one of the two principal poles in India's polity. We also proved that the BJP was capable of leading a stable non-Congress coalition that could not only impart dynamism to India's all-round development but also solve many problems that it inherited from the past.

In 1977, the Janata Party Government was formed with Sri Morarji Desai as Prime Minister. This government lasted for just over two years. In the Sixth General Elections to the Lok Sabha, the Janata Party had secured an impressive tally of 295 seats. But in the Seventh General Elections, its strength slumped steeply to just 31 seats! Smt. Gandhi and her Congress scored a resounding victory. The general talk in the country then became that there is no alternative to Ms Gandhi and there is no alternative to the Congress.

The first annual session of the BJP in December 1980 was presided over by Sri Atal Behari Vajpayee. The 50,000 delegates who had assembled at Bandra in Mumbai for the session felt thrilled when they heard Justice M.C. Chagla declare at the session that he saw in the BJP the only alternative and the only challenge to the authoritarian and corrupt Congress, and that he could clearly see Shri Vajpayee as India's future Prime Minister, a forecast we all have seen actually being realized.

In free India's political history, the launching of the BJP in 1980 has really proved a landmark event. The Indian polity has undergone a radical metamorphosis in these past twenty-five years.

Personally, I deem it a proud privilege that while the First Session was presided over by Shri A.B. Vajpayee, the Party's Silver Jubilee Session being held this December at Mumbai is going to be presided over by me. I had accepted this responsibility as Party President in October 2004 because Shri Venkaiahji had some personal problems. I have decided, however, that after the Mumbai session, I shall demit office, and the party's stewardship should be taken over by some other colleague.

From time to time, and depending on the issue at hand, the BJP leadership has had no hesitation in consulting the RSS functionaries. After such consultations, the Party takes its own independent decisions. Some of these decisions may differ—and have indeed differed—from the stated positions of the RSS and certain constituents of the 'Sangh Parivar'.

But lately an impression has gained ground that no political or organizational decision can be taken without the consent of the RSS functionaries. This perception, we hold, will do no good either to the Party or to the RSS. The RSS too must be concerned that such a perception will dwarf its greater mission of man-making and nation-building. Both the RSS and the BJP must consciously exert to dispel this impression.

We feel that the RSS should continue to play its role to strengthen the ethical, moral and idealistic moorings of the workers as well as functionaries of the BJP, as in the past, and this is in the larger interest of the nation.

The BJP greatly appreciates the continuing interaction we have been having with the RSS and with other organizations in the Sangh Parivar. Their views provide valuable inputs for our decision making process. But the BJP as a political party is accountable to the people, its performance being periodically put to test in elections. So in a democratic, multi-party polity, an ideologically driven party like the BJP has to function in a manner that enables it to keep its basic ideological stances intact and at the same time expand itself to reach the large sections of the people outside the layers of all ideology.

It is in protecting the ideological moorings of the BJP and in articulating it in an idiom and language that the people understand that great care is needed. For us in the BJP, Pandit Deendayal Upadhyaya has been a model ideologue. We have seen him interpret the party's ideological commitments, as for example in respect of 'Akhand Bharat', with remarkable clarity and conviction, and yet with flexibility and finesse.

The RSS is a nationalist organization whose contribution to character-building of millions and towards inculcating in them the spirit of patriotism, idealism and selfless service of the motherland has been incomparable. It is this organization that has inspired tens of thousands of public-spirited persons to serve the nation through the medium of politics. Those in the political field and those who are serving the society in other fields have to function with unity and trust like a family to ensure that the country secures its rightful place in the comity of nations.

11

Jammu & Kashmir

Jammu and Kashmir (J&K) has been a focal point for Hindu nationalism ever since Partition. For the ideologues of this movement, as for so many Indians, the state became the bone of contention *par excellence* with Pakistan. While Jinnah and the Muslim League considered that J&K, being a Muslim-majority state, should have been part of Pakistan and that Partition would remain unachieved so long as the whole of Kashmir remained under Indian rule, for the Hindu nationalists the state was inseparably a part of India.

They could have looked at this issue from a different perspective: they could have developed a purely ethno-religious approach and argued that India should have become more homogeneous via the transfer of Muslim-dominant districts of Kashmir to Pakistan. Interestingly, that was a proposition the Hindu Sabhaites made at the beginning of the twentieth century. Around 1910 Bhai Parmanand, an Arya Samaji who was to preside over the Hindu Mahasabha in the 1930s, suggested that 'the territory beyond Sind should be united with Afghanistan and the North West Frontier Province into a great Musalman kingdom. The Hindus of the region should come away, while at the same time Musulmans in the rest of India should go and settle in this territory.'[1]

Yet the official approach of the Hindu Mahasabha and the Sangh Parivar regarding Jammu & Kashmir has always been the opposite. Why? The answer is that the transfer of one more state to Pakistan would make this hostile country stronger and India weaker; such a

---

[1] Bhai Parmanand, *The Story of My Life* (Delhi: S. Chand, 1982), p. 36.

transfer would deprive many more refugees of their goods and posses-
sions, as had happened to the Hindus from West Punjab and Sindh
who were, in large numbers, within the Hindu nationalist fold; and
finally because international law seemed to be in favour of the Indian
position. Also, we have seen earlier that there is a strong element of
territoriality within the ideology of Hindu nationalism. As previously
noted in our discussion of Savarkar's ideas, the notion of Hindutva is
not only based on ethno-religious categories but also on the belief that
India occupies a sacred land whose frontiers matter as much as religion
and language. Hence the demand for Akhand Bharat (complete, undivided India), which emerged in the 1950s and which implied that
Partition should be undone to restore the natural extension of the
sacred land that is Bharat.

S.P. Mookerjee mobilized for the defence of J&K in a very determined way after Partition. Exemplifying the *bhadralok* elite of
Bengal—he was the son of Ashutosh Mookerjee, probably the most
outstanding and active Vice-Chancellor of Calcutta University—
Mookerjee had himself been appointed Vice-Chancellor of Calcutta
University at the very young age of 33, in 1934.[2] He worked in this
capacity till 1938, when he became deeply involved in politics. He
had been a member of the Hindu Mahasabha since 1937—the year
Savarkar was appointed at the helm of the party—but was returned
to the Bengal Legislative Council on a Congress ticket in 1939.[3] He
resigned when Congress decided to boycott the assembly but was re-
elected as an independent. More and more active in the Hindu Mahasabha, he became its president in 1943–5. Mookerjee then appeared
to be more moderate and open minded than most other Hindu
nationalist leaders, so much so that he was Minister for Industry and
Supply for three years (1947–50) in Nehru's first government, which
was intended to incorporate the broadest array of political positions.
Immediately afterwards he tried to liberalize the Hindu Mahasabha—
more so after the assassination of the Mahatma, which had radically

[2] L. Chatterjee and S.P. Mookerjee, *Representative Indians* (Calcutta, The
Popular Agency, 1936), pp. 97–145.
[3] On his career during the late 1930s and early 1940s, see S.P. Mookerjee,
Leaves from a Diary (Calcutta: Oxford University Press, 1993).

tarnished the image of Hindu nationalism.[4] Mookerjee argued in favour of opening up the party to non-Hindus, but the old guard—including Moonje—successfully resisted this move. Mookerjee resigned from the Hindu Mahasabha in November 1948 and considered launching a new party. He approached RSS leaders in 1949 and succeeded in setting up the Bharatiya Jana Sangh just before the first general elections in 1951. Two years later, he took part in a week-long demonstration against 'Kashmir separatism', dying mysteriously in detention after illegally entering the state of Jammu & Kashmir.[5]

Extract of a Speech by Shyama Prasad Mookerjee, in the Lok Sabha, on 7 August 1952

I agree with the Prime Minister that the matter of Kashmir is a highly complicated one and each one of us, whatever may be his point of view, must approach this problem from a constructive standpoint. I cannot share the view that we are creating a new heaven and a new earth by accepting the scheme which has been placed before the House on the motion of the Prime Minister. The question can be divided into two parts. One relates to the international complications arising out of Kashmir and the other relates to the arrangements that have to be made between Kashmir and ourselves regarding the future Constitution of Kashmir.

It has been said that I was a party when the decision was taken to refer the Kashmir issue to the UNO . . . That is an obvious fact. I have no right and I do not wish to disclose the extraordinary circumstances under which that decision was taken and the great expectations which the Government of India had on that occasion, but it is a matter of common knowledge that we have not got fair treatment from the United Nations which we had expected. We did not go to the UNO with regard to the question of accession, because accession then was

[4] B. Graham, 'Syama Prasad Mookerjee and the Communal Alternative', in D.A. Low, ed., *Soundings in Modern South Asian History* (Berkeley: University of California Press, 1968), pp. 334–74.

[5] B. Madhok, *Portrait of a Martyr: Biography of Dr Shyama Prasad Mookerji* (Bombay: Jaico Publishing House, 1969).

an established fact. We went there for the purpose of getting a quick decision from the UNO regarding the raids which were then taking place by persons behind whom there was the Pakistan Government. The raiders merely acted on behalf of somebody else . . . Somehow, we should withdraw ourselves, so far as consideration of the Kashmir case is concerned, from the UNO. We can tell them respectfully that we have had enough of the UNO and let us now consider and try to settle the matter through our own efforts. I am not suggesting that India should withdraw from the UNO. The only matter regarding which the dispute still continues is about the one-third territory of Kashmir which is in the occupation of the enemy. The Prime Minister said today that portion is there. It is a matter for national humiliation. *We say that Kashmir is a part of India. It is so. So, a part of India is today in the occupation of the enemy and we are peace-lovers, no doubt. But peace-lovers to what extent?—that we will even allow a portion of our territory to be occupied by the enemy?* Of course the Prime Minister said: thus far and no further. If the raiders enter into any part of Kashmir, he held out a threat of war not in relation to Pakistan and Kashmir, but war on a bigger scale between India and Pakistan. Is there any possibility of our getting back this territory? We shall not get it through the efforts of the United Nations: we shall not get it through peaceful methods, by negotiations with Pakistan. That means we lose it, unless we use force and the Prime Minister is unwilling to do so. Let us face facts—are we prepared to lose it? It has been said that there is some provision in the Constitution, that we are bound by the pledges which have been given. Pledges? Undoubtedly, so many pledges we have given. We gave a pledge to Hyderabad. Did we not say that there would be a Constituent Assembly for Hyderabad. It was followed by another pledge that the future of Hyderabad would be decided by the Legislative Assembly of Hyderabad. But is not Hyderabad already a part of the Indian Union? We gave pledges also to those princes whom we are liquidating in different forms today. If we talk of pledges we have given pledges on many other occasions. We gave pledges to the minorities in East Bengal. That was given after the attainment of independence. *The Prime Minister said the other day that even if Kashmir had got acceded to India, when Kashmir was attacked by the raiders on humanitarian grounds the Indian army could have marched to Kashmir*

*and protected the distressed and oppressed. I felt proud. But if I make a
similar statement, or even a similar suggestion for the purpose of saving the
lives and honour of nine million of our fellow brethren and sisters—
through whose sacrifices to some extent at least freedom has been achieved—
I am a communalist, I am a reactionary, I am a war-mongar* [sic]!

Pledges? Undoubtedly pledges have been given. I am also anxious
that pledges should be respected and honoured. What was the nature
of the pledges? We did not give any new pledge to Kashmir. Let us be
clear about it.

What was the set-up we accepted when the British withdrew from
India? There was the Indian India divided into India and Pakistan and
there was, if I may call it, the Princely India. Every one of those five
hundred rulers got theoretical independence and they need have
acceded to India only with relation to three subjects. So far as the rest
was concerned it was purely voluntary. That was the pattern which we
accepted from the British Government. So far as the 498 states were
concerned, they came to India, acceded to India on the 14th August
1947 in relation to three subjects only, but still it was accession, full
accession. Later on, they all came in in relation to all these subjects and
were gradually absorbed in the Constitution of India that we have passed. Supposing some sort of fulfilment of the pledge that we are thinking
of so literally in relation to Kashmir was demanded by these states,
would we have agreed to give that? We would not have because that
would have destroyed India. But there was a different approach to the
solution of those problems.

They were made to feel that in the interest of India, in their interest,
in the interest of mutual progress, they will have to accept this Constitution that we are preparing and the Constitution made elaborate
provisions for nationally absorbing them into its fabric. No coercion;
no compulsion. They were made to feel that they could get what they
wanted from this Constitution.

May I ask—was not Sheikh Abdullah party to this Constitution?
He was a Member of the Constituent Assembly; but he is asking for
special treatment. Did he not agree to accept this Constitution in
relation to the rest of India, including 497 states. It is good enough for
all of them, why should it not be good enough for him in Kashmir? We
are referred to the provision in the Constitution. The Member from

Bihar . . . said there was going to be compulsion; that we are going to hold a pistol at the head of Jammu & Kashmir saying that they must accept our terms. I have said nothing of the kind. How can we say that? What is the provision we have made in the Constitution? Article 373—read it and read the speech of Shri Gopalswami Ayyangar when he moved the adoption of that extraordinary provision. What was the position then? All the other states had come into the picture. Kashmir could not because of special reasons. They were: firstly the matter was in the hands of the Security Council; secondly, there was war; thirdly, a portion of Kashmir territory was in the hands of the enemy and lastly an assurance had been given to Kashmir that Constituent Assembly would be allowed to be formed and the wishes of the people of Kashmir ascertained through a plebiscite. Those were the factors that had yet to be fulfilled and that was why a permanent decision could not be taken. It was a temporary provision.

He said categorically that he and also the Kashmir Government hoped that Jammu & Kashmir would accede to India just as any other state has done and accept the provision of the Constitution. It is not a question of compulsion on our part. The Constitution of India does not say that whatever the Constituent Assembly of Jammu & Kashmir would ask for India would give. That is not the provision. The provision is—agreement, consent. Certain proposals have been made today. Some of us do not like them. What are we to do? If we talk we are reactionaries, we are communalists, we are enemies. If we keep quiet and if a catastrophe comes after a year, then you were a party to it, you kept quiet—therefore, you are stopped from saying anything. I am most anxious, as anxious as anybody else that we should have an honourable, peaceful settlement, with Kashmir.

I realise the great experiment which is being made on the soil of Kashmir. Partition did not help anybody. I come from an area where sufferings are continuous, they are going on. We feel every day, every hour, the tragic effects of partition, the tragic possibilities of approaching this national problem from a narrow, communal and sectarian point of view. Why did we not utter a single word against the policy of Sheikh Abdullah so long? I could have spoken. I came out of this Government two and a half years ago. On the other hand, I supported, wherever I spoke publicly the policy of the Kashmir Government. I said that this was a great experiment which was going on and we have to keep quiet and see that the experiment is made a success. We must be able to show that India is not only in theory, but also in fact, *a country where Hindus, Muslims, Christians and everyone will be able to live without fear and with equality of rights.* That is the Constitution that we have framed and which we propose to apply rigorously and scrupulously. There may be some demands to the contrary here and there. But do not regard that, whenever an attack is made on certain matters of policy, some narrow, sectarian, communal motive is prompting us. Rather it is the fear that history may repeat itself. It is the fear that what you are going to do may lead to the 'Balkanisation' of India, may lead to the strengthening of the hands of those who do not want to see a strong United India, may lead to the strengthening of those who do not believe that India is a nation but is a combination of separate nationalities. That is the danger.

Now, what is it that Sheikh Abdullah has asked for? He has asked for certain changes to be made in the Constitution. Let us proceed coolly, cautiously, without any heat or excitement. Let us examine each of them and ask him and ask ourselves: if we make an allowance in respect of these matters do we hurt India, do we strengthen Kashmir? That will be my approach. I shall not say anything blindly because it transgresses some provisions of this book, the Constitution of India. I would not do so. I would have liked the Prime Minister to have sent for some of us in the Operation when Sheikh Abdullah was here. He faces us today with his decisions. I do not like these public discussions because I know their repercussions may not be desirable in some quarters. He might not have accepted our suggestions, but I would have liked to have met him—those of us who differ from the Prime Minister's attitude on this question. I met him at a private meeting and we had a full and frank discussion. But we would have liked to have met Sheikh Abdullah and others in a friendly way and explained our point of view to them. *We want to come to an agreement, an agreement which will make it possible for India to retain her unity and Kashmir to retain her separate existence from Pakistan and be merged with India.*

Since when did the trouble start? Let us look at it dispassionately. Since Sheikh Abdullah's return from Paris some time ago statements started to be made by him which disturbed us. Even then we did not speak out. His first statement he made in an interview which he gave when he was abroad about his vision of an independent Kashmir. And then when he came he amplified it then again retracted from it and gave an explanation, and then the speeches which he has made during the last few months were of a disturbing character. If he feels that his safety lies in remaining out of India, well, let him say so; we will be sorry for it, but it may become inevitable. But if he feels honestly otherwise, as I have always hoped and wished, then certainly it is for him also to explain why he wants these alternations to be made. . . . Sheikh Abdullah spoke in the Constituent Assembly of Kashmir, about three or four months ago, words which have not been withdrawn, but words which created a good deal of misgivings in the minds of all Indian [sic] irrespective of party affiliations. I do not know whether the Prime Minister saw this: 'We are a hundred per cent sovereign body. No country can put spokes in the wheel of our progress. Neither the Indian Parliament nor any other Parliament outside the state has any jurisdiction over our state.' It is an ominous statement. I shall make an offer to the Prime Minister and to Sheikh Abdullah. I shall give my full, whole hearted support to the scheme as in [sic] interim measure . . . The Prime Minister said today that nothing is final. It cannot be final, because things have to be discussed in their various details. But even then, I am prepared to give my support. Let two conditions be fulfilled.

Let Sheikh Abdullah declare that he accepts the Sovereignty of this Parliament. There cannot be two Sovereign Parliaments in India. You talk of Kashmir being a part of India, and Sheikh Abdullah talks of a Sovereign Parliament for Kashmir. It is inconsistent. It is contradictory. This Parliament does not mean a few of us here who are opposing this. This Parliament includes a majority of people who will not be swayed by any small considerations. And why should he be afraid of accepting the Sovereignty of this Parliament of Free India?

Secondly, it is not a matter of changing the provisions of the Constitution by the President's order. Let us look at some of the changes which are being sought for. We are supporters of the Maharaja! That is what is said against us. I have never met the Maharaja. I do not know him personally. We are not supporters of this Maharaja, or of any Maharaja as such. But the Maharaja is there not by his own free will. The Parliament of India, the Constitution has made him what he is, namely, the constitutional head of Jammu & Kashmir. And what is the irony? At present Sheikh Abdullah's Government is responsible to this Maharaja according to the Constitution, responsible to one who is being described as a wretched fellow who has to be turned out lock, stock and barrel. The Maharaja is there as a constitutional head. If you feel that this should be taken out, change your Constitution. Say that there will be no hereditary Rajpramukhs. It is a matter worthy of consideration. Let us consider it. But see the way in which it has been put: a Hindu Maharaja is being removed. That is one of the war cries in Pakistan. But who finished the royal powers of Hindu Maharajas? Not Sheikh Abdullah, but the Constitution of Free India. We did it. We said that no ruler would have any extraordinary powers, that he will be just head of the government which may be technically responsible to him but later on responsible to an elected legislature. But now great credit is being taken that a unique performance is being done in Kashmir. In every speech of his he gave it: the Maharaja, the Dogra *raj* is being finished. Is that a propaganda? Is that necessary? You are flogging a dead horse. It is finished. What is the use of saying it?

What about the elected Governor? . . . I have got here the proceedings of the Constituent Assembly. The Prime Minister will remember that in our own Constitution we at first made a provision for an elected Governor, and then later on Sardar Patel and the Prime Minister and others felt that in the democratic set-up that we contemplated an elected Governor had no place. Read the speech. It was stated that the Governor will be there to act as the representative of the President and if the Governor is elected by the people or the legislature the Chief Minister also will be elected: as such there is every likelihood of a clash, then again, the Governor will be a partyman. And the Prime Minister pointed out all these considerations and claimed that there was very special reason why in order to retain the unity of India and contact between the Centre and all the States the Governor should be nominated by the President. You just ignore these basic points because Sheikh Abdullah says: 'I want an elected head now.' Why can you not tell him and others what you have done in the Constitution, that originally we provided for an elected Governor but after a good deal of thought we did away with that? Even then I say if today in your wisdom you feel that an elected head is a necessity and it will help you, consider it. Bring it up as a specific proposal. Let us discuss the pros and cons of it. But suddenly my friend *Mr Hiren Mukherjee says: people are clamouring for an elected head. People are clamouring for an elected head everywhere. Are you going to have elected heads everywhere? In fact, as things are happening we may abolish Governors altogether. Governorships are often reserved for various classes of persons—disappointed, defeated, rejected, unwanted Ministers and so forth. We need not have this class at all. Or, if you want to have them, have them. I am not particularly interested. But this is a change for which no justification is given.*

And then the flag. The flag has a significance. It will not do for the Prime Minister to say that it is a matter of sentiment. It was announced in the papers three days ago that the Indian flag will fly only on two ceremonial occasions and otherwise the state flag alone will fly there. If you feel that the unity and integrity of India are not affected and it will not lead to fissiparous tendencies being generated, accept it and do it for all. But why do it as a matter of surrender to Sheikh Abdullah's demand?

He wanted to call himself the Prime Minister. That is how he first started. Some of us did not like it. We know one Prime Minister of India including Kashmir, that is the Prime Minister who is sitting here. How can you have two Prime Ministers, one Prime Minister in Delhi and another Prime Minister in Srinagar who will not call himself the Chief Minister, but a Prime Minister. At first I thought it was a small matter and we should not look at it but see how the process is developing—some sort of special treatment at every step and he must be treated in a very different way. Look at the citizenship rights and fundamental rights. What is it that we are doing? Has the House considered? Has the House discussed the pros and cons of the recommendations which have been made. You are changing without giving much thought to the provisions of the Constitution regarding citizenship. It was said that rich people are rushing to Kashmir and purchasing property. As the Prime Minister mentioned in his statement, in article 19(5) there is a provision.

We discussed this article threadbare when we framed the Constitution. There were attempts made by various provinces and they wanted to have some special protection against unauthorized purchases of land on a large scale. What is it that we have said? We have said that any state legislature may pass a law, imposing reasonable restrictions regarding acquisition of property or movement from one part to another in the public interest or in the interest of Scheduled Castes and Scheduled Tribes. If Sheikh Abdullah feels that in Kashmir some special restriction should be done, the clause is there. I would like to ask the Prime Minister categorically about this. He has not mentioned it. He has skipped over it. Is it intended that the restrictions which the Kashmir Assembly will impose will be in accordance with this exception or is it proposed to give it something more? There are four classes of citizens. I have got the details, but I have not the time to go through them. But those were done in the time of the much cursed Maharaja. Are they to be maintained or are they going to abolish the four different categories of citizenship? I am reminded of a story which was written by Lord Curzon in a book. A distinguished nobleman from England went to the court of Shah of Persia 50 or 60 years ago accompanied by his wife. Both of them were presented and the Shah was a bit inattentive and the secretary asked: 'What should be the honour done to the lady?' There were three different categories of Order of Chastity and the award was made 'Order of Chastity—class three'. That is how the order came out and then it was realized that something had been done which was of a staggering character, and of course amends were made after the damage was done. *Four classes of citizenship in Jammu & Kashmir—what for? They should be abolished. There should be only one class of citizenship. Would Indians take all your property? It was not suggested that Indians should go and purchase property as they liked. Supposing some Indian comes and purchases some property, you may have legislative measures. We have accepted it. What is the fear? We have a Kashmiri Prime Minister of India. We have a Kashmiri Home Minister of India. We are happy in India. We do not mind it. We welcome them. What is the fear? Is it feared that Indians will go and invade Kashmir and one of them will become the Chief Minister of Jammu & Kashmir?* We are not going to raid Jammu & Kashmir. I have never visited this beautiful part. I would like to go and stay there for some time. I have not got the money to purchase a house. In any case, I would like to go there. This is what you have in regard to fundamental rights. You are having new changes there which are very difficult to justify. The Prime Minister mentioned 2 or 3 things—scholarship and services etc. What is this

'etc.'? And why Services? In services, do you want to make a difference
between one citizen and another. Even there, as you know, in our
Constitution, Parliament and Parliament alone has the right to make
special provision regarding entrance to services for those who have to
be protected. Now there are similar demands made in the South. I
have been going through their demands during the last few weeks.
They also feel perturbed by the strict operation of some of these provisions. When you throw open the doors to them, they also will want
similar protection.

There is another thing to which Prime Minister has not referred. I
was really amazed to find how a special provision could be made. As
you know two lakhs of people have gone away to Pakistan. There is a
provision that a special law will be incorporated to get these people
back to Kashmir. War is still going on. On the one hand Fundamental
Rights regarding civil liberty are proposed to be made more strict, and
on the other, you are going to throw open the door and allow Pakistanis
to go to Kashmir; for this there is to be a special law and there is a
special agreement. Why this anxiety on the part of Sheikh Abdullah to
make a special provision for getting back those who ran away to Pakistan
and who are not prepared to come. Is there any point in it? How will
it affect security? . . . Those who have been killed cannot go back.
Those who are alive can come back tomorrow if they honestly believe
in India and if they really want to live in Jammu. They must be tested.
Let them come back. No special provision is needed for it. So far as
Jammu is concerned, as you know, it was a most tragic state. It was
done by both sides. There were Muslims who were bitter and there
were Hindus who were bitter. That was a dark period when many
parts of India were like that, but today, what is the position? You have
allowed how many thousands. I forget the number. They have come
away from Jammu & Kashmir and are a burden on India. Why should
not there be a special provision here in the agreement that promptly
[*sic*] they will be taken back to Jammu & Kashmir? There are several
thousand of them who have come.

Why are they not going back. I do not know how many pandits
have come away from Kashmir. They also must go back to Kashmir.
So far as the other portion is concerned, that also is a serious matter.

In the one-third portion of Jammu & Kashmir which is now under Pakistani occupation, nearly 1 lakh of Hindus and Sikhs have come and taken shelter, within the Kashmiri territory. What will happen to them? They will have to be taken care of. You are thinking of those who have become Pakistanis for the time being. You will reconvert them and reconfer on them the status of Kashmiri citizens but those unfortunate beings who today have taken shelter, how will they be given accommodation? Is there land enough for them? These are matters which had not received any attention. As regards the emergency provision, it is an amazing stand. If there is an emergency on account of internal disturbance, the President of India will not have the last say. Why this fear of the President of India? Can you contemplate a more gratuitous insult to the President of India? Here the Kashmir Government must conform to the Constitution. Why should they request if there is an internal disturbance which is the creation of their misdeeds? Why should they request you if, for instance they are in league with others from the upper side, China or Russia, through our other friends? Why should they come and request you for your interference? I would expect the Prime Minister to tell whether the other emergency provisions apply or not. As you know, there are two other very important emergency provisions in the Constitution. Article 354 relates to application of provisions relating to distribution of revenues while a Proclamation of Emergency is in operation and the other article is 356 relating to provisions in case of failure of Constitutional machinery in states. Has Sheikh Abdullah accepted the application of article 356 or has he accepted the more important provision contained in article 360—provisions as to financial emergency. Has he accepted that provision? The Prime Minister does not make any reference to it. The Supreme Court's jurisdiction also has not yet been accepted.

I shall conclude by making this constructive suggestion. These comments which I made, naturally I had to make without commenting in detail on the reactions of Sheikh Abdullah. He wrote to me and said that he would like to meet me when he was in Delhi last time. I was not here on that day. So I could not meet him. I sent him a friendly reply. Perhaps I would meet him some time. It is not a question of his meeting me or I meeting him. I submit that we must proceed according to certain standards. First of all there is no question of the President by virtue of his power to make orders altering the provisions of the Constitution in material respects.

If the Prime Minister feels that a case has been made out for re-examination of certain important provisions, for instance land, if you feel that land should be taken without payment of compensation, provide for it in the Constitution. You consider all these items and make your provisions so elastic that you can apply them either to the whole of India or you can apply them to only such parts where this Parliament of India will feel that such special treatment is necessary. Proceed in accordance with a constitutional manner, not just play with the Constitution. It is a sacred document, and it is a document on which much labour and much thought were bestowed. If you feel some changes are necessary in order to take into consideration the new set-up that is slowly developing in India, whether in Kashmir or other parts of India, by all means let the people of the country have a chance to express their opinion.

Lastly a charge was levelled that some of us have advocated separate consideration of Jammu and Ladakh. I would assure you and the House that I do not want that Jammu & Kashmir should be partitioned. I know the horrors of partition. I know the results which may ensure [sic] if partition comes. But the responsibility for preventing partition will rest on those who are today the masters of Jammu & Kashmir and are not prepared to adopt the Constitution of India. What is the crime if today the people of Jammu claim that they should be treated separately, in the sense that they should be allowed to join fully with India—mark it, it is not a question of running away from India—if they say that they would like to accept in toto the Constitution of free India, is there any crime that they then commit? I am not suggesting that you partition Jammu & Kashmir. I am not suggesting that you send Kashmir or Kashmir Valley out of India. And it is not for me or for us sitting in this House to decide this matter. As the Prime Minister pointed out very rightly, it is the people of that territory who will have to decide. Now suppose the people of Jammu and Ladakh feel that either it should be full accession in relation to the whole of Jammu & Kashmir, or if that is not acceptable to Sheikh Abdullah, then, at least these two Provinces, the two separate entities could be justified historically or otherwise, that they should be allowed to join with India. Let

Kashmir continue in any way that it likes, even with more autonomy, with less possibility of interference by India; that is a possibility which we cannot rule out. I hope that this question will be considered in its full possible implications.

Preface to *BJP on Kashmir*[6]

In Jammu & Kashmir the country faces to-day the gravest ever threat to the national unity and integrity. It is a dismal tale of criminal apathy, negligence and credulity.

If we analyse briefly the reasons that have brought Jammu & Kashmir to its present pass, we shall find New Delhi's benign neglect and policy bankruptcy all converging on their ostrich like attitude towards the hard realities of the situation, being responsible for it. It is the cumulative result of Government of India's mishandling of the Kashmir issue from the very outset in 1947.

Within weeks of the Instrument of Accession being signed on 26 October 1947, Dr Ram Manohar Lohia, then a member of the All India Congress Committee, on his return from Srinagar, sent a note to the Prime Minister Shri Jawahar Lal Nehru on 2 December 1947. He wrote: 'Undoubtedly, the most significant factor in the battle of Kashmir is Sheikh Abdullah. I am, therefore, notifying you of my talks with him. Sheikh Abdullah suggested that perhaps the best way out would be for India and Pakistan to achieve an understanding on Kashmir's neutrality and independence. Sheikh's Communist assistant encouraged him in this idea. I am amazed.' Not only did his warning remain unheeded, but also the despatches sent by Shri G.C. Bail of the Intelligence Bureau and Kanwar Sir Dalip Singh, the Agent General of India in the state, reporting the designs and the misdoings of Sheikh Abdullah and his Administration failed to evince any interest from the Government of India. The seeds of alienation and separatism were sown right then.

The people of Jammu and Ladakh never had any misunderstanding about the Sheikh's intentions. People from both regions passed resolutions, sent memoranda and delegations to impress upon New Delhi as to what was happening in the state. They cried themselves hoarse to

[6] Preface to The Study Committee on Kashmir Affairs, *BJP on Kashmir* (New Delhi: BJP Publications, 1995).

draw Government of India's attention to the 'Anti India' slant of the policies of the state leaders and the J&K Government. But there was none to help them although the then Congress President Shri Pattabhi Sitaramaiah, the Congress General Secretary Shri Acharya Kripalani and the Home Minister Sardar Patel agreed and sympathized with them in private. They told these delegations in no uncertain terms that the J&K State was Pt Nehru's personal domain where they could not intrude.

Having failed to convince the Government of India about the designs of Sheikh Abdullah and his team, the people of Jammu decided to take their country-men into confidence. A six month long agitation started by the Jammu Praja Parishad and led by Pandit Prem Nath Dogra for the first time brought out in public the existing and other potential dangers of the policies of the Government of India and the designs of the Sheikh. The common man for the first time came to know that an Indian needed a permit to visit Jammu & Kashmir, an integral part of India and that he had to pay custom-duty on goods being taken from 'India' to that state. It was news for them to know that Indian Tricolour was not permitted to be flown on the State Government Offices and buildings. Having personally convinced himself of the genuineness of the issues raised by the Praja Parishad and Pandit Prem Nath Dogra, Dr Syama Prasad Mookerjee, who by that time had formed the Bharatiya Jana Sangh, took up and pleaded their cause in and outside Parliament. He toured the country extensively and told people about the conditions prevailing in the J&K State and the wrong policies being pursued by the Government of India. In its Kanpur Session the Jana Sangh resolved formally to support the Praja Parishad agitation aimed at forcing the state and the Central Governments to shed their policies which were undermining the unity and integrity of the country. The country vibrated with the slogan 'Ek Desh Mein Do Nishan, Do Vidhan, Do Pradhan—Nahin Chalenge, Nahin Chalenge'. For the first time people came to know about the duplicity of Sheikh Abdullah and became apprehensive about his designs and of his coterie. Serious doubts started arising in the people's minds about the correctness of the policies being pursued hitherto by Pt Nehru and his Government as regards Kashmir.

In early 1952, Sheikh Abdullah's game plan was clearly exposed when in the J&K Constituent Assembly he said: 'We are a hundred per cent sovereign body. No country can put spokes in the wheel of our progress. Neither the Indian Parliament nor any other Parliament outside the state has any jurisdiction over our state'. Instead of bridling the Sheikh, Pandit Nehru defended him in and outside Parliament and projected him as a great patriot. It was Dr Syama Prasad Mookerjee who on 7-8-1952 cornered the Prime Minister in Parliament by asking him, pointedly, if the Sheikh was prepared to accept the supremacy of the Indian Parliament. Dr Mookerjee said: 'Let Sheikh Abdullah declare that he accepts the sovereignty of this Parliament. There cannot be two Sovereign Parliaments in India.'

Dr Mookerjee was prepared to support Sheikh Abdullah provided he agreed to accept the sovereignty of the Indian Parliament. Pt Nehru had no answer.

Credit goes to the Praja Parishad and the martyrdom of Dr Mookerjee that the Indian tricolour flies high today on the Government Offices and buildings in the J&K State, the Governor and not the Sadr-e-Riyasat is the Head of the state, the obnoxious permit system and the levying of custom-duty are abolished. Not many in the country know that this could be possible only after thousands courted arrest, from Jammu & Kashmir and from all states of India, during the Praja Parishad agitation and 15 Praja Parishad workers were shot dead while hoisting the Indian tricolour on the State Government Offices in Jammu and Kashmir. It was only after that the jurisdiction of the Supreme Court, the Planning Commission, the Finance Commission, the Election Commissioner, the Census Commissioner and the Comptroller and Auditor General of India had been extended to the state. Alienation of the Valley's population, thus, is not a recent development. It is the sad and inevitable outcome of Government of India's inclination despite all talk of opposition to the two-nation theory to treat the state as a Special State only because it is a Muslim majority state. Indeed New Delhi's handling of Kashmir is tantamount to a de-facto recognition of the two-nation theory. It is this perverse attitude that is responsible for the present mess in the J&K State.

The seeds of this alienation were sown the very day Article 370 was adopted and incorporated in the Indian Constitution. Shri Gopalaswamy Ayyanger, who moved this Article, was not oblivious of its mischief potential. The title of this Article reads: 'Temporary provisions with respect to the State of Jammu & Kashmir'.

Gopalaswamy Ayyanger, while placing Article 430 before the Indian Constituent Assembly, had expressed the hope on behalf of 'everybody here that, in due course, even Jammu & Kashmir will become ripe for the same sort of integration as has taken place in case of the other states.'

It is an irony that the present day so-called progressives, intellectuals and the 'secular' parties swear that this Article is sacrosanct and cannot be touched or changed.

It is significant that efforts in various forums and guises are on putting the clock back and on restoration of pre-1953 position.

There is no doubt that Pakistan has been a major contributor towards the subversion of peace and order in J&K, and naturally tries to fish in troubled waters, but the follies of the Government of India and its acts of omission and commission, are no less responsible for the present impasse in the state. Right since 1947 New Delhi has been committing egregious blunder after blunder which have resulted in keeping the Valley out of the Indian mainstream. No serious attempt has been made for the emotional integration of the people of the state with the rest of the country. On the contrary Article 370 has acted as a big psychological barrier apart from creating vested interests who flourish economically and politically in such an environmental ambivalence.

At the same time the separatist forces and Sheikh's political goons were allowed to act freely and sow the seeds of discontent and alienation. Rampant corruption, gross mal-administration, nepotism, favouritism and rigged elections became handy tools in their hands. Article 370 provided an effective protective cover on the misdeeds of anti-national elements as well as on the masterly inactivity of the Government of India, since Nehru's time.

For the last over four decades, hundreds of 'Madarsas', 'Maktabs', high schools and colleges run by various theological organizations and the Jamat-i-Islami have been systematically sowing in the minds of the young generations of the Valley the seeds of religious fundamentalism and separatism making the alienation total. Pakistan has naturally taken full advantage of this situation.

To realise its ambition of seizing Kashmir, Pakistan has waged three wars with India. In the first war it occupied one third of Jammu & Kashmir State. In the second and third wars it was trounced on the battle-field. For the last few years it has been doggedly pursuing its un-fulfilled ambition by financing, arming and training terrorists in J&K State and creating pockets of subversion. Recently a new dimension has been added to this proxy war, waged by Pakistan. Mercenary mili-tants from various Muslim countries, after the withdrawal of Soviet Army from Afghanistan, have joined this fray.

No doubt, Kashmir has witnessed large scale militancy, terrorism and subversion, particularly during the last five years. But the ominous portents had been clearly visible for quite some time. The State Gov-ernment was deliberately neglectful of the situation. The Government of India remained as usual blind, deaf and dumb.

It was on 15 August 1983 that a major bomb explosion rocked Sri-nagar. In quick succession during the same year there were series of explosions in the Valley. It was in this year that Kapil Dev and his team were subjected to the worst kind of humiliation. Ever since the police and the civil services have been systematically infiltrated by the terrorists and their henchmen. The State Government was rendered politically impotent and administratively helpless.

India's political leadership barring BJP's has always chosen to turn a blind eye to all these serious developments. The reports sent by the intelligence agencies about the activities of the separatists and the connivance of the State Administration were put on the shelf. The despatches and reports in the national newspapers about the gravity of the situation and looming dangers were ignored. Even the large scale destruction of the temples, attacks on the Hindus houses and looting of their properties in 1986 failed to arouse the authorities from their slumber. The despatches sent by the then Governor Shri Jagmohan in early 1988 reporting the fast deteriorating situation and requesting immediate action failed to evoke any significant response from the Union Government.

The Bharatiya Janata Party has all along been warning the Govern-ment of India about the dangerous conditions in the Valley. It had to pay a very heavy price for its forthrightness and frankness. With the murder of Shri Tika Lal Taploo, Vice-President of the J&K State BJP on 14 September 1989, a new phase started in the Valley. Selective killings of the prominent Hindus, abduction and rape of their women-folk, torching of their properties and threats issued to them on the loudspeakers and through media made over fifty thousand families flee from there. They have been made refugees in their own country. But even their sad plight did not elicit any meaningful sympathy or support of either the secularists or the Government agencies. The apathy in political echelons as well as the Government and inertia in administration continue unabated.

There must not remain any ambiguity, as is being deliberately done through all kinds of disinformation and insinuation about the motivation behind the present day terrorism and militancy in Jammu & Kashmir. To believe that some frustrated and disgruntled youth have taken to gun because they are jobless and unemployed, will just be to indulge in an exercise of self-deception. Militancy cannot be curbed and contained unless the moles in the Civil and the Police Services are weeded out. It is unfortunate that under the garb of providing employment to the unemployed known militants are being inducted into these services even to-day. The terrorist violence in Jammu & Kashmir is committed to the Islamization of the state. The terrorist organisations never made any secret of this and have given openly and frequently ample expression to their ideological stand to establish Nizam-e-Mustafa in the state. Ethnic extermination and cleansing the state of the Non Believers, therefore, has become the natural consequence of that fanatical commitment. The strategies they adopted to this end included:

(a) Selective killings of Hindu leaders to create an atmosphere of terror;

(b) Deportation for force, fear of death, conversion and criminal assault on women;

(c) Destruction of Hindu places of Worship; and

(d) Burning down and forcible occupation of the houses, shops and business establishments of the Hindus.

Operation TOPAC, as envisaged by Pakistan, is being implemented in Jammu & Kashmir. Having thrown out the Hindus from the Valley the Operation is on to force the Hindus to flee from the Doda District of Jammu region. Actually this process of squeezing out Hindus from the Valley started much early, immediately after Sheikh Abdullah took over the State Administration. Taking over their lands and denial to them of jobs in the State Government services and admission to the professional colleges, irrespective of their better merit forced the Hindus to move out of the state and find for themselves avenues of livelihood elsewhere. They were discriminated against not only in the allotment of quotas, permits, licences and loans, but even ordinary facilities, making it difficult for them to stay there. Forcible occupation of temple properties, changing names of hundreds of villages and towns, showing their Hindu lineage and communalising the entire State Government machinery created a psychological atmosphere where Hindus found it difficult to breathe freely and ultimately moved out. The happenings in February 1986 when hundreds of Hindu houses were looted were an indicator of how frightful the situation was. It is tragic that the so-called secular press should try to put a lid on these unfortunate happenings.

In 1947 the population of the Hindus in the Valley was 15 per cent, it came down to 5 per cent in 1981 and was reduced further to 0.1 per cent in 1991. The continued discrimination and policy of squeezing them out brought the percentage of Hindu Government employees in the Valley to less than 4 per cent in 1989. During the last five years a large number of them—over four thousand—too, have retired while not one new incumbent has been inducted. Obviously within a span of the next few years there will not be a single Hindu employee in State Services in the Valley.

The situation in the Jammu region is not very different. It is an undisputed fact that the percentage of the Hindu employees in the state has been declining gradually during the last over four decades.

The country does not know fully as to what has been really happening in the Valley during the last five years, it has not been projected objectively and adequately.

The Government of India has failed badly in taking the nation into confidence and come out with the chilling facts of brutality and dastardly atrocities the terrorists perpetrated on the innocent citizens. Rather, efforts have been made to hide the truth or bring out only distorted versions, at times based on half truths or untruths. Surprisingly, our friends from the Human Rights Organisation have been in the forefront in spreading such palpable falsehoods. It is an irony that these activists, who have been very vocal about the protection of the Human Rights of the terrorists, day in and day out, denounced the security forces for violating these rights, initially did not utter a word of condemnation of the terrorists for their acts of murder, rape and torture or express a word of sympathy for the victims of their brutality. Only severe public censure subsequently could bring them to their senses and they relented to some extent.

Truth must come out and the nation must be told that the killings in Jammu & Kashmir were brought about by such inhuman practices as:

(a) Strangulation by steel wire;

(b) Hanging;

(c) Branding with red hot irons;

(d) Burning alive;

(e) Lynching;

(f) Gouging of eyes before assassination;

(g) Slicing;

(h) Dismemberment of bodies;

(i) Drowning alive; and

(j) Slaughter.

Rape is the worst form of torture that terrorist victims faced. Who will cry for Smt Girja and others who met this fate? Such abominable things happened and the Government of India slept.

An organised plan to oust the Hindus from the Valley by selectively killing the Hindu leaders, started with the murder of Shri Tika Lal Taploo, Vice-President of the J&K unit of the Bharatiya Janata Party on 14 September 1989. Next to be killed were Pt Neel Kanth Ganjoo, Pt Prem Nath Bhat, Pt Lassa Kaul, Shri Sarva Nand Premi and many others.

Similarly in Doda District of Jammu region, Shri Santosh Thakur, General Secretary of the Distt, unit of the BJP was the first to be shot dead on 13 February 1992. The spate of selective killings in the district goes unabated. Prominent among the murdered are Shri Satish Bhandari, Shri Swami Raj Kattal, Shri Ruchir Kumar, Shri Praveen Kumar. What about their families? What about the conscience and sensitivity of those crying hoarse about Human Rights in J&K?

The militancy was allowed to spread and escalate in the Jammu region in spite of the warning from time to time of the Bharatiya Janata Party leadership. Important information in this regard was passed on to the State Authorities and the prime minister as early as 1991 but to no avail.

The people of Jammu and Ladakh regions have been agitating for long seeking justice for their regions. They have serious complaints of their regions being discriminated against in all matters pertaining to development, representation in services, representation in the State Legislature or in parliament. Their prolonged and loud protests forced the State Government to appoint commissions headed by Supreme and High Court Judges to look into their complaints. Commissions headed by Gajendragadkar and Wazir found many complaints to be genuine and made certain recommendation to meet them. Unfortunately the same have not been implemented in the Jammu region while it has been done in the Valley giving rise to the already injured feelings of the people of these regions. It is all a matter of history. But Government of India is blind to its lessons.

The discrimination against people of Jammu, which still persists, is evident from the fact that the Valley with a population of 32 lakhs is proposed to be represented by 46 legislators in the State Legislature while the Jammu region having population of over 29 lakhs will have only 37 legislators. In the densely populated Valley which has very well connected roads and transport system, on an average legislative assembly constituency will have 90,000 population while in the Jammu region where the terrain is difficult, area far flung and transport system highly unsatisfactory each assembly constituency will have on an average a population of 1,10,000. No wonder that they feel cheated and dissatisfied.

In Jammu & Kashmir, during the last five years more than 15,000 people have lost their lives, apart from over three lakhs who have been rendered refugees in their own country; about ten thousand properties belonging both to the Hindus and the Government have been burnt down. Timber worth hundreds of crores has been destroyed. The weapons captured during this period by the Army and the Security Forces can very well arm an army Division. It is no secret that the number of arms still with the terrorists is many times more than what the Security Forces have captured.

In 1989, in Ladakh the people came out with the demand that Ladakh should be made Union Territory and they would like to part company with the Valley. They launched a very powerful agitation and kept paralysed the State Administration. The Government of India was forced to intercede. More than two years back, after a series of meetings with their representatives, they were promised that to meet their demand, a District Development Council would be formed. Unfortunately even that paltry assurance or promise has not been implemented so far. The anger of the people of Ladakh is understandable. Apart from the fact that the region has remained neglected, Ladakh a Buddhist majority area in 1947, has got transformed now into a Muslim majority area, giving them ample grounds to worry about their uncertain and bleak future.

Any attempt to foist on the people of Jammu & Kashmir those very politicians who stand discredited in their eyes will be counter-productive. It cannot restore their eroded confidence in the fair play of the Government of India. For them they are stooges and agents of New Delhi who have looted and deprived the common people of the benefits of the thousands of crores of rupees meant for the development of the state. They have to be convinced that they can have the government of their choice in the state. They have to be assured that they are part and parcel of the great Indian heritage and that being equal partners, justice will be done to them in all regions of the state. The present policy of drift and complacency combined with spurts of activity in the name of accelerating development and resuming the political process in the state does not carry conviction with any section of the people in the state.

Attempts are being made to create an impression as if the situation has considerably improved in Jammu & Kashmir. Ground realities are very different.

Things have not changed a bit. The recent (January 1995) bomb-blasts on the Republic Day, the recent developments with militancy having its sway in Chirrar Sharif in the Valley and the fact that in the month of January 1995 alone the militants had over 150 strikes on the Security Forces tell a very different story. It betrays the Government's wilfull lack of appreciation of the situation on the ground. It is only a pitiable attempt to mislead the people. Even today the writ of the terrorists runs there. Fear of the gun still persists. The hollowness of the claim of improvement in the situation in Jammu & Kashmir can be gauged by the fact that the work on the three Central Government projects in Doda District—multi thousand crore rupee Dul Hasti

Hydro Project, the Kishtwar Pangi Road and the important Defence Road Link, the Doda-Sarthal-Banni-Basohli Road still remains abandoned and unfinished for the last over two years because of the fear of the terrorists.

Unless the gun is silenced and its fear vanishes, no political process worth the name can be started in the state. With over 3 lakh Kashmiri Hindus still in forced exile, and with collusive and demoralised administration the atmosphere there is not at all conducive for the elections. On the contrary during the last two years such occasional announcements of holding elections in the state and then shelving them have been counter-productive, leading further loss of credibility of the Government of India. It has sent wrong signals. While the terrorists have felt elated, the nationalists have felt let down and demoralised.

Such bungling on the part of the Government of India smacks of the unimaginative, casual and mechanistic manner in which the problem of Kashmir has been handled all along. Even the gains of an unprecedented military victory in the 1971 war with Pakistan were allowed to be squandered away. Here was an occasion when Pakistan could have been forced to come to a full and final settlement of the Kashmir problem. Alas we failed. Haji Pir and Titwal—our own territory retrieved by our valiant Jawans after great sacrifices—was returned to Pakistan. In return we got a still-born Simla Agreement.

Insurgency cannot be fought with kid gloves on. A war has to be fought like a war. And, it needs proper and correct perception of the situation. More than that is needed the will to fight to win. Unfortunately New Delhi lacks both. The war against the separatists and the terrorists being fought in Jammu & Kashmir can be won. It has to be won. It must be won and it can be done only if the Government of India demonstrate the hitherto lacking determination and will to win it. It has only to implement the nation's solemn resolve as has been reflected in the resolution passed last year unanimously by both Houses of Parliament.

It may not be necessary to go further into this sorry story of governmental apathy and culpability responsible for the present agony of the Kashmiri Hindus and the upsurge of anti-national forces in the State of J&K. From the very beginning the BJP have drawn attention of the people in the country and of the government to the deteriorating political situation, but in vain.

12

The National Language

Language is one of the touchstones of Hindu nationalism, as is evident from the key position of Sanskrit and Hindi in the thought processes of the founders of this ideology. Sanskrit has taken on such a major role because, after the European orientalists identified its affinities with other Indo-European languages, it became a major source of pride for Hindu nationalists—this already sacred language rose in their eyes to the status of mother of all languages.

Hindi benefited from this aura because it is the vernacular (Prakrit) that descends most directly from Sanskrit. Before independence, militant Hindus lobbied actively in favour of Hindi through organizations such as the Hindi Sahitya Sammelan (HSS: or Conference of Hindi Literature), founded in 1910 by Madan Mohan Malaviya. Though the traditional idiom of men like Lajpat Rai was Urdu (the language of the intelligentsia in Punjab), they all promoted a sanskritized form of Hindi. Within the HSS Gandhi opposed this viewpoint and advocated the case of Hindustani, a mix of Hindi and Urdu with some words coming from Sanskrit and others from Persian and Arabic.[1]

After independence, Hindu traditionalists from the Congress and Hindu nationalists from the Hindu Mahasabha joined hands within the Constituent Assembly to make Hindi the national language of India.[2] But the constitution, promulgated in 1950, took into account the fears of non-Hindi-speaking states—especially those in the South—

---

[1] J. Das Gupta, *Language, Conflict and National Development* (Berkeley: University of California Press, 1970).

[2] See, for instance, the speeches by Seth Govind Das on the one hand, and

and gave English an extended lease as India's official language for an interim period of fifteen years. After that period it was to be succeeded by Hindi, which by then should have spread sufficiently to make it practical. But in 1963 Nehru, who wanted to defuse tensions with the Dravidian states, had the Official Language Act passed, whereby English was retained as 'associate additional language'. The ruling Congress sealed the fate of Hindi in 1967 by reiterating that English would remain an official associate language through the Official Languages (Amendment) Act.

The Jana Sangh fought against the dilution of Hindi in many different ways: it organized demonstrations against the legislation mentioned above and denounced the redrawing of the administrative map which, after 1956, gave birth to linguistic states—and, according to Hindu nationalists, to 'sub-nationalisms'.[3] But in 1967 the party's position began to shift. It had obviously realized that it would alienate large sections of the public by sticking to a 'Hindi only' position. The South, in particular, would remain out of its sphere of influence if the Jana Sangh did not acknowledge the role of regional languages and English. Interestingly, the first sign of change occurred during the 1967 election campaign, when the Jana Sangh tried to woo new voters. In its election manifesto it conceded that the public service entry examinations could be taken in the regional languages. It also declined to set a deadline for making Hindi the national language and insisted that, in any case, its adoption had to be voluntary. This evolution was consummated in December 1967, during the party plenary session in Calicut (its first session in South India), where the turn towards a more pragmatic approach became clear: after the Congress's electoral setback the Jana Sangh had decided, in order to form coalition governments, to make alliances with parties which did not share its ideology, including the Communists and the Akalis, against whom it had fought earlier, during their 'Punjabi Suba' campaign. The Sangh Parivar has not returned to its all-Hindi policy since that time.

---

those of S.P. Mookerjee on the other, in *Constituent Assembly Debates* (Delhi: Lok Sabha Secretariat, 1989).

[3] In the 1960s the Jana Sangh argued against the carving out of a Punjabi-speaking state.

Extracts from Bharatiya Jana Sangh,
Party Documents Vol. 5: Resolutions on Education, etc. and Party Affairs[4]

Language Policy

The Working Committee expresses its deep dissatisfaction upon the complete lack of interest shown by the Government of India in the implementation of that part of the Constitution which requires that Hindi should take the place of English as the language of the Union within 15 years. It condemns the antipathy of the Education Ministry towards Hindi and calls for a thorough overhaul of that department which is manned by persons who have no heart in the job.

Common Script

With regard to the Language Policy to be adopted in the educational and administrative fields the committee lays down the following essentials:

(1) That mother tongue should be the medium of instruction at the primary stage.

(2) That the regional language should be the medium for secondary and higher education, Hindi being a compulsory subject for study throughout.

(3) That for post-graduate and specialised scientific studies Hindi alone should be the medium.

(4) That the government should establish a commission of linguists representing all regional languages to draw up a lexicon of technical and scientific terms based on Sanskrit and other spoken Indian languages. The terminology so drawn up will be the common property of all Indian languages.

(5) That steps should be taken for the adoption of Devanagari as the common script for all Indian languages.

(6) That Devanagari should likewise be adopted for the dialects of undeveloped areas which have no script of their own, irrespective of the fact that in certain areas Roman script has been sought to be imposed on them by foreign missionaries.

[4] Bharatiya Jana Sangh, *Party Documents, Vol. 5* (Delhi: 1954), Resolution of 8 May 1954. The extracts are drawn from pp. 21–50 and 56–61.

(7) That the use of Hindi in Central and inter-state communications should be started immediately. Its use should be made compulsory for all ceremonial occasions and Hindi alone should be used on foundation stones and other permanent inscriptions.

(8) Such of the personnel in the services of the Government of India as are not due to retire by the time limit fixed for the replacement of English by Hindi should be given compulsory courses in Hindi in a planned manner at the cost of the government.

The Committee is of the firm opinion that Urdu is the language of no region in India, it being only a foreign and unacceptable style of Hindi with a foreign script and a foreign vocabulary imposed on India during a period of foreign domination and now being supported by some communal elements.

Colonialistic Language Bill[5]

Negation of Democracy—The Jana Sangh views with greatest concern the forthcoming Associate Languages Bill which is a misnomer for a colonialistic language Bill, intended to continue by statutory force the language of the colonial regime. Under the bad provisions of this mischievous Bill, English will be used by the Central and Provincial Governments for all such purposes for which it was used during the hay days [*sic*] of British colonialism. English will have the monopoly and Indian languages will remain suppressed and dominated, relegated to peripheral uses only. 98 per cent of India's population will thereby be reduced for an indefinite period of time to the status of hewers of wood and drawers of water, diggers of mines and cultivators of dusty soil. They will not be able to enter the portals of governmental machinery, not even as clerks. Education and Law, Commerce and Industry will be open to those who have spent 10 to 15 years of their precious youth with the mystery of the most vagrant language, English.

The Jana Sangh cannot support the Government in its persistence in such anti-National and anti-Democratic outlawing of Indian languages. It is only the Indian languages which can be the media of India's

[5] Resolution of 6 April 1963, in idem.

development, each provincial language in its own province and the link language Hindi at the Centre. Those who oppose Hindi at the Centre are unwittingly opposing Tamil in Tamilnadu, and Bengali in Bengal as well. We proclaim to the Nation that there is no conflict between the Indian languages. Whatever conflict is sought to be created and voiced is artificial and is based not on love but on hatred. Emotional integration of the Indian people includes love and reverence for each other's language as well.

We call upon the people and their representatives sitting in the Parliament to realise the historical dimensions of the denationalising process that will be furthered by this language Bill and to oppose it and thereby restore to the Indian languages their due position in the country.

Two per cent Anglocrats—If the government using its brutal majority does succeed in passing the language Bill, the fight against the domination of English will have to be intensified and continued as long as English is not removed. The battle against English is a battle against the biggest monopoly ever established, a monopoly of all the good things of life by less than 2 per cent anglocrats, excluding all others.

Egalitarianism thro' Indian Languages—It will be an economic fight inasmuch as today 3000 crores of rupees are spent annually by the English-media monopolists. The non-English-knowing get only crumb in the form of unskilled labour at an average rate of Rs 2 to 3 a day. Higher emoluments go to the English knowing 2 per cent or less. Fight against English will be a fight for social egalitarianism as against the high-browed supercastes of English-knowing men and women. It is they who have usurped all positions of prestige in the society, others being almost denied and debarred.

Birthright for Education thro' Mother Tongue—Fight against English will be a fight for educational opportunities for those who do not or cannot afford to spend the best part of their youth to the cramming of the most ideosyncratic [*sic*] language of the world. Every Indian has the birthright to receive education and reach the highest echelons in the national life through his own mother tongue. Battle against English will be a battle for democracy. A democracy cannot be carried on in any language save the language of the people. How can road signs and parliamentary debates, law courts and banks be allowed to operate in an alien tongue.

De-Indianisation—Finally it will be a battle against de-Indianisation that is being effected through an all-out emphasis on an alien language, literature, tradition, moods and behaviours and through a corresponding denigrating of Indian literature, traditions, moods and behaviours. Thereby the development of the Indian personality is being kept stunted and submerged. The Jana Sangh warns the nation that the fight may be a long and arduous one but it also wishes to bring confidence to the people in the ultimate victory of nationalism over colonialism.

Official Languages in States[6]

In pursuance of its policy of displacing Indian languages by English for purposes of official use, the Government of India, after first adopting the Official Languages Bill at the Centre, has now issued a directive to the State Governments to initiate legislation in their respective legislatures which would enable the use of English in the states after 26 January 1965 and whereby the English version alone of State Bills and enactments would be deemed authentic. This directive should serve as an eye-opener for those persons who had been supporting the use of English at the central level under the illusion that thereby only the status of Hindi would be affected while the regional languages would continue to be used freely as official languages in their respective spheres. The Bharatiya Jana Sangh has been stressing from the outset that this is a struggle not between Hindi and English but between all the Indian languages on the one hand and English on the other. Among the Indian languages there was no *inter se* clash of interests at all. An argument advanced against the use of Hindi at the Centre has been that such use would entail practical difficulty for non-Hindi-speaking persons who had not yet picked up Hindi adequately. But evidently, no such difficulty can be pleaded in the case of the regional languages. It is obvious that the Central Government's directive is an index only of its deep-rooted antipathy for Indian languages and its infatuation for English. It is the duty of all independent and freedom loving elements to realise the baneful gravity of this attitude and to oppose it strongly. The Jana Sangh urges upon the State Governments to give to their respective regional languages their rightful place in overall work and to emancipate themselves completely from the stranglehood [*sic*]

[6] Resolution of 12 August 1963, in idem.

of English by 26 January 1963. Let no Bill to grant a fresh lease to English be introduced in any state legislature.

Language Policy[7]

On 26 January 1965, the 15-year Constitutional lease granted to English as the country's Official Language comes to an end. After this date, administrative work at the Centre should be carried on in Hindi, and in the states in the respective state languages. It is extremely regrettable that the government has failed to take necessary steps for the change-over. But the lapses and laxity of the government cannot hold back the nation from taking this imperative step which would veritably mark the fulfilment of its freedom fight. It is the duty of the people to struggle for the emancipation of the Government of India from the shackles of English. The Bharatiya Jana Sangh will spearhead this struggle. Jana Sangh workers must see to it that for all official work Hindi is used at the Centre and the various state languages in their respective spheres.

Some quarters have been frantically exerting to impede this process and even to turn the clock back. They want to retain English. For the realisation of this objective they have been sowing in the country the poison-seed of disruption and division. All forces which stand for the country's unity must stand together and ensure that these evil efforts are checkmated.

It is preposterous to suggest that English can serve to promote Indian unity. The absurdity of this suggestion would become apparent if we realise that an analogous plea might well have been made even to advocate continuation of the British Rule in India. After all, enduring national unity can be built up only on factors which contribute to the flowering of the national genius and ethos. For the last two centuries, the imposition of English has stunted the growth of national consciousness and thus served only to divide the nation. It is essential, therefore, for the unity of the country that English must go.

The use of Hindi at the Centre is the result of a natural historical process. So is the use of the various state languages in their own regions. All these are Official Languages having equal status. Their use in administration must be governed by the provisions of the Constitution.

[7] Resolution of 24 January 1965, in idem.

Sindhi should be included in the list of languages enumerated in the Eighth Schedule of the Constitution.

Sanskrit Broadcasts—To Sanskrit, however, belongs the status of India's National Language. This is a historical fact. So, while in the matter of general administrative work, Hindi should be used at the Centre and the state languages in the provinces, on ceremonial occasions and special functions, Sanskrit also ought to be made use of. There should be Sanskrit broadcasts also over the All India Radio.

Thanks to the Government's policies, arrangements that ought to have been completed by now for a switch-over to Indian languages have not been made. This has created misgivings in the minds of some people that the change would adversely affect their prospects in the services. The Jana Sangh would like to reassure these people that this would not be allowed to happen. At the same time, it expects everyone to equip himself soon so as to be able to carry out his obligation properly.

Replacement of English[8]

The Central Working Committee strongly deplores the violent outbursts in Tamilnadu over the language issue and demands that an enquiry commission be appointed to find out the elements who have exploited the real or imaginary apprehensions of the people in the matter of Official Language and incited them into violence, killings and arson.

The attack on the Aurobindo Ashram in the course of the riots, the organised raids on railway stations and post offices, the demolition of Gandhiji's statues, desecration of the State Flag, the burning of Dr Radhakrishnan's English Library—all these happenings show that the language issue came just as a handy excuse for anti-social elements. Their real aim was to challenge the authority of the society and the State and to create conditions of anarchy. If India is to protect its freedom and integrity, it must with a firm hand suppress and root out such tendencies and forces. There is no place for violence in a democratic set-up. The disturbances in Tamilnadu are a grim warning which cannot be ignored.

[8] Resolution of 3 April 1965, in idem.

When the Constituent Assembly resolved unanimously to make Hindi the country's Official Language in place of English, it was prompted by the noble feeling that no foreign language can serve to manifest the national Self. A nation's cultural, educational or even economic development is not possible through an alien tongue. The draft Constitution envisaged continuation of English for a period of 5 years only. But on the insistence of the non-Hindi-speaking members—particularly the members from Tamilnadu—this period was extended to 15 years. If the Central and State Government had systematically exerted for the development of the Indian languages and for their increasing use, 26 January 1965 would have dawned as a historic day as by then we would have been completely emancipated from the shackles of a foreign language and Indian languages would have been able to come to occupy their rightful places. But because of the government inertia and ineptitude, the country does not find itself ready today for a complete switch-over from English to the Indian languages. The dominance of English continues not only at the Centre, but in the states too. In some spheres the use of English has actually increased after 26 January 1965 and Indian languages are despised and ignored. This state of affairs is totally intolerable. It cannot be allowed to continue.

Linguistic Freedom and Mother Tongue—The nation needs to reaffirm our faith in linguistic freedom and the sacred pledge to secure the supremacy and usage of *Swabhasha* (mother tongue) in all walks of life. There is no question of retreating from the provisions of the Constitution. We have to go forward. Today 96 per cent of the people have been reduced to second grade citizens because of their ignorance of English and for no fault of theirs they have absolutely no voice in public affairs. We have to ensure that they are able to partake as equal co-sharers with the rest in administration and in public life.

To make the switch-over from English to Indian languages smooth the Constitution had provided on the one hand continuance of English for a period of 15 years and on the other a provision to permit, if necessary, the use of English in certain spheres even thereafter. With intent to ensure that the non-Hindi speaking do not suffer, the Official Language Act, 1963 has provided for the continuance of English as associate language. Any amendment in this Act which goes counter to the ultimate objective that we have placed before ourselves, namely replacement of English by the Indian languages both at the Centre and in the states cannot be accepted.

The Working Committee demands that:

(1) In the states English must be forthwith replaced by the respective regional languages and all administrative work be carried on in these languages. There is no justification whatsoever of continuing English in the states any longer and the people must not allow it.

(2) For the convenience of those employees at the Centre who do not know Hindi and who have not been able to prepare themselves during these 17 years to be able to work in Hindi, the use of English should be permitted for 10 years.

(3) All Indian languages should be permitted as media for UPSC examinations. For Hindi-speaking examinees there should be a compulsory paper in one other Indian language and for non-Hindi-speaking examinees there should be a compulsory paper in Hindi.

(4) All Indian languages are national languages. They have an equal status, and it is the responsibility of the government to ensure the proper development of all. The government must draw up a planned programme to fulfil this obligation effectively so that these languages are able to contribute to the enrichment of national life.

Official Language[9]

Incomplete Swarajya—The Congress Working Committee's recent resolution on language which is going to be the basis of Government's policy has come as an utter disappointment to all those who have longed to see *Swarajya* manifest itself in the sphere of language too. It is a matter of regret that the resolution fails to outline any steps towards the fulfilment of the constitutional provisions in respect of language. The resolution provides for the continued use of English

[9] Resolution of 10 July 1965, in idem.

but gives no indication as to how and when Hindi would become the official language of the country. To say that English should continue at the Centre so long as even a single non-Hindi state desires, is an index that the Congress Working Committee does not honestly desire the replacement of English by Hindi as the Centre's Official language. When the Constituent Assembly unanimously resolved to have Hindi as the Centre's Official language, the inspiration and logic behind its decision was that a nation's cultural, educational and economic development cannot be brought about through the instrument of a foreign language. The people had been eagerly looking forward to 26 January 1965 as a historic day, on which India's national languages would secure their rightful places. Unfortunately, this resolution of the Congress party gives the impression that English is going to continue for all time to come and that Indian Languages would never be allowed to assert themselves.

The steps taken prior to 26 January 1965, by various departments of the Central Government in regard to the growing use of Hindi in administrative work have now been put off. If the present situation continues, it would be sheer hypocrisy to say that ultimately Hindi was going to be the Official language.

Three-Language Formula—The Bharatiya Jana Sangh strongly deplores this state of affairs and demands:

(1) Let there be an unequivocal declaration that from 26 January 1965, Hindi is the Official Language of the country and that there shall be no restrictions whatsoever on its use in Central Government affairs. Those officials and employees in the Central Government who have not learnt Hindi as yet, will be permitted to use English for a period of 10 years. At the same time planned efforts should be made to teach them Hindi.

(2) All Indian languages should be declared as recognised media of UPSC examinations, which should be conducted from right now through such languages as have been accepted already as media of University examinations in their respective states. As and when the remaining languages also become University media in their spheres, the UPSC should make necessary arrangements to hold examinations in these languages.

(3) English should not be a compulsory subject for study. It should be taught as an optional foreign language.

(4) The three-language formula should include the following languages:

   (i) Mother tongue,

  (ii) Sanskrit, and

 (iii) Hindi (for those whose mother tongue is Hindi, any other modern Indian language).

Education Through Regional Languages

Media for Highest Education—The Central Working Committee welcomes the decision of the Committee of Members of Parliament on Education and the Education Ministers Conference to adopt regional languages as media of education up to the highest level. This decision has been substantially endorsed by the Vice-Chancellors' Conference also.

The deliberations of these bodies have incidentally revealed that the need of a link language is universally acknowledged, and further that a clear consensus exists that Hindi alone can serve as the link language. This Committee is sure that this decision in respect of regional languages, by emancipating the younger generations from the shackles of a foreign tongue, will lead to a full flowering of their genius. It will also create a climate for the fullest development of our languages, whose progress has hitherto been thwarted by the dominance of English.

Apprehensions have been voiced that this decision will jeopardise the country's unity and obstruct inter-state communion. The presumption underlying these misgivings is that English is the bond of unity which holds the country together today. The presumption is entirely fallacious. India has been one and united centuries before English came to this country and India shall remain one and united after English has ceased to occupy the prominent place here that it has today. At best, English serves as a bond of communion for just 15 per cent of the country's population.

The changeover to the regional media instead of weakening of our bonds of unity will, on the contrary, lead to their strengthening inasmuch as most of our national languages derive their vocabulary by and large from one common mother-language—Sanskrit—and therefore have a common heritage.

The Working Committee notes with satisfaction that despite the strains generated on the issue of language in the past 2 years, all political parties have been successful in arriving at a unanimity on the question of regional languages. All those interested in the country's unity must exert to ensure that this resolve in [*sic*] faithfully carried out.

Official Language[10]

Perpetuation of English—By foisting the recent language law on the people, the Government of India has done a disservice to the country. The law has engendered needless strains among different linguistic groups and at places led even to deplorable incidents of violence and lawlessness. Secondly, by overlooking the stultifying effect which perpetuation of English would have on the natural development of Indian languages, the law has set up an obstacle in the way of implementing the unanimous decision of major political parties that regional languages should be made the media of education up to the highest level and that administration in all states should be carried on through the languages of the people.

In its election manifesto for 1967, the Jana Sangh had very clearly spelt out its approach to the question of Official language. The four planks of its language policy are:

(1) Immediate steps should be taken to make the regional languages the official languages in their respective states.
(2) In Central Departments like Railways, Post Offices, etc; [*sic*] which come into direct contact with the people, regional languages should be used along with Hindi.
(3) Hindi should be the Official language at the Centre but this should not handicap those who do not know Hindi; such employees should be permitted the option of English during the period of transition.
(4) Regional languages should be made the media of Union Public Service Commission examinations.

[10] Resolution of 26 December 1967, in idem.

Unfortunately, the Government of India's approach to the issue has been singularly inept. The Constitution enjoined on Government that it should make adequate arrangements for a switchover from English to Hindi within 15 years of the enactment of the Constitution. The Government of India failed to fulfil this obligation. It was the Government's failure which was primarily responsible for arousing in the minds of some non-Hindi sections apprehensions that there was going to be an abrupt changeover and as a result of which they would be placed at a disadvantage. The genuine misgivings of this section, coupled with the machinations of elements who have developed a vested political, economic or administrative interest in the continuation of English, led to serious disturbances in Madras, way back in February 1965. Ever since, the Government of India have lost all sense of direction and proportion in so far as the language question is concerned. All its subsequent decisions are merely in the nature of *ad hoc* reactions to the pressures working on it at a particular time. The language law, as enacted, is a striking specimen of its confused thinking. In the name of reflecting the consensus of opinion of all sections, it has only invited the hostility of every single section. It solves no problem; it creates many. To the extent that it permits the use of English in the Central administration along with Hindi, this Act adds nothing new to what had been already provided under the Official Languages Act of 1963. Looked at from the point of view of Central employees not knowing Hindi, therefore, it was entirely unnecessary [*sic*]. It even violates the Constitution, which confers on Parliament the 'exclusive right' to legislate in respect of the Union subjects. This law denigrates the sovereign authority of Parliament and, in an extremely perverse manner, gives to even a single and small state the right to veto Parliament's decision on language. The Official Languages (Amendment) Act, thus, is ill-conceived, uncalled for and unconstitutional.

No Language Imposition—Hindi must grow on the basis of voluntary acceptance. At the same time, English also cannot be imposed on any section of the people against its will. We are confident that if the Central Government's decision in regard to the media of University education, endorsed by the Education Ministers' Conference and the conference of Vice-Chancellors is sincerely implemented, the language controversy will gradually die down. As the regional languages get their rightful place as the languages of administration in their respective states, and Hindi becomes the sole Official language at the Centre, the people of India would really experience a sense of participation in the democratic governance of the country. The nation eagerly looks forward to that day.

Meanwhile, the Jana Sangh favours the following measures in regard to Central Services:

(1)   Immediate steps must be taken to enable candidates appearing for Union Public Service Commission examinations to appear through the media of regional languages.

(2)   The knowledge of neither English nor Hindi should be compulsory at the time of recruitment. The appointees, however, should be required to get a working knowledge of either Hindi or English during the probation period.

(3)   Appointees, whose mother-tongue is Hindi, must acquire a working knowledge of one additional Indian language, besides Hindi, during the probation period.

13

Conversion and the Arithmetic of Religious Communities

Hindu nationalism and the conversion issue are intimately related. This ideology crystallized largely in reaction to the proselytizing activities of Christian missionaries. Socioreligious reform movements such as the Brahmo Samaj and revivalist neo-Hindu movements like the Arya Samaj were partly formed to cope with often-aggressive religious propaganda. The latter initiated a Hindu conversion technique—which was in fact imitated from the Christian missionaries but shaped along the lines of a traditional ritual—called Shuddhi.[1] This purification ritual is resorted to by upper-caste Hindus affected by 'polluting' contact. But the Arya Samaj used it to reconvert—that is, to purify and reinstate in their caste—ex-Hindus who had become Christians, Muslims, or Sikhs. The first Shuddhi movement gained momentum in the 1920s in reaction to forced conversions which took place during the Khilafat movement—it subsided soon after.

Conversions became a major issue again after independence when Hindu nationalists lobbied the government to prohibit missionary activity by law: while they could not expect any move in this direction from the British, the Congress government they hoped would be more

[1] C. Jaffrelot, 'Militant Hindus and the Conversion Issue (1885–1990): From Shuddhi to Dharm Parivartan: The Politicization and Diffusion of an "Invention of Tradition" ', in J. Assayag, *The Resources of History: Tradition and Narration in South Asia* (Paris: EFEO, 1999), pp. 127–52.

responsive. Indeed, Hindu traditionalist Congressmen like K.M. Munshi argued (in vain) during the Constituent Assembly debates that conversions should be regulated, and the Indian Constitution eventually emphasized that 'all persons are equally entitled to freedom of conscience and to the right freely to practise and propagate religion' (Article 25). However, at the state level things were different. In Madhya Pradesh, for instance, the conversion of large numbers of tribals to Christianity resulted in the mobilization of Hindu nationalists. In 1952 the Vanavasi Kalyan Ashram (VKA—Centre for Tribal Welfare) was founded in Jashpur (today's Chhattisgarh) by R.K. Deshpande, an RSS man who wanted to counter the growing influence of Christian missionaries among the Adivasis. Interestingly, the RSS does not use the word 'adivasi'—literally, those who, according to them, were here before—because the autochthones of India, according to the Hindu nationalist reading of history, were not tribals—who were in the forest: hence the expression 'Vanavasis'—but rather the Aryans of Vedic times. To attract the tribals the VKA established free hostels, hospitals, and schools. In fact, the VKA imitated the Christian missions, which were adept at this kind of philanthropic work, in order to counter them more effectively.[2] In 1954 the Jana Sangh organized an 'Anti Foreign Missionary Week', but the local Congress immediately appointed an inquiry committee. Thus, the Niyogi Committee prepared the ground for a law against conversion, the Swatantra Dharm Act, which was promulgated in 1968.

The issue reappeared during the Janata government phase when ex-Jana Sanghis were in a position to exert pressure on the central government. They introduced a 'Freedom of Religion Bill' which prohibited 'conversion from one religion to another by the use of force or inducement or by fraudulent means'. This piece of legislation could not fructify because of the fall of Morarji Desai's Janata government.

However, the Hindu nationalist point of view gained some respectability and legitimacy in 1981 after a thousand Dalits converted to

[2] The former Maharaja of Jashpur supported the VKA in the 1960s and then joined the Jana Sangh. His son, Dilip Singh Judeo, took over from him in both capacities in the 1980s: as patron of the VKA he launched operations of reconversion in the tribal belt and as political leader he contested elections on the BJP ticket—before becoming union minister in the Vajpayee government.

Islam in a small town of Tamil Nadu, Meenakshipuram. Research carried out by Abdul Malik Mujahid showed that those who were converted were mainly concerned with the need for their family and themselves to escape from the caste system.[3]

Hindu nationalist organizations reacted immediately. The VHP was at the forefront of this mobilization—it had been launched in 1964 to federate the different sectarian streams which cohabit within Hinduism and to cope with Christian missionary activities.[4] One of the VHP's responses consisted in integrating Dalits more intimately into Hindu society in order to dissuade them from converting to Christianity or any other religion. For instance, religious leaders from the VHP accepted eating with Dalits.

The same response was promoted by Lala Lajpat Rai at the beginning of the twentieth century when Hindu nationalists were prepared to relax the traditional orthodox attitude in order to stop the flow out of Hinduism. At the time they were all the more anxious to put an end to this phenomenon for the demographic strength of the religious communities mattered a lot: the British counted heads for defining quotas in the assemblies and even in the administration.

Lala Lajpat Rai on Dalits and Conversions[5]

There can be no denying the fact that the rigidity of the Hindu caste system is the bane of Hindu society. It is a great barrier in the way of

---

[3] A.M. Mujahid, *Conversion to Islam. Untouchables' Strategy for Protest in India* (Chambersburg, PA: Anima Books, 1988) and G. Mathew, 'Politicisation of Religion—Conversion to Islam in Tamil Nadu', *Economic and Political Weekly*, 19 June 1982.

[4] C. Jaffrelot, 'The Vishva Hindu Parishad: A Nationalist but Mimetic Attempt at Federating the Hindu Sects', in Vasudha Dalmia, Angelika Malinar, and Martin Christof, eds, *Charisma and Canon: Essays on the Religious History of the Indian Subcontinent* (Delhi: Oxford University Press, 2001), pp. 388–411; and 'The Vishva Hindu Parishad: Structures and Strategies', in Jeff Haynes, ed., *Religion, Globalization and Political Culture in the Third World* (London: Macmillan, 1999), pp. 191–212.

[5] Extract from Lala Lajpat Rai, 'The Depressed Classes', *Modern Review*, Calcutta, July 1909; rpnt in Devendra Swarup, ed., *Politics of Conversion* (Delhi: Deendayal Research Institute, 1986).

the social and national progress of Hindus. It confronts them at every step and slackens the speed with which, otherwise, the nation would climb up to the heights of national solidarity. The condition of the 'low' castes, sometimes described as '*untouchables*', at other times as the '*depressed classes*' is nothing short of disgraceful. It is a disgrace to our humanity, our sense of justice, and our feeling of social affinity. It is useless to hope for any solidarity so long as the depressed classes continue to be so low in the social scale as they are. The intellectual and moral status of the community as a whole cannot be appreciably raised without the co-operation of all the classes forming the community. So then, as there are classes amongst us who are untouchable by the so-called superior classes, because of their having been born of certain parents, the moral and intellectual elevation of the community as a whole can only proceed by slow, very slow, degrees. The condition of the depressed classes is a standing blot on our social organisation, and we must remove that blot if we are really desirous of securing the efficiency of our social organism. All parts of the whole must be raised, not necessarily to the same level but to a level from which they can, by their individual efforts, talents and achievements, rise to the highest possible position, within the reach of members of the social organism.

The present arrangement is a cruel and unjust arrangement. Besides, it is both economically and politically unsound. A community which allows so much valuable human material to rot in a state of utter depression and helplessness, cannot be said to be economically wise. As to the political danger involved by the continuance of these classes in their present condition, one need only look at the arguments advanced by our friends of the Muslim League in support of their contention for a larger representation on the Legislative Councils than they are entitled to by virtue of their numerical strength. Quite ignoring the fact that they are as much affected by these classes as the Hindus, they make it a point to say that in counting the Hindus for the purposes of representation the untouchables enumerated with them should be excluded. Whatever may be the value of this argument for the purpose for which it is used, there can be no doubt that the existence of these classes in their present deplorable condition is a menace to the power and influence of the Hindu community. The line of argument adopted by our Muslim friends and by some missionary critics of the Reforms

Scheme, ought to open the eyes of the Hindus to the absolute necessity and urgency of raising the social status of their fellow-religionists, called and known as the members of the depressed classes. Thus from every point of view, whether that of humanity, justice or fair play, or that of self-interest, it is the bounden duty of the so-called high-caste Hindus to give a helping hand to their brothers of the 'low castes' and raise them socially as well as intellectually. We are living in a democratic age. The tendencies of democracy are towards the levelling down of all inequalities.

That there are forces working amongst us which will sooner or later demolish all artificial barriers due to accidents of birth between man and man, is patent to all far-sighted people. Under any circumstances, then, the day of the depressed classes is bound to come. If so, would it not be wise to take time by the forelock, and to take in hand, in all willingness, what other forces, which are not in our control, must perforce bring about? I say this not because I have the least doubt about the shocking injustice involved in the existing arrangements, but because it is perfectly legitimate to point out the moral of our neglecting [sic] to do what is right and by the weight of that moral to ask people to avoid the evil consequences of letting the forces of nature to have their own revenge. Morality requires that we should take to the work of elevating the depressed classes out of a sheer sense of justice and humanity regardless of any outside considerations. But to appeal in the name of expediency, when the latter strengthens the demands of morality and humanity, involves no breach of principle, and we may very well point out that the communal interest of the Hindus also lies that way. There are agencies at work which are doing their best to remove these Hindus from the pale of Hinduism, which, bereft of these classes, might live, but only as an exhausted frame. The classes themselves are anxious to remain Hindus even though the latter may not promise them the fullest social privileges which they may be in a position to obtain by change of religion. The only thing for Hinduism to do is to meet them halfway at once and remove at least the principal grounds of their depression. The least that we can do without delay is to make the untouchables touchable and take away the sting out of their names. Hindu [sic] who is not prepared to do even this is an enemy to the community, however unconscious he may be of the great injury he is causing it thereby. I confess, we, the educated Hindus, are not doing our duty in the matter honestly and manfully. Most of our time and energies are employed in agitating for trivial political rights, the good of which can at best be remote, to the neglect of questions upon the right solution of which depends our immediate safety as a nation. I am only repeating what I have already said times out of number, that the work of nation-building must be begun from below. The nation that has to be built up lives in huts and not in palaces. Legislative Councils principally composed of the latter are not likely to be the best instruments of building the nation from below. I say this without in any way disparaging the agitation to obtain more legislative powers. But I cannot help saying that to me there seems to be a lack of proportion in the importance that is being attached to a scheme which for the present at least altogether ignores the masses as well as the lower middle classes.

II

In educated circles there seems to be fairly practical unanimity as to the inherent injustice and monstrosity of the existing system; nay, even further, there seems to be an agreement as to the desirability of taking steps to elevate the moral, material and social condition of the caste system. What stands in the way of progress in this direction, however, is the prejudice of the illiterate and the apathy of the educated classes. The former are wanting in that broad outlook on human affairs without which the consciousness of a sense of corporate social responsibility is slow to awaken, the latter lack in that backbone without which it is impossible to bring about changes which look radical but the absence of which blocks the avenues that lead to national consciousness and national solidarity.

For the latter purpose what is required is fairness and humanity at least, if not perfect equality in the relations of the different units that compose the social organism.

At the present moment the greatest strength of the Hindus consists in their number. It is true that intellectually and educationally, in trade and commerce, in brain and body, in mind and muscle, in the arts of peace and war, they are second to none. But in their numerical strength lies that power which is not shared by any other community in this country. This numerical strength, however, may easily be converted into the chief source of their weakness if not properly organised for national purposes. At first sight the Hindus look a heterogeneous mass of untidy humanity without any ties to bind them to one another. Their lack of homogeneity is their curse. To an outsider they seem to agree in nothing. Caste and inter-caste jealousies block the way to progress. The energies which should be spent in bringing about solidarity are being spent in rearing up individuality in the different social units which make up the community. The Brahman, the Khatri, the Banya, the Kayastha, the Rajput, the Jat; among Brahmans the Gaur, the Sandhya, the Nagar, the Kanaujia; &c &c. are all dominated by separatist tendencies. Their collective ambition moves in the circumscribed circle of their own little group, which gives a sectional or rather only a sub-sectional colour to their patriotism or nationalism, but what is even worse is their attitude towards the lower classes and the latter's attempt to retaliate. The former's denial of equal or any opportunities of worship to the latter in their temples or shrines is a standing disgrace to the good name of Hinduism. The so much boasted of tolerance of the Hindus disappears the moment that tolerance is demanded by the classes lower in the social scale. The high-caste Hindus of the present day, men who have received their education under Western ideals, are often heard to speak with pride of the spirit of toleration possessed and shown by Hinduism towards other religions and other communities, but a critic may very well say that this toleration is the offspring of fear or greed. You dare not be uncivil or unkind to Mohammedans or Christians because they can make matters unpleasant for you, but you are insolent towards your own people, whom you think you can defy without any fear of retaliation. The consequences are plain and can be seen even running. The Hindus are going down in numbers. Your insolence towards the lower classes of Hindus is being repaid by the latter running [sic] their back on you. Mohammedanism and Christianity are extending their arms to embrace them and indications are not wanting of the readiness of the lower classes of Hindus to accept the hospitality of non-Hindu religions and social systems. Why, the reason is obvious. As a Hindu you won't touch him; you would not let him sit on the same carpet with you, you would not offer him water in your cups, you would not accept water or food touched by him; you would not let him enter your temples, in fact you would not treat him like a human being. The moment, however, he becomes a Mohammedan or a Christian, without even giving up his ancestral occupation you are all smiles to him, you welcome him to your home; and have no objection at times to offer him drink and food in your utensils etc. It is a deep-rooted sentiment that has so far prevented the depressed classes of Hindus from deserting Hinduism en-masse [sic]. Sentiments are, however, melting away before the matter-of-fact civilization of the West. The time does not seem to be very distant when sentiment will cease to control the desire of the depressed classes to better their social position, if it cannot be had otherwise than by a change of faith. There are circumstances and causes in the environments of these classes which are working with effect to bring about that consummation and if the Hindus want to avoid that catastrophe, it is time that they subordinated there caste-pride to the exigencies of the situation and took time by the forelock.

III

Commenting on the figures of the Census of 1901, giving the respective strength of the three principal religions of India, Sir H. Risley remarks:

'During the ten years preceding the census of 1901, the Mohammedans increased by 9 per cent, and the Christians by nearly 28 per cent. Hinduism is the dominant religion of India; in all its developments it is intimately associated with caste, and the two sets of factors, the social and the religious, can hardly be considered apart. The two rival creeds, Christianity and Islam, for Buddhism may be left out of account, avowedly reject the principle of caste, and have been affected by its influence solely through their contact with Hinduism. So long as Hinduism shows no decline from its present strength, caste will preserve its ancient reign, and nothing short of a great accession of strength to either Islam or Christianity can materially modify the social and religious future of India. Are there any signs of a tendency in this direction? Can the figures of the last census be regarded as in any sense the forerunners of an Islamic or Christian revival which will threaten the citadel of Hinduism or will Hinduism hold its own in the future as it has done through the long ages of the past?

'The statistics of the last census show that during a decade of famine the Mohammedans in India increased by nine per cent. No doubt these proportions were affected by the fact that the famines were most severe in those parts of the country where the Mohammedans are relatively least numerous, but in the fertile and wealthy region of Eastern Bengal, which has never been touched by real famine, though people on small fixed incomes suffer from high prices, their rate of increase was 12.3 per cent or nearly double that of the Hindus. The figures illustrating the proportion of children tell a similar tale, and indicate that in that part of India the Mohammedans are not only more enterprising and therefore better off than their Hindu neighbours, but also more prolific and more careful of their offspring.'

Sir H. Risley then explains the reasons for these conditions, with some of which we are not directly concerned just now. One of the causes contributing to the increase in the number of Mohammedans is said to be conversions to Islam, about which he remarks:

'Conversions from Hinduism to Islam must also contribute in some degree to the relatively more rapid growth of the Mohammedan population. Here no appeal to statistics is possible, but a number of specific instances of such changes of religion were extracted by Mr Gait, CIE, from the reports of Hindu and Mohammedan gentlemen in 24 Districts and published as Appendix II to the Bengal Census Report of 1901. The motives assigned in various cases—names and particulars are usually given—may be grouped somewhat as follows:

'1. Genuine religious conviction of the purity and simplicity of Islam, derived from study of the Mohammedan scriptures or from the preaching of the Maulvies who go round the villages.

'2. The growing desire on the part of lower Hindu castes to improve their social position leads individuals among them to embrace a creed which seems to offer them a fair chance in life. Malis, Kahars, Gowalas, Napits, Kans, Baildars and other castes of similar status furnish numerous illustrations of this tendency.

'3. Census connected with taboos on food and drink and with various caste misdemeanours have also to be taken into account. Hindus in sickness and distress are tended by Mohammedans and take food and water from their hands; the caste excommunicate them and they join the ranks of a more merciful faith.

'It is needless to observe that none of these causes, nor all of them taken together, exercise an influence wide and potent enough to bring about a great Islamic revival in India. The day of conversions en masse has passed, and there are no signs of its return. Nevertheless certain tendencies are discernible which may add materially to the number of individual conversions. On the one hand, the Mohammedans may raise their standard of education, they may organize and consolidate their influence, they may establish their claim to larger representation in the Legislative Councils and in Government service, and they may thus come to play in Indian public life a part more worthy of the history and traditions of their faith. On the other hand, the spread of English education among the middle and lower ranks of the Hindus may lead to a revolt against the intolerance of the higher castes, and in particular against their virtual monopoly of place and power.

'In Southern India whole castes have been known to become Mohammedans because the Brahmans would not allow them to enter Hindu temples and compelled them to worship outside. It is conceivable that other parts of India will some day realize that for the low-born Hindus the shortest road to success in life, whether at the bar or at the public service, may lie through the portals of Islam.

'Faithful to its earliest traditions, Christianity in India has from the first devoted itself to the poor and lowly, and its most conspicuous successes have been attained among the Animists and the depressed of Hinduism. To the Animist haunted by a crowd of greedy and malevolent demons ever thirsty for blood, like the ghosts that flocked round Ulysses, Christianity opens a new world of love and hope. To the Pariah, the Mahar, the Dher and a host of other helots, it promises release from the most searching and relentless form of social tyranny—the tyranny of caste; it offers them independence, self-respect, education, advancement, a new life in an organised and progressive society. "These People", says Mr Francis, writing of the pariahs of the South, "have little to lose by forsaking the creed of their fore-fathers. As long as they remain Hindus they are daily and hourly made to feel that they are of commoner clay than their neighbours. Any attempts which they may make to educate themselves or their children are actively discouraged by the classes above them; castes-restrictions prevent them from quitting the toilsome, uncertain and undignified means of subsistence to which custom has condemned them, and taking to a handicraft or a trade; they are snubbed and repressed on all public occasions; are refused admission even to the temples of their gods and can hope for no more helpful partner of their joys and sorrows than the unkempt and unhandy maiden of the paracheri with her very primitive notions of comfort and cleanliness. But once a youth from among these people becomes Christian his whole horizon changes. He is as carefully educated as if he was a Brahman; he is put in the way of learning a trade or obtaining an appointment as a clerk; he is treated with kindness and even familiarity by missionaries who belong to the ruling race (!!); he takes an equal part with his elders and betters in the services of the church; and in due time he can choose from among the neat-handed girls of the Mission a wife skilled in domestic matters and even endowed with some little learning. Now-a-days active persecution of converts to Christianity is rare. So those who hearken to its teaching have no martyr's crown to wear, and sheltered, as they often are, in a compound round the missionary's bungalow, it matters little to its adherents if their neighbours look askance upon them. The remarkable growth in the numbers of the native Christians thus largely proceeds from the natural and laudable discontent with their lot which possesses the lower classes of the Hindus, and so well do the converts as a class use their opportunities that the community is earning for itself a constantly improving position in the public estimation."

Making a sufficient allowance for the Padri's anxiety to paint thick—Hinduism black and the chances afforded by conversion to Christianity bright—there remains enough to put the thoughtful Hindu to shame. We do not mind those cases of apostacy from Hinduism where the change of religion results from a change of religious convictions, but we have every reason to be ashamed of those conversions that are the direct result of our insolence and inhumanities towards the so-called lower classes. It is high time that our indifference to the lot of the depressed classes ceased and we gave them a new start in social life.'

These quotations should leave no doubt in the mind of any Hindu as to the urgency and importance of the question of improving the lot of the depressed classes and of raising their social status. I am of opinion that the matter should be taken in hand in each province by influential provincial committees composed of men of provincial reputation.

Depressed classes missions for smaller area should be organised under the guidance and control of these committees and the work pushed through with earnestness and zeal. The sympathies of young men should be enlisted, from whom eventually some may be inclined to make it their life-work. The subject has an important bearing on famine relief and the development of home industries, from which point of view I intend to discuss it in another article.

Extract from Raj Eshwar, *Paravartan* (*Back to Hinduism*): *Why and How* [An RSS Publication][6]

Part I—The Prelude: The Preliminary Dialogue between the Worker and the Missionary on Paravartan and the Continuously Falling Percentage of Hindu Population

Question I: (Worker to the Missionary)—When I hear about the glorious past of Bharat, I feel highly proud of it but when I hear about the decline of Hindu population I get very much worried. I have learnt that you are engaged in Paravartan work for the last 57 years and that you have already reconverted hundreds of Muslims and Christians into Hindu Dharma. I want to know from you the reasons for the continuous fall in the population of Hindus and how ideologies of Hinduism, Islam and Christianity differ in their origin, Paravartan and other allied subjects and also want to know more about the superiority of Hindu Dharma. How did you start the dialogue and what actually you talked to them to make them agree to your proposal. I shall be putting many other questions to you, please answer them in detail telling me also some other useful points on this subject. First of all please tell me whether the work of Paravartan is easy or very difficult. Can I do it? Will it not create an obstacle in my worldly progress?

Answer I: (Missionary to the Worker)—The work of Paravartan is easy. It can be done by every Hindu, whether he may be a student, an employee or self-employed. It enhances one's self-confidence and also provides impetus to his worldly progress. However one must know

[6] Raj Eshwar, *Paravartan (Back to Hinduism): Why and How* (New Delhi: Suruchi Prakashan, 1999), pp. 9–19.

broadly principles of Hindu Dharma, Islam and Christianity which I would tell you in detail while answering your questions.

Question II: (Worker to the Missionary)—Tell me the reasons of decline of Hindu population in terms of percentage, its consequences, the remedies to check it.

Answer II: (Missionary to the Worker)—History is witness to the fact that in whichever part of India the percentage of Hindu population declined, it was cut off from national mainstream and eventually seceded from the country. Only a few thousands of years back, Hindus were holding a religious empire all over the world. It is for that reason that people from distant lands such as China, Japan, Vidalaksh (Europe), Patal (America) and Gandhar, etc. had participated in the war of Mahabharat. Dissemination of Dharma was our policy in those days. Various tribes like Shakas, Huns, Kushans, Tatars and Mangols came to Bharat and we assimilated them. Afghanistan was part of Bharat till AD 1063. When we gave up the policy of propagation of Hindu Dharma, our number started decreasing.

In AD 1200 the percentage of Muslims in undivided India was 1.85 per cent and that of the Hindus 98.15 per cent. During the period from AD 1200 to AD 1600 the population of Muslims increased by 1.9 per hundred years and during the period from 1600 to 1800, 2.21 per cent per hundred years. This fact has been clearly indicated in the book title *Growth of Muslim Population in India 1000–1800* by Shri K.S. Lal as detailed below:

Year	The population percentage of Muslims in undivided Bharat	The growth percentage of Muslims per hundred years in undivided Bharat
1200	1.6 to 2.1 or 1.85	—
1600	9.58	1.93 (The average from 1201 to 1600)
1800	14.00	2.1 (The average from 1601 to 1800)
1901	21.88 (The figure according to the British census of 1901)	7.88 (Census difference between 1801 and 1901)

By the year AD 1800 a large number of Hindus had embraced Islam for fear of atrocities and tortuous death at the hands of barbarous Muslim rulers. Under the British Rule the first census was carried out in AD 1881. According to the census of AD 1901, the population of Muslims in India was 21.88 per cent i.e. there was an increase in Muslim population by 7.88 per cent during the century between 1801 and 1901, Christians also formed 0.98 per cent. During the century Hindus embraced Islam or Christianity either due to fear of death or various allurements or because of the tyranny of the caste system.

In undivided Bharat, since 1881 to date there has not been a single census which has not recorded decrease in the percentage of Hindus and increase in that of Muslims. (See Appendix A) (The word Hindu includes Sikhs, Jains and Buddhists.) The country was divided in 1947. The Muslim majority areas formed Pakistan. About five lakh Hindus, irrespective of their political, social or sectarian affiliations, were brutally massacred and they lost property worth millions of rupees.

After the Partition in 1947, the first census of divided Bharat was carried out in 1951. According to that census, the population of Hindus in the country was 84.98 per cent (including Sikhs, Jains and Buddhists it was 87.12 per cent) and that of the Muslims 9.91 per cent and Christians 2.35 per cent. On adding the population of Assam for 1991, these figures were recorded as 82.29 per cent, 11.73 per cent and 2.49 per cent respectively whereas in West Pakistan where killing of Hindus had taken place on a large scale, the Hindu population declined from 3 per cent to 1 per cent and in East Pakistan (now Pakistan) it declined from 30 per cent to 12 per cent.

The increase in the percentage of Muslims in comparison to Hindus in the decade 1981–91 is more alarming:

As per the Census in 1991 the population of Muslims during 1981–91 increased by 32.7 per cent more in comparison to 1971–81. The combined population of Hindus, Jains, Buddhists and Sikhs increased by 22.39 per cent. The difference is 10.31 per cent. As per the article by Shri S. Niyogi, published in *Organiser* dated 25.6.95—13 lakh Bangladeshi Muslim intruders came to Bharat illegally. If this population be deducted from the Muslim population then the percentage of increase is 31.08. This percentage is more by 8.69 per cent of the combined population of Hindus, Jains, Buddhists and Sikhs. This difference during 1961–71 was 6.97 per cent and during 1971–81 was 6.08 per cent. The average of the same is 6.53 per cent.

The population of Muslims was 10.65 crore in the year 1991. Now in January 1999 the population is 13.49 crore as per the calculation of 1981–91 percentage increase. Accordingly till January 1999 the Muslim population increased in comparison to Hindus by 11,72,841 every year at the rate of 8.69 per cent. The policy of expansion of education among women gave success to the Family Planning Programme during the Congress rule. The same policy has been adopted by the United Front government and the BJP-led coalition government. To educate women is no doubt beneficial but the political aim of the Muslims is that the percentage of increase in the number of Muslims may always remain more than the Hindus. To achieve this goal they adopt all possible measures of conversion. Muslims are least interested in family planning. Besides they continue to practise polygamy. Muslims are least interested in educating their women. It is often seen that Muslim women having higher education give birth to more children in comparison to Hindu women as is very clear from the following Survey Report.

National Family Health Survey (Family Planning) India made a survey in 1992–3, published by International Institute for Population Sciences, Mumbai, in August 1995 which shows that average number of children ever born to women in the age group of 15 years to 40–9 years onwards is 6.06 in the case of illiterate Muslim women and 5.18 in the case of illiterate Hindu women i.e. a difference of 0.88 more children. And with education up to high school and above, comparatively, participation of such Muslim women in family planning programme has further decreased as compared to such Hindu women, making a difference of 1.25 more children as is clear from the education-wise position given below:

	Muslims	Hindu	Difference
I Illiterate	6.06	5.18	0.88
II Middle school complete	4.59	3.73	0.86
III High school & above	4.04	2.79	1.25

It is clear from the analysis of figures appearing in the Census for the period from 1881 to 1981 that in comparison to pre-Pakistan period, the post-Pakistan period has registered the percentage of population growth of Muslims compared with that of the Hindus at a high rate of 21.62 per cent (approximately one and a quarter times more) (see Appendix B). The main reasons for the increase in Muslim population are as follows:

(i) According to the analysis done by the Registrar General and Census Commission of India, an average Muslim does not participate in family planning whether he may be a city-dweller or a villager, literate or illiterate and may belong to any profession. Although, irrespective of religion, family planning is necessary for everyone yet there is difference in the approach of a Hindu and that of a Muslim to this subject.

(ii) In India Muslims indulge in polygamy whereas in other Muslim countries its prevalence is negligible. On the other hand, after the enactment of Hindu Marriage Act, a Hindu cannot have more than one wife.

(iii) For the two reasons noted above an average Indian Muslim produces more children than a Hindu. Besides that, every Muslim supports *Tablig* (Conversion) of Hindus in every possible way. He looks upon conversion as a noble task. According to the Census reports of 1961, 1971 and 1981 the Muslim population has increased in comparison to the Hindu population by 6.42 per cent, i.e. the Muslim population of 10.48 crores in the year 1990 increased by 6,73,000 during the year 1991. Their number will go on increasing at the rate of 6,73,000 per year. (See Appendix C.) According to the World Christian Encyclopedia 1901–80 of Roman Catholic Christians published in 1982, there were 1,20,479 missionaries in India including 5979 foreign missionaries engaged in the conversion of Hindus and they convert 1,75,000 Hindus to Christianity every year. As per details published in *Christian Mission Handbook*, California, U.S.A., 1986, various Christian organisations send their missionaries to foreign lands to spread Christianity and to convert the natives of those countries according to a well-worked-out plan. America sends one missionary for every 4800 heads of the country's population, Switzerland one for every 2400, France one for 2300, Holland one for 1300, Spain one for

1260 and Ireland one for 328. There are 43 (53 after the disintegration of Russia) countries in the world whose state religion is Islam whereas 66 counties have Christianity as state religion; combined together they remit approximately 1440 crore rupees every year to India for the conversion of Hindus. In September 1987, the Minister of State for Home Affairs admitted in the Lok Sabha that according to government records 450 crore rupees were received from foreign countries and much more has been received surreptitiously. Hindu organisations that are working in the field of 'Paravartan' have not been able to reconvert more than 11,000 people a year during the past one decade.

All Hindus have to make up their mind to work for Paravartan to save themselves from this alarming situation. We will have to inform our posterities of the glory, the scientific nature and the quality of eternal quest for truth of Hindu Dharma. We have to be united and disciplined. We must accept that caste system based on birth is outdated. Forgetting all our social and economic differences we must wipe out the scourge of untouchability from society as soon as possible and forever by shaping the ideals of our families in such a way that no dalit Hindu may ever think of his conversion to any other faith and may not feel isolated from the mainstream. A comprehensive plan for eradication of untouchability has been given in Appendix 'D' for the swayamsevaks of Rashtriya Swayamsevak Sangh. If the various Shakhas of Rashtriya Swayamsevak Sangh adopt this programme, they can bring about a revolution in India. It is essential that every Hindu probes into the mind of those Muslims or Christians who come in contact with him or who can be approached to know whether he can be persuaded to re-embrace Hinduism. If he can become Hindu, further talks may be carried on. If he is fanatic, the matter may be dropped to be taken up some time later. Every Hindu can easily reconvert at least five Muslims or Christians to Hinduism or can save Hindus from getting converted to other religions. They have been converted from amongst ourselves. Every Hindu should persuade them with love, revive in them the Hindu culture and the spirit of nationalism and inspire them to get reconverted individually or collectively.

In the beginning, efforts should be made to ensure that out of the yearly increase in population of 6,73,000 among the Muslim and 1,75,000 among the Christians at least half, i.e. 4,24,000, are reconverted to Hinduism every year. Every Hindu will have to work in this direction otherwise the very entity of Hindus would be lost under the democratic system of the country and all Hindu institutions would be destroyed. Paravartan is a programme of national welfare, in which all Hindus must participate. Democracy and secularism can be saved in India only if the Hindus retain their majority in all parts of India not-withstanding different economic policies and ideologies pursued by the political parties that be in power from time to time for taking the country to the peak of prosperity.

India is an agricultural country. Most of the Muslims and Christians eat beef. If a Muslim or a Christian eats beef twice a week on an aver-age, he would consume five cows in his life time. It leads to a great loss to agriculture and decline in milk production. We Hindus revere cow as our mother because it is a very useful animal. If a Hindu succeeds in reconverting a Muslim or a Christian to Hinduism, he immediately earns the gratification of saving the lives of five cows. The ancestors of the Muslims and Christians were all Hindus: if they come back to their Hindu fold, it would bring peace to the tormented souls of their ancestors.

If possible, those who are engaged in Paravartan work should read chapters 13 and 14 of *Satyarth Prakash*, written by Swami Dayanand Saraswati. Some very useful facts about Christianity and Islam have been given there. Both the chapters comprise a book of 73 pages of normal size.

Paravartan does not require violence at any stage. When Ashoka propagated Buddhism, he did not adopt any violent means and was able to spread Buddhism almost in the whole of India, Sri Lanka, Indonesia, Indo-China, Java, Sumatra, China, Japan and Somalia, etc. Today Christian and Muslim governments all over the world are making all-out efforts to convert and to divide India into small parts through the use of huge amount of money and a large man power. On the one hand, there are zealous missionaries of Islam and Christianity, with limitless funds at their disposal, engaged in the conversion of Hindus and on the other hand, India is a pseudo-secular country where the affluent Hindus can provide very little sums for Hindus Dharma activities because of the faulty system of taxation. With such paucity of funds, the only way out is that all Hindus should devote some time daily, at least the time we otherwise spend in gossiping, for the noble work of Paravartan.

Muslim countries openly encourage those Hindus to embrace Islam who go there for employment and punish them even for keeping and reading their holy books. Saudi Arab is an example in this respect. *Sarvdeshik Patrika* dated 5.10.1986 had published a report that Shri Ram Kumar Bhardwaj had gone to Dahran in Saudi Arab as an employee of a construction company on 2.2.1986. One day he was reading his religious book *Satyarth Prakash* during his leisure time. One of his Muslim friends informed the government about it. Consequently, Ram Kumar was arrested and sent to jail. Somehow Ram Kumar informed of his ordeal to Sarvadeshik Arya Pratinidhi Sabha, Ram Lila Maidan, New Delhi. Shri Ram Gopal Shawlwale, the then President of the Sabha, sent a letter dated 28.5.86 to the Ministry of Foreign Affairs. The Ministry of Foreign Affairs sent a reply dated 4.9.86. The relevant paragraph of this reply has been reproduced below:

> You (addressed to Ram Gopal Shawlwale) are aware that Saudi Arab does not permit anybody to have faith in any religion other than Islam and propagate it. To bring any religious literature or material in that country is totally prohibited. You may please inform the members of your Sabha and bring it to their knowledge that according to the laws of Saudi Arab, to follow any religion other than Islam is prohibited and to bring other religious literature or material in that country is violation of law.

To lead Bharat to material and spiritual glory, all the Swayamsevaks of the Shakhas of Rashtriya Swayamsevak Sangh (RSS) and all other allied organisations which have been organised by the Swayamsevaks for undertaking the allied activities, must take up the work of reconverting the Muslims and Christians through affectionate dealings and persuasion. Similarly Paravartan should become an essential part of activities of Sanatan Dharma Arya Samaj and other religious institutions and temples. Mere collective singing of religious songs and performing of the *Yajna* i.e. making offerings to the sacrificial fire, will not help. We the Hindus have been performing *Shuddhi* i.e. Paravartan since the ancient time. According to the *Bhavishya Puran* the sage Kanav had initiated 10,000 natives of Egypt into Hindu Dharma. During the invasion of Mohammed Bin Kasim in AD 712 many Hindus in Sindh were converted to Islam through questionable means. All of them were reconverted to Hinduism on the authority of Deval Smriti written by Deval Rishi whose abode was on the banks of Sindhu river. Thereafter for 300 years the Muslims never dared attack India. Shri Vidyaranya Swami, Shankaracharya of the head religious seat founded by Adi Shankaracharya had reconverted Shri Harihar and Shri Bukkaroy who were princes and had converted to Islam earlier. They together founded the famous Vijayanagar empire in the Southern part of India. Among Shivaji's Eight Chief Councils, one known as the Council of Repentents was headed by Pandit Rao. The Nawab of Bijapur had converted one Maratha Chief Nimbalkar to Islam and had even married his daughter to him. When he expressed his desire to return to Hindu Dharma, he was reconverted to Hindu Dharma with the consent of Brahmins and under the protection of Shivaji's mother, Jijabai. Shivaji got Nimbalkar's son married to one of the girls of his family. (Pages 286–7 of *Hindu Pad Padshahi.*)

In the modern times Maharashi Dayanand and followers of Arya Samaj founded by him, took up the work of Paravartan on a large scale. The role of Swami Shraddhanand in the field of Paravartan is worth mentioning. During eight years from 1923 to 1931, two lakh Muslims were brought back to the Hindu fold. During this very period 60,000 Hindus, who are called untouchable, were saved from getting converted. Dharam Bhaskar Vinayak Maharaj of Ramdasi Ashram at Mysore reconverted 20,000 Christians in the Portuguese state of Goa in the third decade of the nineteenth century. These Christians had been converted from Hinduism 400 years back. These days the Paravartan work of Arya Samaj has slowed down. The leading revolutionary Hardayal had said in 1937 that Paravartan is the most important task. It i like Sudarshan Chakra and there are four basic measures to protect the Hindus—(1) Paravartan (2) Uniting the Hindus (3) Propagation of Hindu Culture (4) To apprise foreign countries of sublimity of Hinduism. While undergoing imprisonment in the notorious Andaman Jail, Veer Savarkar said, 'If the Hindus are to be saved, the Paravartan work has to be done with a greater speed.'

During the reign of Maharaja Ranvir Singh, the Muslims of Kashmir, who were actually the converts from the erstwhile Brahmins, desired to return to the Hindu fold but Kashmiri Pandits refused to reconvert them to Hinduism. This was a great blunder as a result of which today Hindus have been forced to leave Kashmir, their homeland, despite the presence of Indian Army and the rule of Indian government. The humiliation they and their womenfolk have undergone at the hands of Muslims is beyond description. If every Hindu belonging to any state, faith or political party does not come forward to perform Paravartan, the Hindus in the whole of India would suffer the worse fate than that of the Hindus of Kashmir.

Our Hindu community is badly afflicted by the evil of dowry although it is against the teachings of the Vedas. (See Part 3, subject 4 regarding marriage.) There have been instances where parents did not agree to give their daughter in marriage to the boy of another caste although he was compatible with the girl by virtue of his character, nature, temperament and actions. In such cases, the field of their choice is narrowed down and the parents have to face the demands of heavy dowry. In such cases if demands are not met, they fail to get their daughter married in their caste. Such girls under the misconception that all religions are equal, get easily seduced by unscrupulous Muslim or Christian youths. This is not unnatural in the young age when heart prevails over the mind and the girls agree to marry such youths without caring for the consequences of extra-religious marriages. Muslim and Christian youths are very fanatic about their religious faiths. They first get the girl converted to their religions and then marry her according to Civil Law or according to Muslim Law. The parents of such girls find themselves helpless. Some of the parents support such marriage on the ground that they will not have to give dowry. Once Swami Anand Bodh Saraswati, President of the International Aryan League came to see me. Eventually, the talks came around to the subject of Paravartan. He said that one of his friends had a Muslim employee, one day he returned late from his Namaz (Prayer) on a Friday afternoon. His employer jokingly asked if he had gone to Pakistan. The Muslim youth replied that it would not be necessary now for him to go to Pakistan as very soon this land (Bharat) would also become another Pakistan. He disclosed that a Jaini Hindu had come to Jama Masjid with his five young daughters and told the Imam that due to high demands for dowry he was unable to marry them in his own community. His financial position did not allow him to meet such demands.

He had no objection to his daughters being converted to Islam if they would be married to some eligible Muslim youths. Within minutes five young boys offered themselves to marry them. Needless to say that those helpless girls were converted to Islam and marriages were performed.

[Appendices to this text have not been reproduced.]

14

Reservation and Social Justice

Hindu nationalism is imbued with the Brahminic ethos. Its chief ideologues all come from this milieu. The thinkers cited in the first part of this reader are, for example, all Brahmins, excluding notably Lal Chand, Lajpat Rai, Balraj Madhok, and Arun Shourie—of Punjabi origin—and one Vaishya, H.B. Sarda.[1] The belief system of the Arya Samaj and the Sangh Parivar borrows many of its features from Brahminism. For instance, the key notion of Shuddhi or *samskar* in the discourse of the Arya Samaj and the RSS echoes that of sanskritization: new converts to Hinduism accede to this religion through a purification process invented by (and for) upper-caste men; and, in the RSS shakhas, swayamasevaks are requested to emulate Brahminical values as embodied in their pracharaks. While the RSS is virtually open to each and every caste, its modus operandi implies imitation of 'the purest'.

The upper-caste dimension of the Sangh Parivar is largely due to the circumstances in which the RSS was born. In the 1920s Dalits had begun to organize themselves—especially in Maharashtra, the crucible of the RSS—under the auspices of B.R. Ambedkar. The shakhas, therefore, were also intended to train Brahmin youth to react to the growing Dalit assertiveness, and possibly to defuse their aggressiveness by co-opting them through sanskritization.

Though some low-caste people have joined the RSS, the organization has failed to attract them in large numbers. Dalits have remained especially hostile to Hindu nationalism. The elitist profile of the Sangh Parivar explains its reluctance towards positive discrimination. But

[1] And except Rajendra Singh (a Rajput), all the RSS chiefs so far have been Brahmins.

the eagerness of the organization to defend the interests of the social groups it represents does not say everything: the RSS is also hostile to reservations because they are caste based, which means that poor Brahmins cannot benefit from these measures and—more importantly—that the Hindu nation it is building is challenged by divisive caste identities. The RSS sees that caste affiliations cannot be transcended if castes have a vested interest in their caste identity because of the benefits to them from reservations. This stand harks back to the basic notion of Hindu nationalists, namely that the Hindu Rashtra forms an organic totality relying on the virtually harmonious collaboration of all limbs of society.

Therefore the RSS has always been one of the most vocal opponents of positive discrimination in India. It immediately criticized V.P. Singh's announcement on 7 August 1990 that the recommendations of the Mandal Commission report would be implemented, which meant that 27 per cent of central administration posts would be reserved for Other Backward Classes (OBCs, the list of which was in fact a list of low castes). *The Organiser* attacked not only this decision, denouncing it as the pampering of vote banks, but also the whole policy of positive discrimination from an organicist angle: 'The havoc the politics of reservation is playing with the social fabric is unimaginable. It provides a premium for mediocrity, encourages brain-drain and sharpens caste-divide.'[2] In 1994 Rajendra Singh, then chief of the RSS, even considered that 'there should be a gradual reduction in the job quotas',[3] even for the Scheduled Castes.

The BJP did not react to the Mandal affair in the same way as the RSS. The party, and its predecessor the Jana Sangh, have been popularly known as 'Banya/Brahmin' parties. In fact, as evident from election surveys, they have primarily attracted upper-caste white collars, professionals, merchants, and other middle-class groups: what Bruce Graham has described, with reference to the Jana Sangh, as the intermediate world.[4] In 1990, certainly, the BJP also disapproved of caste-based quotas and made a strong plea in favour of economic criteria in

[2] *The Organiser*, 26 August 1990, p. 15.

[3] *The Organiser*, 18 December 1994, p. 20.

[4] B. Graham, *Hindu Nationalism and Indian Politics*, vol. 7, no. 17, 3 September 1990, chapter 6: 'The Jana Sangh and Interest-group Politics'.

the framing of affirmative action programmes.[5] Simultaneously L.K. Advani's Rath Yatra relaunched the agitation around Ayodhya to reunite Hindus and make OBCs regard themselves as Hindus first and foremost. While one of the objectives of the Rath Yatra was to defuse caste feelings, many upper-caste people and non-OBC 'Shudras' became supporters of the BJP at the time because they knew the BJP was much more reluctant about reservations than it stated publicly. However, the BJP could not avoid addressing the Mandal issue.

The main advocate of a more sympathetic attitude *vis-à-vis* the lower castes was K.N. Govindacharya, himself a Brahmin and one of the BJP general secretaries. He called this policy 'social engineering'. However, his strategy was opposed by some of his colleagues, including by M.M. Joshi, who objected on principle to any artificial transformation of the so-called social equilibrium and did not want to give new importance to caste as a result of the 'Mandal affair'.[6] In 1996 the BJP's election manifesto reflected this ambivalence. It promised that, if voted to power, it would continue the reservation system for OBCs 'till they are socially and educational [*sic*] integrated with the rest of society'; but it also announced a 10 per cent reservation on the basis of economic criteria to all economically weaker sections of society, apart from the Scheduled Castes, Scheduled Tribes, and OBCs.[7] The BJP had admitted the inevitability of quotas for OBCs but it tried to combine the criterion of caste with socio-economic criteria.

After the 1998 elections the BJP formed a coalition, the National Democratic Alliance (NDA) which enabled Vajpayee to become prime minister. This alliance was formalized before the 1999 elections, to such an extent that the party did not prepare any election manifesto for itself: there was only one manifesto for the NDA. Being now the pivotal force of a larger coalition whose components were often less elitist than the BJP itself, the party tended to further dilute its stand

[5] This is evident from the BJP's bulletin, *About Us*, 3 September 1990, pp. 6–7, and from interviews of some of its leaders: see L.K. Advani's interview in *Hindustan Times* (Sunday Supplement), 23 September 1990, p. 2.

[6] Interview in *Sunday*, 26 January 1997, p. 13.

[7] Ibid., p. 62. This programme recalls the Social Charter adopted by the 1993 plenary session of the BJP, where L.K. Advani succeeded M.M. Joshi as party president. *India Today*, 15 July 1993, p. 39.

regarding the reservations issue. In the NDA election manifesto one could read: 'If required, the Constitution will be amended to maintain the system of reservation [. . .] We are committed to extending the SC/ST reservation for another 10 years. Reservation-percentages above 50 per cent, as followed by certain states, shall be sanctified through necessary legislation measures.'[8]

Vajpayee himself, while campaigning in Rajasthan, declared that his government 'would implement the reservation policy in right earnest'.[9] Obviously, the BJP leaders had become more responsive to OBC demands, not only because of their coalition partners but also in order to attract more OBC voters.

Extract from *RSS Resolves: Full Text of Resolutions from 1950 to 1983*[10]

The Issue of Reservations in Gujarat in the 1980s

The ABPS feels deeply perturbed over the explosive situation in Gujarat and elsewhere arising out of the issue of reservation.

As one believing in the indivisible unity of the entire Hindu Society including Harijans and tribals, the RSS has consistently been endeavouring to arouse this inherent spirit of oneness. The RSS considers it necessary that reservation be continued for the present with a view to bringing all these brethren of ours who have remained backward in educational, social and economic fields over the centuries at par with the rest of society.

The ABPS is of the opinion that the policy of reservation has, because of its wrong implementation, become a tool of power-politics and election-tactics instead of serving the purpose for which it was framed. And this has resulted in generating mutual ill-will and conflict in our society in several parts of the country. In the considered opinion

---

[8] National Democratic Alliance, *For a Proud, Prosperous India—An Agenda. Election Manifesto, Lok Sabha Election, 1999* (New Delhi: Bharatiya Janata Party, for and on behalf of the National Democratic Alliance, 1999), p. 8.

[9] Cited in *The Hindu*, 25 August 1999.

[10] *RSS Resolves: Full Text of Resolutions from 1950 to 1983* (Bangalore: Prakashan Vibhag, RSS, 1983), pp. 103–4.

of this Sabha, the national resolve of building up a harmonious and egalitarian society cannot be achieved on the strength of constitutional and political measures alone. The Sabha therefore suggests the constituting of a committee of non-partisan social thinkers which will study in depth all the problems arising out of reservations and suggest positive steps for the uplift of Harijans and tribals. The committee should also recommend necessary concessions to the other economically backward sections with a view to ensuring their speedy development.

The ABPS agrees with the Prime Minister's viewpoint that the reservation cannot be a permanent arrangement, that these crutches will have to be done away with as soon as possible, and that because of this arrangement merit and efficiency should not be allowed to be adversely affected. The Sabha appeals to all other political parties and leaders as well to support this viewpoint and initiate measures to find a solution to the problem.

The ABPS believes that the desired result can be achieved only through the combined efforts of social and Governmental agencies. The Sabha exhorts the people and in particular the Sangh Swayamsevaks to strive to create social harmony and goodwill, so that our society becomes capable of solving its problems without giving rise to mutual bitterness or conflicts and be in a position to defuse the tension if and when such occasions arise.

Extracts from 'BJP Election Manifesto', 1991 Lok Sabha Elections[11]

Scheduled Castes and Scheduled Tribes

The BJP sincerely believes with all its heart in the upliftment of SC and ST. To this end we will:

1. Energetically enforce anti-untouchability laws;
2. Make free legal aid available to SC in cases under these laws;
3. Make all village wells available to all castes and communities;
4. Set up a financial agency on the lines of NABARD to cater to the credit needs of SC & ST;
5. Promptly fill up the shortfall in jobs reserved for SC and ST;

[11] Pamphlet of Manifesto, no publisher, author's copy.

6. A befitting memorial would be constructed in honour of Dr Ambedkar;
7. Evolve a new forest policy based on a partnership between the forest tribals and the forest authorities;
8. Protect SC and ST from exploitation and indebtedness;
9. Formulate a sub-plan for the economic development of Scheduled Tribes;
10. Remove all impediments in the speedy development of hill and forest tribal areas.

Other Backward Castes

The BJP is pledged to the socio-economic uplift of Other Backward Castes particularly the more backward among them. BJP in its 1985 resolution and subsequently in its 1989 Election Manifesto commended the following reservation policy:

1. Reservation should be continued for the Scheduled Castes and Scheduled Tribes as before;
2. Reservation should also be made for other backward classes broadly on the basis of the Mandal Commission Report, with preference to be given to the poor among these very classes; and
3. As poverty is an important contributory factor for backwardness, reservation should also be provided for members of the other castes on the basis of their economic condition.

In view of the shocking manner in which the National Front government implemented the Mandal Commission Report which resulted in self-immolation of youths and pitted caste against caste and community against community, BJP feels that the reservation policy should be introduced taking into consideration socio economic ethos. Reservation policy should be used as an instrument of social justice and promoting social harmony as well. The question of reservation has to be viewed with open mind free from all prejudices of any kind.

In addition, BJP:

1. Will start a chain of first class residential schools where the really bright children of really poor families of all castes and communities will be admitted, educated and otherwise looked after, to

come into their own and enter Services, Business and Professions in open competition;

2. Most of the non-agricultural OBSCs are artisans. Foreign and metropolitan competition has hurt these people badly. BJP will train and equip them, so that they can find a place of honour in the new social economy.

Extract from 'BJP Election Manifesto', 1996 Lok Sabha Elections[12]

Harmony and Equality through Integral Humanism: The Bharatiya Janata Party's social philosophy, which is the bedrock of its social agenda, is rooted in integral humanism. It rules out contradictions between society and its various components, as also between society and the individual, or, for that matter, between the family, the basic building brick of our social structure, and the individual. From this stems the BJP's commitment to the eradication of social and economic disparities that have prevented India from emerging as a modern, dynamic nation; to the creation of a socially integrated Bharatiya society which can proudly enter the new century. The BJP will help all socially and economically weak and backward sections of society, through special welfare and other schemes, to reach their full potential. For us, it is a historic task which we are resolved to fulfil.

Equity and Equality

1. The BJP will adhere, through its policies and programmes to the ideals, principles and goals of equity and equality as enshrined in our country's Constitution.
2. The BJP will promote a casteless socio-economic order which will effectively provide access to equal opportunities to all citizens, irrespective of their caste, creed, religion or gender.
3. The BJP will ensure that the place of an individual in society will not be determined on the basis of his birth.
4. The BJP will dismantle practices, customs, beliefs, usages and institutions which are divisive and discriminatory, and which in any manner hurt the dignity of the individual.

[12] Pamphlet of Manifesto, no publisher, author's copy.

Untouchability

1. The BJP condemns unequivocally the practice of untouchability which is not only against the law of the land but runs counter to the very concept of integral humanism. Not surprisingly, the first brick of the Ram temple at Ayodhya was laid by a member of the Scheduled Castes, Kameshwar Chaupal.
2. The BJP will endeavour to create an ethos of equality in social and inter-personal relationships.

Weaker Sections

1. The BJP will make the existing institutions and Constitutional safeguards for Scheduled Castes and Scheduled Tribes operationally more effective.
2. The BJP views the provision of special facilities and special opportunities, including reservations, in the Constitution as practical steps to advance the deprived and under-privileged sections of society. The BJP will continue with the existing policy on reservations till social and economic equity is achieved.

Our Scheduled Castes and Scheduled Tribes

The BJP's goal is to achieve social equality for all Scheduled Castes and Scheduled Tribes through political and economic empowerment. To achieve this goal, the BJP will:

1. Stringently enforce laws against untouchability;
2. Inquire into all cases of atrocities, publish the findings, punish the guilty and rehabilitate the victims as expeditiously as possible;
3. Lay stress on education, vocational training and skill upgradation;
4. Take prompt action to fill up the backlog in jobs reserved for Scheduled Castes and Scheduled Tribes. The reservations policy will be backed up with a statute;
5. Set up a financial agency on the lines of NABARD to cater to the individual and institutional credit needs of Scheduled Castes and Scheduled Tribes;
6. Provide more facilities for greater participation of Scheduled

Castes and Scheduled Tribes in small scale, cottage and rural industries, as well as in trade and commerce;

7. End the pernicious practice of carrying night soil and accelerate the rehabilitation of those engaged in scavenging;

8. Wipe out the evil of bonded and child labour and rehabilitate the victims;

9. Launch a massive housing programme for the homeless in villages;

10. Allot pattas for land, home site and homes in the name of wives/widows/daughters;

11. Take necessary steps to protect tribals from exploitation, especially by contractors, and indebtedness;

12. Amend the existing forest policy to restore to the Vanvasis their rightful share of forest wealth and produce, as well as provide viable marketing facilities;

13. Expedite the processing of the claims of Vanvasis and Girijans for pattas in forest and hill areas;

14. Disallow the diversion of monies from Plan and Tribal Sub-Plan funds meant for the welfare and development of Vanvasis and Girijans;

15. Prevent land alienation through conversion of tribal lands for industrial and other purposes;

Extract from 'BJP Election Manifesto', 1998 Lok Sabha Elections[13]

Our Social Philosophy: Rooted in Integral Humanism

The Bharatiya Janata Party's social agenda flows from its ideology of Integral Humanism. Our ideology rules out contradictions between society and its very components, as also between society and the individual. Our concern for the last man in the last row is as deep as that for the first man in the first row, if not more. The BJP's concept of social justice, therefore, does not seek to create rifts and schisms between various sections of society, but aims at removing social and economic disparities that have resulted in denial of a share in power,

[13] Pamphlet of Manifesto, no publisher, author's copy.

impoverishment and erosion of human dignity. An ideal society is not one that is compartmentalized in segments, but is an integral whole, harmonious and conflict-free. Hence, we subscribe to *Samajik Samarasata* (social harmony) and *Samajik Nyaya* (social justice) and strive to avoid social strife.

Equal Rights for all in Satta (Power), *Sampatti* (Prosperity) *and Samman* (Dignity)

1. The BJP will actively promote a casteless socio-economic order that will effectively provide access to equal opportunity for all citizens, irrespective of their caste, creed, religion and gender.
2. The BJP will, if necessary through legislation, dismantle practices, customs, beliefs, usages and institutions, which in any manner hurt the dignity of an individual.
3. The BJP will ensure that the place of an individual in society is not determined on the basis of his/her birth.

Untouchability: A Crime Against Humanity

1. The BJP will remove the last vestiges of untouchability, which we believe is an unpardonable crime against humanity.
2. The BJP will strive to inculcate an ethos of equality in social and inter-personal relationships.
3. A befitting National Memorial in honour of Dr Babasaheb Ambedkar, who dedicated his life to the cause of social justice, will be erected at Chaityabhoomi in Mumbai on the lines of national memorials like Raj Ghat, Shanti Van and Vijay Ghat.

Our Commitment to the Welfare of Scheduled Castes and Scheduled Tribes

Nearly four-and-a-half decades of Congress rule and the recent United Front regime have failed to empower the Scheduled Castes and the Scheduled Tribes. While thousands of crores have been spent, ostensibly for their welfare, Scheduled Castes and Scheduled Tribes face increasing impoverishment and marginalization. Eighty per cent of members belonging to these sections of Indian society have been pushed below the poverty line. The BJP is committed to the social, economic and political empowerment of the Scheduled Castes and Scheduled Tribes, so that the wrongs of the past are corrected in a time-bound manner for a better future. To fulfill our commitment, we will be guided by a policy whose highlights are as follows:

1. Existing institutions and Constitutional safeguards for Scheduled Castes and Scheduled Tribes will be strengthened and made operationally more effective.

2. The provision of special facilities and preferential opportunities, including reservations, will be implemented in a manner so as to benefit the broadest cross-section and largest number of SCs and STs.

3. The reservations policy will be backed up with a statute and all backlogs will be cleared within a specified time-frame. Special tribunals will be set up under CAT to expeditiously deal with complaints of non-implementation of the reservations policy and related grievances.

4. All cases of atrocities against members of the Scheduled Castes and Scheduled Tribes will be promptly inquired into and the guilty punished through special courts.

5. A comprehensive development package will be introduced for the economic empowerment of Scheduled Castes and Scheduled Tribes. The highlights of this package will include:

    (a) Setting up of a credit agency on the lines of NABARD to meet individual and institutional credit needs;

    (b) Vocational training, skill upgradation and financial assistance to encourage greater participation in cottage and rural industries and other means of self-employment;

    (c) Food-for-education schemes to raise literacy levels;

    (d) A comprehensive national programme of minor irrigation facilities for irrigable land held by SCs and STs;

    (e) Endowing every landless rural family of the SCs and STs with land and ensuring sustenance level of income through requisite facilities;

    (f) Amending the existing forest policy to provide Vanvasis their rightful share of minor forest produce;

   (g) Processing claims of Vanvasis and Girijans for pattas in forest and hill areas promptly; and,

   (h) Separate development plans for tribals living in the plains.

6. The specified allocation for the Special Component Plan (17 per cent) for Scheduled Castes and the Tribal Sub-Plan (8 per cent) for Scheduled Tribes within the total Plan allocation will be strictly followed both at the Centre and in the States. Every effort will be made to ensure that allocated funds do not lapse and are spent as per Plan provisions.

7. The pernicious practice of carrying night soil will be eliminated and all those engaged in scavenging rehabilitated.

8. Allotment of pattas for land, home site and homes in the names of wives/widows/daughters. These will be properly drawn up and handed over to actual beneficiaries;

9. Unifying the Banjaras under a common category and ensuring that they are benefited by the Minimum Needs Programme;

10. Necessary steps to stop the exploitation of tribals by contractors and to free them from indebtedness. We will consider enacting a law whereby the outstanding debts of those tribals who have paid back the principal amount and 50 per cent of the capital as interest, will be written off;

11. Stringent action to prevent tribal land alienation through conversion of tribal land for industrial and other purposes;

12. A National Policy for the 'total rehabilitation' of families displaced by development projects. The policy will include social, economic, educational, environmental, occupational and cultural aspects;

13. An engineering and a medical college will be set up in the national capital in honour of Maharishi Valmiki and Babasaheb Ambedkar. Fifty per cent seats in these institutes will be reserved for students from Scheduled Castes, Scheduled Tribes and OBCs;

14. Panchayat institutions in scheduled areas and tribal areas will be made effective and functional in the light of Bhuria Committee's recommendations;

15. Claims for inclusion into the ST list by erstwhile 'criminal' tribes and others will be entrusted to a commission for recommendations.

Our Commitment to the Welfare of Socially and
Educationally Backward Classes

The BJP is committed to ensuring social and economic justice to the
Other Backward Classes. This is integral to our concept of Social Harmony (Samajik Samarasata). We reject the divisive and casteist politics
of our adversaries that have neither economically empowered the bulk
of the OBCs nor reduced their educational backwardness. We propose
to:

1. Continue with the current reservations policy for the Other Backward Classes till they are socially and educationally integrated with
   the rest of society;
2. Provide training, financial support and management facilities for
   upgradation of skills in traditional industries and professions of
   OBCs;
3. Take corrective and remedial measures in view of recent macro-
   economic policy decisions that have rendered several sections of
   people belonging to the OBCs jobless;
4. Make the National Backward Classes Finance Development Corporation fully operational.

Extract from 'NDA Election Manifesto',
1999 Lok Sabha Elections[14]

SCs, STs and Backward Classes

The interests of Scheduled Castes, Scheduled Tribes and Backward
Classes will be adequately safeguarded by appropriate legal, executive
and societal efforts and by large scale education and empowerment.
We will provide legal protection to existing percentages of reservation
in government employment and educational institutions at the Centre
and State level. If required, the Constitution will be amended to maintain the system of reservation. We will continue to offer all assistance
to the SCs, STs and Backward Classes to ensure their speedy socio-
economic development. We will remove the last vestiges of untouchability from our society. Further, we will present a National Charter
for Social Justice (Samajik Nyaya) based on the principle of social

[14] Pamphlet of Manifesto, no publisher, author's copy.

harmony (Samajik Samarasata). We are committed to extending the SC/ST reservations for another 10 years. Reservation percentages, above 50 per cent, as followed by certain states shall be sanctified through necessary legislative measures.

'Extract from 'NDA Election Manifesto', 2004 Lok Sabha Elections[15]

Social Justice and Empowerment

1. A Monitoring Committee for Elimination of Social Disparities will be set up to focus on social and economic justice for SCs, STs, OBCs, denotified and nomadic tribes, and the poor among forward classes and minorities. States will be encouraged to set up similar committees.

2. A National Tribal Policy will be enunciated for the all-round socio-economic development of our vanvasi brethren.

3. Regularization of land rights of tribals living on forest land and promotion of their livelihood activities based on forest produce, if necessary by suitable amendments in the forest laws.

4. Provisions of the policy on reservations will be strictly implemented. A major drive will be launched for filling up all backlogs in jobs and promotions for SCs and STs. Private sector enterprises will be given incentives for creating more educational, training, employment and entrepreneurship opportunities for SCs and STs.

5. Functioning of various Commissions and Finance Corporations for the development of SCs and STs will be improved.

6. Laws to check atrocities against SCs, STs, and other weaker sections will be strictly enforced.

7. The newly announced Commission for Nomadic and Denotified Tribes will be made operational.

8. Reservations for the poor among 'Forward Classes' will be introduced after receiving recommendations of the Commission set up for this purpose.

9. Special encouragement will be given for preservation of the artistic and cultural traditions of SCs and STs, and for honouring their heroes.

[15] Pamphlet of Manifesto, no publisher, author's copy.

15

Education

E ducation occupies a central position in the Hindu nationalist agenda since it pertains to the very mission of the RSS that Hedgewar and his successors defined as 'character building'. In the shakhas, the daily reshaping of minds suggests forms of brainwashing. Naturally, leaders of the Sangh Parivar would find their task much easier if the official curriculum taught to Indian schoolchildren echoed their worldview instead of the secularism mandated by the Indian constitution. In order to cope with this issue, the RSS has set up a network of schools.

A pracharak from Maharashtra, Nanaji Deshmukh, who had been sent to Uttar Pradesh, initiated the first component of this new offshoot of the RSS in 1952 in Gorakhpur under the name 'Saraswati Shishu Mandir' (temples of the pupils of Saraswati). These 'mandirs' were federated and put under an umbrella organisation called Vidya Bharti (Indian Knowledge) in 1977, headquartered in Delhi. At that time, Vidya Bharti ran 700 schools.[1] In the early 1990s the organization was responsible for managing 5000 schools with 1.2 million pupils enrolled and 40,000 teachers employed.[2] In 2003 it had 14,000 schools, 73,000 teachers and 1.7 million pupils.[3]

However, Hindu nationalist leaders were keen to influence the national public education system in order to make a bigger impact. Every time they have had access to power, at the centre or state level,

[1] *The Organiser*, 19 November 1978, p. 1.
[2] N. Khanna, 'Education: The RSS Way', *Sunday*, 1 December 1991, pp. 22–3.
[3] http://www.rss.org/New_RSS/parivaar/History.jsp

they have tried to promote their own idea of education. In 1977–9, during the Janata phase, Hindu nationalist leaders targeted three history textbooks—*Ancient India* by Romila Thapar, *Modern India* by Bipan Chandra, and *Freedom Struggle* by A. Tripathi, Barun De and Bipan Chandra—which they wanted to withdraw from the curriculum. They resented the failure to condemn the Muslim invasions of India and the use of derogatory terms—or sheer neglect—in relation to Hindus they regarded as heroes, such as Aurobindo and Tilak. *The Organiser* orchestrated the campaign against these books, whose authors were all described as communist intellectuals.[4] In July 1978 the government banned one more textbook, *Ancient India* by R.S. Sharma, another 'communist' historian who had also been relieved of his post as head of the Indian Council of Historical Research (ICHR).[5] The early fall of Morarji Desai's government foiled the Hindu nationalists, but history repeated itself when the BJP came to power in the 1990s.

Murli Manohar Joshi (1934–), who was Minister of Human Resource Development and Sciences & Technology with the explicit approval of the RSS, between 1998 and 2004 appointed personalities who had been close to the Sangh Parivar as heads of various directive bodies, such as ICHR and the Indian Council of Social Science Research (ICSSR).[6] For the National Council for Educational Research and Training (NCERT) he selected Krishna Gopal Rastogi, a former RSS pracharak. Marxism was dropped from the class XII political science curriculum in English. After the left protested in parliament, the Central Board of Secondary Education said the omission was a printer's mistake,

---

[4] A.R.G. Tiwari, 'A True History of India is Yet to be Written', *The Organiser*, 23 July 1978, pp. 8–9.

[5] On the controversy regarding history textbooks during the Janata phase, see L.I. Rudolph and S. Hoeber Rudolph, 'Cultural Policy, the Textbook Controversy and Indian Identity', in A.J. Wilson and D. Dalton, eds, *The States of South Asia* (London: Hurst, 1982).

[6] The apprehensions aroused by the placement in key positions of RSS fellow travellers began to materialize in February 2000 when the ICHR 'suspended' two volumes of its series called 'Towards Freedom', those edited by Sumit Sarkar and K.N. Panikkar, who were known for being highly critical of the Sangh Parivar.

but the episode exacerbated apprehensions among left-oriented intellectuals.[7]

M.M. Joshi, who also promoted Sanskrit and astrology at the university when he was Minister, joined the RSS when he was ten years old. A professor of physics, he taught at Allahabad University, where he had been the student of another professor of physics, Rajendra Singh, who had succeeded Balasaheb Deoras as the RSS chief. Joshi was active within the ABVP and then in the Jana Sangh. He was elected to the Lok Sabha for the first time in 1977 and for the second time in 1996, when he was made Home Minister in Vajpayee's first 13-day government. He was appointed president of the BJP in 1991 but served only one term because he was too representative of the party's right wing at a time when the Sangh Parivar was trying to project a more moderate face in order to make allies.

Extracts from Murli Manohar Joshi: 'Reorienting Education'[8]

Considering the supreme importance of the role of education in national development, it is distressing that our educational endeavours in the last five decades should have been characterised by evident infirmity of purpose. We inherited from our colonial past a largely imitative system of not very high quality, and even that quality seems to have declined in recent years. It would be interesting to have a glimpse of the state of education in India when the British came.

Mahatma Gandhi stated in October 1931 at Chatham House, London that, 'India today is much more illiterate than it was before fifty years ago.' The statement was challenged by Sir Philip Hartog one of the founders of the School of Oriental and African Studies, London.

---

[7] One of them, Romila Thapar, echoed these feelings in a press interview: 'Schoolteachers I've been in touch with, those teaching history, are very concerned about what to teach the children. Because if they teach from the textbooks we have written, the kids will be penalized in the exams.' Interview in *Outlook*, 6 December 1999, p. 11.

[8] Murli Manohar Joshi, 'Reorienting Education', *Seminar*, Delhi, no. 417, May 1994, pp. 26–9.

But the reports of William Adam (1835) provide unimpeachable evidence in Gandhiji's support. The Adam Reports on indigenous educational institutions in Bengal and Bihar have long been recognised as a unique record of these institutions before the British influence extended to all the interior villages.

William Adam had observed in 1835 that there seem to exist about 100,000 village schools in Bengal and Bihar around 1830. A few years earlier G.L. Prendergast had stated that in the newly extended presidency of Bombay 'there is hardly a village, great or small throughout our territories, in which there is not at least one school and in larger villages more'. The same state of affairs had been affirmed by Thomas Munro when he reported in 1812–13 that 'every village had a school'. Dr G.W. Leitner observed as late as 1882 that the spread of education in Punjab around 1850 was to a similar extent.

The thousands of schools which Adam saw and meticulously reported reflected the rich diversity of Indian culture. These institutions were entirely supported by local resources unaided by government in any way. They revealed an underlying harmony in which various religious groups studied with and were taught by teachers of different backgrounds and castes. Dharmpal, in his famous book *The Beautiful Tree* (1983), has made a comprehensive study of archival materials and has shown that the indigenous system at the end of the 18th century had a high percentage of students belonging to those communities now characterised as scheduled castes. Dharmpal also proved that the Indian education system during the early 19th century was comparable to that obtainable elsewhere and the British education system was in no way superior.

When the British took hold of India, they decided to impose Western education through the English language and thus destroyed the indigenous system. No single decision has done more to cut off the vast majority of Indians from their great national heritage and values and also deprive poor villagers from access to the most prestigious jobs in government and industry. The Kothari Commission later suggested that if education was not in coherence with our great national heritage and cultural values, it would not serve as the foundation for the full development of an individual's personality nor could it provide an instrument for the nation's progress, welfare and security. The education system, therefore, needs a drastic reconstruction.

The BJP would suggest a bold and imaginative educational programme, which

- is directed towards the full development of individual personality, so as to equip him to contribute his best to enrich the quality of life in Indian society and attain those standards of material, intellectual and cultural advancement which the country wants to achieve;
- helps in modernising society and in the quick assimilation of science and technology, with work experience and dignity of manual labour as an essential part of education, taking care to understand that all that is western is not modern;
- inspires confidence in the future of India as a nation, cherishes the best of Indian traditions and heritage, develops pride in its achievements, and offers internationally comparable standards of training so as to produce world leaders in different fields;
- is related to productivity, and leads to eradication of poverty;
- leads to the adoption of democracy as a way of life, helps in the establishment of an egalitarian society, fosters national and social integration and promotes a healthy international outlook;
- inculcates necessary and desirable moral, social and cultural values and self-discipline;
- creates faith in the dignity and liberty of the individual and brings the realisation that individual fulfilment is best achieved through social advancement.

Poverty and illiteracy go hand in hand. The main thrust of any educational programme should be the simultaneous eradication of both. Education should cater both to the needs of life and living. With this in view, expansion programmes of education should take into account man-power requirements and the educational needs of each region.

Each district should prepare a blueprint of these requirements and plan for the establishment of institutions for imparting both general and vocational education. There is need to provide technical education at various levels and a complex of agro-industrial polytechnics should be established in each district. Courses in home science and home industry should be made available to girls.

It is a pity that even after forty-seven years of independence, India's record of fulfilling the Constitutional directive regarding free and compulsory education for the 6–14 years age group has been extremely poor. The BJP believes that an Adult Education Programme should form an essential component of a massive literacy drive, and universities, voluntary organisations, and social activists must be involved in this endeavour. A blind adoption of the standards of affluent societies with regard to educational buildings and equipment will not help implementing the Constitutional obligation. The party would instead emphasise a teacher-oriented education expansion programme suitable to Indian conditions and traditions.

Agencies at both state and central levels should be created for constant review and framing of the school curriculum. A significant feature of the syllabus should be to acquaint the student with the Indian contribution to the advancement of world civilisation and with the history of India's struggle for freedom from foreign rule.

Special funds should be earmarked for the search and development of sports talent. Physical education, including yogic exercise, should be designed to ensure balanced growth and development of character.

Science education and work experience should be an important ingredient of the curriculum and no school curriculum would be complete without giving some place to personal hygiene, the obligations of a citizen, environmental studies and population education.

Education in moral and spiritual values must be properly integrated with the curriculum. Information about various religions, and the lives of great saints should be given so as to promote respect for all religions.

The BJP supports the principle that people have a right to be educated and run the administration in their own language. It is therefore necessary to provide, in every linguistic region, adequate arrangements for teaching various Indian languages so that persons knowing different languages are available in every region. The party would pursue a policy of providing full assistance for the development and growth of Sanskrit and also such other Indian languages which are not state or regional languages but have contributed to the growth of Indian culture.

The school system as it exists today is divisive in its impact on the young. The good quality schools are expensive and are available only to the affluent sections but a vast majority has to remain content with schools of poor quality. Under the provisions of the Indian Constitution, religious and linguistic minorities are allowed to run their own schools. But this right does not prevent the state from prescribing norms of academic standards and fair employment practices or to bring the institutions run by non-governmental agencies under the network of a national/common school system. In the opinion of the BJP, the education system should lead to national integration by effectively eliminating the divisive trends. The state and district level education boards as recommended by the Kothari Commission should ensure that the schools are imbued with the sense of a common purpose. BJP would favour a National School Board to coordinate the work of State Boards.

The University Grants Commission, as envisaged in the Constitution, should function as an effective agency for determining and coordinating the standards of higher education and as a national accreditation authority, instead of paying excessive attention to the disbursal of grants. Freedom and accountability must be the hallmark of the higher education system. The universities should be endowed with utmost possible autonomy, and the participation of the entire academic community, that is teachers and students, in various decision-making processes be ensured in meaningful ways.

The BJP would pursue a policy of promoting close interaction between educational institutions and the community with a view to provide a critical and objective assessment of the strength and weaknesses of the social order. The universities should on the one hand cater to what society wants and on the other also suggest what it 'should want'. The BJP would suggest that the teachers should be free to exercise their civic rights and as suggested by the Kothari Commission, they should be eligible to hold public offices at all levels.

A convention of representatives of students, teachers, guardians, political parties and the administration should be called at least once a year, at the state level, to consider problems of common interest and to discuss ways and means for ensuring that the academic calendar is not disrupted and the campus remains peaceful. The students union should be associated with the management of student welfare pro-grammes. It is for each university to determine the way its students are associated with the decision-making process at different levels.

The BJP recognises the symbiotic relationship between educational expenditure and national well-being; the party would strive for progressively increasing allocations for education till it reaches a level of 6 per cent of the GNP.

Under the British administration, educational institutions were expected to teach loyalty to the colonial rulers rather than develop a spirit of national consciousness. During the freedom struggle, efforts to instill a love for one's country and countrymen were largely made outside the educational system. These efforts were inspired by a renewed belief in the value of Indian culture and a pride in India's past achieve-ments. It was recognised by the leaders of the independence movement that in the interaction between India and the West, India had also something worthwhile to give in return and that Indians should try to maintain the precious elements in their own ancient culture and tradi-tions while accepting all that was good in the rest of the world. It was interpreted by certain sections as an attempt to slide back to medieval ages which it was not. It was an attempt to refuse to be blown off one's feet even when all the windows of one's house were thrown open from every corner of the world.

It has been well recognised all over the world that schools and uni-versities can play a dominant role in the regeneration and progress of a nation and in providing the necessary psychological energy needed for the advancement of the people. Unfortunately the colonial edu-cational system inherited by us had no such tradition. The system needs to be reoriented for this prime responsibility of awakening and strengthening the national spirit, it has to be transformed into an effective instrument for this purpose.

With this in view when certain steps were initiated by the BJP governments in UP and MP much noise was made against them. The existing syllabi were reviewed and some additions to supplement them were suggested. Vedic mathematics was introduced as a technique for quick computation. Its incorporation in the syllabus did not displace any of the contemporary methods, rather it was presented as an alter-native system. Its introduction acquainted the students with the capacity of Indian seers to discover such a unique system in what has been hitherto understood as an exclusive domain of western scientists and also provided a sense of respect for India's ancient wisdom and heritage.

The sixteen aphorisms of Vedic mathematics are not related to any ritual, they have been termed Vedic because the seer who discovered them did so in the same manner in which the Vedic sages perceived the Vedic *rishis*. In a sense its introduction could motivate the students to think about the holistic approach of ancient Rishis and compare it with the reductionist approach of the Newtonian science. It may be recalled that the work of scientists like David Bohm, Bell, Capra and others have pointed out the limitations of the Cartesian approach and have pointed out that in many respects the eastern holistic approach provides a deeper understanding of the universe.

Sanskrit language is the repository of ancient Indian contributions to the field of science, philosophy, literature, architecture and various performing arts. Kautilya wrote his famous treatise in Sanskrit and works of Arya Bhata, Varahmihira, Brahmagupta, Bhaskaracharya and a host of mathematicians cannot be properly understood without Sanskrit. The vast literature of Kalidasa, Bhavabhuti, Magh and others alongwith the Indian contributions to the field of technology, chemistry, astronomy, horticulture and agriculture cannot be appreciated without knowing Sanskrit. The moment a student comes to know about the rich Indian heritage in these fields a sense of self-confidence is generated in his own capacities. This releases immense psychological energy for the development of his own capabilities to take up any challenge.

The story of India's independence movement will remain incomplete without mentioning the contribution of Ambedkar, Mahatma Phule, Veer Savarkar, Chandra Shekhar Azad, Sardar Bhagat Singh, K.B. Hedgewar and others who were not given their due place in the history of the freedom struggle. Without deleting anything from the textbooks, brief contributions by these great sons of mother India were incorporated. The coming generation should know about all those who had a burning passion for freedom but did not agree in full with the policies of the Congress. It was thus only a small addition to remove certain distortions from the syllabus. To introduce the teachings of Vivekananda or the singing of Vande Mataram has nothing to do with forcing any religious ritual down the throats of the students; it is to acquaint them with the urges and inspirations behind the freedom struggle.

Although the theory of the Aryan invasion of India is no longer tenable, and even western scholars do not subscribe to it, yet many textbooks failed to mention its infirmity. Perhaps no other theory had harmed the cause of national integration than this one. Attempts were made to inform the students about later developments in the field so that they could critically examine the entire evidence. This is how a sound academic foundation can be laid.

The BJP recognises that we are on the threshold of great changes in the world. The permeation of science and technology to an extent unknown in history has thrown open immense opportunities for material development. The speed with which knowledge is advancing and the amazing developments in the field of cybernetics have pushed us into the technotronic age. The world situation is becoming increasingly unpredictable and the scenario is fast changing. With rising waves of prosperity and increasing consumption levels, many contemporary societies are under stress and stains [*sic*] of a value crisis. Application of science has no doubt produced affluence but at the cost of the human spirit. Blending of science and spirituality is thus both a challenge and opportunity for India. The BJP will strive to create an educational system capable of restoring the balance between atom and ahimsa.

16

Ayodhya, the Babri Masjid, and the Ramjanmabhumi Dispute

Ayodhya is the name of a small town of Uttar Pradesh in Faizabad district. It is known in the Ramayana as the capital of Lord Rama, the place from where he ruled as the ideal Hindu king. In the eighteenth century the common belief was, apparently, that the birthplace of Rama was marked by a small platform near the Babri Masjid, a mosque built in 1528 under the auspices of the first Mughal emperor, Babur.[1] But in 1853 Hindu ascetics from the Bairagi order claimed that the mosque was built on Rama's birthplace itself.[2] However, a compromise was found whereby Hindu devotees were to worship Rama on the platform (*chabootra*) near the mosque. It was here that, in 1883, a local pandit asked for a temple to be built—a demand that the British rejected because of its proximity to the mosque.

The issue resurfaced after sixty years of peaceful coexistence in the tragic context of post-Partition India. On the night of 22–23 December 1949 someone broke into the mosque and there installed the idols of Rama and Sita. The following day thousands of local Hindus assembled

---

[1] This is inferred from the testimony of a Jesuit missionary who visited Ayodhya in 1786: G. Deleury, *Les Indes florissantes. Anthologie des voyageurs français 1750–1820* (Paris: Flammarion, 1991), p. 737.

[2] Most of the information regarding this historical overview is drawn from S. Gopal, ed., *Anatomy of a Confrontation. The Babri Masjid-Ramjanmabhumi Issue* (New Delhi: Viking, 1991). See also S. Srivastava, *The Disputed Mosque: A Historical Inquiry* (New Delhi: Vistaar Publications, 1991), and Asghar Ali Engineer, ed., *Babri Masjid/Ramjanmabhoomi Controversy* (New Delhi: Ajanta Publications, 1990).

and proclaimed this event a miracle. The Chief Minister of the United Provinces (today's Uttar Pradesh), G.B. Pant, asked the District Magistrate to remove the idols but the man refused to obey—his wife was elected MP from Gonda on a Hindu Mashasabha ticket two years later, and it seems plausible the ploy had been masterminded by activists of this party. But Nehru prevented the Mahasabha from exploiting the issue by ordering preventive arrests and getting the gates of the mosque sealed in 1950.

The Ayodhya issue was conveniently revived in 1984 by the VHP, which had become the preferred offshoot of the RSS for public agitation after the dilution of their ideological agenda by the ex-Jana Sanghis who had formed the BJP. In July 1984 a Sri Ramjanmabhoomi Mukti Yagna Samiti (Committee of Sacrifice to Liberate Rama's Birthplace) was formed, soon after the establishment—still under the aegis of the VHP—of a brigade-like body called the Bajrang Dal.[3] In July 1984 it organized a long procession which set off in Bihar and which was intended to reach Delhi to 'liberate' Rama, prisoner of the Babri Masjid in Ayodhya.[4] The procession was supposed to arrive in the capital of India in December, before the general elections, but the assassination of Indira Gandhi transformed the political agenda of the country.

Interestingly, the issue was revived just before another election, in 1989, in a completely different context: this happened when the BJP, which had stayed aloof from the Ayodhya campaign till then, under the impulse of L.K. Advani (who had succeeded Vajpayee as party president), joined the movement. The party passed an important resolution formalizing this shift during the Palampur (Himachal Pradesh) meeting of its national executive in June 1989, where the decision to finalize an alliance with the Mumbai–Maharashtra–centred Hindu party, the Shiv Sena, was also made. At the same time, all components of the Sangh Parivar embarked on a new programme, the Ram Shila Pujans, which consisted in parading bricks marked with the name of Rama through thousands of towns and villages in order to mobilize Hindus in favour of the construction of the Rama Mandir in Ayodhya.

---

[3] The word *bajrang* (strong, sturdy) is used here with reference to Hanuman, the monkey god who led Rama's army into battle.

[4] P. van der Veer, ' "God must be Liberated!" A Hindu Liberation Movement in Ayodhya', *Modern Asian Studies*, vol. 21, no. 2, 1987.

Taken in local processions, these bricks were consecrated by sadhus of the VHP, and devotees could contribute Rs 1.25 to participate in the enterprise. These processions were responsible for a wave of communal riots inasmuch as they were true shows of strength that provoked Muslims.

The BJP benefited from this Hindu mobilization and the polarization of the electorate through violence. The party won 88 seats (as against 2 in 1984) and became part of the coalition supporting the V.P. Singh government.

While V.P. Singh played the OBC card, no solution could be found in Ayodhya. The BJP then appropriated this issue further as it had, for some of its leaders, the potential of a mass movement. Soon after V.P. Singh announced the implementation of the Mandal report in August 1990, L.K. Advani took the lead in a 10,000 km procession, which was intended to mobilize the Hindus (and transcend caste divisions that way) in favour of the Rama Mandir in Ayodhya. K. Govindacharya, one of L.K. Advani's lieutenants, compared it in importance to Gandhi's salt march in 1931.[5] This Rath Yatra, and the final attack of the Babri Masjid by Hindu nationalist militants (including Bajrang Dalis) once again triggered Hindu–Muslim riots all over India. The Chief Minister of UP, Mulayam Singh Yadav, had saved the mosque from such assailants in 1990; his successor, a BJP man who had won the state elections in 1991, Kalyan Singh, could not, or did not try to: on 6 December 1992 the Babri Masjid was razed to the ground by militants who replaced it by a makeshift temple where statues of Rama and Sita were immediately installed. Riots occurred once again all over India after Muslims attacked symbols of the state which had not been able to protect the mosque. Hundreds were killed in retaliation, mostly by the police, in Bombay, Bhopal, Surat and other places.

While the BJP benefited from voter polarization along communal lines in the course of the Ayodhya movement, it was not able to satisfy those who supported it for this cause when it took power in the late 1990s. It had to dilute its stand on Ayodhya to make allies and form a ruling coalition, the National Democratic Alliance, so much so that its plan to build a Rama Mandir was not even included in the election

---

[5] K.N. Govindacharya, 'Future Vistas', in J. Bajaj, ed., *Ayodhya and the Future India* (Madras: Centre for Policy Studies, 1993), pp. 181–212.

manifesto of the NDA in 1999. Other components of the Sangh Parivar—including the VHP—strongly resented what they called the betrayal of the Hindus by the Vajpayee government. While the BJP stood by its new, moderate approach to politics, after its unexpected May 2004 electoral defeat it was under pressure to revert to its old plank regarding Ayodhya from the VHP and the RSS, which attributed the party's setback to the dilution of its ideology.

Extract from an Interview of L.K. Advani[6]

Q5: What; according to the BJP, is the main issue in the coming elections [of 1991]?

Advani: The main issue is going to revert back to what was being talked about two months back. Mainly how can the unity of this country be preserved? What is nationalism? How do you ensure social harmony? Communal harmony? And in that context what is secularism? These issues have been there all along but have been very sharply focussed as a result of Ayodhya. I view this not as an issue of Ayodhya, though at the level of the common man, the common voter, it will continue to be Ayodhya. I view it in this context. And this I believe is going to be the principal issue in this election.

Q9: How do you square a purely religious ritual like temple building with the larger Hindutva concept?

Advani: I would like to answer this question by recalling Sardar Patel's approach to Hindu–Muslim problems. His approach was that this is broadly a Hindu country and the tendency to shy away from Hindu feeling is not secularism. Take the case of Somnath, something like that could not have happened now. Some might say it was the aftermath of Partition and therefore it (the reconstruction of Somnath) took place. I would say no. It was because of Patel. Nehru did not like it even then.

Q10: How do you justify the BJP stand that the Rama temple issue is a matter of faith?

[6] G. Vazirani, *Lal Advani: The Man and His Mission* (New Delhi: Arnold Publishers, 1991).

Advani: There was that theft of the Prophet's hair at the Hazrat Bal shrine in Srinagar. Now if someone complains that the relic has been stolen and the state must exert its entire energy to see that it is recovered, and someone counters: 'Can you prove that this is the Prophet Mohammed's hair?' Would it be a right question? But I for one would say, that as my Muslim brethren believe that it is the hair of the Prophet, I respect their sentiments.

Similarly if crores of Hindus believe that it is the birthplace of Rama, I would expect the State as well as other sections of opinion in this country, especially the minorities, to respect that sentiment and say 'Well, if you believe it to be the birthplace of Rama, it is the birthplace of Rama, we are not asking you to prove this.'

Q11: Isn't upholding the cause of temple construction communal? What about the Muslims' claim that it is the site of a mosque?

Advani: How do you explain the total apathy to the pulling down of temples in Kashmir? In 1986, 55 temples were destroyed in Anantnag. Last year too, temples were gutted. Why is it that all political parties, Hindus in general, and the media, are indifferent to it.

As for the Ayodhya site for 54 years no one has offered *namaz* there. From 1949, 40 years now, regular *poojas* are going on. On should end the dispute on this. Moreover the VHP has offered that, if you are attached to the bricks and mortar, which you call a mosque, we are willing to reverently shift it to another site where you can construct another mosque, we would even contribute to its construction. It would be an amicable solution and settlement of the problem.

Q12: How do you relate your demand for the construction of the Rama temple at Ayodhya to the larger issue of secularism? How do you propose to dispel the misgivings among the Muslims on this score?

Advani: I am fighting against the attitude of politicians and political parties that anything associated with Hindu is communal, their allergy to it and their idea that if you cherish this allergy, only then your secular credentials are proved.

I have not made it a temple issue. I have made it an issue of secularism, of national unity. I am also trying to convert it into an issue pertaining to the welfare of so-called minorities—that this is not in their (minorities') interest. These days Muslims meet me and say 'humko kahan phasa diya. Humko pata bhi nahin tha ki hum wahan jaa bhi nahin sakte.'

And these political parties have done a singular disservice even to the reputation of the country by propagating that the Hindus have suddenly gone mad under the leadership of the BJP and they want to pull down a 500 year old mosque and build a temple in its place. If the facts were to be presented, the impression would be totally different. Hindus have not become fundamentalists. Not at all. It is a remarkable though happy fact that there are 35 mosques in Ayodhya apart from the controversial one. Not one of them was touched during these months of turmoil. Lakhs of people visited the place. All of them extremely devout and passionate. Not one of them was touched. Why is it that no Muslims were killed in Ayodhya? No riots took place in Ayodhya, Why?

It is our responsibility to see that the misgivings which have been deliberately created by our adversaries are removed. But at the same time the efforts to remove these misgivings should not tend to make us apologetic and defensive about our basic beliefs.

Q13: Don't you think that a democratic India cannot be a Hindu-oriented country or Hindu Rashtra?

Advani: Every country has a certain cultural ethos. Even if Italy is called a Catholic State or Great Britain a Protestant one, they are still regarded as liberal. But if India is called a Hindu State, or a Hindu Rashtra, why does it become communal?

In the pre-Independence Congress, the dominant ideology used to be that of Gandhiji. Before that, it was of Tilak. Gandhiji, Rajaji, Sampoornanand, Rajen Babu, Sardar Patel, Purshottamdas Tandon, all represented one school of thought. Gandhiji had no inhibitions in saying that he wanted to establish Ram Rajya, which was synonymous with his concept of an ideal State. He had no reservations in having the audience at his evening meetings chant *Raghupati Raghava Raja Ram*. But that did not mean he wanted to establish a theocratic State.

Q14: What do you mean by positive secularism?

Advani: Positive secularism flows from our commitment to national unity which is an article of faith for us and not just a slogan to be converted into slick spots for the TV. Our Constitution seeks to strengthen this unity by rejecting theocracy and by guaranteeing equality to all citizens, irrespective of their religion. These are the two principal facets of secularism as our Constitution makers conceived them. For most politicians in the country, however, secularism has become just a device for garnering block minority votes.

A desire to appease the minorities often makes these politicians flaunt their allergy to Hinduism and everything associated with the word Hindu. Privately, many of them share our respect for the RSS, and our views on Article 370, on the need to replace the Minorities Commission with the Human Rights Commission, on Rama Janma Bhoomi, and even on the desirability of having an honourable electoral arrangement with the Shiv Sena in Maharashtra. But publicly they keep criticising us on these issues because they think that it is an easy way of proving their secular credentials, and gaining the support of the minorities. I think that thereby they are doing a disservice to the country, and ill serving the minorities as well.

I wish the country's political leadership, irrespective of party affiliation, could realise that the utterances and activities of some elements among the minorities are becoming increasingly aggressive and are ominously reminiscent of the pre-1947 years. These elements must be isolated, not propitiated. If these elements are allowed to grow, the consequences can be extremely dangerous for national integrity. Appeasement failed to avert partition. Appeasement is no way of combating the present threats to national unity. These threats have to be met head-on, and squarely spiked.

The BJP believes in Positive Secularism; the Congress-I and most other parties subscribe only to Vote Secularism. Positive Secularism means: justice for all, but appeasement of none. In the ensuing elections, let this become the BJP's distinctive message to the nation.

Q15: How is the Somnath experience relevant today in the context of the Ayodhya controversy?

Advani: I have already explained my view of secularism in the Indian context. Now I will take you back to what had happened at Somnath to put the matter in the correct perspective.

Prabhas Patan, the Somnath temple site was in Junagarh State. On the eve of Independence day, the Nawab of Junagarh announced that Junagarh had acceded to Pakistan. A shocked population rose in revolt and set up a parallel government headed by Samaldas Gandhi. Several parts of the State fell into the hands of the Samaldas Government. One night the Nawab quietly decamped to Pakistan, and the provisional Government formally invited New Delhi to take over.

On 9 November 1947, Union Home Minister, Sardar Vallabhbhai Patel, accompanied by N.V. Gadgil, Minister of Works, Mines and Power, came to Saurashtra. The first thing Sardar did was to visit Prabhas Patan. At a public meeting there Sardar Patel announced that now that Junagarh had formally acceded to India, the first Government of free India would reconstruct the great temple of Somnath, then reinstall therein the *jyotirlinga*. In the bureaucracy there were some who did not quite relish the idea, though they dared not say anything directly contrary to the Sardar's wishes.

When Sardar Patel reported to Gandhiji that the Government of India had decided to reconstruct Somnath, Gandhiji blessed the move. He suggested, however, that funds for its reconstruction be raised from the people. Sardar Patel readily accepted the suggestion. However, the reconstruction of the temple proceeded under the overall supervision and guidance of an official committee with Union Food and Agriculture Minister, Dr K.M. Munshi, as Chairman, and the Director-General of Archaeology as Convenor. The reconstruction completed, the deity was formally installed by the country's President, Dr Rajendra Prasad. No Aurangzebi Masjid Samiti was constituted at the time to protest that secularism had been thrown overboard, and 'Hindu Chauvinism' had taken over the State apparatus!

Pandit Nehru, of course, did have reservations about the President going to the installation ceremony. He tried, in vain, to dissuade him from going. Later, in a lengthy letter addressed to Pandit Nehru, Dr Munshi pointed out that 'everything (in respect of the temple's reconstruction) was done from the very beginning in accordance with the decision of the Cabinet taken under his (Nehru's) guidance'. In the course of this letter, Munshi very forcefully argued against the concepts which had started taking root after Gandhiji and Sardar Patel (and which continue to distort the thinking of the Indian elite till this day), whereby secularism became only a euphemism for an allergy to Hinduism. In this letter, Dr Munshi said:

You pointedly referred to me (yesterday) in the Cabinet as connected with Somnath. I am glad you did so; for I do not want to keep back any part of my views or activities, particularly from you who have placed such abundant confidence in me all these months . . . I can assure you that the 'collective sub-conscious' of India today is happier with the scheme of reconstruction of Somnath sponsored by the Government of India than with many other things that we have done and are doing.

Yesterday you referred to Hindu revivalism. I know your views on the subject. I have always done justice to them. I hope you will equally do justice to mine. Many have been the customs which I have defied in personal life from my boyhood. I have laboured in my humble way through literary and social work to shape or reintegrate some aspects of Hinduism, in the conviction that that alone will make India an advanced and vigorous nation under modern conditions . . .

It is my faith in our past which has given me the strength to work in the present and to look forward to our future. I cannot value freedom if it deprives us of the Bhagavad Gita or uproots our millions from the faith with which they look upon our temples, and thereby destroys the texture of our lives.

V.P. Menon, who was at that time Adviser to the States Ministry, after reading the letter wrote to Munshi saying: 'I have seen your masterpiece. I for one would be prepared to live, and, if necessary, die by the views you have expressed in your letter.'

If the controversy in Ayodhya were simply one between a temple and a mosque, it would not have been that intractable. Those campaigning for Babri Masjid should realise that they are wanting the country to choose not between a masjid and a mandir; they are pitting Babar against Rama. When the British Viceroys used to tell Jinnah that India should do this or India should do that Jinnah immediately reacted—Which India are you talking about? There are two Indias. Hindu India or Muslim India? Jinnah's two-India thesis resulted in Pakistan. It is time the thesis is finally buried, and it is accepted that there is but one India, and that this India, and its entire population, Hindu or Muslim, can identify itself only with Rama and not with Babar.

Q16: Why do you say that the courts cannot settle the dispute about the Ayodhya site? Why are you not prepared to abide by a judicial verdict?

Advani: My party has never said that we will not accept a court verdict. What we have said is that the nature of the controversy is such that a court verdict will not solve the problem. That is all that I say. Further, I say, let us understand that this present turmoil, the present acute controversy has itself arisen from court verdicts. It has not arisen because of any agitation as much as it has arisen out of court verdicts—two court verdicts, one of 1951 and the second of 1986.

The 1951 case was Gopal Singh Visharad *versus* Zahoor Ahmed and others, and the court was that of the Faizabad Civil Judge. The Judge observed in his judgement of 3 March 1951 that, 'At least from 1936 onwards, the Muslims have neither used the site as a mosque nor offered prayers there and that the Hindus have been performing their pooja, etc.' on the disputed site. And on that basis, he granted a temporary injunction, against removal of idols, though for considerations of law and order he said that locks should be imposed on the gates, the pooja should be done from a distance, people need not go inside. In 1986, the District Judge, Faizabad, referred to this 1951 order and directed that, 'As for the last 35 years Hindus have had an unrestricted right of worship at the place', the locks put on two gates in 1951 on grounds of law and order should be removed. This is Civil Appeal No. 65/1986. It is after this appeal that suddenly the controversy became very acute, very bitter. Shortly after this, the Babri Masjid Action Committee was formed.

Now the people are asking why are these locks there even after 40 years, why are we not allowed to have pooja without any hindrance, without any difficulty? I for one am of the view that if the Central Government had taken note of the problem that obtained in Prabhas Patan, a seaside place in Gujarat in Saurashtra, where at one time there was that ancient Somnath Temple which was razed to the ground many times, destroyed many times, reconstructed many times, it would have been different.

Q17: What is wrong in making a national monument of the Ayodhya site so that it will be neither Hindu nor Muslim but will be purely of archaeological interest?

Advani: A similar suggestion was made in the case of Somnath also. Many bureaucrats were unhappy over the decision of the Government to reconstruct the temple. The Department of Archaeology itself suggested that the site at Prabhas Patan—where originally, there was the Somnath Temple and subsequently there was a graveyard—should be declared a 'protected monument'. The then Home Minister, Sardar Patel, put down in writing his reaction to the proposal. The Hindu sentiment in regard to this temple is both strong and widespread. In the present conditions, it is unlikely that this sentiment will be satisfied by mere restoration of the temple or by prolonging its life. The restoration of the idol would be a point of honour and sentiment for the Hindu public.

Extract from L.K. Advani, 'The Ayodhya Movement'[7]

Last year, a Calcutta daily asked me to identify a day or moment in my life which I regarded as my happiest. I named 30 October 1990, and more specifically, the moment I heard the BBC broadcast that *kar sevaks* had overcome all obstacles and broken all barriers put up by the Mulayam Singh government, penetrated into Ayodhya and performed *kar seva*.

Ironically, this year's *kar seva* day at Ayodhya, 6 December, turned out to be one of the most depressing days in my life. Of course, most others there were ecstatic with joy, a mood I just could not share. I have seldom felt as dejected and downcast as I felt that day.

My sadness, however, did not stem from any disenchantment with the Ayodhya movement, or with the path the party had chosen for itself, or, as the trite phrase goes, that we had been riding a tiger which we could not dismount. In fact, the post-demolition developments have fully vindicated our misgivings about the opponents of this movement, and have reinforced our resolve to pursue the path more vigorously.

There were three very specific reasons for my distress.

Firstly, I felt sad that the 6 December happenings had impaired the BJP's and RSS's reputation as organisations capable of enforcing discipline. True, a very large percentage of the over two lakhs assembled at Ayodhya were not members either of the BJP or of the RSS. But that did not absolve us of our responsibility.

---

[7] First published in *Indian Express*, 27 December 1992. Cited in *The Five Hours and After* (Madras: Vigil, 1983).

Secondly, I felt sad that a meticulously drawn up plan of action whereunder the UP government was steadily marching forward towards discharging its mandate regarding temple-construction, without violating any law or disregarding any court order, had gone awry.

Delinking Move: The BJP's action plan contemplated delinking the dispute about the structure from commencing construction at the *shilanyas* site (within the 2.77 acres of acquired land), negotiating about the structure while the construction work proceeded apace, and, if negotiations failed, resorting to legislation. If State legislation was blocked by the Centre, we intended to seek a national mandate. We were thus working towards achieving our objective peacefully, and by the due process of law. Not only the BJP, but the RSS, the VHP and the *sants* were all agreed on this approach. If the exercise contemplated has now been shortcircuited in a totally unforeseen manner, the above organisations can certainly be blamed for not being able to judge the impatience of the people participating in the movement. No one can deny that the manner in which courts had been dragging their feet on all issues relating to Ayodhya, and the obstructive and obtuse role of the Central Government had tried the patience of the people to the utmost limit.

The third and most important reason for my unhappiness that day was that, in my perception the day's incidents would affect the BJP's overall image (not electoral prospects) adversely, and, to that extent, our cause would suffer a temporary setback.

When I speak of a setback I am not at all thinking in political terms. In fact, politically, these events have boosted the BJP's poll prospects no end. The Congress, the JD, the Communists all are frantically exerting to ensure that no elections are held for at least a year. After the three State Assemblies controlled by the BJP were dissolved, Congress spokesman V.N. Gadgil said that elections would be held within six months. It did not take Mr Arjun Singh even 24 hours to come forth with a contradiction, saying that polls in these three states would be held after one year! In a recent article (*The Hindustan Times*, 17 December 1992), Mr S. Sahay, former editor, *The Statesman*, has noted: 'The feedback is that were elections to be held today in Uttar Pradesh, Congress candidates would find it difficult to retain their deposits.' Reports pouring in from other parts of the country are no different.

Despite what our adversaries have been saying about us day in and day out, we have never regarded Ayodhya as a ladder to power. Through this movement the BJP has only intensified its ongoing crusade against the politics of vote-banks, and the politics of minorityism, which we believe is gravely undermining the fabric of national unity.

A Mass Movement: The Ayodhya movement, according to the BJP, is not just for building a temple. It is a mass movement—the biggest since independence—to reaffirm the nation's cultural identity. This reaffirmation alone, we hold, can provide an enduring basis for national unity, and besides, the dynamo for a resurgent, resolute and modern India.

It is slanderous to say that the Ayodhya movement is an assault on secularism. It is wrong to describe even the demolition of the Babri structure as negation of secularism. The demolition is more related to lack of a firm commitment in the general masses to the Rule of Law, and an exasperation with the frustrating sluggishness of the judicial process.

I remember very well the Bhagalpur episode of some years back. The whole country felt outraged that undertrial prisoners—they may have been notorious dacoits—should be so cruelly blinded by policemen. But when I visited Bhagalpur I was surprised to find that among the people at large there was little disapproval of what the police had done. Many lawyers of Bhagalpur actually came out in defence of the police action!

The BJP is unequivocally committed to secularism. As conceived by our Constitution makers, secularism meant *sarvapantha sama bhava*, that is, equal respect for all religions. Secularism as embedded into the Indian Constitution has three important ingredients, namely (i) rejection of theocracy; (ii) equality of all citizens, irrespective of their faith; and (iii) full freedom of faith and worship.

We also believe that India is secular because it is predominantly Hindu. Theocracy is alien to our history and tradition.

Indian nationalism is rooted, as was India's freedom struggle against colonialism, in a Hindu ethos. It was Gandhiji who projected *Rama Rajya* as the goal of the freedom movement. He was criticised by the Muslim League as being an exponent of Hindu Raj. The League did not relish the chanting of *Ram Dhun* at Gandhiji's meetings or his insistence on *Goraksha* (cow-protection). The Muslim League at one of its annual sessions passed a formal resolution denouncing *Vande Mataram* as 'idolatrous'. All this never made leaders of the freedom struggle apologetic about the fountainhead of their inspiration.

Unfortunately, for four decades now, in the name of secularism, politicians have been wanting the nation to disown its essential personality. For the left inclined, secularism has become a euphemism to cloak their intense allergy to religion, and more particularly, to Hinduism.

Pseudo-Secularism: It is this attitude which the BJP characterises as pseudo-secularism. This attitude is wrong and unscientific. Coupled with the weakness of political parties for vote banks, it becomes perverse and baneful.

In October 1990, the day Mr V.P. Singh stopped the *Rath Yatra*, and put me and my colleagues in the *Yatra* behind bars, Mr A.B. Vajpayee called on the Rashtrapati, and informed him that the BJP had withdrawn support to the National Front Government. It was obvious to all that VP's Government had been reduced to a hopeless minority. But VP did not resign. Instead, he convened a special session of Parliament to vote on a confidence motion tabled by him. He said he was doing so mainly to precipitate a debate on secularism and communalism. We welcomed the debate, and challenged VP not to confine it to the four walls of Parliament, but to take it to the people.

VP was defeated in Parliament that day. But he shied away from accepting our challenge. Events nevertheless moved inexorably towards the trial of strength we had asked for. Seven months later people went to the polls to elect the country's Tenth Lok Sabha. Unlike as in 1989, when we were part of an opposition combine, the BJP fought the election all on its own and emerged the principal opposition party in the Lok Sabha.

What has gratified us all along is not merely that our numerical strength in Parliament and the State Legislature has been growing at a rapid pace, but that acceptance of our ideology in all sections of society and at all levels has been simultaneously growing.

A silent minority even among the Muslims has been building up which appreciates that the BJP is not anti-Muslim as its enemies have been trying to depict it, and more importantly, the BJP leadership means what it says, and says what it means, and is not hypocritical like other political parties. The BJP Government's track record in the matter of preserving communal peace in their respective States has added considerably to the BJP's credibility in this regard.

It is the process of widening acceptability of the BJP's ideology within the country, and also among people of Indian origin overseas, which has upset our opponents the most. It is this process precisely which may be somewhat decelerated by the 6 December events. I have little doubt, however, that the party can, with proper planning and effort, soon get over this phase.

It is sad that over one thousand persons have lost their lives in the aftermath of Ayodhya. It is certainly a matter of anguish. But when one compares this time's fallout with what has been happening in earlier years over incidents which can be considered trifling, this time's has been a contained one. And in most cases the deaths that have occurred have been the consequence not of any clash between communities but of security forces trying to quell the violence and vandalism of frenzied mobs.

I wonder how many in Government, in politics and in the media realise that their stubborn insistence on calling this old structure (which was abandoned by Muslims 56 years back and which for 43 years has been a de facto temple) a 'mosque' has made no mean contribution towards building up this frenzy. Even so, there is little doubt that the 6 December happenings have given our opponents a handle to malign the Ayodhya movement as fundamentalist and fanatic.

Voices of Reason: Amidst the hysterical breast-beating that has been going on for over a fortnight now, there have been in the media voices of reason, a few distinguished journalists who have tried to put the events in proper perspective, and to emphasise that the happenings are unfortunate, but that it is no occasion either for gloating or for self-condemnation. In an excellent article written for the *Free Journal*, Bombay (17 December 1992), Mr M.V. Kamath, former editor of *The Illustrated Weekly India*, has written: 'Let it be said even if it hurts many secularists: in the last five years, several temples have been demolished in Kashmir without our hearing one word of protest from them. There has been no hue and cry made about such wanton destruction . . . We are lectured to by Iran and some other Muslim countries on our duties. Has Iran ever been ruled by Hindu monarchs, and had its masjids pulled down to make place for temples to Shiva or Vishnu? . . . We should not bear the burden of history. But neither should we be constantly pilloried. There has to be some way to heal past wounds, but reviling the BJP or the VHP is not the best way. The anger of the *kar sevaks* has to be understood in this context. They have not gone around demolishing every mosque in sight. It might even be said that they were led down the garden path by Mr P.V. Narasimha Rao who kept promising that a solution was near, even while he was trying to pass the buck onto the judiciary.'

Feeble Voices: For four decades, the pseudo-secularists have commanded undisputed supremacy in Indian politics. Jana Sangh's and BJP's was, at best, a feeble voice of dissent. Ayodhya has enabled our viewpoint to become a formidable challenge.

Unable to meet this challenge at the ideological and political level through discussion and debate, the Government has pulled out of its armoury all the usual weapons used in such situations by repressive regimes—arrests, ban on associations, ban on meetings etc. Demolition of the Babri structure is only an excuse to carry out what they have been itching to do for quite some time. After all, all this talk about the need to have BJP derecognised or deregistered has not started now. Mr Arjun Singh had formally petitioned the Election Commission in this regard more than a year back. The Election Commission rejected his plea. Ever since, the ruling party has been toying with the idea of amending the Representation of the Peoples Act to achieve this objective. Without naming either the BJP or the RSS, Mr Narasimha Rao himself, in his Presidential address to the Congress Session at Tirupati, had endorsed the idea. When I met him and registered my protest, he tried to backtrack, and maintained that he had in mind only organisations like the Majilis (of Owaisi)!

Elementary political prudence should have restrained the Prime Minister from taking the series of unwise steps he has taken after 6 December: banning the RSS and VHP, dismissing BJP Governments of Rajasthan, HP and MP and promising to rebuild the demolished 'mosque'. But then, history keeps repeating itself in a quaint fashion.

Left to himself Shri V.P. Singh may not have obstructed the *Rath Yatra* of 1990. But the internal politics of Janata Dal forced his hand.

To prove himself a greater patron of the minorities than Mulayam Singh, VP asked Laloo Prasad to take action before the UP Chief Minister did so. Laloo did as he was told, and became instrumental for terminating VP's tenure. This time it has been Mr Arjun Singh who has played Mulayam Singh to P.V. Narasimha Rao. The denouement may well be the same.

Prime Target: In Parliament, as well as outside, a prime target of attack for our critics has been Mr Kalyan Singh. He is being accused of betrayal, of 'deceit', of 'conspiracy' and what not. The general refrain is: Kalyan Singh promised to the courts, to the National Integration Council, to the Central Government, that he would protect the structure, New Delhi trusted his word; he has betrayed the trust. None of these Kalyan-baiters even mentions that along with every assurance, there was an invariable addendum: that he would not use force against the *kar sevaks*, because he would not like to see any repetition of the traumatic happenings which took place in 1990 during Mulayam Singh's tenure. This has been stated even in the affidavit given to the Supreme Court by the UP Government.

On 6 December, Mr Kalyan Singh stuck to this stand. When informed that all efforts at persuading the *kar sevaks* to desist from demolishing the structure had failed, and that protection of the structure had become impossible except by resort to firing, he forthwith resigned.

When political leaders have been driven into such difficult corners, they have been generally inclined to issue oral orders. Bureaucrats have often had to pay the price for such deviousness. In contrast, Mr Kalyan Singh acted in an exemplary manner. He put down his orders about not using force in writing so that the officers were not punished for what was entirely a political decision.

I shudder to think what would have happened that day at Ayodhya if firing had taken place. Jallianwala Bagh would have been re-enacted many times over. There would have been a holocaust not only in Ayodhya but in the whole country. Mr Kalyan Singh acted wisely in refusing to use force.

It is significant that the last phase of the demolition, the clearing of the debris, installation of the Ram Lalla idols with due ceremony, and erection of a temporary temple to house the idols, all this happened after New Delhi had taken over the State administration. Yet, wisely again, the Narasimha Rao Government made no attempt to use force to prevent this happening.

No doubt, it was Mr Kalyan Singh's duty to protect the Babri structure. He failed to do so; so he resigned. Protection of the country's Prime Minister is the responsibility of the Union Home Minister. The country should not forget that Mr P.V. Narasimha Rao was the Home Minister when Mrs Gandhi was brutally killed. It can be said that P.V. failed to protect more than 3,000 Sikhs who were killed in the wake of Mrs Gandhi's death. Today, I am not arraigning him for failing to resign on that score. I am only trying to point out how outraged he would have felt if, say, in 1984 he had been accused not just of a failure to protect, but of actual complicity in the perpetration of those horrendous crimes!

Political observers who have been feeling baffled by the abrupt change of mood of the BJP-RSS-VHP combine from one of regret on 6 December to one of 'determined belligerence' from 8 December onward, must appreciate that it is a similar sense of outrage over all that the Government and our other opponents have been saying and doing that fully accounts for it.

Let it also be realised that once you start circulating conspiracy charges with irresponsible levity, the distrust generated will ultimately boomerang, and get back to its source. I was really amused to read a column by Tavleen Singh in which she summed up the attitude of Congressmen towards Mr Narasimha Rao in these words: 'Those who are still with him charge him only with being indecisive and weak. Those who are against him are saying much more. Even ministers are admitting, albeit privately, that the Prime Minister had adequate information, before 6 December, to be prepared for what eventually happened. Some go so far as to charge him with collusion with the BJP on the grounds that he is not interested in a Congress revival in North India as this would make it harder for a Prime Minister from the South.' (*The Observer*, Dec. 18.)

Some of our critics have been comparing the demolition of the Babri structure with the assassination of Mahatma Gandhi. The comparison is ludicrous. But from a purely personal angle, I can establish a nexus. I was 20 years old at that time, and an RSS *pracharak* in Rajasthan. Mahatmaji's murder also was followed by a ban on the

RSS. I was among the tens of thousands of RSS activists jailed at that time. I recall that the accusations and calumny heaped on us then were far more vile and vicious than we are having to face today. The trial of Godse and the Commission of Inquiry set up later nailed all the lies circulated, and completely exonerated the RSS from the libellous charges hurled at it. The RSS emerged from that first major crisis in its life purer and stronger.

It is not without significance that one of those who was spearheading the anti-RSS campaign in 1948, Mr Jayaprakash Narayan, later became one of its most ardent admirers and protagonists.

When the RSS was banned the second time in 1975, JP and RSS became comrades-in-arms waging an unrelenting battle for the defence of democracy.

In one of his speeches in 1977, the Loknayak observed: 'RSS is a revolutionary organisation. No other organisation in the country comes anywhere near it. It alone has the capacity to transform society, end casteism, and wipe the tears from the eyes of the poor. May God give you strength and may you live up to such expectations.'

Lemming Complex: Self-preservation is a basic instinct of all living beings. Only a human being can think of, and commit, suicide. There is, however, a rodent found in Scandinavian countries, called Lemming, which in this context is supposed to be unique among animals, and behaves unnaturally. *The Concise Oxford Dictionary* describes Lemming as a 'small arctic rodent of the genus Lemmus . . . which is reputed to rush headlong into the sea and drown during migration.' To me, it seems the Congress Party these days is in the grip of a terrible *Lemming complex!*

Let the Congress do with itself what it wishes. For the BJP, the situation poses a challenge which, if tackled wisely, with determination and readiness, if need be, to wage a protracted struggle, can become a watershed in the history of independent India. Let us also realise that intolerance and fanaticism are traits which may appear to give a cutting edge to a movement but which actually causes great damage to the movement.

They have to be consciously eschewed. Once that happens, even our Muslim brethren would appreciate that in India there can be no firmer foundation for communal harmony than cultural nationalism.

The present situation presents to the country a unique opportunity. Let us grab it by the forelock. December 6 did not turn out to be as we expected; we did not want it to happen that way.

But then, as the famous essayist Sir Arthur Helps has said: 'Fortune does not stoop often to take anyone up. Favourable opportunities will not happen precisely in the way that you imagined. Nothing does.' Or, as Goswami Tulsidas has put it in a somewhat different vein: '*Hoi hai soi jo Rama rachi rakha!*'

17

Defence

In complete opposition to Gandhi's ahimsa-based pacifism,[1] and Nehru's aversion to any form of militarization,[2] the Hindu nationalist movement has always promoted an aggressive defence of Hindus and India. 'Aggressive defence' is not a contradiction in terms for Hindu nationalists since their aggressiveness is all the more vehement as their feeling of vulnerability runs high. Hindu nationalism itself stems from the idea that Hindus may be stabbed in the back by others—Muslims, Christians—and that Hindus must equip themselves to cope with these threatening others, at home and abroad.

As early as the 1920s the Hindu Sangathan programme included the promotion of a martial ethos: the RSS shakhas were immediately intended to endow swayamsevaks with fighting techniques (including plying the *lathi*), allegedly to resist Muslims during riots. When the Second World War broke out the Hindu Mahasabha offered support to the British, hoping that the government would recruit Hindus and teach them the art of war. Savarkar's motto at the time was 'Militarise Hindudom!'[3]

Besides the hereditary foe, Pakistan, the arch-enemy of Hindu nationalism has always been China, and as early as the 1950s, the Jana

---

[1] Mahatma Gandhi once said that if a pilot flew over India to launch a nuclear bomb, he would change the pilot's heart from a distance and dissuade him.

[2] Nehru called this approach into question after the 1962 attack on China which showed that India had foolishly neglected its military establishment.

[3] C. Jaffrelot, 'Opposing Gandhi: Hindu Nationalism and Political Violence', in D. Vidal, G. Tarabout, and E. Meyer, eds, *Violence/Non-Violence. Some Hindu Perspectives* (Delhi: Manohar, 2003), pp. 299–324.

Sangh was worried about the growing influence of Peking in Tibet. In 1959 its Working Committee reacted to the Chinese incursions along the Indo-Tibetan border by demanding from Nehru's government 'that national security be accorded total priority' and that the territories that had been occupied be liberated.[4] When the first signs of the Chinese invasion appeared in May 1962 with the capture of two Indian frontier posts, the Jana Sangh called for massive reprisals and the breaking-off of diplomatic relations.[5] When the Chinese operation gained momentum, the party could pride itself on having always given warning of a Chinese threat to a prime minister whose idealism had led him to underestimate it.[6]

The Jana Sangh continued in that vein in the domain of internal security, but it could not derive much dividend from the 1965 war against Pakistan, when Prime Minister Shastri reacted exactly the way the party would have had it been in office.[7] Similarly, Indira Gandhi's rescue of East Pakistan forced them to praise her during the 1971 crisis. Vajpayee then described her as Durga, the female divinity embodying Shakti or cosmic energy. In 1965 and 1971 RSS volunteers offered their services to maintain law and order in Delhi and to donate blood.

National security remained a focal point of the BJP's discourse in the 1980s and 1990s, when the party leaders arraigned the Congress regime for letting defence expenditures decline (as a percentage of GDP) and for abstaining from the nuclear tests that many experts considered absolutely necessary to upgrade India's arsenal. When A.B. Vajpayee became prime minister in 1998, nuclear testing was the first significant decision he made a few weeks after taking office. This gesture was greatly appreciated by the RSS. In his yearly report before the Akhil Bharatiya Pratinidhi Sabha in March 1999, H.V. Seshadri, the

[4] Resolution of 20 September 1959, in *Party Documents*, vol. 3 (New Delhi: Bharatiya Jana Sangh, 1973), pp. 66–8.

[5] Resolution of 24 May 1962, in ibid., p. 86.

[6] S. Gopal, *Jawaharlal Nehru—A Biography*, vol. 3, pp. 212 and 224.

[7] The Jana Sangh Working Committee admitted that 'never before in these 18 years of independence, have the government policies and actions been so completely in accord with the people's will as they have been during these past few weeks' (Resolution of 27 September 1965, in *Party Documents*, vol. 3, pp. 128–9).

RSS joint general secretary, highlighted the achievement of Vajpayee's government in the field of security issues:

> The series of 5 nuclear blasts at Pokharan on May 11th and 13th of last year, carried out on the strength of entirely indigenous input by way of materials and also of sheer scientific and technological excellence placing Bharat at the top of nuclear world on par with any of the giants in that field, the absolute secrecy maintained all through until it was broadcast on the TV by our Prime Minister, the political grit and courage displayed by the central leadership in taking that historic decision in the light of our national security requirements, and the way it has acted as a great morale booster not only to our army but to all our patriotic country-men—all this has proved to be the one greatest moment of all-round national jubilation and celebration during the Golden Jubilee Year of our Independence.[8]

In August 1999 the 27-member National Security Advisory Board that had been appointed by the Vajpayee government spelt out a 'nuclear doctrine' that was not formally endorsed by Vajpayee but made public by his National Security Adviser, Brajesh Mishra. This doctrine pointed out that India would develop a credible minimum nuclear deterrent by weaponizing a triad of aircraft, mobile land-based missiles and sea-based assets. Simultaneously, Vajpayee's government decided to speed up the missile programme by developing Agni II and to strengthen the army on the front of conventional forces. About 20 Agni ballistic missiles with a range of more than 2000 km were to be manufactured by 2001 and the Prithvi missile was to be upgraded from 150 km to 350 km.

National security remained the BJP trademark during the Kargil war which broke out in Spring 1999 after Indian troops discovered infiltrations of Pakistani regular soldiers and Islamist paramilitary. The blitzkrieg which followed was commented on in the press as testimony of A.B. Vajpayee's coolheadedness, determination, and

---

[8] *The Organiser*, 4 April 1999, p. 12. The RSS has always favoured the development of nuclear weapons. In the early 1990s Rajendra Singh—himself a nuclear physicist—had declared that: 'The day Pakistan comes to know that we also have a nuclear bomb, there would be an end to the possibility of a Pakistan nuclear bomb being dropped here.' R. Singh, *Ever-Vigilant We Have to Be* (New Delhi: Suruchi Prakashan, n.d.), p. 9.

moderation. This military victory was one of the reasons for the BJP's electoral success a few months later.

In February 2000 the first budget of the second Vajpayee government took one step further by increasing the share of defence expenditures by 28 per cent. The man who played a major role in the Prime Minister's team, as far as defence and foreign affairs were concerned, was Jaswant Singh. A retired army major with an aristocratic background—he belongs to a Rajput family related to the dynasty of Jodhpur in Rajasthan—Singh had resigned his commission to enter public life. He was one of the first ex-army men to join the BJP. Many more were to follow. He was given a party ticket for the Rajya Sabha election in 1980 and remained a member of the upper house till 1989, when he contested a Lok Sabha seat and won the first of his six terms. Vajpayee appointed him first Deputy Chairman of the Planning Commission— he had wanted to include him in his governmental team but had to bow to RSS opposition—and then as Minister of External Affairs, and finally Finance Minister. As Minister of External Affairs Jaswant Singh played a major role in the Indo-American rapprochement, via almost a dozen rounds of discussion with Strobe Talbot, Assistant Secretary of State in the Clinton administration, who, eventually, became convinced that India should become a strategic partner of the United States in Asia.

Extract from Jaswant Singh, *Defending India*[9]

The May Tests and After

The end of the Cold War marks a watershed in the history of the 20th century. While it transformed the political landscape of Europe it did little to ameliorate India's security concerns. Early and mid 1980s, and the period roughly upto 1995 was, in fact, a greatly troubling period for India. The relative order and absence of conflict that arrived in the Americas and Europe was also not replicated in other parts of the globe. At the global level there is no evidence yet on the part of the nuclear weapon states about taking decisive and irreversible steps and moving towards a nuclear-weapon-free world. Instead, the NPT, in 1995, was extended indefinitely unconditionally, perpetuating the existence of nuclear weapons in the hands of five countries who are

---

[9] Jaswant Singh, *Defending India* (London: Macmillan, 1999), pp. 326–37.

also engaged in programmes for modernisation of their nuclear arsenals. At this juncture, and after over 2000 tests had been conducted, a Comprehensive Test Ban Treaty was opened for signature in 1996, following two and a half years of negotiations in which India had participated actively. This treaty was neither comprehensive nor was it related to disarmament.

The range of options for India had, by then, narrowed critically. India had to take necessary steps to ensure that the country's nuclear option, developed and safeguarded over decades, was not permitted to erode by a self-imposed restraint. Indeed, such an erosion would have resulted in an irremediably adverse impact on national security. The Government of India was thus faced with a difficult decision. The only touchstone that could determine its decision remained national security. The tests conducted on 11 and 13 May had by then not only become inevitable, they were, in actuality a continuation of the policies set into motion, from almost the earliest years of independence.

An examination of the first fifty years of Indian independence reveals that the country's moralistic nuclear policy and restraint did not really pay any measurable dividends. Consequently, this resulted in resentment within the country; a feeling grew that India was being discriminated against. In the political market place of India, nuclear weaponisation gained currency, and the plank of disarmament began to be argued that if the Permanent Five's possession of nuclear weapons is good, and confers security to their respective countries, then how is the possession of nuclear weapons by India not good, or how does the equation reverse simply in this instance? There is also the factor of the currency in the form of nuclear weapons: as an international communicator of force then how is India to voluntarily devalue its own state power, which it has to, after all, employ for its own national security? It is this reasoning that lies behind the evolution of Indian nuclear thought in the past fifty years. India has also learnt from the experience of the West, their approach to, attitudes about and application of nuclear policy. Deterrence works in the West, or elsewhere, as it so obviously appears to otherwise why should these nations continue to possess nuclear weapons at all. Then by what reasoning is it to be asserted that it will not work or cannot work in India? To admonitorily argue, thereafter, that India has to now 'fall in line' because there is now a new international agenda of discriminatory non-proliferation, pursued more on account of the demands of the political market place of some of these countries, as an extension also of their own internal agendas or political debates, is to assert the unimplementable. The rationale behind nuclear weapon powers continuing to have, and preaching to those that do not have, to have even less, leaves a gross imbalance between the rights of and obligations of nation states of the world community. Either India counters by suggesting global, non-discriminatory disarmament by all; or, equal and legitimate security for the entire world.

That alone is why, and it bears repetition, India since independence has been a consistent advocate of global nuclear disarmament, participating actively in all such efforts, convinced that a world without nuclear weapons will enhance both national and global security. India was the first to call for a ban on nuclear testing in 1954, for a non-discriminatory treaty on non-proliferation in 1965, for a treaty on non-use of nuclear weapons in 1978, for a nuclear freeze in 1982, and for a phased programme for complete elimination in 1988. Unfortunately, most of these initiatives were not accepted by the nuclear weapon states who still consider these weapons essential for their own security. What emerged, in consequence, has been a discriminatory and flawed non-Proliferation regime which affects India's security adversely. For many years India conveyed its apprehensions to other countries but this did not lead to any improvement in its security environment. This disharmony and disjunction between global thought and the movement of India's thought is, unfortunately, the objective reality of the world. In the totality of state power, nuclear weapons as a currency of it is still operational. Since this currency is operational in large parts of the globe, therefore, India was left with no choice but to update and re-validate the capability that had been demonstrated 24 years ago in the PNE of 1974.

In undertaking these tests, India has not violated any international treaty obligations. The Comprehensive Test Ban Treaty, to which India does not subscribe, also contains provisions permitting states parties to withdraw if they consider their supreme national interests being jeopardised. In any event, in the evolution of the present South Asian situation 1995 was a watershed year. By forcing an unconditional and indefinite extension of the Non-proliferation Treaty on the international community, India was left with no option but to go in for overt nuclear weaponisation. The Sino-Pakistan nuclear weapons collaboration, continued with in violation of the NPT, made it obvious that the NPT regime had collapsed, and critically in India's neighbourhood. Since it is now argued that NPT is unamendable, it is obvious that the legitimization of nuclear weapons, implicit in the unconditional and indefinite extension of the NPT, is also irreversible. While India could have lived with a nuclear option but without overt weaponization in a world where nuclear weapons had not been formally legitimised, that course was no longer viable in a world of legitimised nuclear weapons. Unfortunately, the full implications of the legitimisation of nuclear weapons were not debated either in India or abroad. This fatal setback to nuclear disarmament and progress towards delegitimisation of nuclear weapons was hailed by most of the peace movements abroad as a great victory.

In negotiations on the CTBT, for the first time the Indian Ambassador's statement of 20 June 1996 in the Conference of Disarmament stated 'that the nuclear issue is a national security concern for India and advanced [that] as one of the reasons why India was unable to accede to the Comprehensive Test Ban Treaty'. Presumably this persuaded the nuclear hegemons to introduce a clause at the last minute, 'that India along with 43 other nations should sign the treaty to bring it into force. This clause was coercive and a violation of the Vienna Convention on Treaties which stipulates that a nation not willing to be a party to a treaty cannot be imposed obligations arising out of the treaty. It should be remembered that this clause was [introduced] at the insistence of China—the nuclear proliferator to Pakistan. The international community approved that coercive CTBT.' That was a major deterioration in India's security environment.

As the decade of the nineties advanced the situation for India became more pressing. In 1997 more evidence surfaced on China-Pakistan proliferation linkage and about US permissiveness. The very fact that the US administration insisted on a separate agreement with China, during President Jiang Zemin's visit to Washington, on its proliferation to Iran and Pakistan, and that the Chinese signed such an agreement, instead of protesting their innocence establishes that Chinese proliferation was a reality affecting India's security. After all these assurances, according to a testimony given by the US Deputy Assistant Secretary of State for Non-proliferation to the House of Representatives on 4 February 1998, it had to be asserted that though China did not proliferate MTCR class missiles it was continuing to proliferate missile technology and components to Pakistan. Despite this, US Administration continued to express willingness to certify that China was not proliferating, or, for India, worse, that the US was either unable or unwilling to restrain China. As the range of options for India narrowed so, too, did the difficulties of taking corrective action.

Today, India is a nuclear weapon state. This adds to its sense of responsibility as a nation that is committed to the principles of the UN Charter and to promoting regional peace and stability. Efforts for closer engagement will, of course, have to be intensified covering the entire range of issues which require collective consideration. During the past 50 years there have been a number of decisive moments. 1968 was one such moment in India's nuclear chapter; as was 1974, and now 1998. At each of these moments, India took the decision guided only by national interest, and supported by a national consensus. The May tests of 1998 were born in the crucible of earlier decisions and made possible only because those decisions had been taken correctly, and in time.

Let it be repeated that India's nuclear policy remains firmly committed to a basic tenet: that the country's national security, in a world of nuclear proliferation lies either in global disarmament or in exercise of the principle of equal and legitimate security for all. The earliest Indian articulations on the question of nuclear disarmament were admittedly more moralistic than realistic. The current disharmony, therefore, between India's position and the position that the rest of the globe has seemingly adopted is that whereas India has moved from the totally moralistic to a little more realistic, the rest of the nuclear world has arrived at all of its nuclear conclusions entirely realistically. They now have a surplus of nuclear weapons, also the technology for fourth generation weapons, and are now thus beginning to move towards a moralistic position. It is of this that is born lack of understanding about the Indian stand. The first and perhaps the principal obstacle in understanding India's position lies in an absence of due and proper recognition of the country's security needs; also in this nuclearised world for a balance between the rights and obligations of all nations;

of restraint in acquisition of nuclear weaponry; of ending this unequal division between nuclear haves and have-nots. No other country in the world has demonstrated the kind of restraint that India has for near about a quarter of a century after the first Pokhran test of 1974. In the years preceding that PNE and in subsequent decades, consistently, India continued to advocate the basic tenet of its nuclear strategy.

Now, in the nineties, and as the century turns, the country was faced by critical choices. India had been witness to decades of international unconcern and incomprehension even as the overall security environment of the country, both globally and in Asia, deteriorated. The end of the cold war resulted in the collapse of the then existing bipolarity, it created the appearance of unipolarity but it also led to the rise of additional power centres. The fulcrum of international balance of power shifted from Europe to Asia; Asian nations began their process of economic resurgence. Asia-Pacific as a trade and security rim became a geo-political reality. In 1995, the Nuclear Non-proliferation Treaty, essentially a cold war arms control treaty, with a fixed duration of 25 years, was extended indefinitely and unconditionally. This legitimised, in perpetuity, the existing nuclear arsenals; in effect an unequal nuclear regime. Even as nations of the world acceded to the treaty, the five nuclear weapon powers states were also unable to subscribe. Meanwhile, in the intervening decades had persisted reports of the transfer of nuclear weapon powers technology from declared nuclear weapon powers to preferred states. Neither the world nor the nuclear weapon powers succeeded in halting this process. NPT notwithstanding, proliferation in the region spread.

Since nuclear weapon powers that assist proliferation, or even condone it are not subject to any penalty, the entire non-proliferation regime became flawed. Nuclear technologies became, at their worst, commodities of international commerce, at best lubricants of diplomatic fidelity. Such proliferation in India's neighbourhood has been enumerated in strategic literature and cited in numerous Congressional testimonies. India noted with concern that not only did the CIA refer to them, indeed, from the early nineties onward the required presidential certification in this regard could not be provided. India is the only country in the world to be situated between two nuclear weapon powers.

Today most nations of the world are also the beneficiaries of a nuclear security paradigm. From Vancouver to Vladivostok stretches a club: that of a security framework with four nuclear weapon powers as partners in peace providing extended deterrent protection. The Americas progress under the US nuclear deterrent protection as members of Organisation of American States. South Korea, Japan and Australasia also have the benefit of US extended deterrence. By itself, China is a major nuclear weapon power. Only Africa and southern Asia remain outside the exclusivity of this new international nuclear paradigm, where nuclear weapons and their currency in international conduct is, paradoxically, legitimised. How to accept these differentiated standards of national security or a regime of international nuclear apartheid is a challenge not simply to India but to the inequality of the entire non-proliferation regime.

In the aftermath of the cold war a new Asian balance of power is emerging. Developments in this region create new alignments, new vacuums. India, in exercise of its supreme national interests, has acted, and timely, to correct this imbalance, to fill a potential vacuum. Its endeavour is to contribute to a stable balance of power in Asia, which it holds will contribute meaningfully to a furtherance of the democratic process.

On India's western flank lies the Gulf region, one of the most critical sources of the world's energy States, a yet to be fully developed reservoir. With both these regions India has ancient linkages. It also has extensive energy import requirements. The Gulf provides employment to Indian labour and talent. However, this region too, and its adjoining countries have been targets of missile and nuclear proliferation. Long range missiles of 2500 km range were proliferated to this area in the mid-1980s. Unfortunately, from 1987 onwards nuclear proliferation, with extra-regional assistance, has continued unchecked.

Faced as India was, with a legitimisation of nuclear weapons by the haves, by a global nuclear security paradigm from which it was excluded, trends towards disequilibrium in the balance of power in Asia, and a neighbourhood of two nuclear weapon countries acting in concert, India had to protect its future by exercising its nuclear option. By doing this India has brought into the open the nuclear reality which had remained clandestine for at least the last eleven years. India could not accept a flawed non-proliferation regime, as the international norm, when all objective realities asserted conclusively to the contrary.

India's policies towards its neighbours and other countries have not changed. The country remains fully committed to the promotion of peace, stability, and resolution of all outstanding issues through bilateral dialogue and negotiations. The tests of May 11 and 13, 1998 were not directed against any country; these were intended to reassure the people of India about their own security. Confidence building is a continuous process, with India remaining committed to it.

India is now a nuclear weapon state; as is Pakistan. That is a reality that can neither be denied, nor wished away. This category of a Nuclear Weapon State is not, in actuality, a conferment; nor is it a status for others to grant, it is an objective reality. This strengthened capability adds to India's sense of responsibility; the responsibility and obligation of power. India, mindful of its international obligations, is committed to not using these weapons to commit aggression or to mount threats against any country; these are weapons of self-defence, to ensure that India, too, is not subjected to nuclear threats or coercion.

India has reiterated its undertaking of a 'no-first-use' agreement with any country, bilaterally or in a collective forum. India shall not engage in an arms race; of course, it shall also neither subscribe to nor reinvent the sterile doctrines of the cold war. India remains committed to the basic tenet of its foreign policy—a conviction that global elimination of nuclear weapons will enhance its security as well as that of the rest of the world. It will continue to urge countries, particularly other nuclear weapon states to adopt measures that would contribute meaningfully to such an objective. This is the defining difference; it is also the cornerstone of India's nuclear doctrine.

That is why India will continue to support such initiatives, taken individually or collectively, by the Non-Aligned Movement which has continued to attach the highest priority to nuclear disarmament. This was reaffirmed most recently at the NAM Ministerial meeting held at Cartagena soon after India had conducted its present series of underground tests. The NAM ministers 'reiterated their call on the Conference on Disarmament to establish, as the highest priority, an ad hoc committee to start in 1998 negotiations on a phased programme for the complete elimination of nuclear weapons with a specified framework of time, including a Nuclear Weapons Convention'. This collective voice of 113 NAM countries reflects an approach to global nuclear disarmament to which India has remained committed. One of the

NAM member initiatives, to which great importance is attached, was the reference to the International Court of Justice resulting in the unanimous declaration as part of the Advisory Opinion handed down on 8 July 1996, that 'there exists an obligation to pursue in good faith and bring to a conclusion negotiations leading to nuclear disarmament in all its aspects under strict and effective international control'. India was one of the countries that appealed to the ICJ on this issue. No other nuclear weapon state has supported this judgment; in fact, they have sought to decry its value. India has been and will continue to be in the forefront of the calls for opening negotiations for a Nuclear Weapons Convention, so that this challenge can be dealt with in the manner used in the scourge of other weapons of mass destruction—the Biological Weapons Convention and the Chemical Weapons Convention. In keeping with its commitment to comprehensive, universal and non-discriminatory approaches to disarmament India is an original State party to both these conventions. In recent years, in keeping with these new challenges, India has actively promoted regional cooperation—in SAARC, in the Indian Ocean Rim Association for Regional Cooperation and as a member of the ASEAN Regional Forum. This engagement will also continue. The policies of economic liberalisation introduced in recent years have increased India's regional and global linkages and India shall deepen and strengthen these ties.

India's nuclear policy has been marked by restraint and openness. It has not violated any international agreements either in 1974 or now, in 1998. This restraint exercised for 24 years, after having demonstrated a capability in 1974, is in itself an unique example. Restraint, however, has to arise from strength. It cannot be based upon indecision or doubt. Restraint is valid only when doubts are removed. The series of tests undertaken by India have led to the removal of doubts. The action involved was balanced, in that it was the minimum necessary to maintain what is an irreducible component of the country's national security calculus.

Subsequent to the tests the Government of India has already stated that it will now observe a voluntary moratorium and refrain from conducting underground nuclear test explosions. It has also indicated willingness to move towards a de-jure formalisation of this declaration. The basic obligation of the CTBT is thus met: to refrain from undertaking nuclear tests.

India has also expressed readiness to participate in negotiations in the Conference on Disarmament, in Geneva, on a Fissile Material Cut-off Treaty. The basic objective of this treaty is to prohibit future production of fissile materials for use in nuclear weapons or nuclear explosive devices. India's approach in these negotiations will be to ensure that this treaty emerges as a universal and non-discriminatory treaty, backed by an effective verification mechanism.

India has maintained effective export controls on nuclear materials as well as related technologies even though it is neither a party to the NPT nor a member of the Nuclear Suppliers Group. Nonetheless, India is committed to non-proliferation and to the maintaining of stringent export controls to ensure that there is no leakage of its indigenously developed know-how and technologies. In fact, India's conduct in this regard has been better than some countries party to the NPT.

India has in the past conveyed its concerns on the inadequacies of the international nuclear non-proliferation regime. It has explained that the country was not in a position to join because the regime did not address the country's security concerns. These could have been addressed by moving towards global nuclear disarmament, India's preferred approach. As this did not take place, India was obliged to stand aside from the emerging regime so that its freedom of action was not constrained. This is precisely the path that it has continued to follow, unwaveringly, for the last three decades. That same constructive approach will underlie India's dialogue with countries that need to be persuaded of India's serious intent and willingness to engage so that mutual concerns are satisfactorily addressed. The challenge to Indian statecraft remains that of reconciling India's security imperatives with valid international concerns in regard to nuclear weapons.

What collapsed prior to the Pressler Amendment cannot now be reinvented. Let the world move towards finding more realistic solutions: to evolving a universal common security paradigm for the entire globe. Since nuclear weapons are not really usable, paradoxically the dilemma lies in their continuing deterrent value; and this paradox further deepens the concerns of public men having the responsibility of governance: how to employ state power in service of national security and simultaneously address international concerns. How, thereafter, to evolve to an order that ensures a peaceful present and an orderly future. How then to reconcile with an objective global reality that as these weapons do have a deterrent value, some are the owners of this value, others not; yet a lasting balance has to be found even then. For, though humanity is indivisible, national security interests, as sovereign expressions, have not the same attribute.

18

Secularism

Though it made its appearance in the Indian constitution through a late amendment to its preamble during the Emergency at Indira Gandhi's initiative, secularism is one of the keystones of post-independence Indian polity. It does not imply separation of religion and politics, but rather the benevolent attitude of the state *vis-à-vis* all religious communities. Moreover, Article 30(2) of the constitution emphasizes that 'The state shall not, in granting aid to educational institutions, discriminate against any educational institution on the ground that it is under the management of a minority, whether based on religion or language.'

Ironically, Hindu nationalists have always looked at themselves as more sincere secularists than have Congressmen. They denounced the Congress Party as 'pseudo-secular' because of its bias in favour of religious minorities. As early as the 1950s the Sangh Parivar criticized the Hindu Code Bill which reformed Hindu customs of marriage, adoption, and inheritance, whereas the shariat and the personal laws of other religious minorities remained untouched. This issue resurfaced in the 1980s during what is known as the Shah Bano affair, when the Congress was accused of pampering its Muslim vote bank by reaffirming the status of the shariat in regulating the private sphere of this minority.

In contrast, Hindu nationalists claim they are the true secularists because Hinduism ignores theocracy: in their view the traditionally weak role of the state *vis-à-vis* the social order is in harmony with a loose religious organization—Hinduism in their view ignores church-like hierarchies and has always accommodated a plurality of spiritual streams. According to them, religious minorities benefit from this traditional tolerance in a Hindu-dominated polity. This line of thought is disputed on the ground that if Hinduism ignores orthodoxy, it relies on strict orthopraxy through the caste system, which implies that religious minorities should pay allegiance to the value system of Brahmins; besides, Hindu nationalism has always assumed that religious minorities may practice their rituals freely in the private sphere but should respect Hindu customs in the public sphere.

One of the personalities the Sangh Parivar projected as the moderate face of Hindu nationalism, Atal Behari Vajpayee, articulated the official view of secularism of his ideological milieu in a systematic way. Born in Gwalior, the capital of one of the largest princely states of North India, Vajpayee first came under the influence of Congress and the Arya Samaj. He studied in the DAV College, Kanpur (where he earned an MA in Political Science) and became General Secretary of the Arya Kumar Sabha of Gwalior in 1944. He had joined the RSS earlier and was sent to UP as a *vistarak* in 1946. He worked for Deendayal Upadhyaya's newspaper in the late 1940s and eventually became editor of *Panchjanya*. He then followed Upadhyaya into the Jana Sangh. He became S.P. Mookerjee's secretary and assisted Upadhyaya in the party headquarters after Mookerjee's death. He remained party secretary from 1956 to 1966. He ran for office for the first time in 1957 and won a seat in the Lok Sabha—he was re-elected ten times. He succeeded Upadhyaya as president of the Jana Sangh after the latter's assassination in 1968 and was re-elected between 1969 and 1972 without interruption. He was the leader of the Jana Sangh parliamentary group from 1957 to the mid-1970s, when the party merged with the Janata Party. He was then appointed Minister of External Affairs in Morarji Desai's government. After the disintegration of the Janata Party he was the first president of the Bharatiya Janata Party between 1980 and 1986. After ten years in a less prominent position, he was appointed Prime Minister for 13 days in 1996, leader of the opposition in Parliament in 1996–7 and then Prime Minister in 1998, and again over 1999–2004. He was appointed chairman of the parliamentary group of the BJP after the defeat of his party in the 2004 elections.

Extract from Atal Behari Vajpayee,
'The Bane of Pseudo-Secularism'[1]

National integration is a continuing process. It is a feeling that has to be kindled with effort and fostered with care. In a big country like ours, which has always been full of variety and which is now going through a period of economic and social transition, it is impossible to check occasional communal incidents. But the very fact that we stopped our efforts at National Unity when it was automatically born as a reaction to foreign aggression and have now revived them as an antidote to communal riots at some places shows how unrealistic and illogical the thinking on the problem of National Unity has become.

The Basic Truths of National Integrity

We have to accept some basic truths for the protection and fostering of national integrity. The first among them is that from Kashmir to Kanya Kumari Bharat is one nation and not a group of different nationalities. Those according to whom different language groups are different nations are the agents of disintegration and destruction, so let us beware of them. Secondly Bharat is an ancient nation; so we are not engaged in creating a new nation but in preparing our old nation to face the new challenges. Our nationalism is as old as the Vedic declaration: 'The earth is my mother and I am her son.' For Western scholars, nationalism may be a modern concept, but for us it is as old as our life in this land.

Bharat or the Indian nation is basically a cultural unit. It was on the basis of this cultural unity that we have attempted to establish political, economic and social unity. Whenever these attempts failed, the country was divided into different kingdoms, but our cultural unity continued and it formed the basis on which we fought for unity in other fields. Even today we are not one because we are citizens of one State. Rather Bharat is one State because we are one.

Our national life is full of variety. There are many languages, many sects, many modes of life and many styles of art and literature. This

---

[1] Atal Behari Vajpayee, 'The Bane of Secularism', in S.S. Bhandari, ed., *Jana Sangh Souvenir* (Delhi: BJP, 1969), pp. 55–8.

variety is the symbol of the richness of our life. We have to protect as
well as foster it. And it is in this variety that we have to find and consolidate our unity.

Invidious Distinction of Majority/Minority

To divide the people of this country on the basis of language, regions
[*sic*], sect, community or profession into majority and minority is still
more dangerous. Those who are true to India are all Indians, whatever
their religion or language. So on the one hand we have to rise above
small loyalties and make our country our prime loyalty, while on the
other hand we have to wean some people from extra-territorial loyalties.
Freedom of worship is an integral part of Indian culture. The Constitution of India also contains this freedom. Indians have never discriminated on the basis of sect or religion. In the future too nobody wishes
to have such a distinction. At the same time to base a minority or a
majority on modes of worship is both illogical and harmful to national
unity. The Muslims and Christians for whom India is a home have not
come from outside. Their ancestors were Hindus and Hindu blood
flows in their veins. A change in religion does not mean a change in
nationality or culture. Culture is related to the soil and nationality to
loyalty. The Muslims of East Bengal and Pakhtoonistan follow the
same religion but their cultures are different. On the other hand those
who forsake their loyalty to the nation become enemies even when
they follow the same religion. Bharatiya Jana Sangh believes in bringing
about a society and state in which all citizens will have equality of opportunity without discrimination. Language and religion would not
form the basis of any discrimination whatsoever.

What is Secularism?

The policy of encouraging fissiparous tendencies in the name of
secularism would be detrimental to national unity. Communalism
has already led to one partition of the country. Now let us stop this
unfortunate history from repeating itself. Secular just means pertaining
to this world. According to Hindu polity, the State came into being
for the fulfilment of earthly functions. Unlike in the west, in Bharat
there was no conflict between the State and the religious order. Secular
does not mean anti-religious or non-religious. In fact the people of

India can never be secular in this sense. Secularism just means an impartial attitude of the State towards all modes of worship. The Jana Sangh champions the cause of such an impartial state and does not believe in adopting any one mode of worship as the religion of the State. At present some elements which are trying to draw us away from our glorious past, our noble ideals of life and from our great men and seers in the name of secularism are gaining strength. But we must remember that if we break with our past we would neither be able to face the challenge of the present nor have strength to build the future. We have to make India a modern nation. We have to see that the latest research in the field of science and technology serves to make the life of the common man happy and prosperous. But we shall never accept denying our past and our traditional culture as a price for bringing this about. The stream of our life has been flowing since Vedic Time and we want to give it still more strength so that it can assimilate into it many tributaries from many directions.

Muslims in India

The communal riots that have taken place in different parts of the country are a matter of some concern. Before 1947 we thought we had done our duty when we put the blame of such disturbances on the British. But the very fact that 20 years after our attaining freedom and establishment of Pakistan such riots take place indicates that we are mistaking the symptoms for the disease and are still not prepared for some basic thinking in this respect. We must seriously try to find out why quarrels among individuals deteriorate into communal riots. The shouting of pro-Pakistani slogans and radio reports of such riots from Pakistan immediately after they take place have added an element of greater difficulty to an already difficult problem.

During the last some years there has been a great increase in Muslim organisations seeking to foster separatism. Some of them, like the Jamiat-i-Islami, openly declare that Muslims can be safe and happy only in a State which runs according to Shariat. In addition, there are also secret societies which operate from schools and places of worship and keep promoting the nefarious idea that Muslims have no future in India. To say that minorities are not secure or have no future in the country in which the President himself, the Chief Justice of the Supreme

Court, and many Central as well as State Ministers, Ambassadors and high Government officials are Muslims is nothing but to discredit India in the eyes of the world. As a matter of fact all Indians, irrespective of their religion or language, are facing the same kind of problems. These problems have arisen out of economic backwardness. Giving it a religious, linguistic or regional colour is not only creating an interference in the way of national integrity but making the solution still more difficult. It is the duty of political parties to educate the people and save them from such selfish and separatist elements. It is a matter of surprise that the party which declares its secularism from house tops and is the first to berate communalism not only compromises with communal elements for political ends but unashamedly supports minority demands in the guise of protecting minority interests. If the country is to be saved from the tragedy of communalism, all parties must pledge to cleanse their minds of all communal virus.

We are Determined . . .

The solution of all problems of Bharat lies in arousing a strong sense of nationalism. Single-minded devotion to the nation and a readiness to sweat and if necessary also to give up everything can alone enable us to rise above sectarian, linguistic and religious considerations and behave like citizens of one great nation. The Bharatiya Jana Sangh has devoted itself to this mission. It is determined to confront and defeat all divisive elements, and their supporters—with the help of others, if possible, alone, if necessary.

Extract from Atal Behari Vajpayee, 'Secularism, the Indian Concept'[2]

. . . Today, after four decades of India becoming free, we find the word 'secular' has become the main subject of a political debate. There is no unanimity as to what does the word 'Secular' actually mean. One political party calls it 'secularism', while the other party calls the same as 'pseudo-secularism'. What has been described as positive secularism

---

[2] Atal Behari Vajpayee, 'Rajendra Prasad Lecture', 1992, All India Radio, copy of broadcast.

by one party, the other party calls the same as communalism. Parliament witnesses frequent exchanges between the political parties calling themselves 'secular' and the parties whom they do not recognise as 'secular'. 'Secular' and 'secularism' were used on a wide scale during campaigns in the last general elections. The same can be said about newspapers. It is, therefore, essential that we should crystallise our views on the concept of secularism. In this process, we shall first have to understand the western concept of secularism and its background.

The New Encyclopaedia Britannica Micropaedia volume 9 (1978) describes secularism as a movement towards ecclesiastic from the non-ecclesiastic. It also says that secularism came into being as a reaction to the tendency of the mediaeval period to regard the activities of human life in this world as insignificant and to devote all attention to God and the life beyond. According to the *Concise Oxford Dictionary*, the word secular means 'related to or pertaining to this world. . . . not to church.' *The Chambers Twentieth Century Dictionary* defines 'secular' as 'pertaining to the present world, or to things not spiritual, not concerned with religion, civil, not ecclesiastical.'

Therefore, it can be said that in substance, secularism means pertaining to the human existence in the present world and it should be understood that it does not require any reference to religion. Secularism is something different from religion, without religion or temporal. It is said that the word secularism was first used by Holioke. He differentiated between secularism and atheism. It is often the impression that an atheist neither believes in God nor in morality. One who believes in secularism lays emphasis on morality independent of God and religion. Secularism is said to have been in Europe during the Renaissance. *The Encyclopaedia of Social Science* (vols 13–14) tells us that while the success of the reform movements in various countries of North Europe led to the consolidation of irrational faith, the scholars and philosophers of the Italian Renaissance took the logical and empirical investigation to new heights. Their unrelenting quest for unfolding the secrets of nature and human life shifted the emphasis from the metaphysical to the physical world.

The origin of the modern concept of secularism can be traced back to mediaeval Europe when the Roman Catholic Church was dominant. The Head of the Roman Catholic Church, the Pope, then not only enjoyed the religious power but also non-ecclesiastical and State power. Just like any other ruler, the Pope absorbed smaller independent or semi-independent 'Jagirs' into what he had got by way of inheritance. The conduct of the Pope was just like any other Head of State. There existed a well-knit system establishing the stranglehold of the Church. On the basis of continuity and tradition, the psychological and political influence of the Church crossed the state boundaries and extended to the entire Europe. Everyone from top to bottom, be it a king or a slave, claimed to be loyal to the Church. There was the threat of punishment by the Church. And this fear was always undercurrent [*sic*].

The Pope, in fact, is a political power even in the present time. The Vatican City is an independent State and the Pope is its Head. There is an ambassador of the Pope in New Delhi.

The Christian Church, as an organised force, reached its zenith of power during the reign of Pope Innocent III (1198–1216) in the Western hemisphere. The Pope could easily establish his hold on the rulers of England and France. He enthroned or dethroned three monarchs of the Holy Roman Empire and brought most parts of Italy under his personal control. He took a number of decisions which were adopted in toto in the judicial system of the Church. This resulted in human life coming under the purview of the Church.

Boniface VIII became the Pope in 1281. Maximum amount of bitterness was generated during this period because of his conflict with Philip of France. Ultimately, armed men sent by King Philip attacked the Summer Palace of the Pope. They could have captured or harmed the Pope. But they did not do so and went back. The shock of the humiliation was too great for the Pope who died after a month of the attack.

The struggle between the Pope and King Philip of France illustrates the struggle between the Church and the State. The basic question was as to whose writ would run? Would it be the political authority of the country, the ruler or the king, or would it be the religious authority headed by the Pope? A study of the struggle between France and the Pope helps us to understand the real nature of the conflict. King Philip of France and King Edward I of England were at war. Philip needed funds to meet the war expenditure. He demanded parsons to pay 10 per cent of their annual income for this purpose. The priesthood promptly complained against it to the Pope. The Pope issued an edict—a 'bull' which declared that a state is unquestionably under the supreme authority of the Church and as such no king or any other worldly power has the authority over the subjects of Church or their property.

This edict was applicable to both the kings, Edward and Philip. However, King Edward of England forced the priesthood to part with the fifth portion of their annual income. A threat was held out to the priesthood that anyone who disobeyed the command would be held prisoner. If anyone belonging to the Church did not hand over the money as stipulated, his property would be confiscated. It was asserted that King Edward's suzerainty over such properties was beyond any doubt. It is noteworthy that the King had the support of his people in making such assertions.

However, the situation in France was different. King Philip retaliated against the Pope's edict by banning the entry of any foreigner into France. It implied that the envoy of the Pope or any other official could not enter France. Even the English were not allowed. King Philip subsequently banned export of gold, silver and defence supplies from France. This choked the supply line to the Pope from an important source.

The Pope adopted the posture of compromise. But King Philip made his stand clear by bringing out a pamphlet, though it did not carry any name. The pamphlet propounded the theory that the authority of the temporal king had ascendency over the authority of the Church so far as the masses are concerned. According to the pamphlet, the priesthood should follow the dictates of the temporal ruler in all worldly matters. It said that the priesthood also was a part of the State like the general public and everyone was obliged to support the State.

Peace prevailed for almost a year. But after some time, the conflict again came to the fore. In an edict the Pope wrote to King Philip, 'My dear son, you should not be misled by anyone to believe that there was no one above you on this earth nor should you think that you are not subordinate to the supreme head of the Catholic Church.' This edict was read out to King Philip. The king's associates were furious to be told that their king was not free to act in the way he wanted.

Philip called a joint meeting of the representatives of the priests, feudal lords and of the middle class and thus created a platform from which an advisor of Philip made a forceful appeal to French nationalism.

A reply was given to the Pope. It said that they (those in the court of King Philip) did not accept the authority of anyone in worldly matters. The reply emphasised that whatever was theirs was under the authority of the Crowned King. Insulting expressions were used for Pope Boniface such as 'no salutation to one who calls himself the Pope'. It is important that all the three groups, the priesthood, the middle class and the feudal class, supported the king. The flame of French nationalism had been lit.

In Rome, at a religious congregation, the Pope read out an edict which clearly stated that all temporal kings were under the authority of the Pope. The edict spelt of [sic] the belief there was only one holy inspiration and it was that of the Catholic Church. There was no salvation outside the Church nor any forgiveness by the Pope. It further said that the Church had two swords—one that of the spirit and it is in the hands of the priesthood and the other sword was that of this world which was in the hands of the kings and the soldiers. This sword, too, should be used only with the concurrence of priests. The edict goes on to say 'we declare that every human being should follow the Pope for his salvation.'

When the King of France heard about the declaration, he promptly despatched orators to different parts of the country to project the view that the French people should be free from the bondage of the lecherous and spendthrift Pope. The feelings of nationalism of the French people were exploited in a very shrewd manner and the common reaction was in favour of the king. Allies of the king were aware that the Pope would excommunicate him. The order of excommunication was to be issued on the 8th of September. A day earlier, the Summer Palace of the Pope was stormed. The incident has already been mentioned earlier.

We find that the conflict between the Church and the State led to the generation of nationalist sentiments which played a major role in the conflict. The same feelings led to the emergence of nation states in Europe and it was a significant development. We find that King Philip could defeat the Pope because he had the support of the French people. The same is true of King Edward of England who succeeded in either ignoring or opposing the Pope and the Church. Therefore, we can say that the emergence of nation states was a secular development.

The Pope was of the view that all Christian countries were under his control as he had the supreme authority over all the followers of Christianity. The jurisdiction of the nation states was limited to their boundaries only. As the head of the state, the king or anyone else could have only political authority. The authority of the Pope was of a religious nature and it transcended national boundaries. The authority of the head of a state was temporal in nature and was confined to the people of the state irrespective of their religion. Thus, the Pope or Church was essentially a religious entity whereas the State was 'secular or independent of religion.'

So far as India is concerned, there had been no question of the supremacy of temporal or political authority, whatever might have been the nature of the political system of the country, autocratic, capitalist or democratic. The temporal or political power of the State maintained its equipoise because of the teachings of the Acharyas. This balance was the result of the moral and altruistic outlook. We have had the tradition of discipline and not the rule by religious leaders.

Indian political ideology has accepted the supremacy of the political system but they have never supported autocratic dictatorship. There is a need to put some check on the political authority. This check is that of law. Even during the Vedic period, the importance of law was recognised. The cycle of seasons, as conceived during the Vedic period, was based on the concept of law which regulates the entire world. It is said in the 'Rigveda' that the earth remains firm in its position because of the law (Niyam), the same law keeps the sun in its position in the sky. Similarly, the State has to function according to the law or 'niyam'. These laws provide the foundation for the concept of Dharma. The moral and material well being of the people can be ensured by the State by acting according to Dharma.

We find that Dharma is used in the Indian thought in a much broader sense and in different contexts than the word 'religion', though often Dharma and religion are used as synonyms. The word Dharma has been derived from 'Dhri/dhatu', which means 'to hold'. Thus we can say that anything that helps to keep something in its original form is its Dharma. The natural tendency of any object (or an individual) and its qualities denote its Dharma. Dharma is also used in the sense of duty. Therefore, in the social context, Dharma is important. Dharma is the ensemble of the rules and regulations followed in various facets of human life of an individual and the society as a whole. Indian traditions lay utmost importance on the following of Dharma. Dharma allows freedom of thought and faith but as long as you are following your Dharma or act according to your Dharma, you are on the right track.

We must realise the difference between Dharma and religion. Religion is related to certain definite beliefs. As long as one shares those beliefs, he remains a member of that faith, religion or 'mazhab'. No sooner does one give up those beliefs than he ceases to be a member of that religion. Dharma is not entirely dependent upon beliefs. A person may not have any religious faith but still he could be called 'Dharmik'. That means he has good qualities. Essentially, Dharma is the way of life. It is something more than just living according to certain beliefs. The practice of adding adjectives to Dharma is rather new. Dharma is neither related to a country or a period nor is it confined to a specific community. When Dharma gets associated with a particular community, it becomes religion. It also becomes religion when it is institutionalised.

Scholars speak of two categories of Dharma 1—General Dharma and 2—Special Dharma. Manusmriti speaks of ten attributes of Dharma like patience, forgiveness, compassion, honesty, purity, control over senses, wisdom, knowledge, truth and non-violence. All these are related to the conduct of man. Stress has been laid in the Shantiparva of the Mahabharata that a man should speak the truth, give donations, do hard work and should have purity, forgiveness and concern for others. He should be straight in his dealings, and should act with wisdom. He should also have the capacity and tendency to concentrate and to maintain peace.

The Mahabharata reminds us that a Brahmin who had the arrogance of his asceticism was obliged to go to a butcher to learn Dharma. Also in Mahabharata, Yudhishthira had said that the question as to who is high or low can be decided only by judging the conduct of a person.

One who acts according to his Dharma, acquires the power of 'Punya'. The story of 'Savitri–Satyavan' can be cited as an example. Savitri is not depicted as any scholarly or a wise lady. She is great only as a wife because she had followed the 'Pativrata Dharma' and this gave her the extra-ordinary power that she could bring her dead husband back to life. We have many other such examples which point out that the family an individual is born in or the caste of an individual are immaterial.

'Shatpath Brahmin' says that 'Dharma is the Ruler of a Ruler, the supreme authority lies in Dharma'. The Mahabharata also provides evidence that the king had to follow the authority of Dharma. At the time of coronation, the king had to take a pledge that he would follow Dharma and would not act in an autocratic manner. The pledge was:

प्रतिज्ञा चावरोहस्व मनसा कर्मणा गिरा ।
पालयिष्याम्यहं भौमं ब्रह्म इत्येव चासकृत ।
यश्चात्र धर्म इत्युक्ते दण्डनीतिव्यपाश्रयः ।
तमशंकः करिष्यामि स्ववशोन कदाचन् ।

In the 'Aranya Kanda' of Ramayana, sages preach Shri Rama Chandra:

अधर्मः सुमहात्ताथ भवेत तस्य तु भूपतेः
यो हरेत बलिषड्भागं न च रक्षति पुत्रवत् ।।

'A king who realises taxes from his subjects but does not protect them as his own son, commits great Adharma.'

The same idea is expressed in different words in the Bhagwat. It describes the Dharma of the king as:

सर्वा समुद्धरेद्राजा पितेव व्यवसनात्प्रजाः ।

'The king has to protect his subjects from calamities as a father protects his son.'

Maharishi Vedavyas described the attributes of a noble king in the following words:

पुत्र इव पितुगृहे विषये यस्य मानवाः
निर्भया विरिष्यंति स राजा राजसत्तमः ।

'The best king is one in whose empire all subjects live without fear, as a son lives in the house of his father.'

It was the responsibility of the king not only to maintain peace and order in his kingdom but also to ensure that his subjects are not subjected to any hardships.

According to the 'Aapastamba' Dharmasutra:

न चास्य विषये क्षुधा रोगेण हिमातपाभ्यां नावसीदेत कश्चित् ।

'The king is bound by the Dharma to ensure that no one in his kingdom goes without food, no one meets an untimely death because of any disease or as a result of extreme cold or heat. It is the duty of the king to protect people against epidemics and famine.'

A king is also advised to protect his subjects from the atrocities and excesses of State officials:

राज्ञो हि रक्षेधिकृतोः परस्वाकांक्षिणः शठाः
भृत्या भवन्ति प्रायेण तेभ्यो रक्षोदिमाः प्रजाः

'State officials often become corrupt. They swallow the money that belongs to the people. The king should ensure that such corrupt officials are not kept in a position where they can indulge in undesirable activities.'

Referring to the treatment such officials deserve, it goes on to say that:

तेषां सर्वस्वमादाय राजा कुर्यात् प्रवासनूम् ।

'The king should take away everything whatever such officials have and then throw them out of his kingdom.'

The purpose behind the reference to the Dharma of the king as enunciated in our scriptures is just to bring home that Dharma essentially means Karma or duty. Anyone who ignores his duty i.e. Karma cannot follow his Dharma.

An analysis and comparative study of the Western and Indian concept of secularism leads us to the conclusion that the European secularism is something of this world and is independent of the Dharma or religion. On the other hand, a common man in India talks of life beyond this life and takes the belief as a matter of course.

We in India have an ancient religious and spiritual tradition. This tradition has left a deep imprint on the Indian psyche though it is true that the Indian philosophy also has schools like materialism and atheism.

Mahatma Gandhi describes the correct attitude towards religion as 'Sarva Dharma Sambhava', equal respect to all religions. The concept of 'Sarva Dharma Sambhava' is somewhat different from the European secularism which is independent of religion. In fact by propounding the theory of Sarva Dharma Sambhava, Gandhiji continued the age-old Indian tradition which can be traced to the ancient saying of 'Ekam Sadavipra Bahudha Vadanti'. We may say that the Indian concept of secularism is that of Sarva Dharma Sambhava. This concept reminds us of the ancient Indian tradition of liberalism and tolerance. Gandhiji's great stress on Sarva Dharma Sambhava was reflected in our freedom struggle. Our objective was to free ourselves from the colonial rule and to establish democracy. Under the democratic system, every citizen has a vote and thus he is an equal partner in the election of a Government. There is no discrimination on the basis of his religion.

'Sarva Dharma Sambhava' is not against any religion. It treats all religions with equal respect. And, therefore, it can be said that the Indian concept of secularism is more positive. It is specially suited to India as followers of different faiths had been living in India since time immemorial, long before the advent of Christianity and Islam. The translation of the word 'secular' as dharmanirpeksha has caused some confusion. Dharmanirpeksha appears somewhat negative. It creates an impression that it negates something. Secondly, dharmanirpeksha has been taken to mean that it is unconcerned about or indifferent to religion. We should not ignore the fact that the Indian society is basically oriented to Dharma and has faith in it.

After a decade of the framing of the Constitution, Nehruji thought of this aspect while writing the preface of the book entitled *Dharma-nirpeksha Rajya* (Secular State) by Shri Raghunath Singh (M.P.) Nehruji said that the word Dharmanirpeksha does not fully convey the idea behind the English word 'secular'. Some people think that it is something against religion. Obviously, it is an erroneous impression. The correct interpretation of the Secular State would be that all dharmas or religious faiths are treated with equal respect. This way, Nehruji also supported the Sarva Dharma Sambhava. The education and upbringing of Nehruji was in modern and western background. He envisaged an ideal society which sought solutions to its social and economic problems by making full use of science and technology.

Despite his modern outlook, Nehru never wanted to cut himself off from India's past. In his will and testament, Nehru wrote that he was proud of the glorious heritage which was ours and has been ours. He said that he realised that he, like all others, was a part of the long unbroken chain which takes us back to the hoary past, from times immemorial to the beginning of the early history. He saw that he would never break this chain as it is precious and he draws inspiration from it.

Nehruji wrote a letter to Bernard Hollywood in 1959. He said, 'No doubt, progress depended upon physical well-being, education, health facilities and industries etc'. However, he anxiously hoped that 'this progress would not be achieved at the cost of ethical values or to put it rather vaguely, by foregoing the spiritual attitude towards life and its problems.' He said 'he never meant that India acted on a high moral or spiritual plane. But certainly, India had continued to deliberate on such values and, at least, in principle, endorsed them.' It would be unfortunate, he said, if India forgot these values in its pursuits of physical well-being.

So, we find that Jawaharlal Nehru was deeply committed to the old Indian tradition of spirituality.

Delivering the convocation address at the Aligarh University in 1948, Nehruji had said that he was proud of India, not only because of its glorious heritage, but also because of its extraordinary capacity to add something to it; to keep open the doors and windows of its mind and spirit, so that refreshing air is kept blowing into it from distant lands.

He further said that he was proud of this heritage and also of our ancestors who provided intellectual and cultural prominence to India. He put a question to his audience, 'What do you feel about the past. Do you feel that you too are a part of it and India's past belongs as much to you or you push it aside to go forward without realising or feeling the thrill that comes with the realisation that we are the inheritors and trustees of a great heritage.' [. . .]

. . . Nehruji said, 'You are a Muslim and I am a Hindu. We may have different religious faiths or we may even not have any religious faith, but our cultural heritage remains the same. It is as much yours as mine.'

Now we should ponder as to what extent our Constitution provides for a state which is based on secularism or Sarva Dharma Sambhava. We have already discussed secularism and Sarva Dharma Sambhava. Articles 14, 15, 16 and 25 of the Constitution propound Sarva Dharma Sambhava. According to Article 14, specific provision is made that all citizens would have equal legal rights and the State would not deny them any protection as provided under the law. According to Article 15, the State would not discriminate against any citizen on the basis of religion. Article 16 makes provision for equality in matters of employment for any post under the State or controlled by it. Article 25 provides equal rights to all citizens to follow or propagate any religious faith and the freedom of conscience. In fact, the Preamble of the Constitution speaks of providing equal opportunities and status. It also says that this equality has to be ensured for all citizens.

This way, our Constitution provides equal opportunities and equal protection under the law for all citizens and is against religious discrimination. It also guarantees equal status and equal opportunities to all citizens irrespective of their religion. In this context, it is understandable that the makers of the Constitution did not feel it necessary to add separately the word 'secular' in the Preamble of the Constitution.

But a decision was taken to add the word 'secular' by amending the Constitution 25 years later. Then there was a state of emergency. The Lok Sabha had completed its term of five years and was surviving on the extended life of one year. Most of the prominent leaders of the opposition parties were behind the bar. Even, some leaders of the ruling party who dared to oppose were put in jail. The press was under censorship. The freedom of expression was curbed. Complaints were voiced in Parliament that the Administration did not grant permission for holding even those meetings which were arranged for discussing the proposed constitutional amendment. The Law Minister tried to defend the Government by saying that such meetings were planned for some other purpose.

In reality the purpose of the constitutional amendment was not merely to add a few words in the Preamble. The statement of aims and objects which was attached to the Constitutional Amendment Bill stated that the Government's aim was 'to bring about a social and economic revolution in the country.' Constitutional amendment was necessary to remove the hurdles that obstructed the ushering in of the revolution. The Government had come out with a statement that 'vested interests are busy advancing their interests, at the cost of the public.' In a statement, the Law Minister Shri Gokhale said, 'Certain things have become inevitable for the Government. Therefore, the high ideals of socialism, secularism and national integrity are being explicitly mentioned in the Constitution.'

We all know that the purpose behind the constitutional amendment was to give precedence to the Directive Principles over the Fundamental Rights, to establish the prerogative of Parliament to amend the Constitution and finally to curtail the right of the judiciary to declare any law as unconstitutional.

Introducing the Constitutional Amendment Bill in the Lok Sabha, the Law Minister Shri Gokhale had said that the addition of the words 'socialism and secularism' was not just a play of words. He however, did not elaborate on the need to include these words. It may be noted that he had mentioned socialism and secularism in one breath. There was no separate discussion on them nor was any attempt made to define these two words. Shri Gokhale said that the two isms had been before us. We have tried to follow them and now we will follow them still more. He himself commented that one could say that the two terms could not be defined and then proceeded to say that even the concept of democracy could not be defined. It is interpreted in different countries in different manners. However, he said, we do know as to what 'socialism and secularism' mean.

During the course of discussion on the bill in the Lok Sabha, several members wanted to know the need for including the word 'secularism' in the Constitution. Shri Indrajit Gupta of the Communist Party of India even went to the extent of saying that India was already a Secular Republic. The State provided equal status and rights to the followers of different religions. Even those who did not believe in any religion got equal treatment. Shri Indrajit Gupta then said the only purpose of adding the word 'secular' in the Constitution one could make out was that we wanted to strengthen the secular character of our Republic and to give an assurance to the followers of all religions that the element of secularism would be underlined. He further said that India, unlike its neighbours, was not a theocratic State. He insisted that the Government should spell out exactly what assurance it wanted to give to the followers of different faiths especially the minorities by adding the word 'secularism'.

Many members who took part in the debate did not utter a single word on the inclusion of secularism. Shri K. Hanumanthaiah was one of them. What conclusion can be drawn from it? Does it mean that such members did not consider the subject important enough to be commented upon? Perhaps it would be rather unfair to them to think in this way.

Even those members who supported the move to declare India a secular republic, emphasised that we should not be guided by the dictionary meaning of the word 'secular'. The most outstanding speech during the debate was that of Sardar Swaran Singh. He had headed the Government Committee on the constitutional amendment. In his speech, he clarified that the word secular as given in the dictionary was not the same as what we had in our perception. He even went to the extent of saying that as far as he was concerned the word secular, as defined in the dictionary, was not a concept that could be highly spoken of. He then referred to the conflict between the Church and the State in Europe and said, 'Given this background, the Western secular concept was not acceptable to us.' Sardar Swaran Singh said that the word secular has acquired a definite connotation in our country. And it means that, under the Constitution, followers of different religions are on an equal footing before the law of the land. He said, 'Our secularism would not have the slightest suggestion that it was anti-religion. Secularism as we understand provides for equal respect for all religions.'

Shri Suleman Sait of the Muslim League welcomed the inclusion of the word 'secular'. He however, interpreted that its inclusion would fortify the rights of the minorities. Shri Sait quoted from the speech delivered by Smt Indira Gandhi in April 1976 and said according to her, 'We are striving to provide Indian versions of socialism and Communism'.

One of the debates in the Constituent Assembly was nearest to the Indian concept of secularism. This debate was held on the report of the Advisory Committee which had been constituted to go into the question of the minorities and their fundamental rights. Specially, some Muslim League members of the committee had demanded that there should be a separate electoral college for the Muslims. Sardar Vallabh Bhai Patel was the Chairman of the Committee. While presenting the report and subsequently replying to the debate, he had made important points. It is worthwhile to go into some details.

Sardar Patel emphasised the country's objective to ensure equity for all the citizens and to remove all divisions, classifications and privileges in the shortest possible time. He reminded both the majority and minority communities of their responsibilities and said it was in the interest of all that a real and strong foundation of the Secular State was laid. In conclusion, he said 'We all should forget about the majority and minority communities and should think only in the terms of one Indian society.'

During the debate, a Muslim League member again raised the issue of separate representation. He moved an amendment demanding the continuation and endorsement of proportionate representation in the Central and state legislatures (according to the population of Muslims). But the amendment was opposed by some other members of the Muslim League. They included Begum Aizaz Rassol, Col. Zaidi, and Maulana Hasrat Mohani. The tenor of the speeches made by those who had supported the amendment was such that even a leader of Sardar Patel's mettle got perturbed. He made a speech which has acquired historical importance and it is as relevant today as when it was made.

Whatever he said is being reproduced: 'Sir I would not take much time. I am pained to learn that this question has been taken seriously. This question was put forth in the Advisory Committee also but it had not generated as much debate as today. My friends in the Muslim League present here, those who moved the amendment and supported, had felt that they, in a way, had to discharge a duty. They had been pressing for the system of separate electorate. They had been used to it for a long time and they felt that the system should not be discarded all of a sudden. They could have simply put the amendment to vote. However, when I listened to their detailed speeches, I became aware that I was living in the period when the question of communalism had become a matter of controversy for the first time.

'I did not have the occasion to listen to the speeches which propounded the theory of communal system of elections in the Congress
in the early days. However, several prominent Muslims have expressed
their view in writing that the greatest harm has been done to India by
the communal electoral colleges. The communal approach to the election process has injected poison in the body politic of our nation.
Many of the Britishers, who had been responsible for introducing the
system themselves, accept this fact. This communal system had led to
the division of the country. Realising this consequence, I could never
think that any such proposal could be put forward with any serious
intent. Or if put forth it would be taken seriously.

'When the creation of Pakistan was accepted it was also accepted
that the remaining India, 80 per cent part of India, would be one
nation and no one would indulge in the talk of two nations. There is
no gainsaying that the separate electoral system is being demanded as
it is in our interest. We have heard enough. We had been hearing of
this for years and as a result of this agitation we find today that we are
a separate nation. The agitation had centred around the argument that
they were a separate nation. Separate electoral colleges or any provision
of special status or privileges were not good enough for their security
and were not acceptable. They needed a separate state. Ultimately, we
had to say "alright, you take a separate state". But the rest of the country 80 per cent of it would remain one nation. Do you agree to this?
Or do you still want that we should raise the question of two nations
even here? I oppose separate electoral system. Can you name a single
independent country which has such separate electoral system? If yes,
I would be prepared to accept the system. But the country be damned
if such a separate system is to be continued in this unfortunate land
even after the division of the country. The country would no longer be
worth living in. I therefore, say not only in my interest but also in your
interest that you please let bygone be bygone. We all can get united
one day. I wish Pakistan well. May it be a success. May it build itself
up in its own way and be prosperous. We may compete for achieving
prosperity but surely we may not have a rivalry as is being witnessed
in Pakistan these days. You do not know, in Delhi we are sitting on the
top of a volcano. You do not know as to how much pressure is being
put on us on account of what has been happening around us. My

friends, the movers of the amendment say that the Muslim community is united today. Fine, I am happy to learn about it. You would no longer require our support. (Thumping of desks) However there are other minorities which are not organised. They deserve special facilities and protection. We want to be liberal towards them. At the same time, you want that we should accept reservations on the basis of population, for you have taken advantage of it for a long time and do not realise that discrimination is implicit in the system. Do other independent countries in the world have any system of reservations of this type? I am asking you, would you please tell me? You are an organised community. Then why do you act like a lame? You are organised. Be brave and strong. Stand on your own feet. Think of the nation we are trying to build. With the new Constitution we have laid the foundation of the nation. Chaudhary Khali-quzzama has said that the British element is no more and we should forget all apprehensions. The British have left but they have left behind a mischief. We do not want to make it a permanent mischief (Hear, Hear). When the British introduced this element, they had not thought that they would have to go so soon. They had done so with a view to ruling over us with ease. It is true that it is their legacy, but do we have to discard it or not? For this very reason, I am asking you, I am making an appeal to you to please think about it. Do you expect that there is even one individual in the country outside the Muslim League who would advocate the separate electoral system? Then why do you do this? If you say that you want to remain loyal to this country, I would like to ask as to how do you define this loyalty. Do you want to encourage loyalty for the other side? I had no intention to speak on the subject. But when the mover of the amendment motion spoke at such length and his party leader supported him, I felt that there was something wrong somewhere in the country. Therefore, my friends, I put this question to you. Do you want peace in the country? If yes, then please leave all this. You can neither do harm to Pakistan nor to India. The only thing that you can do is to make such things happen all over the country as are happening today around us. If you really want this you can have it. But I appeal to you that at least from our side we should prove that we have forgotten the things of the past. If you want to forget the past, we will have to forget what was done in the past and also as to who was responsible for the present sorry state of affairs. I would once again appeal to you to please withdraw the amendment and pass the motion unanimously to prove to the world outside that we are united.'

Immediately after the speech of Sardar Patel, some members made a strong demand for the withdrawal of the amendments. This was not done. The amendments were put to vote and rejected.

There was unanimous opinion in the Constituent Assembly as indeed all over the country, that the State should be secular in the sense that there would be no State religion nor would there be any discrimination of its citizens on the basis of religion. The question now arises as to why do we have this sharp controversy over secularism full four decades after the framing of the Constitution?

It seems that there are three main reasons. In principle, it was accepted that the Indian concept of secularism would draw its inspiration from the Sarva Dharma Sambhava—equal respect for all religions. It would not be anti-religion. Still the Government followed such policies and implemented them in such a manner that gave rise to the apprehension that the State wanted to keep away from the religion and treated it as a hurdle in the way of progress. The equality of all religions and also of their followers as implied in the Sarva Dharma Sambhava was not put into practice. Right or wrong, both the majority and minority communities started feeling that the scales were tilted one side or the other in view of political expediency and for the quest of power. The scheme of providing incentives and dis-incentives to tackle the problem of population explosion was not implemented on the ground that it would hurt the religious feelings of some groups. Such an interpretation makes the very concept of secularism ludicrous. A bride in the ancient times was given blessing with the expression of the wish that she may bear eight sons (Ashta-Putravati). Such a blessing was treated as in accordance with Dharma or religion. In the present times, if we start practising what we were told, you can well imagine what would happen to the country in a matter of few years.

The Directive Principles of the Constitution say that the State should make efforts for evolving a comm1on civil code. The Government's failure in this regard has also helped strengthen the impression that no efforts are being made to achieve this as it may annoy some groups and hurt the election prospects of the ruling party. The objection to the national song 'Vande Mataram' betrays the same mentality that had resulted in the unfortunate division of the country. The idea behind secular India was that the country once already divided would not have any further division and there would be no demand for its division in the name of religion, community or language. The violent disturbances created by the divisive elements in different parts of the country have given a blow to the feeling of one nation and some people have started wondering if the path we decided to follow in 1950 was correct. The public mind also gets influenced by what happens in India's neighbourhood and what political systems are being followed by the neighbouring countries. The emergence of religious fundamentalism in some parts of the world and its alliance with terrorism has generated new fears.

I feel that had we translated the word 'secular' as 'Sampradaya-nirpeksha' or 'Pantha-nirpeksha' instead of 'Dharma-nirpeksha', in the very beginning, many apprehensions would not have arisen. Whatever might have been the differences of opinion on the interpretation of the word 'secular', all, however, agreed that the State should be non-communal. Even today there is unanimity on this question. The new Hindi edition of the Constitution has translated the word 'secular' as 'Panth-nirpeksha' and thus tried to make amends for the past mistake. What is needed now is that we all should adopt this correct translation and popularise it.

In the absence of the correct understanding of the secular concept, some elements adopt a negative approach on some emotive issues placing a question mark on the concept itself. Practices like lighting a lamp at the inauguration of State functions or breaking a coconut at the time of launching a new ship are not connected with the rituals of any religion but are a part of Indian culture and tradition. 'From darkness to light'—'Tamso Ma Jyotir Gamaya' is the guiding spirit of man's progress. Right from ancient times, man has challenged the forces of darkness by lighting a small lamp. Lighting of a lamp at public functions is thus symbolic. Similarly, I would pose a question to those who oppose chanting of Vedic hymns on such occasions. Could there be any objection to any mantra which exhorts to walk hand in hand and to speak and think with a feeling of oneness?

On occasions, unnecessary controversies are created about national festivals. Social festivals like Diwali, Dussehra and Holi should not be associated with any specific form of worship. These festivals have manifested our cultural wealth and its diversity right from the days of 'Puranas'. Almost all festivals are associated with the change of the season and the advent of the new crop. Also alongwith these festivals there has been a tradition of folk-songs and folk-dances. Baisakhi in Punjab, Bihu in Assam, Onam in Kerala, Ugadi and Pongal in Tamil Nadu and Andhra are such festivals. The celebrations of Id and Christmas festivals generate goodwill and social intercourse. Now Ganeshotsav and Durga Puja are also being celebrated on a national scale. We have to differentiate between the religious practices and rituals which have got associated with the festivals and their social aspects to facilitate their transformation into national festivals.

The main issue in the present debate on secularism is that of special provisions for the minorities on the basis of religion. Article 30(1) of the Constitution provides special rights to minorities on the basis of religion or language. According to the provisions of this article, all religious and linguistic minorities have the right to establish and manage educational institutions of their choice. I would like to confine myself here to religion as we are discussing secularism.

The Supreme Court has given judgement in several cases pertaining to the fundamental rights enshrined under Article 30(1).

It is said that the article makes provisions for two rights; 1) to establish educational institutions of one's choice and 2) to manage them. The right to establish means to bring into existence. Justice Khanna in the case of Saint Xavier's College v/s Gujarat State has elaborated that the right to manage an institution refers to the right of functional management. There should be no control over the management so that the founders of the institute or those nominated by them are left free to shape the institution in a manner they think fit and according to their perception as to what would be in the common interest of the community and the institution itself. The words 'educational institution of their choice' qualify the institution. The provision does not say that the institutions established and managed by minorities should necessarily belong to one group only. Minorities have the freedom and the right to establish and manage educational institution of their choice.

Hence, Article 30(1) provides autonomy to a religious minority to manage educational institutions. At the same time, it has been categorically stated there is no restriction on the State imposing reasonable restrictions on such educational institutions. The right to manage can never include the right to mismanage. The state can exercise some control to ensure maintenance of the standard of the institution. Prescribing standards or objectives of educational institutions does not violate the right of a minority to manage educational institutions. In the case of Kerala State v/s Ati Shraddheya Mother Provincial, the representatives of the minority group, who were petitioners, had agreed that reasonable controls could be exercised in matters relating to the terms and conditions of employment of teachers, students' health care and their physical education. It was also stated that the standards of education and objectives were not part of the management.

When the President had referred to the Supreme Court the questions arising out of certain sections of the Kerala Education Bill for eliciting its opinion it was stated that the State, before providing any grant to any educational institution could insist on effective measures to protect it from mismanagement and this right of the State did not contravene the right of a minority group to manage its educational institutions.

At the same time, it was stated that a State legislature cannot make indirect use of its legislative powers to deny the fundamental rights. As the legislature does not have any direct power in this regard, it cannot have any indirect power as well. On the question of granting recognition to institutions run by minorities, the Supreme Court has held that the minorities did not enjoy any fundamental rights to get their institutions recognised by the Government. However, denial of recognition on the grounds which may tantamount to forsaking the right to manage will in fact be violative of Article 30(1). It was stated that the right of the minorities to manage their educational institutions is not in conflict with the right of the state to ensure their protection from mismanagement. Thus the Article, as interpreted by the apex court, gives full guarantee to a religious minority to manage educational institutions.

The State can specify reasonable regulations. For instance, it may mean that minimum qualifications can be laid down for the appointment of teachers and principals. This however, does not ensure that only the most deserving would be appointed. An institution may appoint a person who may not be as deserving as some other as it may feel that such a person would be more appropriate. For instance, a college run by Christian religious minority may impose a condition that only a Christian would be appointed principal of the College. I feel it would amount to discrimination on the basis of religion and, therefore, it would be against secularism or the Sarva Dharma Sambhava.

In this context, it would be relevant to refer to the observations made by Justice Khanna in the case of Saint Xavier's College v/s Gujarat State. Referring to the Constitution of the United States and the Canadian Bill of Rights, he said that the constitutional provision of religious freedom simply abolishes religious descrimination, it does not provide any new privilege. It provides for equality of religious but does not mean that the citizens have no obligations. Justice Khanna further says that the contention cannot be objected to. It is a practical guide and several examples can be cited in its support but difficulties arise when we talk of precedents which are not so clear.

There is no doubt that any provision for removing disabilities does not create any positive privileges. Sometimes the two aspects get so mixed up that it is apprehended that non-observance of what appears to be a privilege disturbs the arrangement made for removing some disability and thus ends the Constitutional guarantee about it.

Justice Khanna has made an important observation. He says, 'In spite of this position and irrespective of the position in the United States and Canada, we in our Constitution have some Articles which not only provide for removing disabilities of the minorities but also are applicable for the generation of their positive rights. Article 30(1) falls in this category.'

I feel that we need to have a second look at provisions like Article 30(1). All citizens should be given equal rights in educational matters. There should not be discrimination between minorities and the majority in their right to establish and manage educational institutions of their choice.

Way back in 1929, Shri Jawaharlal Nehru, in his Presidential address at the Lahore Session of the Congress, had stressed that no religion should get any specific privileges nor should any community be denied its reasonable rights.

Justice Khanna has also referred to the first amendment in the Constitution of the United States which lays down that the US Congress would not make any law which would put any religion on a higher pedestal or prohibit the following of any religion of their choice by the citizens. The US Supreme Court in the case of 'Renalds v/s the United States' had commented upon this amendment and said that the amendment did not affect the power of the State to punish anyone for acts which were against the social order or tended to destroy it.

In that case, the petitioner had claimed that polygamy was a part of his religious faith and the ban by the Congress on it amounted to negation of his right to freely follow his religion.

Speaking on behalf of the US Supreme Court Justice Roberts in 'Cantwell v/s Connecticut' had this to say on the first amendment:

'This amendment has two aspects—freedom of faith and freedom of action. The first freedom is absolute whereas the second cannot be so.'

In my speech, I have given the comparative analysis of the Western and Indian concepts of secularism. This analysis leads us to the conclusion that 'Sarva Dharma Sambhava' finds the correct expression of the Indian concept of secularism. The concept of Sarva Dharma Sambhava has inspired us from the Vedic period to the modern time. The 'Atharva/Veda' is said to be 5000 years old. The Prithvi Sukta of the Atharva/Veda speaks of the different faiths prevalent in the world and wishes their co-existence. The Prithvi Sukta says:

जनविभ्रति बहुधा विवाचसम् ।
नानाधर्माण पृथिवी यथौकसम् ।।

'Let this earth, where people of different faiths live peacefully like a family, give happiness to all of us.'

Dr Shankar Dayal Sharma while assuming office of the President spoke at length of the Indian tradition of Sarva Dharma in his speech. In his words 'Sarva Dharma Sambhava has been a part of the Indian thought.' He referred to Jain, Buddhism and Sikh religions, and said Sarva Dharma Sambhava teaches us the way of life. He quoted from a verse of Guru Govind Singh and exhorted all Indians to remember those lines. They are:

देहरा मसीत सोई, पूजा ओ नमाज ओई,
मानस सभै एक, पै अनेक को प्रभाव है ।
अलख अभेख सोई, पुराण ओ कुरान ओई,
एक ही सरुप सभै, एक ही बनाव है ।

'There is no difference between a mandir and a mosque, between puja and Namaaz, and between the Puranas and Quran. All human beings are equal and are the creation of one God.'

It is gratifying to note that Dr Shankar Dayal Sharma lends grace to the office of the President when the country celebrates the 108th birthday of Dr Rajendra Prasad, the first President of Independent India. We find that unflinching faith in Dharma is common to both. We find the same commitment to Sarva Dharma Sambhava in both the Presidents which is manifested through their words and deeds.

Several dramatic changes have taken place in the world. No one could have ever even imagined of such changes a few years ago. Some changes augur well, but there are also changes which spell uncertainty. The end of the cold war gives rise to the hope that the world community would move fast towards achieving the goal of disarmament and some part of the heavy expenditure on defence equipment would now be made available to the third world countries for their economic development. However, the emergence of religious fundamentalism and its alliance with terrorism in some parts of the world have caused serious apprehensions. It is a serious situation. While keeping a watchful eye on the developments in neighbouring and other countries, we have to remain firm in maintaining our traditions and culture. We have to give a concrete shape to our resolve to build an India where there is no discrimination on the basis of the community or the way of worship. Our Republic rests on the foundation of the guarantee that all citizens have equal rights, equal opportunities and equal status. By strengthening this foundation only can we face successfully the serious challenges, from within and without, to our national unity and integrity.

19

The Economy

The importance attached by the Sangh Parivar to decentralization down to the village level and its distrust of the state as opposed to society explains its hostility towards Nehru's economic policy. In the 1950s Upadhyaya articulated with great clarity the Jana Sangh's opposition to the pattern of state-owned economy he was implementing: the role of the Planning Commission was too big, the nationalizations were too many, and the development of cooperatives in the rural sector reflected an illegitimate, interventionist philosophy.[1]

At the same time, the Hindu nationalist movement did not advocate the case of the corporate sector in a liberal vein. The Jana Sangh was not as close to the business world as the Swatantra Party. Certainly, the party wanted to protect the private sector from state intervention, but it also wanted the state to prevent business conglomeration so that family enterprise might flourish.[2] In fact, its model remained the cottage industries which were developed in rural India. As Deepak Lal has noted, the views expressed in the socio-economic programme of Hindu nationalists were 'close to those espoused by Gandhi'.[3] Indeed, Hindu nationalism has affinities with Gandhism since it is also in favour of economic nationalism through protectionism, a notion encapsulated

---

[1] D. Upadhyaya, *The Two Plans—Promises, Performances, Prospects* (Lucknow: Rashtradharma Prakashan, 1958).

[2] Jana Sangh, 'Manifesto—1951', *Party Documents, 1951–1972*, vol. 1 (New Delhi: Bharatiya Jana Sangh, 1973), p. 52, and 'Manifesto—1954', ibid., p. 64.

[3] D. Lal, 'The Economic Impact of Hindu Revivalism', in M.E. Marty and R. Scott Appleby, eds, *Fundamentalism and the State* (Chicago: University of Chicago Press, 1993), p. 418.

in that key word 'swadeshi'. While this one-word slogan emerged in the public sphere in the years 1905–8 when the first Swadeshi Movement for the boycott of foreign goods imported by the British was on, it has remained associated with Gandhi, who relaunched a similar movement in the 1920s and implemented it himself by replacing his Western clothes with Indian ones.

Within the Sangh Parivar, the staunchest advocate of Swadeshi has been its trade union, the Bharatiya Mazdoor Sangh founded by D.P. Thengadi in 1955. The primary mission of the BMS is to fight Marxist unions—the red unions—by arguing that class struggles should be replaced by a harmonious collaboration of all components of society.[4] After the economic turn in India in 1991, the RSS expressed its 'deep concern at throwing open the door for foreigners and multinational companies in the name of economic liberalisation.'[5] It also created another front organization, the Swadeshi Jagaran Manch (SJM).[6]

In the opposition the BJP stuck to the economic dimensions of Swadeshi agenda while admitting that it appreciated the liberalization of the economy. Its National Executive declared in 1992 that it stood for 'liberalisation with self reliance or, to stress the *Swadeshi* angle, self-reliance with liberalisation'.[7] In fact, the party dissociated domestic liberalization, of which it fully approved, from the integration of India with the global market, which it regarded with caution.

When it came to power the BJP realized that such a dissociation was not feasible, and in any case some of its leaders were eager to fully liberalize. In 1993 Jaswant Singh declared at the National Conference of the Confederation of Indian Industry—one of the major federations of chambers of commerce and industry—that 'the BJP would welcome foreign capital in all spheres of national endeavour'.[8] Jaswant Singh,

---

[4] C. Jaffrelot, 'The Bharatiya Mazdoor Sangh', in C. Jaffrelot, ed., *The Sangh Parivar: A Reader* (Delhi: Oxford University Press, 2005).

[5] *The Organiser*, 4 July 1993, p. 9.

[6] See I. Bouton, 'The Swadeshi Jagaran Manch: An Economic Arm of the Hindu Nationalist Movement', in C. Jaffrelot, ed., *The Sangh Parivar: A Reader*, pp. 393–410.

[7] BJP, *National Executive Meeting. Resolutions, 22–24 August 1992* (*Bhopal*) (New Delhi: BJP, 1992), p. 19.

[8] *BJP Meets Indian Industry* (New Delhi: BJP, 1993), p. 9.

who was close to Vajpayee, eventually became Finance Minister despite RSS opposition, but he was not the only member of government who lobbied for more liberal measures—the Minister for Disinvestment, Arun Shourie, did the same for instance. As a result, new public sector firms were privatized and new sectors (such as insurance) were opened up to foreign investors.

The BJP was immediately attacked by the BMS and the SJM, which both denounced its economic policy. As early as September 1998 the SJM accused the Vajpayee government of pursuing an 'anti-swadeshi and anti-people's economic agenda'.[9] Things grew worse with time. In 2001 D.P. Thengadi, the senior BMS leader, declared that the Finance Minister, Yashwant Sinha, was 'a criminal', and Murlidhar Rao, the SJM convenor, went so far as to say that 'the government is not being led by political leadership but by people who are insensitive to national interest'.[10]

Economic issues are among those which most affect Sangh Parivar unity today. This is evident from the conflicting views expressed by S. Gurumurthy and Arun Shourie in the following pages.

S. Gurumurthy belongs to the RSS. He has been seconded by this organization to the SJM, to which he has contributed in collaboration with senior swayamsevaks such as D. Thengaoli, the founder of the BMS. A co-convener of the SJM, Gurumurthy had always had relations with major figures of the corporate sector such as Goenka (the owner of the *Indian Express* in the 1970s–1980s) and Rahul Bajaj. He remains one of the most active advocates of Swadeshi within the Sangh Parivar.

Arun Shourie (1941–), a journalist by profession and an economist by training, though a special invitee of the RSS to some of its major functions, has never formally belonged to that organization. But he has been a BJP Rajya Sabha member since 1998 and a member of the Vajpayee government from 1999 till 2004. Among the portfolios he held, the post he kept for the longest period was Minister of Disinvestment. A prolific and articulate writer, he has been one of the most convinced defenders of economic liberalization of the NDA coalition.

[9] *Hindustan Times*, 2 September 1998.
[10] *The Hindu*, 7 July 2001. See his 'Foreword' to M.G. Bokare, *Hindu Economics: Eternal Economic Order* (New Delhi: Swadeshi Jagaran Manch, 1993).

Extract from S. Gurumurthy, 'Swadeshi and Nationalism'[11]

Even five years back, the idea of *swadeshi* was considered outdated. To the economist it was anti-economics, to the intellectual it was anti-modern, to the industrialist it was anti-technology, to the media it was amusement, to the policy-maker it was socialism in disguise, and to the politician it was an embarrassment. The combined calumny of all these powerful groups created deep prejudice against the idea of swadeshi in India and outside.

But now the swadeshi view has overcome all unfair attempts to label it as irrelevant and harmful to India. Today many intellectuals admit that swadeshi is not such an inelegant idea after all. Many define it as an 'India-first' approach, like the 'America-first' approach in USA, for they need a foreign lead to define swadeshi. Many industrialists agree on swadeshi as the idea of strengthening Indian industry and creating Indian multinationals. Even the media and commentators are not as hostile to the idea of swadeshi as they were and have begun to view it more seriously. Many political parties and leaders openly support the swadeshi viewpoint. The media now talks of swadeshi shares as distinct from MNC shares in the stock market. The takeover of various corporates by MNCs is not just regarded as anti-swadeshi, but also against national interests. So the idea of swadeshi, interpreted by everyone in their own light, is now very much in the Indian mind.

What is it that turned the Indian mind towards swadeshi when just five years ago it had virtually been consigned to the dustbin of history? Before tracing how swadeshi began to reassert itself in India, it is necessary to recapitulate how socialism forced its way into the Indian polity, and what it meant in contrast to present-day market capitalism.

When at the beginning of this decade the Berlin Wall collapsed and the Soviet Union disintegrated, virtually the entire world defected from socialism to capitalism. The premise was that if socialism failed, capitalism must succeed. During the Cold War, the operating principle was that capitalism and socialism were competing ideologies. In truth, they were two sides of the same coin.

[11] S. Gurumurthy, 'Swadeshi and Nationalism', *Seminar*, no. 469, Delhi, September 1998.

Both view human beings as purely economic creatures and are based on the abrahamanic worldview that the world is secular and materialist, that there is nothing sacred about anything. Both agree that men and women pursue, in the main, economic prosperity and nothing else; both rule out the existence of God except as the personal view of the believer. Both regard human beings as essentially atomised individuals and do not recognise any natural, cultural and social human collectivities having common faiths, ideals, goals, or way of life. Capitalism believes in sharing the burden of the state with the market, and trusts the market more than it believes in the state as the delivery mechanism. But socialism does not believe in the market and believes only in the state. This is the sole difference. Thus, capitalism and socialism are the same content in two different containers. And yet the world for almost the whole of the 20th century believed that they represented conflicting ideologies.

This was why Mahatma Gandhi told Pandit Nehru that although the latter believed that the capitalist system was the cause for the ills of industrialism, the truth was that the fault lay in industrialism and no amount of socialisation would cure its ills. The dialogue between Gandhi and Nehru on industrialism, socialism and capitalism dates back to 1928.

Pandit Nehru first wrote an angry letter to the Mahatma accusing him of exaggerating the faults of western industrial civilisation, and belittling its achievements. Nehru also told the Mahatma that the idea of *Ramrajya* was no good in the past, nor would he want it back. He was blunt that whether one liked it or not, western civilisation would gradually overtake India. The Mahatma, stunned by Nehru's angry outburst, wanted to make public the differences between the two, saying that he never imagined that the differences between him and Nehru were so unbridgeable. He also advised Nehru to carry on open warfare with him, because if he (Gandhi) was wrong, he was causing irreparable harm to national interest. But, Nehru successfully avoided the debate.

Once again, 17 years later, in 1945, Nehru ridiculed the Mahatma for his ideas on *gramswaraj* and swadeshi. Here too Gandhi suggested an open debate, but Nehru avoided the dialogue remarking that the elected representatives of independent India would discuss and decide the direction in which the country should move. So the all-important debate between the mentor (Gandhi) and the disciple (Nehru) never took place.

Neither did the dialogue, which Pandit Nehru had promised to the Mahatma that the elected representatives of independent India would carry on take place. There was no debate at the national level about whether the ideas of swadeshi, *swavalamban* and gramswaraj articulated by the Mahatma were outdated and irrelevant. There was no discussion on whether India should pursue the free market motto if it discarded the swadeshi view or the socialist model, and whether socialist philosophy would suit the Indian psyche. The leadership adopted socialism without a debate, without understanding what it entailed and what changes and adjustments it would impose on our society, polity, ethos and religion.

We assumed that purely through the political process, that too in a democratic polity, we could remould the society to abandon its age-old traditions, beliefs and lifestyle and switch over to socialism. The result was a dual life—a formal modern life as the veneer and the age-old beliefs as the core. The traditional views and lifestyle were pushed underground—seen as illegitimate within the political, economic and modern social intercourse. Alongside, we relegated religion to the sidelines, except to the extent that the system allowed the minority religion and culture to define our new notions of secularism.

This led to a further duality—while paying lip service to socialism for votes, we institutionalised the permit, quota, licence raj in the name of a mixed economy. This promoted corruption and black money and caused serious erosion of national character. Yet, the society remained where it always was and refused to change, but the polity put on a cloak of socialism. The deterioration reached its nadir when Indira Gandhi virtually turned socialism into theatre. She even labelled those who opposed the dishonesty that went on in the name of socialism as anti-poor, pro-rich, even as American and CIA agents. She grafted the slogan of socialism on the Constitution, pressured the Supreme Court into accepting socialism as a constitutional creed to which the rest of the Constitution was subordinate. Thus, phoney socialism became legitimate politics.

While the socialist reign was a general disaster, in specific terms it damaged the economic potential of the country. Indian enterprise and entrepreneurship had dominated world trade before the advent of the

British; it had dominated the trade in East Asia and Africa even after the British left India.

Before the British established their rule in 1830, India's share of the world's production was 19 per cent, that of Britain 9 per cent and of USA 2 per cent; its share in world trade was 18 per cent, that of Britain 8 per cent and of USA 1 per cent. India had higher literacy than Europe. It is colonial rule that eroded our economic base. When the British left, our share of world production and trade was less than 1 per cent. The British demolished the business competence, initiative and self-confidence of Indians; the demolition work continued more efficiently under the socialist regime in India.

The Indian trading communities turned into clerks while the skilled self-employed became unskilled employees, or turned unskilled and unemployed. A country which worshipped money (Lakshmi) as god was persuaded to treat money makers as untouchables. A nation which had a tradition of treating work as worship and which actually worshipped the tools of trade was organised and trained to destroy all work ethic. The public sector was indiscriminately encouraged with the resulting inefficiency concealed by ideological sloganeering. The installation of a socialist regime was collaterally assisted by the godless idea of secularism. Socialism and secularism alienated the Indian state from Indian beliefs, tradition and values.

The Indian state abhorred talented traders as blood-sucking middlemen, astute financiers and bankers as exploiters and accumulators of wealth and power, and astute industrialists as monopolists and profiteers. In fact, Indian businessmen were treated as undesirables, even as untouchables. The socialist regime perpetuated a mindset in which the best minds of India found it advantageous to seek employment rather than turn to employers to provide employment.

In the first two decades after freedom, some of the best minds in the country entered government service instead of setting up business or joining professions that could create wealth and employment; some of them even made business out of the government. That is not all. Socialism made public life government-centric and politics oriented. This disproportionate role for state and politics without any norms to recognise quality and merit, generated a rush into politics for recognition and power. As the society weakened against politics and money, it gradually turned politics into a profitable industry.

Ordinary people as well as the informed ones, whether in towns or villages, were made to believe that it was the state, not society or community, which would deliver. The result was the falling into disuse of all traditional delivery mechanisms like village communities and social and religious institutions. The ensuing public discourse served to move people away from God and even from the very idea of nationalism. The result was an India which was an antithesis of all that the movement for our freedom had envisioned.

If the freedom movement was inspired by the idea of spiritual nationalism as expounded by Swami Vivekananda, motivated by *Sanatana Dharma*, held out by Aurobindo as our nationalism, fertilised by the enchanting *Vande Mataram* of Bankin Chandra, and defined by the ideal of *Ramrajya* as enunciated by Mahatma Gandhi, free India's secular and socialist mix declared every one of these noble and sustaining ideas as irrelevant, unsecular and communal.

It was then that two path-breaking developments took place in the post 1980 years. The Ayodhya movement called the bluff of pseudo-secularism while the collapse of the communist states exposed the socialist rhetoric in India as nothing more than a shadow of the Soviet brand of socialism. This resulted in a massive generation of national self-assertion. The Ayodhya movement restored the pre-independence values eclipsed by the secular socialist regime, and illegitimised pseudo-secular ideas and practices.

With its collapse in Berlin and Moscow, socialism became a dead letter in the Indian polity, notwithstanding the false undertaking given by all political parties to the Election Commission regarding socialism. Overnight, the entire intellectual establishment, including bureaucrats and columnists defected to market capitalism. Narasimha Rao and Manmohan Singh dismantled the entire socialist edifice in pin-drop silence. There was not a word of protest—in the Congress or in the CPM or CPI, the Revolutionary Socialist Party or the different Samajwadi parties. The entire nation witnessed and even rejoiced in the way socialism ceased to figure in the resolutions of political parties and in their election speeches.

When the exponents of socialism abandoned their pet ideology, they swung to the other extreme—they became as ardent and faithful exponents of liberalisation and globalisation as they had been about socialism. They supported every move that dismantled the socialist

establishment, even though many of the moves contributed to a dis-
mantling of the Indian state itself.

Indian businessmen, the middle class and the intelligentsia turned
so hostile to the socialist idea of the past that they viewed with suspicion
any voice of moderation against the thoughtless way in which the entire national course was reversed. They saw every sane voice which
advocated a gradual opening up of the Indian economy to global competition as a conspiracy to retain the socialist establishment.

The result was that just as socialism had become a fad, globalisation
too became an ideological *mantra*. The socialism of the past legitimised
globalisation for the future—without any thought as to what globalisation entailed, and the capacity of the nation to meet it. Anyone who
differed regarding the pace or reach of globalisation was branded as
anti-modern and even anti-growth. There was no debate as to how, in
what stages, in what areas and with what safeguards the change-over
from a socialist regime to a free market economy would take place.

Just as our establishment adopted socialism instantly, without debate, and suffered for 40 years, equally instantly it has adopted market
economy, again without debate. What it has not realised is that just as
40 years of socialism could not penetrate the Indian psyche defended
by its age-old traditions, values and lifestyles, the free market prescrip-
tion too cannot accomplish what socialism did not. But like an allopa-
thic doctor who prescribes antibiotics as an instant cure for illness,
instead of building up of resistance for a long term cure, the Indian
establishment has prescribed free market globalisation as an instant
cure for the ills of socialism.

Free market globalisation which is presented as the cure today, will
eventually prove to be a mere dose of antibiotics—a transitional treatment rather than a durable cure. This is what emerges from the [*sic*]
India's experience—and that of the world—in the 1990s. If swadeshi,
which was eclipsed by socialism for four decades and ridiculed by the
globaliser brigade, is back as India discarded socialism—although with
different meaning and implications for different sections—it means
that the Indian establishment took less time to realise the mismatch
between globalisation and India than it took to understand the
unsuitability of socialist ideas for India.

The present trend to view swadeshi thinking as 'not so terrible' is
indicative of the fact that the present day India is in transition and the

idea of economic globalisation is a transitional flirtation, not a desti-nation. Why is globalisation a transitional flirtation? Not because the intellectuals and elites in India, inspired by an Anglo-Saxon worldview, and who direct the Indian mind in politics and economics, have the vision of a larger philosophic formulation. It is because Indian society's core values, which are not amenable to the Anglo-Saxon traditions, cannot internalise the idea of globalisation. Because the civilisational, cultural and traditional ideas and forces have a resistance which the state directed ideologies cannot overcome.

Remember that despite the unmitigated monstrosity of the com-munist regime in China which organised cultural revolutions to banish Confucian traditions, what emerged unscathed from the blackest period of Chinese history was the very same Confucian tradition. Akio Morita, the doyen of Japanese business, told Group 7 leaders when they met in Tokyo in 1992 that whatever the great political leaders might do to install a global regime, national, traditional and civilisational factors would thwart the so-called 'global system of trade'. The Anglo-Saxon worldview recognised no value other than its own as fit for survival. The basic justification behind the present effort at globalisation is that the West has finally won against the Rest and that the world is finally being restructured on the basis of western civilisational values. Global-isation assumed a world civilisational modelled after the Western.

This is how the West first perceived the post-Cold War world. Francis Fukuyama in his work, *The End of History and the Last Man* declared that the collapse of communism meant that Western civilisa-tion had finally won and that world peace was guaranteed on that ba-sis. But this view did not dominate the field for more than a couple of years. Samuel Huntington, the strategic analyst, came out with his famous theory of 'clash of civilisations'. He forecast not the final victory of the West over the Rest but a West-versus-the Rest scenario. He visualised the post-Cold War world driven by civilisational factors inspired by religion, not by economics or trade. He saw civilisational blocks evolving as trade and political blocs. He advised the West to come to terms with a world of different civilisations which have to live with each other, and not hope for a world civilisation based on the western to emerge.

Alvin Toffler agreed that there would be civilisational clashes, not between civilisations defined by religion but among civilisations, demarcated by economic criteria. He envisioned a civilisationally trisected world—premodern, modern, and postmodern—clashing with one another, in which he perceived the emergence of city states and the collapse of all nation states.

Yet another view, expounded by Lester Thurow, perceived the collapse of the family, community, morals and traditions, leading to the stagnation and decay of capitalism. Thus, the theoretical framework needed for a global regime in trade and politics does not seem to exist. Unless there is a broad theoretical framework in which a world regime can be accommodated, a functional world trade regime cannot be internalised. Therefore, the idea of globalisation fabricated by the West after the Cold War seems to suffer from a myopic vision and ignores the large gaps among nations not amenable to a world regime.

If theory refuses to legitimise a global regime, the functioning of the current global regime equally exposes its disfunctionality. The European monetary crisis, the Mexican crisis and now the South East Asian crisis have rocked the basic assumptions of the global regime under installation. The greatest danger to the world trade regime will come from within the regime—even if the people of the world forget their religious, cultural, national and civilisational identities and resolve not to clash in the interest of money and trade. John Maynard Keynes said: 'Money is essentially a destabiliser, and has to be reined in for economic stability.' This is precisely what the present world regime cannot do.

In fact, the IMF–World Bank–GATT formulation was based on this very idea that money being a destabiliser had to be checked; this applied with greater force to transnational money which worked on the basis of exchange rates between currencies. The IMF was created with the fundamental idea of ensuring stable exchange rates. The world currencies remained firmly linked to the US dollar and the US dollar was linked to gold at a firm rate of 35 USD per ounce of gold.

This system worked well till 1971 when, because of the run of US gold reserves and the world losing confidence in US dollar convertibility, it depreciated from 35 to over 400 per ounce of gold. More significantly, the world shifted to the present system of floating currency values determined by market force of demand and supply of currencies against one another.

It was precisely to avoid this situation that the IMF was set up. The only protection that the weak currencies of the world had against the strong ones was eroded. And now we have a world currency market in which speculative trade in derivatives exceeds 1.2 trillion dollars a day against the annual world trade in goods and services of 4.5 trillion dollars. So, the speculative currency market has emerged as the chief arbiter of transnational and even international economics.

Akio Morita's letter to the G7 leaders pointedly invited their attention to this point. Morita asked them to answer a vital question: if Japan, through efficiency and cost-cutting, increases its production physically by 10 per cent, and if the yen value goes down by 12 per cent, has Japan grown by 10 per cent or fallen by 2 per cent? He asked them another question: Does anyone control the forces that determine currency values? He pointed out that the derivative trading income of Citibank exceeded (in 1992) 150 million dollars a day!

Realising that the great leaders had no answer for any of these questions, Akio Morita argued that a world trade regime required a common world currency. It followed that in the absence of a world currency there cannot be a world trade regime, particularly if the currency for world trade is in the control of one monopoly, country, or in the hands of an oligarchy.

The entire effort of the EC is to evolve a currency to match the dollar. But that would create a competitor for the dollar, not answer the question which Akio Morita had raised. Any long term analysis of the present-day world trade regime would indicate not its durability and stability but its instability and transitional nature. So globalisation and global trade regimes are unstable in their very conception and structure.

The issue is whether a nation should restructure itself to suit the unstable global structure and ever-changing global institutions? That is, should a nation be largely directed by global perspectives and institutions or be mainly guided by factors inherent to itself? In other words, should an ever-changing global agenda lead a nation to marginalise its national ideas, beliefs and institutions, or should it be directed by its own national agenda based on its own ideas, in which the global situation plays a marginal role? If the answer is yes—then it is a return to swadeshi. It is this awareness, both at the national and global level,

which is gradually persuading the Indian establishment not to treat
the idea of swadeshi with contempt.

What we have now is a slow and painfully slow return to swadeshi
and nationalism. That is where the civilisational assertion of India
commenced in the pre-independence days. Swadeshi and nationalism
were the foundation of the Indian freedom movement. They should
have been the foundation of a free India. But the Anglo-Saxon domination of the Indian polity and establishment virtually defeated the
very objective of the Indian struggle for freedom. The result was the
fallacious attempt to westernise India on the socialist model. When
socialism could not scratch the skin of the Indian psyche and collapsed
with the demise of global communism, they swung to another Anglo-
Saxon view, westernisation through globalisation. This too has become
a transition, rather than the destination.

We started the 20th century with swadeshi and natonalism; we are
nearing the end of the century with the very same concepts—swadeshi
and nationalism. The long interlude with socialism and the current
interlude with globalisation are mere flirtations of the Indian elite
establishment lacking in self-confidence. Ultimately, Indian society's
unwillingness to disown its age-old values and traditions is manifest
in the realisation that globalisation cannot be the core thought of
India; it is India which will be the core of India, with the world as a
marginal influence.

Extract from Arun Shourie,
'This is India's Moment, But It's Only a Moment,
Can We Grasp It?'[12]

On the one hand, we have unbounded opportunities and incomparable
advantages to seize them. On the other, there is the fate that will surely
befall us if we falter. Unemployment will reach such proportions that
social unrest will become unmanageable. Similarly, if the rates of growth
of India and China continue to differ by the margins of the past 15
years, within the next 15 years the Chinese economy will be six times
that of India. And the consequences will be worse than we can imagine.

---

[12] A. Shourie, *Listen to the New India* (New Delhi: BJP, 2003).

Economic strength is itself power. To take one instance, because China has been able to attract so many more to invest than we have, China today is able to mobilise so many more—American firms, for instance—as lobbyists—to advance its interests.

Moreover, economic strength gives China the wherewithal to go in for comprehensive modernisation of its armed forces. Indeed, that there is so much talk of China's economic transformation obscures what China is already doing, what its economic modernisation already enables it to in the military sphere.

Will a China six times stronger than India not administer another slap at us? Indeed, will it have to administer a slap? Will an India dwarfed to that extent not learn to pay heed to China's interests subliminally? [. . .] The achievements—the incredible infrastructure built in Shanghai, for instance, themselves remind us of problems it may be storing up: this infrastructure has been built by getting the country's banks to lend money to the special purpose vehicles that were created for building the projects. But everything has to be paid for in economics: what is the rate of return of these projects today, and how does it compare with what is needed to repay the investments?

There is moreover a fundamental issue. The twenty-first century is going to be the century of knowledge—of its continuous unraveling and of its continuous application. One of the central lessons of the twentieth century is that where the state is pervasive, creativity does not flourish. The Chinese have indeed transformed their state. But it remains pervasive. How will they ensure creativity—of the kind, say, youngsters in our IT firms have displayed?

So we have many things working for us. In many ways, this is India's moment, even *vis-à-vis* China. For the first time, observers have begun to voice questions in public about China—its statistics; the fact, for instance, as a German investor said recently at a conference I was deputed to attend, that, 'If you want your factory to come up quickly, go to China; if you want to make money, go to India.' On the other side, everyone's noticing Indians make a mark in every sphere: writers, scientists, doctors, IT, cricket, beauty pageants, chess . . .

So it is the moment for India. It is a moment. But, it is only a moment. What should we do to ensure we grasp it?

First, we should begin to notice what is happening around us. We

have become what an American author calls 'Negaholics'—addicted
to the negative as an alcoholic is to drink. Ever so many of us are un-
aware of even the elementary examples that have been listed above.

Nor is that the result merely of inattention. We look for, we latch
on to the negative; even if some achievement breaks on to our mental
screen it does not percolate into our awareness, we do not see that it
is part of a pattern, that it is not an isolated fluke. Indeed, our instinct
is not to believe evidence of that accomplishment.

Remember how eager many commentators were to find fault with
NSS data that established a steep decline in proportions living below
the poverty line? These are symptoms of a habit. Remember the exercise
that books on creative thinking recommend?

Is there much blue around you? You would not have noticed much.
Now make an effort to look only for blue things around you. You will
notice so many that, though they were lying around, had not registered.
It is especially important that those who are in public life—who hold
public office, who participate in public discourse—break out of this
addiction to the negative. Because of my work, I have had occasion to
travel abroad several times in the past two-three years. Each time I
have been struck by the contrast between the way India is looked upon
abroad, and the way we look upon it here.

There is an equally telling symptom here at home—there is much
greater confidence in the Indian industrial class than there is in the
rhetoric of politicians who ostensibly are shouting on behalf of and to
save that industry!

The result is our discourse continues to be mired in fear, so many
of us just keep repeating slogans of 30 years ago. We should listen to
the new India.

Next we should be alert to what the critics of reform are doing
where they are in power. In New Delhi, the CPI(M) shouts against
even the slightest attempt to reform—for instance, privatise—a public
sector unit, they bring woe upon anyone who may say that repeated
revival attempts having failed, such and such firm has to be shut down.

But in West Bengal the state government has already shut down
two state-owned units, it is disinvesting 10 more. It's just that the state
government does not talk of 'disinvestment', it says it is just turning
the firm over to a joint venture partner!

Remember Ajit Jogi's hysterics over Balco?[13] Remember his threat, 'Should anyone from Sterlite enter Chattisgarh, we will break his legs'? Since then his refrain is, 'Sterlite is scripting the success-story of Chattisgarh'! More important, he is today the leader in public sector reform! Including privatisation! *The Indian Express* reports he has already closed thirty-seven public sector units [as Chief Minister of Chattisgarh].

[. . .] A simple rule of self-denial among political parties would help: 'Do not block another party from doing what your own party is doing where it is in power.' As parties are unlikely to deny themselves even this much, journalists and others should bring the rule into being in effect: keep an eye on what the party is doing where it is in power, recall what it was doing when it was not in power, and, each time the party tries to stop a rival from prosecuting a reform, broadcast those facts, grill its leaders on them.

There is a more intractable problem—a central dissociation between democracy as we know it in India and what is needed for rapid growth.

All change involves dislocation. And this is where the strengths of yesterday become the handicaps of today. BSNL has one of the world's most extensive networks of copper-wire. But people are switching to wireless telephony. Every time there is a proposal for new technology, our first thought is, 'But what will happen to the thousands of crores that have been sunk into that network?'

Nor is the drag confined to governments. As BSNL has been purchasing copper wire worth Rs 2,000 to 4,000 crore every year, 30 or more companies have come up that can survive only if BSNL continues to purchase copper wire! Their owners and the workers employed in them too would rather that the switchover to new technologies is slower.

That is how over the decades the Civil Aviation Policy becomes the policy for Air India rather than for India. That is how our finances get sucked into quicksand—that is how we continue to 'protect' existing producers of wheat and rice with ever higher minimum support prices even as government godowns overflow with stocks, and even though we know that these support prices are in fact preventing the crop

---

[13] Bharat Aluminium Company was one of the firms privatized by the Vajpayee government.

diversification that other programmes of government are trying to promote; that is how a state like Maharashtra brings its finances to the brink by continuing subsidies to sugar growers; that is how over the years we squander Rs 10,000 or 15,000 crores keeping obsolete mills of the National Textile Corporation (NTC) on artificial respirators rather than spend the money to modernise the textile industry; that is how we continue to guarantee procurement of tobacco, of all things, even as we spend crores admonishing people to abjure it; that is how, ostensibly to protect existing tenants, we continue rent control laws, thereby discouraging investment in housing and thus ensure both housing shortage and urban decay.

We block voice-over-internet for long, we set the police upon young-sters who have begun using the technology; for years we won't allow personnel of IT firms to avail of the Closed User Group facility—lest the revenues of BSNL get affected . . . It is as if we were to block the introduction of the automobile to protect carpenters who are making tongas. Without doubt, one of the reasons West Germany and Japan forged ahead of the United Kingdom after World War II was that the entire industrial stock of those two countries had been bombed out of existence while that of the latter had survived.

In the end, all such efforts fail. One cannot block technology any more than one can block time: in the end Bangladesh has had to close down the largest jute mill in the world, in the end we are having to close down NTC mills . . . But over the years we ensure our country's progress is slowed down, and our governmental finances are brought to the brink.

The problem becomes all the more acute in a democracy, all the more so in what we have made of democracy. The electorate has been so fractured by caste and the rest that it does not respond to national issues. To attain office and retain it, therefore, parties have to aggre-gate votes, section by section. Each section liable to be dislocated by change—the tobacco farmer no less than the textile mill owner and the powerloom operator—is able to suborn parties and politicians to block that change.

Of course, in due time a constituency will arise of those who have benefited from the change—the IT professionals, the ones who will prosper if only we were to allow our entrepreneurs to set up institutions of higher learning . . . But they are in the womb of the future. And the ones who will be dislocated are ones who will defeat the party today. As the horizon of political parties seldom extends beyond the forthcoming election, even a bit of aggressive shouting can ensure that reform is deferred.

There is another factor that confounds everyone into submission. All politicians are nervous—witness our nerves before every reshuffle! Politicians faced with elections are more so. And no one quite knows what issues are on the people's mind. So the moment a step is mooted, everyone can, and does, proclaim, 'Not just now, elections are round the corner. People will turn against us.'

Was disinvestment an issue in any of the elections during the past five years? If free power could have won elections, how come the Akalis in Punjab, the DMK in Tamil Nadu were swept away? I well remember a meeting in a state on the eve of elections there, and what was being said 'on the sidelines', 'Please get (the chief minister) to abolish (a local tax) . . . If only it is removed, we will sweep the urban areas.' It was abolished. The urban areas swept away the alliance.

There isn't much that can be done about the politicians' nervousness, except to go on pointing out reforms are not the issue they are made out to be: internal bickering has brought defeat to parties not issues like disinvestment or tariffs.

But the problem—the dislocation that change will cause—is real and we have to attend to it. Four things can help.

We should multiply outlays on activities that will engage large numbers, and are things that we should be doing in any case. The Planning Commission has prepared three first-rate reports, for instance, on biofuels, on bamboo cultivation and products, and on medicinal plants. Each of these can engage millions. As can organic farming, diversification into vegetables and fruit and floriculture. As can water harvesting.

When activities like these flourish, incomes will multiply, nutrition will improve, fewer will flock to urban slums. Indeed, through them the country would register gains even in foreign exchange—outlays on biofuels would save on imported crude; organic farming, medicinal plants would bring foreign exchange.

Similarly, projects that entail huge earthworks—the Prime Minister's Quadrilateral and gram sadak projects, the linking of rivers—can absorb millions who may be dislocated and at the same time unleash the country's productive potential. They are the real social security that will cushion our people.

But the main solutions lie, as usual, not in the economic realm. They lie in political arrangements, in discourse. We must reduce the frequency of elections: schedule elections, as the vice-president and the deputy prime minister have proposed, to state assemblies and to the Lok Sabha simultaneously; fixed terms for legislatures even as individual ministers can be voted away for dereliction.

Even before such changes are put into effect, and even after they have been instituted, we have to make everyone see that change cannot be blocked. The more we succeed within India in delaying it, the greater the lead that others will get over us. Schemes to rehabilitate and reposition workers or farmers who may be dislocated must, of course, be devised and executed. But the project or technology must not be blocked.

Soon enough that project will have to be executed in any case; soon that technology will come to be adopted. Time will have been lost. Resources that could have been used for modernisation of that enterprise, that industry, for the prosperity of that very region would have been wasted in keeping that obsolete technology or enterprise 'alive'.

And we must with evidence induce everyone to see that more often than not the resources needed to take care of and re-equip those who will be dislocated are embedded in the obsolete enterprises themselves. Look at the land NTC's mills have in Mumbai. If only the government would be allowed to sell it, more than enough would be available to retrain and re-equip every single worker in those mills, as well as to modernise the mills that are to survive.

Not the details of economic policy—that is not where the impediments lie. The way we look at things, our discourse, the drag of interests that are vested in the way things are—these are what we need to change.

20

The Diaspora
and Hindu Nationalism

The presence of Hindus overseas is not a new development. The British transferred thousands of Indians in some of their other colonies which were not as populated as the Raj. As a result, coolies, but also traders and professionals, were present in large numbers in the Pacific islands, South East Asia, and East as well as South Africa. Hindu movements paid attention to these groups as early as the first decades of the twentieth century. The Arya Samaj played a pioneering role because many migrants from Punjab, who were overrepresented among these exiled Indians, paid allegiance to this organization. *Updeshaks* travelled to Trinidad but also to South Africa,[1] and subsequently to North America (Canada and the United States), where Lala Lajpat Rai met fellow Punjabis before (and during) the First World War. Hindu nationalists who had opted for the revolutionary repertoire and had suffered from British repression also found refuge in Japan and South East Asia—such as Raj Behari Bose—who set up a branch of the Hindu Mahasabha there in the inter-War period.

However, the chief Hindu nationalist movement, the RSS, ignored overseas Hindus for decades. Its ethnic brand of nationalism should have led the RSS to cater to the needs of their coreligionists outside India, but for decades it did not, a clear indication that the ethnic dimension of the Hindutva movement was mitigated by its territorial dimension: Hindu nationalists identified with their sacred land and

---

[1] Bhai Parmanand travelled to these regions in the early years of the twentieth century. In 1902 he toured east and south Africa. Bhai Parmanand, *The Story of My Life* (Delhi: S. Chand, 1982), p. 272.

neglected their coreligionists overseas. As a result, the RSS sarsangh-chalak did not dare cross the 'Kala Pani' before the 1990s!

Yet, the RSS started to organize shakhas overseas much before the 1990s, while some of its members stated to migrate. The first branch was apparently set up in the late 1940s in Kenya, where two swayam-sevaks had just settled.[2] Since these shakhas were not on 'national' (*rashtriya*) soil, they were rechristened and the RSS abroad came to be known as the Hindu Swayamsevak Sangh (HSS). Senior pracharaks, including Bhaurao Deoras—older brother of the third sarsanghcha-lak—spent years out of India to develop this organization. This trend acquired some additional force during the Emergency when Balasaheb Deoras sent colleagues abroad to seek support after Indira Gandhi had banned the RSS in India. Rajendra Singh created the Friends of India Society International (FISI) in this context in 1976 in the UK, and subsequently in the US. Today the RSS claims that it is active in 34 countries, where it runs 570 shakhas.

But the RSS is not the only Hindu nationalist organization that has gained momentum abroad. Other components of the Sangh Parivar are now prominent too, including the BJP—which has set up units of the Overseas Friends of the BJP in many countries—and the VHP.

The VHP has been especially active in Western countries, where the Hindu diaspora has grown quickly over the last few decades. Today, there are about half a million Indians in the UK and two million in the US. The leaders of the Hindutva movement in India tried to establish contact with these groups in order to enlist their support—in financial terms too: in the US, according to the 2000 census, the revenue per capita of the Indian community is $68,000 a year, more than twice that of the average American. The Vishva Hindu Parishad of America was created in the 1970s as a cultural organization dedicated to the re-Hinduization of a group exposed to the materialistic value system of the amoral West. The *modus operandi* of the VHPA recalls that of its Indian matrix: it uses existing temples and has built new ones to dis-seminate its ideas.[3] It organizes courses in Hindi; it teaches the sacred scriptures to young Hindus, especially those of the second generation,

[2] Jai Prakash, 'The Sangh Fraternity Bringing the World Within its Fold', *The Organiser*, XIVI (40), 7 May 1995, pp. 51–2.

[3] As Sucheta Mazumdar notices, for such purpose 'the temple serves both as a community centre and a social cult'. S. Mazumdar, 'The Politics of Religion

whose parents fear they may learn nothing about their religion; they celebrate Hindu festivals, with which migrants are not always familiar any more. This is especially so on the university campuses, where another Hindutva movement is active too: the Hindu Students Council, founded in 1990. To learn about the Hindu heritage, the VHPA has also initiated summer schools or youth camps.

In addition to this routinized re-Hinduization process, the Sangh Parivar organizes big events. In 1989 it collected funds for the construction of the Rama Mandir in Ayodhya. In 1993 the VHPA organized a World Vision Conference to commemorate the participation of Vivekananda in the 1893 World Parliament of Religions in Chicago. In June 2001 K. Sudarshan took part in an event entitled 'A Hindu Vision for Human Entitlement' in California.

Hindu nationalist propaganda seems to be especially intense and successful in the US, where it can prosper on fertile terrain: while migrants are anxious to keep contact with their culture, this is made possible by the multicultural ethos of American society, as well as by its pervasive religiosity.[4] As a result, the Sangh Parivar has been able to articulate a strong agenda as an ethnic lobby. One of its main demands relates to the rewriting of history textbooks. As in India, Hindu nationalists in the US try to introduce their ideas in the classroom regarding Aryan invasions and the atrocities committed by Muslims in India. This strategy came to light in 2005 in California, when the Board of Education embarked—as it does every six years—on the task of evaluating and modifying instructional materials for one of the core subjects, history. Hindu nationalists from the Vedic Foundation and the Hindu Education Foundation (an affiliate of the Hindu Swayamsevak Sangh of America) started a petition 'to protest unfair and inaccurate depiction of Hinduism in school textbooks'.[5] The Vedic Foundation submitted a report recommending 382 edits in 8 textbooks which were disputed by other Indian organization active in the US, including the Friends

and National Origin: Rediscovering Hindu Indian Identity in the United States', in V. Kaiwar and S. Mazumdar (eds), *Antinomies of Modernity: Essays on Race, Orient, Nation* (Durham and London: Duke University Press, 2003), p. 248.

[4] See the special issue: C. Bhatt and P. Mukta (eds), 'Hindutva Movement in the West', *Ethnic and Racial Studies*, 23 (3), May 2002.

[5] Cited in S. Padmanabhan, 'Debate on Indian History: Revisiting Textbooks in California', *Economic and Political Weekly*, 6 May 2006, p. 1761.

of South Asia (FOSA). For them, these recommendations reflected a fundamentalist agenda they wanted to defeat. The terms of the debate—and its outcome—are summarized below—even while this affair may not yet be a closed chapter.

Documents on the California Textbooks Controversy

Table 1

Edits Recommended by the Hindu Education Foundation

Publisher	Original Text by Publisher	Recommendations by Hindu Education Foundation	FOSA/CAC Comment
Harcourt School Publishers Page 245, 'Review'	'Men had **many more rights** than women. Unless there were no sons in a family, only a man could inherit property. Only men could go to school or become priests.'	Replace with: 'Men had **different** rights and duties than women' and add after last sentence, 'Women's education was mostly done at home.'	This edit attempts the sleight of hand of 'Separate but Equal' by suggesting that women's lack of access to education, property, and to positions of authority made them 'different'; thus it belies the actual position of women that was and is socially inferior to that of men.
Glencoe/ McGraw-Hill Page 245, second paragraph	'Men had **many more rights** than women.'	Replace with: 'Men had **different** duties (dharma) as well as rights than women. Many women were among the sages to whom the Vedas were **revealed.**'	See Note above. In addition, the phrase 'the Vedas were revealed' completely contradicts the evolutionary nature of texts such as the Vedas.
Macmillan/ McGraw-Hill Page 252, last paragraph	'There was one group that did not belong to any varna. Its members were called untouchables. They performed work other Indians thought was too dirty, such as collecting trash,	Delete and replace text with 'There was one group that did not belong to any varna. Its members were called untouchables **because** they performed dirty work such as skinning animals or handling dead bodies.'	The HEF's ideological work—of denying the role of the caste system within Hinduism & within Indian Society—continues through this edit. By adding the word 'because' to invoke a spurious causality, the HEF implicitly suggests that untouchability is the result of contact with taboo substances

Table 1 (contd.)

Publisher	Original Text by Publisher	Recommendations by Hindu Education Foundation	FOSA/CAC Comment
	skinning animals, or handling dead bodies.'		rather than the reverse: that they were assigned such work on account of their degraded social status.
Teachers' Curriculum Institute Page 145, last paragraph	'The caste system is just one example of how Hinduism was woven into the fabric of daily life in India.'	'Delete this part.'	Another example of the HEF's campaign to whitewash Hinduism: their 'Hindu pride' dictates essentially that they hide all information about uncomfortable realities, including the one of caste discrimina-tion.
Prentice Hall Page 181, secomnd paragraph	'Once their society had merged with the local population a late hymn of the *Rig Veda* described the four castes.'	Replace with, 'A late hymn of the *Rig Veda* describes the **interrelationship** and **interdependence** of the four social classes.'	This replacement seeks to depict the caste system as a benign arrangement of mutual benefit & mutual convenience instead of one that creates a distinct hierarchy that is used to justify rank exploitation of the so-called 'lower castes'.
Prentice Hall Page 181, table, last row ('Sudras')	'Native peoples; performed services for members of the three higher castes.'	Replace with, 'Performed services for all classes and did more labor-intensive work.'	This edit is similar to the one above insofar as it implicitly depicts the caste system as beneficial to all castes as opposed to being a system that maintained the privileges of the higher castes.
Prentice Hall Page 182, fourth paragraph	'In modern India, these people are now called **Dalits**, and treating someone as an	Replace with, 'In modern India, treating someone as an untouchable is a crime against the law.'	Note the attempt at a systematic erasure of the very word 'Dalit' from the lexicon of Hinduism. The utter

Table 1 (*contd.*)

Publisher	Original Text by Publisher	Recommendations by Hindu Education Foundation	FOSA/CAC Comment
	untouchable is a crime against the law.'		marginalization of being labeled an 'untouchable' is also left unaddressed.
Oxford University Press Page 76, second paragraph	'The language and traditions of the Indo-Aryan speakers replaced the old ways of the Harappans . . .'	Replace with 'People from elsewhere in India replaced . . .'	This edit does not modify, but actually rewrites history, completely contradicting the intent of the original passage. In this case, the HEF edit rejects the role of Indo-Aryans in ancient India, contrary to prevailing scholarly views on this topic.
Glencoe/ McGraw-Hill Page 238, Second bullet under 'Focusing on the Main ideas'	'The Aryans introduced . . .'	Replace with, 'New ideas and technology were developed in India. (page 242)'	According to all extant evidence, this is not correct, as Chariots, for instance, came from outside of India.
Harcourt School Publishers Page 386, paragraph 5	'The Vedas came to form the major beliefs of the religion called Brahmanism.'	Replace with, 'The Vedas constitute the source of Hinduism.'	This change seeks to conflate 'Brahmanism', a small sub-set of Hindu practice, with the much larger and more diverse practices of 'Hinduism' as a whole. Further it also seeks to elevate Vedic Brahmanism over other forms and sources of Hinduism.

Table 2

Edits Recommended by the Vedic Foundation

Publisher	Original Text by Publisher	Recommendations by Vedic Foundation	FOSA/CAC Comment
Houghton Mifflin/ McDougal Littell Grade 6, p. 229	Indian society **divides** itself into a **complex structure** of social classes based particularly on jobs. This class structure is called the **caste system**.	This sentence, written in the present tense in a textbook describing ancient history, is out of place. It presumes that the caste system is present in India today. According to the Indian Constitution, under the section, Fundamental Rights, the Right to Equality is guaranteed to all citizens, just as the U.S. has enacted Equal Employment Opportunity Laws to prevent discrimination.	This edit seeks to deny that the social hierarchy of the caste system is intact and that it is very much a reality in Indian society today. Over 160 million Dalits routinely face physical and sexual violence that is used to maintain and police the social boundaries of caste. It is also ridiculous to claim that the existence of laws against discrimination means that caste automatically vanishes from Indian society. Such denials constitute, at best, ignorant and wishful thinking, and at worst are another form of violence against the Dalit community.
Teachers' Curriculum Institute p. 144	'Modern day Hinduism is **very complex. Many beliefs**, many forms of worship, and **many gods exist** side by side.'	Remove.	This is a transparent attempt to deny the pluralistic nature of the Hindu Pantheon and to minimize the complex and diverse nature of everyday Hindu spiritual practice.
	'Hinduism . . . has affected how people worship, **what jobs they do** . . . And it has helped to determine the status of people in Indian society.'	Remove.	This edit is a continuation of the VF's denials, made elsewhere, that the Hindu caste system determines one's social status, in addition to shaping one's access to resources in a fundamental way.

Table 2 (contd.)

Publisher	Original Text by Publisher	Recommendations by Vedic Foundation	FOSA/CAC Comment
Teacher's Curriculum Institute p. 143	'Modern Hindus continue to visit temples to express their love of the **gods**.'	Replace with '. . . visit temples to worship and express their love for God.'	Note again the VF's promotion of Monotheism and the reduction of the common Hindu practice of Pantheism (i.e. the acceptance of many gods) into one single 'God' with a capitalized 'G'.
Teachers' Curriculum Institute p. 146	. . . show **gods and goddesses** from popular Hindu **stories**.'	Replace with '. . . show various forms of God from Hindu scriptures.'	This edit is an attempt to mask the pantheistic nature of Hinduism and present it as Monotheistic instead. Monotheism is in fact contrary to the way many Hindus understand and practice their religion.
Teachers' Curriculum Institute p. 146	The heading 'Hindu Beliefs About Multiple Gods'.	Replace with 'Hindu Beliefs About Various Forms of God.'	The sole purpose of this edit is to replace 'god' with 'God', i.e. with a capitalized 'G'.
Teachers' Curriculum Institute p. 146	*Brahman* is the Hindu name for a supreme **power** or a divine **force**, that is greater than all the **other gods**.'	Replace with 'Bhagwan is a word for God in Hinduism.'	The VF is here attempting to replace abstract terms such as 'divine force', 'supreme power' with terms from more devotional, theistic paths. This is a major content innovation.
Teachers' Curriculum Institute p. 146	According to Hindu belief, everything in the world is a **part** of Brahman . . . It is a **part** of Brahman.'	Replace 'a part' with 'the power' and 'Brahman' with 'God'.	See Note Above.
Teachers' Curriculum Institute p. 151	'. . . devote their entire lives to **uniting** with Brahman.'	Replace '. . . devote their entire lives to attaining God realization.'	See Note Above.

Table 2 (*contd.*)

Publisher	Original Text by Publisher	Recommendations by Vedic Foundation	FOSA/CAC Comment
Teachers' Curriculum Institute p. 151	'They use . . . to focus on **Brahman**'	Replace 'Brahman' with 'God.'	This is yet another example of the VF's attempts to move from a spiritual vocabulary to a religious vocabulary in describing Hindu practices and to hijack the space occupied by spiritual practice so as to bring it under the purview of religion.

California Textbook Controversy About Hinduism*

SACRAMENTO, Calif. Following an impassioned [. . .] meeting here Feb. 27 at the California Department of Education, where hundreds of Indian Americans presented their views in front of a Board of Education subcommittee, the five-member panel unanimously voted to recommend adoption of staff recommendations for edits and corrections proposed by the Hindu Education Foundation and Austin, Texas-based Vedic Foundation for its sixth-grade textbooks. [. . .] the recommendations reflect a compromise on a substantial part of the proposed edits following a meeting Jan. 6 between Harvard Sanskrit expert and philologist Prof. Michael Witzel and Cal State Northridge emeritus Prof. Shiva Bajpai; on issues where they couldn't agree, the edits were rejected in favor of the original text. [. . .] Although quite a few disgruntled HEF supporters appeared irate following the announcement [. . .] HEF organizers told *India West* they were pleased that 70 per cent of their changes had been accepted. Meanwhile, Friends of South Asia, an activist group that has opposed the HEF and VF campaign, welcomed the decision as well. 'This decision is a victory for community organizations such as Friends of South Asia, the Ambedkar Center for Peace and Justice, the Federation of Tamils on North America, and the Coalition Against Communalism, who have worked diligently to ensure that ahistorical and sectarian content proposed by Hindu right-wing groups is removed from California textbooks.'

The complete PDF ocument listing the HEF edits and staff recommendations is available at this web link: http://www.cde.ca.goye/agfagldocuments/hssnoticeo227o6a1.pdf

*Excerpt from Newsreport by Ashfaque Swapan in *India West*, 3 March 2006.

Bibliography

I. OFFICIAL ARCHIVES
India Office Library and Records (London)

*Political (Confidential) Proceedings
and Home Department Political Files*

- P/8153 Confidential Proceedings (Political) Proceedings no. 155 October 1909.
- P/8153 Home Department (Political) Proceedings for the Year 1909 [about Savarkar in London].
- P/8430 Home Department (Political) Proceedings for the Year 1910 Pro no. 98 [about Savarkar in London].
- P/8713 Home Department (Political) Proceedings for the Year 1911 Pro no. 47 [about Savarkar in London].
- P/9460 Home Department (Political) Proceedings for the Year 1914 Pro no. 169 [about S.K. Verma in London].

Public and Judicial Department Files

- L/P&J/Coll 117/C/81—The Volunteer Movement in India.
- L/P&J/8/683 Coll 117/D1—Public and Judicial Department—Subject of File: Law and Order. Hindu Mahasabha Copies of Resolutions, etc.
- L/P&J/10/8—Cripps Mission and the Hindu Mahasabha.
- L/P&J/10/51—Cabinet Mission Proper—Minor Parties and Interests.
- L/P&J/8/684 Coll 117/D2—Public and Judicial Department—Law and Order All India Hindu League. Resolutions [Letters by M.S. Aney and M.M. Malaviya in March 1941].
- L/P&J/8/683 Coll 117/D1 Sir F. Wylie's Situation Report (1939) [correspondence of Savarkar with the Viceroy (1939–41)].
- L/P&J/1186 Resolutions, Accounts and Balance Sheet 1935–6 passed by the 18th Session of the Hindu Mahasabha held at Lahore.
- I/P&J/116 Note on the Volunteer Movement 31 December 1938.

– I/P&J/116 Note on the Volunteer Movement 23 August 1940.
– L/P&J/8/683 Coll 117/D1 [Resolution of the Hindu Mahasabha Working Committee—hereafter HMWC (21–22 September 1940) at its session in Nagpur].
– L/P&J/1394 [On the Akhand Hindustan League].
– L/P&J/10/8 [Resolutions of the HMWC sent by Savarkar to Cripps— 1 April 1942].
– L/P&J/10/51 Note of Meeting between Sir Stafford Cripps and Mr A.V. Alexander and the Representatives of the Hindu Mahasabha, Dr S.P. Mookerjee and Mr L.B. Bhopatkar . . . (15 April 1946).

Government of Bombay Political Department

– P/Conf./73 Confidential Proceedings in the Political Department for the Year 1927 [report about communal riots].

National Archives of India (New Delhi)
Home Political Department

– Home Department (Deposit) File no. 52, Nov. 1916 ('Note on the Anti-Cow Killing Agitation in the United Provinces').
– Home Political Department (Deposit) File no. 198 (1924) [on the Annual Session of the Hindu Mahasabha].

II. PRIVATE PAPERS
India Office Library and Records

– Morley Papers (MSS EUR D 573)
– Meston Papers (MSS EUR F)
– Hailey Papers (MSS EUR 2 2017 B)
– Montagu Papers (MSS EUR D 523)

National Archives of India

– Jayakar Papers
– N.B. Khare Papers

Nehru Memorial Museum and Library (New Delhi)

– M.S. Aney Papers
– G.M. Chitnavis Papers

- M.G. Chitnavis Papers
- K.B. Hedgewar Papers (Microfilm Section)
- A. Lahiry Papers
- S.P. Mookerjee Papers
- B.S. Moonje Papers (Microfilms/Manuscripts Section)
- Nanakchand Papers
- V.D. Savarkar Papers (Microfilms Section)
- K.R. Malkani Papers
- C.K. Sarda Papers

Transcriptions of Interviews
(Nehru Memorial Museum and Library)

- Ganpat Rai
- N.B. Khare
- G.C. Narang
- Lala Jagat Narain
- M.C. Sharma

Archives of Political Parties
(Nehru Memorial Museum and Library)

- Hindu Mahasabha Papers ('C' papers are about national affairs whereas the 'P' papers are about provincial branches).
- Madhya Pradesh Congress Committee Papers.

File A-43 (Manuscript Section) [about the relationship between the local branches of the Hindu Mahasabha and the local branches of the Congress.]

Documents by Hindu Nationalist Organizations
and Parties

(1) The Arya Samaj

Crucifixion by an Eye Witness (New Delhi: Sarvadeshik Arya Pratinidhi Sabha, April 1960), 2nd edn.
Narain Swami, *The Daily Prayer of an Arya* (Delhi: 1980).
Chamupati, M.A., *Ten Commandments. Principles of Arya Samaj* (New Delhi: Sarvadeshik Arya Pratinidhi Sabha: n.d.).
———, *Arya Samaj at a Glance* (New Delhi: Sarvadeshik Arya Pratinidhi Sabha, 1973).

————, *Achievements of Arya Samaj—Arya Samaj Foundation Centenary Publication* (New Delhi: Sarvadeshik Arya Pratinidhi Sabha, 1975), 2nd edn.

Shastri, A.V., *Vedic Marriage Ceremony. From Sanskarvidhi of Swami Dayananda Saraswati* (New Delhi: Sarvadeshik Arya Pratinidhi Sabha, 1982), 2nd edn.

————, *Some Points of the Political Philosophy of the Vedas* (New Delhi: Sarvadeshik Arya Pratinidhi Sabha, 1972).

Sri Aurobindo Ghose, *Dayananda and the Veda* (New Delhi: Sarvadeshik Arya Pratinidhi Sabha, 1982), 2nd edn.

————, *Dayananda: The Man and his Work* (New Delhi: Sarvadeshik Arya Pratinidhi Sabha, 1983).

Sudhakar, M., *In Defence of Satyarth Prakash (Light of Truth)* (Delhi: Sarvadeshik Arya Pratinidhi Sabha).

————, *Some Questions on Bible* (New Delhi: Sarvadeshik Arya Pratinidhi Sabha).

Prof. Bhaskaranand, *Understand Arya Samaj* (Patna: 1979).

————, *Vedic Cosmogony* (Patna: 1980).

(2) The RSS

'Untouchability'—A Challenge. The Right Approach (Bangalore: Jagarana Prakashana, 1973).

RSS: A Brief Introduction (New Delhi: Suruchi Sahitya, 1973).

Ram Mohan, ed., *Truth Triumph. What High Courts Say on RSS* (New Delhi: Suruchi Sahitya, 1977).

RSS—A Bird's-eye View (Bangalore: Rashtriya Swayamsevak Sangh, 1978).

Balasaheb Deoras with Delhi Newsmen: In the Press Club of India, March 12, 1979 (New Delhi: Suruchi Sahitya, 1979).

RSS: In the Forefront of Second Freedom Struggle (Bangalore: Jagarana Prakashana, 1979).

RSS: Ready for Selfless Service (Bangalore: Jagarana Prakashana, 1979).

Ram Swarup, *Hindu Dharma and Semitic Religions* (Bangalore: Jagarana Prakashana, 1980).

Seshadri, H.V., *Warning of Meenakshipuram* (Bangalore: Jagarana Prakashana, 1981).

The Shah Bano Case. Nation Speaks Out (Bangalore: Jagarana Prakashana, 1 March 1986).

Golwalkar, Guruji, *Thoughts Excelsior* (Bangalore: Jagarana Prakashana, 1983).

Thengadi, D.B., *Marx and Deendayal—The Two Approaches* (New Delhi: Deendayal Research Institute, n.d.)

Jeelany, Saiffuddin, 'Interview with Shri Guruji', *Shri Guruji on the Muslim Problem* (New Delhi: Suruchi Sahitya, n.d.).

Chitaranjan, *Facts about RSS. Mist of Motivated Propaganda Shattered* (New Delhi: Suruchi Sahitya, n.d.).

(3) Vishva Hindu Parishad

B.S. Mewar, Udaipur, President VHP, Address Delivered at 10th Hindu Conference, New York, July 1984.

Vishva Hindu Parishad, *Hindu Contribution to the World of Science* (New Delhi, 1987).

———, *Thousands of Hands Join in the Service of the Poor* (n.p.: n.d.).

———, *The Hindu Awakening: Retrospect & Promise* (New Delhi, n.d.).

Pandya, A., *Relevance of Hinduism in Modern Age* (New Delhi, n.d.).

(4) The BJS and the BJP

Advani, L.K., *President's Addresses, 1986–1990/1993–1998* (New Delhi: BJP, 2000).

———, *Ramjanma Bhoomi—Honour People's Sentiments*, New Delhi: BJP, 1989).

Bharatiya Jana Sangh, *Party Documents, 1951–1972*, 5 vols (New Delhi, 1973).

———, *Resolutions*, Session in Chandigarh, 18 & 19 July 1970.

———, *The Case for Reservation* (Delhi: BJP Publication, n.d.).

BJP, *Resolutions. Political (1980–1999)* (New Delhi: BJP, 2000).

BJP, *Resolutions. Economic (1980–1999)* (New Delhi: BJP, 2000).

BJP, *Our Five Commitments* (New Delhi, 1980).

———, *Economic Policy Statement* (New Delhi, December 1980).

———, *Heal the Wounds—Vajpayee's Appeal on Assam Tragedy to the Parliament—21 February 1983* (no place, n.d.).

———, *Govern or Get Out—N.D.A. Satyagraha on Punjab* (Delhi: May 1984).

———, *Action Unavoidable Situation Avoidable—Hindu-Sikh Unity at all Cost* (New Delhi: 1984).

———, *Two Years of Congress Misrule. A Charge Sheet* (New Delhi: 1986).

———, *The Tip of the Iceberg. The Story of Three Scandals* (New Delhi: 1987).

——, *Constitution and Rules—As Amended by the National Council* (Vijayawada, 1987).

Gonda Gramodaya Project—Evaluation (New Delhi: Deendayal Research Institute, n.d.).

Jethmalani, R. and Bakht, S., *Jamshedpur Riots—The Truth Unmasked* (New Delhi: BJP Publications, 1981).

Puri, B., *Understanding Punjab—Committee for Dialogue on Punjab* (New Delhi: 1985).

Vajpayee, A.B., *India at the Cross-roads* (Delhi: BJP Publications, December 1980).

III. UNPUBLISHED PhDs

Freitag, S., 'Religious Rites and Riots: From Community Identity to Communalism in North India 1870–1940', University of California, 1980.

Gross, R.L., 'Hindu Asceticism: A Study of the Sadhu of North India', University of California, 1979.

Jayaprasad, K., 'Impact of Hindu Nationalism on Kerala Society and Politics—A Study of RSS', Trivandrum University, 1989.

Reeves, P.D., 'The Landlords' Response to Political Change in the United Provinces of Agra and Oudh—India 1921–1937', Canberra, The Australian National University, 1963.

Thursby, G.R., 'Aspects of Hindu–Muslim Relations in British India: A Study of Arya Samaj Activities, Government of India Politics, and Communal Conflicts in the Period 1923–1928', Duke University, 1972.

IV. UNPUBLISHED PAPERS

Curran, J.A., 'Militant Hinduism in Indian Politics—A Study of the RSS', Institute of Pacific Relations, 1951.

Graham, B., 'The Challenge of Hindu Nationalism: The BJP in Contemporary Indian Politics', *Hull Papers in Politics*, no. 40, October 1987.

Lütt, J., 'Indian Nationalism and Hindu Identity—The Beginnings of the Hindu Sabha Movement', 7th International Conference of the Association of Historians of Asia (Bangkok, 22–26 August 1977).

——, 'The Hindi Movement and the Origin of a Cultural Nationalism in Uttar Pradesh', Second European Conference on Modern South Asian Studies, Copenhagen, 3–7 July 1970.

Saberwal, S. and Hasan, M., 'Communal Riot in Moradabad, 1980: Economy, Policy and Administration Regression', *Occasional Papers on History and Society*, no. 19, Nehru Memorial Museum and Library.

V. Books

Advani, L.K., *The People Betrayed* (Delhi: Vision Books, 1979).

———, *A Prisoner's Scrap Book* (New Delhi: Arnold-Heinemann, 1978).

Agarwala, R.K., *Hindu Law* (1958; rpnt Allahabad: Central Law Agency, 1989).

All India Hindu Conference. *Address of the Maharaja Manindra Chandra Nandy of Kasimbazar, Hardwar, 9 April 1915* (Calcutta: P.C. Das Publisher, 1915).

Anand, V.S., *Savarkar—A Study in the Evolution of Indian Nationalism* (London: Woolf, 1967).

Andersen, W. and Damle, S.D., *The Brotherhood in Saffron—The Rashtriya Swayamsevak Sangh and Hindu Revivalism* (New Delhi: Vistaar Publications, 1987).

An Indian Nationalist, *The Indian War of Independence of 1857*, anonymous edition of the book written by Savarkar in London in 1909.

Apte, S.R., *Bhavganagar Struggle* (Poona: Sadashiv Peth, 1970).

Baker, D.E.U., *Changing Political Leadership in an Indian Province—The Central Provinces and Berar 1919–1939* (Delhi: Oxford University Press, 1979).

Barrier, N.G., *The Punjab Alienation of Land Bill of 1900* (Duke: Duke University Press, 1966).

———, *Banned-Controversial Literature and Political Control in British India (1907–1947)* (Columbia: University of Missouri Press, 1974).

———, ed., *Roots of Communal Politics* (New Delhi: Arnold Heinemann, 1976).

Baru, S., *Last Days of the Morarji Raj* (Calcutta: Ananda, 1979).

Baxter, C., *A Biography on an Indian Political Party—Jana Sangh* (Bombay: Oxford University Press, 1971).

Bayly, C.A., *The Local Roots of Indian Politics: Allahabad 1880–1920* (Oxford: Clarendon Press, 1975).

Bazaz, P.N., *The Shadow of Ram Rajya over India* (New Delhi: Spark Publishers, 1980).

Bhandari, S.S., ed., *Jana Deep Souvenir* (New Delhi: Rakesh Press, 1967).

Bhatt, C., *Hindu Nationalism. Origins, Ideologies and Modern Myths* (Oxford/New York: Berg, 2001).

Bhishikar, C.P., *Shri Guruji. Pioneer of a New Era* (Bangalore: Sahitya Sindhu Prakashana, 1999).

Bokare, M.G., *Hindu Economics* (New Delhi: Swadeshi Jagaran Manch, 1993).

Borthwick, M., *Keshub Chandra Sen: A Search for Cultural Synthesis* (Calcutta: Minerva Associates, 1977).

Brahm Dutt, P., *Five Headed Monster—A Factual Narrative of the Genesis of Janata Party* (New Delhi: Surge Publication, 1978).

Broomfield, J.H., *Elite Conflict in a Plural Society, Twentieth-Century Bengal* (Berkeley: University of California Press, 1968).

Burger, A.S., *Opposition in a Dominant Party System* (Berkeley: University of California Press, 1969).

Carstairs, G.M., *The Twice-Born: A Study of a Community of High Caste Hindus* (Bloomington: Indiana University Press, 1958).

Cashman, R., *The Myth of the Lokmanya* (Berkeley: University of California Press, 1975).

Chand, F., *Lajpat Rai—Life and Work* (Delhi: Ministry of Information and Broadcasting, 1978).

Chand, L., *Self-Abnegation in Politics*, foreword by Bhai Parmanand (Lahore: The Central Hindu Yuvak Sabha, 1938).

Chandra, B., *Communalism in Modern India* (New Delhi: Vani Educational Books, 1984).

Chandra, S., *Communal Interpretation of Indian History* (New Delhi: Sampradayikta Virodhi Committee, 1970).

Chaturvedi, S., *Madan Mohan Malaviya* (Delhi: Government of India, 1972).

Chirol, V., *Indian Unrest* (London: Macmillan, 1910).

Chitra Gupta, *Life of Barrister Savarkar* (1926; rpnt Bombay: Acharya Balarao Savarkar, 1987 (This book was apparently authored by C. Rajagopalachariar. First published in 1926, it had been immediately banned by the British.)

Collet, D., *The Life and Letters of Raja Ram Mohan Roy* (Calcutta: Sadharan Brahmo Samaj, 1962).

Corbridge, S. and Harriss, J., *Reinventing India: Liberalization, Hindu Nationalism and Popular Democracy* (Delhi: Oxford University Press, 2000).

Dar, S.L. and Somaskandan, S., *History of the Benares Hindu University* (Benares: BHU, 1966).

Dayananda, Swami, *The Light of Truth* (*Satyarth Prakash*), transl. G.P. Upadhyaya (Allahabad, 1981).

Deshmukh, N., *RSS: Victim of Slander* (New Delhi: Vision Books, 1979).

Deshpande, B.V. and Ramaswamy, S.R., *Dr Hedgewar the Epoch Maker* (Bangalore: Sahitya Sindhu, 1981).

Dharmaveer Dr B.S. Moonje Commemoration Volume (Nagpur: Birth Centenary Celebration Committee, 1972).

Dhooria, R.L., *I Was a Swayamsevak* (New Delhi: Sampradayikta Virodhi Committee, n.d.)

Dixit, P., *Communalism—A Struggle for Power* (New Delhi: Orient Longman, 1974).

Dube, M., *The Path of the Parivar: Articles on Gujarat and Hindutva* (New Delhi: Three Essays Collective, 2004).

Elst, K., *Ram Janmabhoomi vs Babri Masjid* (New Delhi: Voice of India, 1990).

Farquhar, J.N., *Modern Religious Movements in India* (Delhi: Munshiram Manoharlal, 1967).

Ghai, R.K., *Shuddhi Movement in India* (New Delhi: Commonwealth Publishers, 1990).

Ghose, Aurobindo, *Swami Dayananda Saraswati. An Assessment*, ed. R.R. Bhardwaj, Ambala: Arya Samaj, 1987.

Golwalkar, M.S., *Bunch of Thoughts* (Bangalore: Jagarana Prakashan, 1966).

———, *We or Our Nationhood Defined* (Nagpur: Bharat Prakashan, 1947), 4th edn.

Gopal, S., ed., *Anatomy of a Confrontation* (New Delhi: Viking, 1991).

Goyal, D.R., *Rashtriya Swayamsevak Sangh* (New Delhi: Radha Krishna Prakashan, 1979).

Graham, B., *Hindu Nationalism and Indian Politics: The Origins and Development of the Bharatiya Jana Sangh* (Cambridge: Cambridge University Press).

Grave Danger to the Hindus, by 'An Obscure Hindu' (Puthiyara, Malabar: K.C. Bhalla Harbinger, 1940).

Gupta, S.L., *Pandit Madan Mohan Malaviya—A Socio-Political Study* (Allahabad: Chugh Publications, 1978).

Hansen, Thomas B., *The Saffron Wave* (Princeton: Princeton University Press, 1999).

———, and C. Jaffrelot, eds, *The BJP and the Compulsions of Politics in India* (New Delhi: Oxford University Press, 2001).

Heehs, P., ed., *Sri Aurobindo: Nationalism, Religion, and Beyond* (Delhi: Permanent Black, 2005).

Hindu Mahasabha, *The History of the Bhagalpur Struggle* (Bhagalpur: Madhukari, 1942).

Jaffrelot, C., *The Hindu Nationalist Movement and Indian Politics* (New Delhi: Penguin India, 1999).

Jambunathan, M.R., ed., *Swami Shraddhananda (Autobiography)* (Bombay: Vidya Bhavan, 1961).

Jayakar, M.R., *Social Reform and Social Service* (Madras: Theosophical Publishing House, 1917).

———, *The Story of My Life*, 2 vols (Bombay: Asian Publishing House, 1958).

Jivan Das, ed., *Works of Late Pandit Guru Datta* (Lahore: Punjab Economical Press, 1897).

Jog, N.G., *Lokamanya Bal Gangadhar Tilak* (New Delhi: Ministry of Information and Broadcasting, 1979).

Jones, K., *The New Cambridge History of India III.1—Socio-religious Reform Movements in British India* (Cambridge: Cambridge University Press, 1989).

———, *Arya Dharm—Consciousness in Nineteenth-Century Punjab* (Berkeley: University of California Press, 1976).

Jordens, J.T.F., *Dayananda Saraswati—His Life and Ideas* (Delhi: Oxford University Press, 1978).

———, *Swami Shraddhananda—His Life and Causes* (Oxford: Oxford University Press, 1981).

Justice on Trial. A Collection of the Historic Letters between Sri Guruji and the Government (1948–1949) (Mangalore: Prakashan Vibhag, 1969).

Kanungo, P., *RSS's Tryst with Politics. From Hedgewar to Sudarshan* (Delhi: Manohar, 2003).

Katju, M., *Vishva Hindu Parishad and Indian Politics* (New Delhi: Orient Longman, 2003).

Keer, D., *Veer Savarkar* (Bombay: Popular Prakashan, 1988).

Khare, N.B., *My Political Memoirs or Autobiography* (Nagpur: Joshi JR, 1959).

Kohli, R., *Political Ideas of M.S. Golwalkar* (New Delhi: Deep and Deep, 1993).

Kopf, D., *British Orientalism and the Bengal Renaissance* (Calcutta: K.L. Mukhopadhyay, 1969).

Kotnala, M.C., *Raja Ram Mohun Roy and Indian Awakening* (New Delhi: Gitanjali Prakashan, 1975).

Lajpat Rai, Lala, *The Message of the Bhagavad Gita* (Allahabad: Published by the author, 1908).

———, *Autobiographical Writings*, ed. V.C. Joshi (Delhi/Jullundur: University Publishers, 1965).

———, *Writings and Speeches*, ed. V.C. Joshi (Delhi/Jullundur: University Publishers, 1966).

———, *A History of the Arya Samaj* (1914; rpnt. Bombay: Orient Longman, 1967).

Lal Chand, *Self-Abnegation in Politics* (Lahore: The Central Yuvak Sabha, 1938).

Ludden, D., ed., *Making India Hindu* (New Delhi: Oxford University Press, 1996).

Lütt, J., *Hindu Nationalismus in Uttar Pradesh 1867–1900* (Stuttgart: Ernst Klett Verlog, 1970).

McGuire, J., P. Reeves and H. Brasted, eds, *Politics of Violence. From Ayodhya to Behrampada* (New Delhi: Sage, 1996).

Madan, D.P., *Report of the Commission of Inquiry into the Communal Disturbances at Bhiwandi, Jalgaon and Mahad in May 1970*, 2 vols (no place, n.d.).

Madhok, B., *Portrait of a Martyr: Biography of Dr Shyama Prasad Mookerji* (Bombay: Jaico Publishing House, 1969).

———, *Indianisation? What, Why and How* (New Delhi: S. Chand, 1970).

———, *RSS and Politics* (New Delhi: Hindu World Publications, 1986).

Majumdar, B., *History of Indian Social and Political Thought from Ram Mohun to Dayananda* (Calcutta: Bookland, 1967).

Malaviya, M.M., *Court Character and Primary Education in the North-West Provinces and Oudh* (Allahabad: Indian Press, 1897).

———, *Speeches and Writings* (Moon Light Publishers, 1919).

———, *Speeches and Writings of Pandit Madan Mohan Malaviya* (Madras: G.A. Natesan and Co, 1919).

———, and M.S. Aney, *The Congress Nationalist Party—What it Stands for, Why Every Indian Should Support It* (Benares, 1934).

Marshall, P.J., ed., *The British Discovery of Hinduism in the Eighteenth Century* (Cambridge: Cambridge University Press, 1970).

Malgonkar, M., *The Men Who Killed Gandhi* (Delhi: Orient Paperbacks, 1981).

Malkani, K.R., *The Midnight Knock* (New Delhi: Vikas Publishing House, 1978).

————, *The RSS Story* (New Delhi: Impex India, 1980).

————, *The Sindh Story* (New Delhi: Allied Publishers, 1984).

Miksh, A.K., *Hindu Sabha: Ek Adhyayan* (Delhi: Akhil Bharat Hindu Mahasabha, 1988). Hindi.

Minault, G., *The Khilafat Movement—Religious Symbolism and Political Mobilization in India* (New York: Columbia University Press, 1982).

Mishra, D.N., *RSS: Myth and Reality* (New Delhi: Vikas Publishing House, 1980).

Mookerjee, S.P., *Awake Hindustan* (Calcutta, 1944).

Narain, J., *Report of the Three-Member Commission of Inquiry—Two Communal Disturbances that Took Place in April 1979, In and Around Jamshedpur* (n.p.: 1981).

Nene, V.V., *Pandit Deendayal Upadhyaya: Ideology and Perception—Part II: Integral Humanism* (New Delhi: Suruchi Prakashan, 1988).

Noorani, A.G., *The RSS and the BJP. A Division of Labour* (New Delhi: Leftword, 2000).

Pandey, G., *The Construction of Communalism in Colonial North India* (Delhi: Oxford University Press, 1990).

————, ed., *Hindus and Others* (Delhi: Viking, 1993).

Pareek, R.S., *Contributions of Arya Samaj in the Making of Modern India 1875–1947* (New Delhi: Sarvadeshik Arya Pratinidhi Sabha, 1973).

Parmanand, B., *Hindu Sangathan* (Lahore: The Central Hindu Yuvak Sabha, 1936).

————, *The Story of My Life* (New Delhi: S. Chand, 1982).

Panikkar, K.N., *Communal Threat, Secular Challenge* (Madras, Earthworm Books, 1997).

Panikkar, K.N. and Muralidharan, S., eds, *Communalism, Civil Society and the State. Reflections on a Decade of Turbulence 1992–2002* (New Delhi: Shamat, 2002).

Prakash, I., *A Review of the History and Work of the Hindu Mahasabha and the Hindu Sangathan Movement* (New Delhi: Akhil Cheratiya Hindu Mahasabha, 1938).

————, *A Prophet of Modern India* (New Delhi: Akhil Bharat Hindu Mahasabha, 1975).

————, *Dharamvir Bhopatkar* (New Delhi: Hindu Mission Pustak Bhandar, 1949).

Puri, G., *Bharatiya Jana Sangh—Organisation and Ideology* (New Delhi: Sterling Publishers, 1980).

Raja Narendra Nath, *Memorandum on the Rights Claimed by Hindu Minority in North-West India* (Lahore: The Civil and Military Gazette Press, 1928).

Rajagopal, A., *Politics after Television. Hindu Nationalism and the Reshaping of the Public in India* (Cambridge: Cambridge University Press, 2001).

Raje, S., ed., *Pt Deendayal Upadhyaya—A Profile* (New Delhi: Deendayal Research Institute, 1972).

Ram, Munshi, *The Future of the Arya Samaj* (Lahore: Virajanand Press, 1893).

Rama Deva, *The Arya Samaj and its Detractors: A Vindication* (Dayananda-bad, 1910).

Ramananda Tirtha, Swami, *Memoirs of Hyderabad Freedom Struggle* (Bombay: Popular Prakashan, 1967).

Report of the Commission of Inquiry on Communal Disturbances—Ranchi, Hatia (Aug. 22–29, 1967) (New Delhi: Government of India, 1968).

Report of the Commission of Inquiry into Conspiracy to Murder Mahatma Gandhi, 2 vols (Delhi: Government of India, 1969).

Sampurnanand, *Memories and Reflections* (Bombay: Asia Publishing House, 1962).

Sarda, H.B., *Life of Dayanand Saraswati* (Ajmer, 1968).

Savarkar, V.D., *Hindutva—Who is a Hindu?* (Bombay: S.S. Savarkar, 1969).

———, *My Transportation for Life* (Bombay: Veer Savarkar Prakashan, 1984).

———, *Echoes from the Andamans* (Bombay: Veer Savarkar Prakashan, 1984).

———, *Hindu Rashtra Darshan* (Bombay: Veer Savarkar Prakashan, 1984).

Sen, Amiya, P., *The Indispensable Vivekananda* (Delhi: Permanent Black, 2006).

Sen, K.C., *Lectures in India* (London: Cassel, 1904).

Sen, N.B., ed., *Punjab's Eminent Hindus* (Lahore: New Book Society, 1944).

Seshadri, H.V., *The Tragic Story of Partition* (Bangalore: Jagarana Prakashana, 1984).

———, ed., *RSS, A Vision in Action*. Bangalore (Jagarana Prakashana, 1988).

Seunarine, J.F., *Reconversion to Hinduism through Shuddhi* (Madras: The Christian Literature Society, 1977).

Shah Commission of Inquiry—Interim Report I (New Delhi: Government of India, 11 March 1978).

Shah Commission of Inquiry—Interim Report II (New Delhi: 26 April 1978).

Sharma, J., *Hindutva. Exploring the Idea of Hindu Nationalism* (New Delhi: Penguin, 2005).

Shourie, A., *Religion and Politics* (New Delhi: Roli Books International, 1987).

———, *Missionaries in India. Continuities, Changes, Dilemmas* (New Delhi: ASA, 1994).

Shraddhananda, *Hindu Sangathan—Saviour of the Dying Race* (Delhi: Arjun Press, 1926).

———, *Inside Congress* (Bombay: Phoenix Publications, 1946).

Singh, N.L., ed., *Mahamana Malaviyaji Birth Centenary Volume* (Benares: BHU, 1961).

Srivastava, H., *Five Stormy Years: Savarkar in London* (New Delhi: Allied Publishers, 1983).

Sundaram, V.A., ed., *Benares Hindu University 1916–1942* (Benares, 1942).

Talbot, I., *Punjab and the Raj 1849–1947* (New Delhi: Manohar, 1988).

Tandon, P., *A Punjabi Century* (Berkeley: University of California Press, 1968).

Thengadi, D.P., *Third Way* (Bangalore: Sahitya Sindhu Prakashana, 1998).

The Gurukul through European Eyes—Reprint from The Pioneer of the Notable Articles of M.H. Phelps, with an introduction by Mahatma Munshi Ram (Kangri: Gurukul Press, 1917).

The Rashtriya Swayam Sevak Sangh (anonymous) (Lahore: Government Printing, 1948).

Tilak, B.G., *Srimad Bhagavadgita—Rahasya or Karma Yoga Shastra* (1911; rpnt. Poona, 1965).

———, *The Orion of Researches into the Antiquity of the Vedas* (Poona: Shri J.S. Tilak, 1972).

Upadhyaya, D., *The Two Plans—Promises, Performances, Prospects* (Lucknow: Rashtradharma Prakashan, 1958).

———, *Integral Humanism* (New Delhi: Bharatiya Jana Sangh, 1965).

———, *Political Diary* (Bombay: Jaico Publishing House, 1968).

Vable, D., *The Arya Samaj—Hindu without Hinduism* (New Delhi: Vikas Publishing House, 1983).

Vardarajan, S., ed., *Gujarat: The Making of a Tragedy* (Delhi: Penguin, 2002).

Varma, T.K.C., *Regeneration of the Hindus* (Madras: The Author, 1917).

Varshney, M.R., *Jana Sangh—RSS and Balraj Madhok* (Aligarh: Varshney College, n.d.)

Vazirani, G., *Lal Advani. The Man and His Mission* (New Delhi: Arnold Publishers, 1991).

Vedananda Tirtha, Swami, ed., *Wisdom of the Rishis, or Complete Works of Pandita Guru Datta* (Hindi Electric Press, n.d.).

Veer, P. van der, *Religious Nationalism* (Berkeley/Los Angeles: University of California Press, 1994).

Weiner, M., *Party Politics in India* (Princeton: Princeton University Press, 1957).

Widwans, M.D., ed., *Letters of Lokmanya Tilak* (Poona: Kesari Prakashan, 1966).

Yadav, K.C., ed., *Autobiography of Swami Dayanand Saraswati* (New Delhi: Manohar, 1976).

———, *Elections in Punjab 1920–1947* (New Delhi: Manohar, 1987).

Zaidi, S.A.H., *The New Nazis* (Bharatpur State, 1948).

Zavos, J., *The Emergence of Hindu Nationalism in India* (Delhi: Oxford University Press, 2000).

VI. Essays in Edited Volumes

Brass, P., 'The Politics of Ayurvedic Education: A Case Study of Revivalism and Modernization in India', in S.H. Rudolph and L.I. Rudolph, eds, *Education and Politics in India—Studies in Organisation Society and Policy* (Delhi: Oxford University Press, 1972).

———, 'Elite Groups, Symbol Manipulation and Ethnic Identity among the Muslims of South Asia', in D. Taylor and M. Yapp, eds, *Political Identity in South Asia* (London: Curzon Press, 1979).

Chatterjee, P., 'Agrarian Relations and Communalism in Bengal', in R. Guha, ed., *Subaltern Studies I* (Delhi: Oxford University Press, 1982).

Cleghorn, B., 'Religion and Politics: The Leadership of the All-India Hindu Mahasabha Punjab and Maharashtra 1920–1939', in B.N. Pandey, ed., *Leadership in South Asia* (New Delhi: Vikas Publishing House, 1977).

Datta, V.N., 'Punjabi Refugees and the Urban Development of Greater Delhi', in R.E. Frykenberg, *Delhi through the Ages* (Delhi: Oxford University Press, 1986).

Engineer, A.A., 'Meerut—Shame of the Nation', in A.A. Engineer, ed., *Delhi, Meerut Riots* (New Delhi: Ajanta, 1988).

Frykenberg, R.E., 'The Emergence of Modern "Hinduism" as a Concept and as an Institution: A Reappraisal with Special Reference to South India', in G.D. Sontheimer and H. Kulke, eds, *Hinduism Reconsidered* (New Delhi: Manohar, 1989).

Gould, H.A., 'Religion and Politics in a U.P. Constituency', in D.E. Smith, ed., *South Asian Politics and Religion* (Princeton: Princeton University Press, 1966).

Graham, B., 'Syama Prasad Mookerjee and the Communalist Alternative', in D.A. Low, ed., *Soundings in Modern South Asian History* (Berkeley: University of California Press, 1968).

———, 'The Congress and Hindu Nationalism', in D.A. Low, ed., *The Indian National Congress* (Delhi: Oxford University Press, 1988).

Jaffrelot, C., 'The BJP in Madhya Pradesh: Networks, Strategy and Power', in G. Pandey, ed., *Hindus and Others: The Question of Identity in India Today* (New Delhi: Penguin, 1993).

———, 'The Idea of the Hindu Race in the Writings of Hindu Nationalist Ideologues in the 1920s and 1930s: A Concept between Two Cultures', in Peter Robb, ed., *The Concept of Race in South Asia* (Delhi: Oxford University Press, 1995).

———, 'The Sangh Parivar between Sanskritization and Social Engineering', and 'BJP and the Challenge of Factionalism in Madhya Pradesh', in T.B. Hansen and C. Jaffrelot, eds, *The BJP and the Compulsions of Politics in India* (Delhi: Oxford University Press, 1998).

———, 'The Politics of Processions and Hindu–Muslim Riots', in Atul Kohli and Amrita Basu, eds, *Community Conflicts and the State in India* (Delhi: Oxford University Press, 1998).

———, 'The Vishva Hindu Parishad: Structures and Strategies', in Jeff Haynes, ed., *Religion, Globalization and Political Culture in the Third World* (London: Macmillan, 1999).

———, 'Militant Hindus and the Conversion Issue (1885–1990): From Shuddhi to Dharm Parivartan. The Politicization and the Diffusion of an "Invention of Tradition" ', in J. Assayag, ed., *The Resources of History. Tradition and Narration in South Asia* (Paris: EFEO, 1999).

———, 'The Hindu Nationalist Movement in Delhi : From "Locals" to Refugees—and Towards Peripheral Groups'?, in Véronique Dupont, Emma Tarlo and Denis Vidal, eds, *Delhi: Urban Space and Human Destinies* (Delhi: Manohar, 2000).

————, 'Hindu Nationalism and Democracy', in F.R. Frankel *et al.*, eds, *Transforming India. Social and Political Dynamics of Democracy* (Delhi: Oxford University Press, 2000).

————, 'Hindu Nationalism and the Social Welfare Strategy', in Alain Dieckhoff and Natividad Gutierrez, eds, *Modern Roots. Studies of National Identity* (Aldershot: Ashgate, 2001).

————, 'The Vishva Hindu Parishad: A Nationalist but Mimetic Attempt at Federating the Hindu Sects', in Vasudha Dalmia, Angelika Malinar and Martin Christof, eds, *Charisma and Canon: Essays on the Religious History of the Indian Subcontinent* (Delhi: Oxford University Press, 2001).

————, 'The Rise of Hindu Nationalism and the Marginalisation of the Muslims in India Today', in Amita Shastri and A.J. Wilson, eds, *The Post-Colonial States of South Asia* (Richmond: Curzon, 2001).

Johnson, G., 'Chitpavan Brahmins and Politics in Western India in the Late Nineteenth and Early Twentieth Centuries', in L. Leach and S.N. Mukherjee, eds, *Elites in South Asia* (Cambridge: Cambridge University Press, 1970).

Jones, K., 'Religious Identity and the Indian Census', in N.G. Barrier, ed., *The Census in British India* (New Delhi: Manohar, 1981).

————, 'Socio-Religious Movements and Changing Gender Relationships among Hindus of British India', in J.W. Björkman, ed., *Fundamentalism, Revivalists and Violence in South Asia* (Delhi: Manohar, 1988).

Jordens, J.T.F., 'Reconversion to Hinduism, the Shuddhi of the Arya Samaj', in G.A. Oddie, ed., *Religion in South Asia* (London: Curzon Press, 1977).

Joshi, P.C., 'The Economic Background of Communalism in India—A Model of Analysis', in B.R. Nanda, ed., *Essays in Modern Indian History* (New Delhi: Oxford University Press, 1980).

Lele, J., 'The Two Faces of Nationalism: On the Revolutionary Potential of Tradition', in J. Dofny and A. Aakinowo, eds, *National and Ethnic Movements* (London: Sage, 1980).

Lütt, J., 'The Movement for the Foundation of the Benares Hindu University', in *German Scholars in India* (New Delhi: Cultural Department of the Embassy of Federal Republic of Germany), 1976, vol. 2.

————, 'The Sankaracarya of Puri', in A. Eschmann *et al.*, eds, *The Cult of Jagannath and the Regional Tradition of Orissa* (New Delhi: Manohar, 1978).

———, 'Die regionalen wurzeln der Hindu Mahasabha', in H. Kulke and D. Rothermund, eds, *Regionale Tradition in Südasien* (Wiesbaden: Franz Steiner Verlag, 1985).

Mitter, P., 'Rammohun Roy and the New Language of Monotheism', in F. Schmidt, ed., *The Inconceivable Polytheism* (London: Harwood Academic Publishers, 1987).

Owen, H.F., 'Towards Nation-Wide Agitation and Organization: The Home Rule Leagues, 1915–18', in D.A. Low, ed., *Soundings in Modern South Asian History* (Berkeley: University of California Press, 1968).

Pal, B.C., 'Hinduism and Indian Nationalism', in E. Kedourie, ed., *Nationalism in Asia and Africa* (New York: World Publishing Co, 1970).

Pandey, G., 'Rallying Round the Cow—Sectarian Strife in the Bhojpuri Region, *c.* 1888–1917', in R. Guha, ed., *Subaltern Studies II* (Delhi: Oxford University Press, 1983).

Panikkar, K.N., 'A Historical Overview', in S. Gopal, ed., *Anatomy of a Confrontation—The Babri Masjid–Ramjanmabhumi Issue* (New Delhi: Viking, 1991).

Qurushi, I.H., 'A Case-Study of the Social Relations between the Muslims and the Hindus, 1935–1947', in C.H. Philips and M.D. Wainwright, eds, *The Partition of India* (London: G. Allen and Unwin, 1970).

Roy, R.M., 'A Defence of Hindoo Theism in Reply to the Attack of an Advocate for Idolatry at Madras' (1817), in J.C. Ghose, ed., *The English Works of Raja Ram Mohun Roy*, vol. 1 (Delhi: Cosmo Publication, 1982).

———, 'Translation of Several Principal Books. Passages and Texts of the Vedas', in W.B. Stein, ed., *Two Brahman Sources of Emerson and Thoreau* (Gainesville: Scholars facsimile and reprints, 1967).

———, 'The Brahmanical Magazine of the Missionary and the Brahman Being a Vindication of the Hindoo Religion Against the Attacks of Christian Missionaries' (Calcutta, 1821), in J.C. Ghose, ed., *The English Works of Raja Ram Mohun Roy* (Delhi: Cosmo Publications, 1982).

Rudolph, L.I. and S.H. Rudolph, 'Rethinking Secularism: Genesis and Implications of the Next Text-Book Controversy, 1977–79', in L.I. Rudolph and S.H. Rudolph, eds, *Cultural Policy in India* (Delhi: Chanakya, 1984).

Sarda, H.B., 'Har Bilas Sarda—A Sketch by Ram Gopal', in H.B. Sarda, *Speeches and Writings* (Ajmer: Vedic Yantralaya, 1935).

Srivastava, S., 'How the British Saw the Issue', in S. Gopal, ed., *Anatomy of a Confrontation—The Babri-Masjid–Ramjanmabhumi Issue* (New Delhi: Viking, 1991).

Tripathi, S.K., 'One Hundred Years of Litigation', in A.A. Engineer, ed., *Babri Masjid-Ramjanmabhoomi Controversy* (New Delhi: Ajanta Publications, 1990).

von Stienencron, H., 'Hinduism: On the Proper Use of a Deceptive Term', in G.D. Sontheimer and H. Kulke, eds, *Hinduism Reconsidered* (New Delhi: Manohar, 1989).

VII. Articles

Andersen, W., 'The Rashtriya Swayamsevak Sangh I: Early Concerns', *Economic and Political Weekly*, 11 March 1972.

——, 'The Rashtriya Swayamsevak Sangh III: Participation in Politics', *Economic and Political Weekly*, 25 March 1972.

Baker, D.E.U., 'The Swaraj Parties in the Central Provinces and Berar, India 1924–1926: An Essay on Regional Politics', *South Asia*, vol. 2, nos 1–2, March & September 1979.

Barrier, N.G., 'The Punjab Disturbances of 1907: The Response of the British Government in India to Agrarian Unrest', *Modern Asian Studies*, vol. 1, no. 4, 1967.

——, 'The Punjab Government and Communal Politics, 1870–1900', *Journal of Asian Studies*, vol. 17, no. 3, May 1968.

——, 'The Arya Samaj and Congress Politics in the Punjab 1894–1908', *Journal of Asian Studies*, vol. 26, no. 3, May 1967.

Bayly, C.A., 'Patrons and Politics in Northern India', *Modern Asian Studies*, vol. 7, no. 3, 1973.

——, 'The Pre-history of "Communalism"? Religious Conflict in India, 1700–1800', *Modern Asian Studies*, vol. 19, no. 2, 1985.

Brown, B.N., 'The Sanctity of the Cow in Hinduism', *Economic and Political Weekly*, February 1964.

Chandra, S., 'Hindu Conservatism in the Nineteenth Century', *Economic and Political Weekly*, 12 December 1986.

Copland, I., ' "Communalism" in Princely India: The Case of Hyderabad, 1930–1940', *Modern Asian Studies*, vol. 22, no. 4, 1988.

Das, S., 'Communal Violence in Twentieth Century Colonial Bengal: An Analytical Framework', *Social Scientist*, June–July 1990.

Dua, V., 'Social Organisation of Arya Samaj: A Study of Two Local Arya Centers in Jullundur', *Sociological Bulletin*, vol. 19, no. 1, March 1970.

Dutta, P.K., 'War over Music: The Riots of 1926 in Bengal', *Social Scientist*, June–July 1990.

Fox, R.G., 'Gandhian Socialism and Hindu Nationalism: Cultural Domination in the World System', *The Journal of Commonwealth and Comparative Politics*, vol. 25, no.3, November 1987.

Freitag, S., 'Sacred Symbols as Mobilizing Ideology: The North Indian Search for a "Hindu" Community', *Comparative Studies of Society and History*, vol. 22, no. 4, 1980.

———, ' "Natural Leaders", Administrators and Social Control: Communal Riots in the United Provinces, 1870–1925', *South Asia*, vol 1, no. 2, September 1978.

Frykenberg, R.E., 'The Concept of "Majority" as a Devilish Force in the Politics of Modern Asia', *The Journal of Commonwealth and Comparative Politics*, vol. 15, no. 3, November 1987.

Gordon, R., 'The Hindu Mahasabha and the Indian National Congress 1915 to 1926', *Modern Asian Studies*, vol. 9, no. 2, 1975.

Graham, B., 'The Jana Sangh and Party Alliances: 1967–70', *South Asian Review*, vol. 4, no. 1, October 1970.

Gupta, K.P., 'Religious Evolution and Social Change in India: A Study of the Ramakrishna Mission Movement', *Contributions to Indian Sociology*, no. 8, 1974.

Hardgrave, R.L., Jr, 'The Mappilla Rebellion, 1921: Peasant Revolt in Malabar', *Modern Asian Studies*, vol. 11, no. 1, 1977.

Hasan, M., 'Communalism in the Provinces: A Case Study of Bengal and the Punjab, 1922–1926', *Economic and Political Weekly*, 16 August 1980.

Heeger, G.A., 'Discipline *versus* Mobilization: Party Building and the Punjab Jana Sangh', *Asian Survey*, vol. 12, no. 10, October 1970.

———, 'The Growth of the Congress Movement in Punjab, 1920–1940', *Journal of Asian Studies*, vol. 32, no. 1, November 1972.

Jaffrelot, C., 'Hindu Nationalism: Strategic Syncretism in Ideology Building', *Indian Journal of Social Science*, vol. 5, no. 42, August 1992.

———, 'Hindu Nationalism: Strategic Syncretism in Ideology Building', *Economic and Political Weekly*, vol. 28, nos 12–13, 20 March 1993.

———, 'The Genesis and Development of Hindu Nationalism in the Punjab: From the Arya to the Hindu Sabha (1875–1990)', *The Indo-British Review*, vol. 21, no. 1, 1995, pp. 3–39.

———, 'Madhya Pradesh I—Setback to BJP', *Economic and Political Weekly*, vol. 31, nos 2–3, 13 January 1996.

————, 'The Rise of the Other Backward Classes in the Hindi Belt ', *Journal of Asian Studies*, vol. 59, no. 1, February 2000.

————, 'Sanskritization *vs.* Ethnicization in India: Changing Identities and Caste Politics Before Mandal', *Asian Survey*, vol. 60, no. 5, September–October 2000.

Jha, J.S., 'An Unpublished Correspondence Relating to the Bihar Hindu Sabha', *Journal of Bengal and Bihar Studies*, vol. LIV, parts 1–4.

Jhari, K.D., 'Revealing Details of Pracharak's Life', *Secular Democracy*, June 1970.

————, 'I was a Swayamsevak—II', *Secular Democracy*, Annual 1970.

————, 'Creating the Urge to Kill', *Secular Democracy*, July 1970.

Jones, K., 'The Bengali Elite in Post-Annexation Punjab: An Example of Inter-Regional Influence in Nineteenth Century India', *The Indian Economic and Social History Review*, vol. 3, no. 4, December 1966.

————, 'Communalism in the Punjab—The Arya Samaj Contribution', *Journal of Asian Studies*, vol. 28, no. 1, November 1966.

————, 'Ham Hindu Nahin: Arya–Sikh Relations, 1877–1905', *Journal of Asian Studies*, vol. 32, no. 3, May 1973.

Ketkar, G.V., 'The All India Hindu Mahasabha', *The Indian Annual Register*, 1941, vol. 1.

Kishwar, M., 'Arya Samaj and Women's Education—Kanya Mahavidyalaya, Jalandhar', *Economic and Political Weekly*, vol. 29, no. 17, 26 April 1986.

Kumar, K.N., 'The Ideology of the Janata Party', *The Indian Journal of Political Science*, vol 39, no. 4.

McGinn, P., 'Communalism and the North-West Frontier Province: The Kohat Riots, 9–10 September 1924', *South Asia Research*, vol. 6, no. 2, November 1986.

Mathew, G., 'Politicisation of Religion—Conversions to Islam in Tamil Nadu', *Economic and Political Weekly*, 19 June 1982.

O'Connell, J.T., 'The Word "Hindu" in Gaudiya Vaishnava Texts', *Journal of the American Oriental Society*, vol. 93, no. 3, 1973.

Parel, A., 'The Political Symbolism of the Cow in India', *Journal of Commonwealth Political Studies*, vol. 7, no. 3, November 1969.

Ramdas, R.V., 'Shuddhi Movement—A Brief Survey', *Manthan*, vol. 5, no. 1, May 1983.

Robb, P., 'The Challenge of Gau Mata—British Policy and Religious Change in India 1880–1916', *Modern Asian Studies*, vol. 20, no. 2, 1986.

Saini, M.K. and Andersen, W.K., 'The Basti Julahan Bye-election', *The Indian Journal of Political Science*, July–September 1969.

Saxena, N.C., 'Nature and Origin of Communal Riots in India', *Man and Development*, vol. 4, no. 3.

Sen, A., 'Hindu Revivalism in Action—The Age of Consent Bill Agitation in Bengal', *The Indian Historical Review*, vol. 7, no. 12, July 1980–January 1981.

Sharma, U., 'Status Striving and Striving to Abolish Status: The Arya Samaj and the Low Castes', *Social Action*, vol. 26, no. 3, July–September 1976.

Thapar, R., 'Syndicated Moksha'? *Seminar*, September 1985.

———, 'Imagined Religious Communities? Ancient History and the Modern Search for a Hindu Identity', *Modern Asian Studies*, vol. 23, no. 2, 1989.

Tucker, R., 'Hindu Traditionalism and Nationalist Ideologies in Nineteenth-Century Maharashtra', *Modern Asian Studies*, vol. 10, no. 3, 1976.

van der Veer, P., ' "God must be Liberated!" A Hindu Liberation Movement in Ayodhya', *Modern Asian Studies*, vol. 21, no. 2, 1987.

Yang, A.A., 'Sacred Symbols in Rural India: Community Mobilization in the "Anti-Cow Killing" Riot of 1893', *Comparative Studies of Society and History*, vol. 22, no. 4, October 1980.